AF527877

Ideas for Social Change

Ideas for Social Change

Life and Mission of DR. BINDESHWAR PATHAK

S.P. SINGH

Sulabh International Centre for Action Sociology
Sulabh Bhawan, RZ-83, Mahavir Enclave, New Delhi – 110 045, India

RAWAT PUBLICATIONS
Jaipur • New Delhi • Bangalore • Guwahati • Kolkata

ISBN : 978-81-316-0989-7

First Published 2018

Published by
Sulabh International Centre for Action Sociology
Sulabh Bhawan, RZ-83, Mahavir Enclave, New Delhi - 110 045, India
Tele: (91-11) 25032344, 25038093; Fax: (91-11) 25034014
Email: info@sulabhcentre.org / sicasmail@hotmail.com
Website: www.sulabhcentre.org

Distributed by
Rawat Publications
Satyam Apts, Sector 3, Jawahar Nagar, Jaipur 302 004 (India)
Phone: 0141 265 1748 / 7006 Fax: 0141 265 1748
E-mail: info@rawatbooks.com
Website: www.rawatbooks.com

Also at *New Delhi, Bangalore*, *Guwahati* and *Kolkata*

Printed and bound in India.

Dedicated to
Sulabh Workers

It is not the strongest of the species that survives, nor the most intelligent, but the one which is most responsive to change.

— Charles Darwin

It is about the man and his mission

Richard Holmes, Britain's biographer says: "A biographer has to step back, step up and inside to discover the central fact of the story with empathy". This is the complex fact of friendship which can neither be proved, nor demonstrated but it is all over the book. It is a handshake across time, cultures and faiths – right and wrong. But they existed in ample measures. And, they are true in context and time. Dr. Pathak's life and missions, as I write them, should be read in that context.

The stink has a story !!

Desire creates conflict and conflict creates losers and winners. Winners become masters and losers become slaves and, thus, an unequal society is created, says John Stuart Mill (1806–1873) in his book, *On Liberty*. It is believed that manual scavengers are the earliest losers in the conflict whose history has not changed since, except that of the toilets they cleaned. No wonder, their life begins at the far-end of human sufferings and humiliation. And, this is where Sulabh story begins !!

The ultimate truth is not the reality but ideas.

– Plato

Reflecting Mood of the Times

Victor Vigo (1802-85) says in *Les Misérables*: "As long as there are ignorance and poverty in the world, this book will continue to reflect the mood of the times". However, times change, but human miseries, exploitation and social injustices continue. *Les Misérables* brought in a panoramic social revolution in France in 1862 and Sulabh has produced a huge change in mindset, ending manual scavenging and promoting a new sanitation order by virtually lifting the mountain without raising dust. History never happens; it is made. Hence, this book.

> *" Small steps by good men somewhere turn into a giant leap for mankind everywhere."*
>
> *– John F. Kennedy*

A Life of Leadership

The Sulabh Founder, Dr. Bindeshwar Pathak, has not only offered different technologies and a new vision of sanitation, but also different policy choices and fundamentally different ways of determining sanitation identity. Identity is an umbrella term, which is a collection of ideas, technologies and characteristics that define how we live a clean, healthy and productive life, individually and collectively, specially in a country like India with a richly diverse population, cultural habits, value systems, diverse faiths, languages, customs and cuisine. Dr. Pathak has found a common ground among all movements and blended them together in a fascinating network to make Sulabh a wave of our time. And, while carrying the burden of leadership, he stays focused and fully engaged in the emancipation of manual scavengers in India. Let us know about the man and his mission in perspective.

The man who has no power, money, or inheritance, digs up one pit where one existed before to become the icon of the new sanitation age.

Contents

The continuous search for new ideas has been man's old obsession and older still is to find a blend of ancient values and modern materialism. The Sulabh philosophy is the nearest approximation to it.

Preface

Man and his mystique – a riddle hard to unravel

Writing about life and mission of Dr. Bindeshwar Pathak is like discussing an elusive idea which is hard to define and harder still to put into a theoretical stereotype. It all started from toilet to later expand into a societal culture and a system which produces no winner, no loser – the stuff of which history is made of. While the ideas of the past have shaped the social, political and religious institutions of today's world, new concepts continually challenge our old perceptions, fuel debate and pave way for the future.

Writing Dr. Bindeshwar Pathak's biography is far more difficult than writing about other leaders like Gandhiji, Nehru, Dr. Ambedkar, Ataturk and Lincoln because their lives were full of events which could be counted and the consequences identified. Most leaders knew their enemies; Gandhiji had British Empire, Dr. Ambedkar had untouchability, Lincoln had slavery, Ataturk ended the Ottoman Empire, Churchill had Hitler, and Mandela had apartheid. All these and other leaders had clearly identifiable enemies to defeat or systems to demolish.

Dr. Pathak has none of these. He wants to abolish untouchability without harming the 'touchables'; he seeks to end scavenging by providing an alternative and universally applicable technology and rehabilitate scavengers without dislodging non-scavengers; he seeks for scavengers not reservation at the cost of somebody else but education, training and social mainstreaming. So where is his enemy to beat and land to conquer? Very clearly, it is in the minds of men who have, for historical reasons or social prejudices, ostracised a section of people not for their caste, for they have none, but for their unclean jobs. Once the unclean job was taken over by technology, the boycotted people became friends as the Alwar project has shown. *(See it in later chapters)*. Dr. Pathak's movement is also not about violent social revolution; it is about the system of osmosis and change which is a gradual absorbing of new ideas and adopting new social order–a process of social transformation highlighted in sociology, of which Dr. Pathak has been a student.

The Sulabh Movement is not ideology centric either, capitalist or socialist, though focus is on equality for all, including scavengers. Since these do not yield to violent changes, Sulabh is all about the process of shifting the social system from one stage of evolution to another; it is about changing one thing and the rest will remain changed, a domino effect. Each area of social relationship has, however, to be addressed differently. For instance, if it is manual scavenging, the answer is two-pit technology; if it is untouchability, it is education and entitlement and if it is the environment, sanitation in all its different ways will be the answer. For that matter, Sulabh is more an eclectic philosophy than a road map for revolution.

But, if this is true, what this biography is all about? No man is killed, nor any war won or lost, nor any political systems built or demolished or a new religion founded. So, where is the story? This is what a news reporter asks. Dr. Pathak's profile is not eventful; it could be the story of any middle class Brahmin family which had fallen on hard times. Or, about a Brahmin boy who emerged to oppose and, finally, change the Brahmanical orthodoxy, living and dining with scavengers whom he was not supposed to touch. And, once when he did, he had to swallow cow dung.

A solo effort

Dr. Pathak did the revolutionary work while staying out of power, without money, or traditional support of high-caste people until he and his mission became unstoppable. He fought no election, held no office, launched no campaign, formed no party, nor did he take any money from any government or non-government agency to default on payment and hit the headlines of national newspapers. It has been his solo effort, working with some of those very few committed social workers who stood by him in good times and bad. To be true the Sulabh success story is built on its impact on the lives of people; more than 2 lakh scavengers liberated and rehabilitated; universal acceptance of its technology; over 20 million people using Sulabh toilets everyday, and the wave of social change that Dr. Pathak has created through more than five decades of campaigning and social advocacy. One has to closely watch the happy faces of liberated scavengers which show a new dawn in their lives. Their faces tell the Sulabh story more eloquently than I can write. Dr. Pathak has changed the terms of national dialogue from power sharing to responsibility sharing; of carrying the burden together and lifting society from the bottom, making the last man, the scavenger, as the measure of development. This is what Gandhiji said; this is what Dr. Pathak has done and is doing. And, this is happening for all to see. His biography is all about it, although it is a continuing story.

In sum, Sulabh is a story about the nobility of man, the goodness of human civilisation and the glory of God. It is about the unity of human species, not of a part. "This is the purpose of God for which he has created this world. Time does not pause at any point, it is like a flowing stream, a continuing drama; let us play our part and leave the rest to God", says Dr. Pathak, a believer, who has won the hearts and minds of people by his work, ideas and vision more than any conqueror could do by war. The Sulabh Founder is a role model and that is the stuff this biography is made of.

Dr. Pathak governs by trust and persuasion

Dr. Pathak, a liberal by instinct, is a great man manager, with his mystical skill to emotionally, not only institutionally, manage volunteers and bind them in personal relationship. His easy and simple manners are disarming, radiating innocence of vintage times – a quaint reminder of distant dreams or of unheard songs. He knows most social volunteers by name or those of their village or town and calls them by first name. Through his personal bond, he keeps about 60,000 persons together, working in Sulabh network. In Sulabh, responsibilities are fixed by word of mouth and those who fail in duty have only to explain their conduct before 'Sulabh Darbar', held periodically to review work performance and address complaints. Sulabh, I believe, is the only organisation where accounts are discussed at Darbar before being passed over to authority. The Founder projects himself as a trustee in the Gandhian tradition, and not a 'boss'. He wields no direct control over projects, but governs through persuasion and pressure. And, when he is annoyed, he pulls a long face showing deep visages and, silence descends on the Darbar and the message is reached. His body language is the game-changer, truly a strange way to manage a pan-India organisation. He rules by trust and persuasion.

The fact is that technology and greed have destroyed our innocence. Consequently, those working in modern farms and factories have become cogs in the machine or statistics in accounts books. Not in Sulabh. Here each worker is held in trust and high respect and they are so addressed; for instance, treated as custodians of Sulabh Trust, not inspectors. For that matter, Dr. Pathak is a man born 100 years too late, in a complicated and valueless world where man's worth is measured by the furniture he keeps, or the car he rides. And, in these loveless and troubled times, Dr. Pathak harks back to vintage values by rediscovering the Gandhian concept of trusteeship.

New thinking on Gandhiji

The Sulabh Movement is, however, not entirely the consequence of Dr. Pathak's reaction to the miseries of scavengers when he lived with them in their colonies in Bettiah, Bihar, or to the spectacle of a boy being gored to death by a bull and nobody saved him because he was a scavenger. Or, to the sad situation when a young bride was forced to clean toilets by her mother-in-law because she was a scavenger. To say that these events made Dr. Pathak a social reformer is to believe that Siddhartha became Buddha because he saw a dead man. No. In both the cases, events were only triggers that caused ripple action which itself was a conscious and deliberate decision under intellectual influence of contemporary ideas and social conditions.

It is evident from the thinking and writings of Dr. Pathak that it was the independent influence of ideas, more than social and economic condition of scavengers, that produced the Sulabh Movement which above all else is an ideological road map for social renewal while keeping off the political controversies between parties and social groups. Dr. Pathak, like Gandhiji and John Locke, says: "The government is a trust which will be forfeited by rulers who fail to secure the public good. Nor does the individual surrender all his rights when he enters a civil society. An individual has the rights to withdraw the trust, if the government fails to help the poor and create conditions of social justice". John Locke, much before Gandhiji, expressed the idea that the ruler's authority is conditional, not absolute.

Locke formulated this concept to become the philosopher of the enlightenment, British empiricism and American pragmatism. Social activists used this argument to enforce the rights of civil society and justify civil disobedience. Dr. Pathak has adopted this formulation to provide an intellectual background for the Sulabh Movement. Locke also formulated the classic expression of liberalism which inspired the writers of the American Constitution; Gandhiji did that to empower the weak and poor, which the Sulabh Founder also does although with greater emphasis on the welfare of the scavenger who, he says, is the face of social injustices, inhumanity and all that is wrong and skewed in a democratic polity.

Dr. Pathak says, "History is stories of winners and losers, reducing the whole life to a zero-sum game where one man's loss is another man's gain." And, this has been the source of conflict, first starting in the minds of men to later spill over in battlefields. All the battles recorded in history since Herodotus (5th century BC), from the Peloponnesian War between Athens and Sparta (431-404 BC) to the World War I and II, when the national boundaries were redrawn and new nations created – there has been only one motive all along – to be a winner. And, those who were defeated in World War I, launched World War II to become winner. It is all about winner and loser. The fact is there is no known case in history of war over food, clothes or houses. The poor are too weak, too deprived to fight war which is the privilege of the rich and the strong. Yes, we know of food riots and famines in Bengal, Ireland, Russia and in many countries of Africa, during the World War I, but they were self-limiting social disorders with no global consequences.

This biography may be different from most others, also because Dr. Pathak had packed so many events into his life, a long spell in wilderness, a failed medicine seller, a teacher, an unpaid volunteer, and a social reformer to finally become one of the tallest Indians of our times – the stuff great biographies are made of. History may judge him differently, but Sulabh has set up a benchmark, against which the future sanitation and human rights standard will be measured, so also the social reforms by ending injustice to scavengers for which the Sulabh Sanitation Movement was launched in the first place.

We have to change that. And, this change has to be brought about in attitude, and minds of man. To say this, however, is not to plead for a world of all equals. Certainly, it cannot be. "Men and women are born unequal in strength, capacity to learn new things, physical strength, genetic features, and many other ways, including the environment, upbringing, social conditions and various other factors which cannot be changed by external intervention. But the man-made social inequality, flowing through flawed social structure, convention, religious orthodoxy or prejudices, can be changed and that too without conflict or war," says the Sulabh Founder. What follows is the story of a social reformer, who seeks to make these things happen. His life and mission put in perspective and context is a refreshing thought in these extraordinary times.

How it all began

When I joined Sulabh decades ago, quitting *The Hindustan Times,* I asked Dr. Pathak what would be my duty. He said: "I am not sure myself, but you will know as you grow in the job". Then, Dr. Pathak was a handsome young man in early thirties, young enough to look for pretty things of life, and certainly not to talk about the Gandhian philosophy on austerity, stern living, scavenging and the environment. After joining this prodigious organisation, I supervised toilets cleaning, their maintenance and construction, campaigning for the liberation of scavengers, going to their *bastis* to know their lifestyle, habits, culture and everything else. I have written extended promotional pamphlets, many books, reports, citations and discussion papers for seminars and public talks, besides addressing national and international conferences on the environment and sanitation and editing *Sulabh India.*

It was an exciting experience which I never got tired of, nor did I ever think of exploring other career options which were not entirely closed on me. Working for Sulabh was also emotionally satisfying and intellectually fulfilling with a sense of participating in a social change which I could neither clearly define nor fully explain. But, I had the feeling of an anonymous soldier entering the Menin Gate of Ypres in Flanders (1918) during the World War I, scribbling his message hurriedly on a big billboard as if saying: "You may not know me, nor do I care. For, I will not live to see you again. But I will be the first to see the new dawn breaking in the war trenches which is worth living and dying for."

This was about those soldiers who never returned home from war, not knowing what it was all about. But the Sulabh workers know that they are working with a Promethean responsibility to affirm the human freedom for scavengers against the supposed inevitability of history. Certainly, in Sulabh it is not a job, nor a war to fight in battle gear, or taking out processions on the streets to topple a system. Nothing of these. Yet there is a feeling that you are part of a great social upheaval because you smell it every morning in Sulabh prayer, also composed by its Founder. It is the love of mystery that has driven Sulabh workers to this great human endeavour, of which I have the privilege to be a part. And, that entitles me to tell this story.

While doing all these things, I discovered I was already in the evening of life and the shadow was lengthening by the day. Then I decided to hurriedly write down the story of the Sulabh Movement and about its Founder in this book which turns out to be the collection of a profile, memoir, biography of ideas and technology, a veritable collage of everything that does not fit into a stereotype, leaving it for the younger and wiser minds to complete the story. Whatever one may say about Sulabh, no one can deny the fact that Dr. Bindeshwar Pathak is the prime mover of a massive social movement, next only to the one launched by Gandhiji, to end scavenging and ensure full sanitation for all – rich and poor, in villages and cities. Sulabh also marks the first use of non-sewered, eco-friendly and bio-friendly, on-the-spot waste disposal technology and a seamless change to a social and sanitation order from the old, when toilet was the privilege of the few, to the new Sulabh social order, when it is affordable to all as a matter of human rights and universal commitment of a civilised society.

Sulabh is inseparable from peaceful struggle; it is a process and not conclusion. Sanitation for Sulabh is both the means employed and end attained. "And this peaceful struggle", says Dr. Pathak, "offers a better life for the poor, specially scavengers, and a measure of fulfilment for all". This is the Sulabh objective; the rest is detail. The Sulabh Movement, as a matter of fact, is the result of a historical process which no human agency could have prevented. If there were no Dr. Pathak, history would have invented one. There is no Dickens to write about the miseries of industrialised England, nor a Premchand to write about the degrading poverty in feudal India. Sulabh is a logical response to this historical inevitability, of which I may not be the only man to write about. But, I have collated facts together which will make writing easier for those who do it later.

Thus, I complete the book in a spirit of humility, remembering the words of great historian Arthur Schlesinger, Jr. that "great men and women are not redeemers, but their stories inspire people to make greater efforts than before to create a better and happier world". Clearly, Dr. Pathak cannot make history and write it too. Mine is one such humble attempt.

All flaws and faults in the book are mine and if there is any good thing about the book, it is entirely because of those with whom I have the good fortune to work with, including the Sulabh Founder.

S.P. Singh

Acknowledgements

While doing this book, I depended on long years of my association with the Sulabh Movement during which it had three avatars, Sulabh Shauchalaya Sansthan, Sulabh International and Sulabh International Social Service Organisation. Those were eventful times when I saw the movement rise to great heights despite many setbacks and faltering steps. I have also watched Dr. Bindeshwar Pathak's steps closely; the manner of his taking many crucial decisions, his ability to face challenging moments, and intense moments of grief, none of which, however, changed the course of his action or weakened determination to achieve the Gandhian dreams of setting up a scavenging-free society. A large number of colleagues in Sulabh, and outside it, helped me compile details and check them. I am deeply grateful to Mr. S.P.N. Sinha, IAS (Retd.), Mr. C. Prabhakaran Nambiar, a senior journalist, Late Prof. Sidheshwardhari Sinha, an English scholar, and Mrs. Anita Jha, who have carefully revised the script and made many changes to give a readable shape to the text.

I owe deep gratitude to Mr. B.N. Srivastava who has edited facts, opinions and other details which, but for his diligence, would have escaped into print. Mr. Srivastava has retired as a senior officer in the Government of India and has written books and articles on social issues, including sanitation, untouchability and minority problems. He has also checked the mind-boggling data and figures, collating them in a readable form. Mr. Debabrata Chatterjee, Mr. Sandeep Shankar, an old Sulabh hand, Mr. Shashi Dhar and Mr. Anil Khanna provided support to the writing work for which

I am thankful to them. I am also thankful to Mr. Indrajeet Kumar Jha, photographer, who has provided pictorial support to the book. I have acknowledged the sources quoted in the book for which I record my gratitude to all of them.

To be true, this has been a collective effort, spanning over many years of working together. The draft of the book has been checked by many others and the surviving errors are mine alone.

S.P. Singh

Introduction

In Greek mythology, the song of the Sirens (part women, part birds) was so seductive that the enraptured sailors listened to their songs and let their ships run on to the rocks. In Homer's epic *Odyssey,* Odysseus, the principal character, plugged his sailors' ears with wax and had himself tied to his ship's mast so that he could hear the song without endangering his vessel. And the adventurer king Ithaca safely sailed the ship and won the Battle of Troy. During more than four decades of work, Dr. Bindeshwar Pathak, Founder of the Sulabh Movement, had heard many seductive songs, achieved great name and fame but like Odysseus he remains tied to the Sulabh mast in order to sail the movement through crises and achieve the distinction which this book talks about in detail.

To be true, the book is less about the man and more about his work and the contemporary issues, social reforms and reformers and much else besides which give perspective of the Sulabh Movement. For that reason, it doesn't fit into the template of a biographical story; it is a combination of all these and more, with the Sulabh Founder in the centre of the narrative around whom the story revolves.

Anything worth doing is the work of generations – ending racism, casteism, untouchability, promoting freedom or building nation. America's founders, for example, felt the eyes of their future generations upon them while founding the republic. Alexander Hamilton felt that he was helping to create a great empire; Noah Webster composed his dictionary anticipating that America would some day have 300 million inhabitants, even though at the time it had only 6 million people. These people undertook their grand projects because they were building for their descendants. They were motivated and ambitious leaders, writers and social activists, known for their hunger for immortal fame. Without posterity, there are no grand designs, no high ambitions. If people knew that their nation, group and family were doomed to perish, they would build no buildings, save no money and fight no war to 'make the world safe for our children'.

Dr. Pathak is no exception. He thinks that his is the first step and somebody some day will take the final step to abolish untouchability and social injustice without which a stable social structure cannot be built.

Unlike war heroes, cinema artists or political icons, Dr. Pathak doesn't have dramatic flourishes about his life story or career, neither of which could be a trail blazer in history. It is about an ordinary boy of an average Brahmin family, neither rich nor poor, seeking to change the social asymmetry and put the values in right perspective. And, he has largely succeeded working with about 60,000 volunteers of the Sulabh social service network. Nor had he any inheritance to fall back upon and achieve a head start in his mission which remained defined no more than the career which was never planned. But his wandering life and unorthodox thinking open up new possibilities for future generations.

The Sulabh technology of digging yet another toilet pit where one existed before is neither a complicated physics nor space science. Nor were the inventions of steam engine by James Watt, aeroplane by Wright Brothers (1903) or penicillin by Alexander Fleming. Millions of innovations like these have provided stimulating ideas for scientific renovations and social change which have created the modern world. And, most of these happened by chance. It is also true in Dr. Pathak's case.

The Sulabh two-pit toilet technology has a revolutionary impact on the sanitation situation. More than 20 million people in India alone use the toilets based on the Sulabh technology everyday. For close to 2.5 billion people in the world, who do not have access to safe and hygienic toilet system, the Sulabh technology arguably provides a credible option. This is unlike the sewerage system, which simply transfers the human waste to water areas where either it is treated or, in most cases, discharged raw into water, creating environmental problem. This is a paradigm shift in the sanitation technologies.

Enlightenment, Reformation and Industrialisation in Europe were consequences of the ideas, producing technology and changing attitude. The printing press was evolved during Reformation when Martin Luther translated the *Bible* from Latin, a language of the elite, into other languages. And a new attitude towards religion and social issues evolved. And Protestantism was born which split Christianity.

Slavery was abolished in America not entirely because of the Civil War or the series of anti-slavery laws but largely because of the fact that technologies were developed which replaced slaves for cotton plantation. So demand for slaves was cut off and slavery ended. Similarly, the Sulabh technology has cut off the demand for the services of manual scavengers. And, hence, scavenging is in decline which we hope will end in our lifetime. The epochal social, intellectual and technological developments during these periods were again the consequences of new thinking, inventions and innovations by many great men and women all over the world.

A socially uneventful life and career of Dr. Pathak has made writing his life story more difficult. Newsmen say that reporting war, violence, and social conflicts is easier than writing about peace, or unspoken sufferings, especially of the women who have to wait for the break of dawn or the fall of dusk before they can go out in the dark for open defecation because they have no toilets in their houses. How do you write this tragedy? No shots have been fired nor is anyone injured. But, it is worse than both, a life of quiet suffering which is surpassed in scale and intensity only by that of scavengers who have been socially, culturally and economically disenfranchised for physically cleaning toilets as a job to make a living, hardly enough to keep the head above water.

No clash of cultures

Dr. Pathak lived with scavengers when he was intimately exposed to their miseries and to test his determination if he could stand the test by fire. And, also to relate himself to scavengers, living and eating with them in filthy and stinking areas of Bettiah in Bihar. It was, however, not like Prince Siddhartha becoming Buddha after seeing a dead man, or Ashoka giving up arms after Kalinga. It is a steadily unfolding of the life of an ordinary man becoming an extraordinary crusader for a just social order which has become the rallying cry of most social reforms today specially of the Prime Minister, Mr. Narendra Modi. Unlike most social reforms, the Sulabh Movement is peaceful, inclusive, technology and education-based. Dr. Pathak says it is not necessary to demolish one social system to build another; both can exist together after they are reformed.

Dr. Pathak does not believe in Huntington's clash of civilisations. He says, the history of cultures is one of constant cross-fertilisation, of endless exchange and mutual borrowing. Who would, for instance, say that Christianity, a West Asian product, is not European, or American? Who would say that Buddhism, born in India, has nothing to do with China and Japan? The same can be said about ideologies that have left a profound imprint in different continents and countries. What about a German Jew (Marx) and a Russian revolutionary (Lenin) becoming heroes in China? The fact is that values converge, cross, merge and clash. Although the clash is real, frequent, but it is neither geographical, nor always along cultural, or religious fault lines which exist within each culture, each society, each religion, and even between individuals. How can Europeans deny that Hitler's genocide happened in a Christian and western country? To which 'civilisation' does Adolf Hitler belong? As a child, he attended a Christian church, not an Islamic Madrasa and, Stalin was also a student in an Orthodox Church seminary. Man is a constantly changing species who does not fit into a stereotype; he can be very good and very bad at the same time.

All civilisations are dialogic

Dialogue is a constant mode of relations between different civilisations, cultures, value systems and ideologies. It is the only way to stay out of conflict. What is central to the survival of human civilisation is contact, dialogue and mutual trust. The choice is not between self-contained isolation and hostility, but between conflict and dialogue. Inter-civilisational relations should also be based on the recognition of diversity since it does not limit our ethical recognition of those who are similar to us. In the first half of the last century, the most prominent French thinkers interested in India were Romain Rolland and Andre Gide. But in the second half, Sartre and Camus wrote little about India. The exception was Andre Malraux, the hugely accomplished man of letters and Charles de Gaulle, minister of culture, whose admiration for India's arts, philosophies, plurality, democracy and its composite culture and leaders, notably Nehru and Gandhiji, was quite beyond compare.

When Malraux defended the role of India in the liberation of Bangladesh, and condemned the Chinese attack on India, he was asked how he rated Mao Zedong and Mahatma Gandhi. He said: "Mao's greatness lay in the fact that he made the Chinese people believe in their entitlement to a bowl of rice. And Gandhi's greatness lay in the fact that he made the Indian people believe that they could get rid of the mightiest empire on earth with a pinch of salt. Gandhi promoted composite culture and combined many civilisations into one nation to become an example for other countries, fighting for individual identities." When asked what would happen if one day a pinch of Indian salt were to be added to a bowl of Chinese rice, Malraux replied: "That day will herald the birth of a new world and the smile of the Buddha will become more enigmatic".

This is broadly the composite cultural background in which Dr. Pathak has always lived and sought to build an inclusive culture to give justice to the poor. He had two ways of doing it; try to destroy the old order and build a new one in its place, or re-interpret the positive values in the existing social order and expand it to be inclusive. Hinduism is not a doctrinaire and hide-bound one-book, one-god religion. It has any number of gods and books of religion. *Manusmriti,* which has deeply divided society, does not have the sanction of *the Vedas* and other books which recognise no caste or creed. *The Rig Veda* says "God is a later creation after the universe". That being the central tenet of Hinduism, where is place for casteism and untouchability?

A philosophy becomes Sulabh Movement

When I met Dr. Pathak in 1986, he already had a place in history as one of the tallest Indians of our times; later it was only about finding new frontiers, taking Sulabh torch deeper into 'An Area of Darkness', (a la V.S. Naipaul) winning more people on the side of sanitation, and, thus, making more disenfranchised and disinherited people happier and healthier than before. For that matter, Sulabh philosophy has become a movement which is more a moral enterprise than blueprint of a new sanitation order. Men seldom receive truth from their enemies and it is seldom offered to them by their friends and admirers. However, I have sought to be different, telling the truth of the man and his mission as I saw it. Perception and opinions are entirely mine, but they are also widely shared by others which I have elaborately mentioned in every chapter, if not every page. Many writers take it upon themselves to inform others of the benefits of reading their books, a work which is beyond me to do. Hence, I leave it to the reader to make his own judgment and find out how a bare-footed boy has changed the lives of scavengers which all governments and leaders promised but no one could deliver–an amazing story of persistence, commitment and social service.

S.P. Singh

CHAPTER I

A Trust and Value-Based System of Self-Governance

The global context to Sulabh ideas

India is not alone for sanitation movements to happen. In the pre-industrial societies of the West, open defecation and unsafe disposal of human waste had been common in rich countries also. France had the "flying toilets" (18th Century) when Parisians wrapped up excreta in paper and threw it in the open. There was a "Great Stink" when the Thames was frozen with excreta (19th Century) and the entire Europe had cholera, bubonic plague and other sanitation-related diseases which threatened the Western civilisation. The Sulabh Founder knew these when he launched the Sulabh Movement. It was Dr. Bindeshwar Pathak's historical inheritance.

Great things sometimes emerge from working under pressure. In his first draft of the Declaration of Independence, prepared in mid-June 1776, Thomas Jefferson wrote, "We hold these truths to be sacred and undeniable; that all men are created equal and independent (sic) and from that equal creation man derives rights which are inherent and inalienable. And, among which are the preservation of life, liberty, and the pursuit of happiness." Jafferson also repeated, "We hold these truths to be self-evident, that all men are created equal, that they are endowed by their Creator with certain inalienable rights, that among these are life, liberty and the pursuit of happiness."

Dr. Bindeshwar Pathak, however, has redefined the human rights of manual scavengers and put them on national agenda. He says,

The French Revolution has produced the modern world based on equality for all

"Human rights are not discovered; they existed since birth as natural inalienable, and sacred rights (UN Declaration) that is based on birth, not of French Revolution or American War, the two prime sources of human rights that we know today. Human rights are intellectual and cultural issues which need social reform intervention." And, that is what this book talks about. It is Dr. Pathak's life and mission in a global context that has made him a great social reformer of our times.

One need not have to quote Karl Marx to say that all social and economic changes are rooted in money. Rulers make religious code and punish those who don't follow them. It is true since Jesus Christ who was crucified for defying the Roman code and to the manual scavengers in India, who fought and lost in wars to become untouchables today. The world history since Plato is full of debates on right and wrong. And, nobody has won. The art of association, says Alexis Tocqueville, has therefore become the mother of social peace action because it works between the state and people. The state is too remote for individuals to approach and society is too loosely organised and too powerless to be of any use for the people. Hence, the organised social groups (or NGO) of committed people alone can bring social change, says sociologist Emile Durkheim.

These quotes, although incomplete, define the Sulabh profile though it has now expanded globally to become more of an idea, than an organised group of people committed to seeking change and social justice without violence. Dr. Bindeshwar Pathak, who founded Sulabh International Social Service Organisation in 1970, being a socialist himself, has defined the "social capital", as the ability of people to work together for common purposes in groups and organisations. The concept of "human capital" starts from the premise that since capital today is less about land, factory and machines and more about knowledge and human skill now represented by Bill Gates, Charles Babbage and Mark Zuckerberg and many other knowledge leaders. The human capital is also about people's ability to associate with each other, not only to promote economic life but also to organise peaceful social action like Gandhiji, Nelson Mandela, Lech Walesa, Jayaprakash Narayan and Dr. Bindeshwar Pathak. The governments do not organise movements; they make laws. People associate themselves if they share the same values based on trust. No wonder, the Sulabh Social Movement is a trust and value-based social concept whose slogan is, "Move Forward Together".

Just as Dr. Pathak launched the sanitation movement, Joseph Bazalgette (1819-91) constructed the sewer system in London to end the 'Great Stink' (1858) that had clogged the river Thames, closing down Parliament for several days. Both happened after the Industrial Revolution in two countries about 100 years apart. The Industrial Revolution also transformed global society, and altered the way goods were made. These changes, which began in Britain in 1760, included the use of water and steam power, the invention of new machinery to increase coal and

Joseph Bazalgette - The man who constructed the sewer system in London

iron production, the setting up of factories, and growth of towns. Industrialisation also created new social groups. This change meant that cloth, particularly cotton, could be produced faster than ever before. James Hargreaves, an English weaver, invented the spinning jenny in 1764-1767. Worked by one person, it consisted of a frame and a number of spindles that spun several threads at once. After 1850, industrialisation spread to other countries, including India. This was the time when the Sulabh Revolution was born in Arrah, Patna, in 1970.

Industrial Revolution

The Industrial Revolution also created new social groups, the working class, a new army of industrial workers, railway workers, dockers, textile workers and engineers, along with slums, filth, inequality, exploitation and two global wars. This marks the beginning of the Modern World, wonderful and dangerous. As Britain was the first country to industrialise, it was also the first to experience the disastrous consequences of urbanisation and the first to construct a modern sewerage system to mitigate the resultant unsanitary conditions. During the early 19th century, the Thames was effectively an open sewer, leading to frequent outbreaks of cholera epidemics. Proposals to modernise the sewerage system had been made during 1856, but were neglected due to lack of funds. However, after 'Great Stink' of 1858, Parliament realised the urgency of the problem and resolved to create a modern sewerage system.

In the 16th century, Sir John Harrington invented a flush toilet as a device for Queen Elizabeth I (his godmother) that released wastes into cesspools. Joseph Bazalgette, Chief Engineer of the Metropolitan Board of Works, was given responsibility to lay sewer lines. He designed an extensive underground sewerage system that diverted waste to the Thames estuary, downstream of the main centre of population. Six main interceptor sewers, totalling almost

160 km in length, were constructed, some incorporating stretches of London's 'lost' river. Three of these sewers were north of the river, the southernmost, low-level one being incorporated in the Thames embankment. The embankment also allowed new roads, new public gardens, and the Circle Line of the London Underground.

Sir John Harington, father of the modern flush toilet system

Not by law alone

Dr. Pathak did not say too much when he mentioned in a speech that without government intervention full sanitation would not be achieved as envisaged in the Millennium Development Goals (MDGs) at Johannesburg in 2002. Dr. Pathak is no historian and, for all we know, he has never claimed to be one. However, he has a keen sense of history which enables him to look backward far into the past to sharpen his vision far into the future. For that matter, the Sulabh Movement is an adventure that has succeeded, or a gamble that did not fail! Venezuelan hero Simon Bolivar, standing on the edge of formidable jungle of the Amazon, had cried at his army, "Soldiers, there is no path ahead, but the path is made by walking." Dr. Pathak has walked that untrodden path.

The people and the countries without sanitation (or with an inadequate one) have been mentioned in the position papers, and the UNDP reports, especially of 2006 and 2007. It was reported that about two million children die everyday due to sanitation-related diseases; that every dollar spent on cleanliness saves three dollars in return; that our hospitals are full of diarrhoea patients, and factories marked by low productivity and society by high fecundity. These and many more depressing statics are at best approximation of truth, neither measurable nor verifiable. But, what Dr. A.P.J. Abdul Kalam said in his presidential address about our stinking cities, heaps of uncleared garbage, sick children, coughing women in slums, and the poor weighed down by centuries of poverty, filth and homeless life are the social indicators of poor sanitation, more dependable and verifiable than statistics.

So if we stand for half a minute in memory of each one of those who have died due to lack of sanitation, it will be another 100 years and we will still be standing in silence. Those who die in war, lost or won, are remembered with respect but not those who perished due to cholera in Europe, Spanish influenza in east Russia and any number of cases of plague, and other sanitation-related diseases. They are not even counted; they lie in heaps in history books, uncounted and unremembered. It was in this context Dr. Pathak said that state intervention is necessary to achieve the sanitation goal.

It may be recalled that in the West, sanitation has been a state business. John Harington invented WC in the Queen's Palace and all movements to clean up places after Great London Fire (1666) became the state-sponsored business. Harington had invented the first flushing toilet that used moving parts to remove excreta and refill the water tank. His invention, however, did not take off. Although some of the elite between the 16th and 18th centuries had systems that used water from cisterns to flush their chamber pots, those primitive water closets were hard to install and harder to maintain. But in 1775, Alexander Cummings, an English watchmaker, recognised the economic potential for a functional flush toilet. Cummings drastically simplified Harington's design with a single sliding valve that emptied the bowl, released water from a cistern to clean it, and then refilled the cistern. In 1778, Joseph Bramah converted the sliding valve to a hinge flap, simplifying the mechanism even further. By the turn of the century, Braman's company had sold and installed over 6,000 toilets across England.

How it developed

Significant improvements came 75 years after Braman, during the Queen Victoria's reign. George Adamson incorporated siphonic flush-down, George Jennings improved on it, Thomas Crapper devised the pull-chain method for flushing, and Thomas Twyford encapsulated the whole system into porcelain for easy cleaning and sanitising. While early toilets were by today's measures loud, inefficient, and hard to clean, they sufficed for those who wanted to leave no smear in the WC. In the 19th century, the crap-cleaning capacity of the cities grew ever more strained as population densities skyrocketed. A number of great cholera outbreaks, including the ones in 1831, 1849, 1854 and 1866, ravaged the West. The 1849 outbreaks killed 35,000 in England and Wales, beyond 15,000 dead in London alone. All over the Western world, as endless waves of migrants flocked to the cities for jobs, cholera followed. 2,200 people died in Quebec City in 1832, 8,000 in Havana in 1833, 5,000 in New York City in 1848-49, and 1,000 in Sacramento in 1850.

By the end of the 19th century, reforming the sanitary conditions of the poor became a pet cause of the English bourgeoisie. Led by people such as Edwin Chadwick and Octavia Hill, a movement grew to transfer the responsibility for clean water and sewage disposal from individuals to societies and governments. It may be noted that the Chadwick movement was state-sponsored, so also the other.

Chief among the sanitary reformers' proposals was eliminating the danger of leaching cesspools, open street-level gutters, leaky sewer pipes, and flying faeces dumped from chamber pots, by instituting a system for the simple and efficient removal of flush toilets in all homes, and the water and sewerage system they necessitated. To save the population from the dangers of excreta, the elite's toilet habits had to be disseminated across society.

The English launched massive public works campaigns towards building toilet. Between 1859 and 1865, London city engineers led by Joseph Bazalgette built 100 miles of main sewers, 450 miles of interceptor sewers, and 13,000 million bricks and excavating 3.5 million tons of earth in the process. And in the decades following London's great cholera outbreak in 1866, the state legislated a number of provisions mandating the same kind of amenities for the working class that the middle and upper classes had long since embraced. By World War I, England was a toilet-based society. France, the cleanest city in the world, had "flying toilets" when people wrapped up excreta and flung it around to let it fall on the neighbours' houses or in the street.

US: a different story

America is a different story. It is a country which has not indigenous people of their own traditions. America became the United States in 1776. People mostly from the English-speaking world, brought their own sanitation practices to a huge landmass (4 times of India's size) with 20% of its population. But sanitation is becoming a problem in the US now as is brilliantly discussed by Mr. Dave Praeger in his book 'Poop Culture'. In Europe, the story is more complicated. But, the European captured half the world to keep their cities clean. Britain, France, Germany, Italy, Belgium, the Netherlands, Spain and Portugal governed most of Asia, Africa and Latin America.

Victor Hugo says in his book, 'Les Miserables', "All the rich are alike but the poor suffer in their own ways." The entire West has one sanitation system, the capital and water-intensive sewerage system invented by Harington. And, they flush their waste into places one doesn't know. The places are clean also because of cold climate and high rainfall. For instance, there has never been a problem of houselessness in Europe and America. It was because those who had no place to hide were frozen to death. What a way to solve the problem! Don't cure the patient, kill him. The Roman emperor told Governor Pontius Pilate to restore peace in Judea (now Patestine). Pilate killed all those who could not flee and reported peace to Rome. When Pilate was told by his mistress that among the crucified was Jesus from Bethlehem, he turned to her in sneer and said, "You do not know, darling, how much little wisdom does it take to rule the world."

But, sanitation problem in the poor countries are different. They have different waste disposal systems; hand albution and open defecation in India and stone and bricks are used in many countries of Africa. A large number of different sanitation practices are prevalent in 52 inland countries of Africa, 14 major countries in Asia and South East Asia where they developed their cultural practices in their own ways. But, all these poor countries suffer from insanitation following influx into cities.

A historical ring

In which case what do we do to achieve the MDGs in these poor societies? Dr. Pathak's idea becomes relevant. Nowhere in the world any non-government organisation (NGO), like Sulabh, has worked for sanitation to achieve the level of success which Dr. Pathak has achieved. The Sulabh-created facilities are now used by more than 10 million people a day which is more than the total population of Israel, or those of many small countries, like Monaco, Luxembourg and Liechtenstein, in Europe put together. Never has such a thing happened before that a jobless wanderer boy of India from backwater areas of Bihar tumbled upon a dream which has become the dominant idea of our times. Sanitation is now a slogan, a rallying cry of the poor countries to join together and take up the broom to clean this exploited planet which is the common heritage of mankind.

A historical ring also. After Napoleon won the French Revolution and Europe, he turned to his advisor Talleyrand and asked; "After all, who started it in the first place; of course I didn't. I had came to "Paris for a job. "He was told it was Rousseau, a Geneva-based Parian tramp who wrote a pamphlet "Liberty, Fraternity Equality", to get some money to buy a ticket for Paris. And after that the world was never the same again. This is a story not very dissimilar from Dr. Pathak's who also dug up one more pit where one existed before. And, the world's sanitation situation was never the same again. Thus, he has become a folk hero of our times. History repeats itself but always in a way crazier than before.

Nobody can choose future or destroy; it happens.
— Max Weber

CHAPTER 2

Formative Years: A World of Old Values and New Hope

Being remembered makes one live forever

Dr. Bindeshwar Pathak is like any other man of traditional values except that he thinks differently and says that the only way to find a new future for the country is to rebuild it anew. Very clearly, he has done that in a considerable measure. Dr. Pathak lives by his ethics, hard work, honesty, fair play, courage, loyalty and patriotism, always remaining faithful to the ideals of his forebears, while trying to change social order.

Dr. Bindeshwar Pathak came in the mists of legend as a homespun commoner child who cared little about material rewards and social status only to later become great emancipator of the scavenger, a social pariah, after a veritable civil war to free him from manually cleaning human excreta and, thus, create a new social order. The folk heroes of the legend building histories are not born in palaces but in villages and the prairies. Dr. Pathak is one, honest and compassionate man with deep commitment to the right of all people to elevate themselves in a free society. He is a complex, paradoxical, and a self-made man who is happy about his social commitments, obsessed with his work, troubled with recurring bouts of melancholy, and gifted with a superb talent for communication. One cannot name many names like this in these troubled times.

REFORMERS ARE NOT BORN IN PALACES
The front view of the ancestral house where Dr. Pathak was born

Scavengers have inherited poverty, degradation, indignity and discrimination by birth which have social approval and religious sanction. They are wronged by the chances of history and condemned to a life of depravity because of social indifference and political sleepwalking in a chaotic social order which remains unchanged by time and untroubled by conscience. Just as religious conviction is impervious to logical argument, the event of scavenging has acquired complete independence from the change in government or political system. Democracy had changed everything in India but not the scavenging which persists despite many laws and tall claims. "When the GDP is growing at a high rate, a small problem like scavenging can wait", seems to be the argument of the neo-liberals and growth wizards. Dr. Pathak rejects this argument and says, "Glittering growth graphs, social and political spectacles, high-rise buildings, electric light, and blazing metro will not add up to the world of my dream if the system cannot end the immoral and inhuman practice of scavenging which is a civilisational problem". Very clearly, the Sulabh Founder is the friend of the poorest and the lowliest and the lost – the scavengers.

Dr. Pathak's life has been shaped by his experiences, intellectual curiosity or simple pragmatism – all rolled into one. During the formative years he was no different from any of his time and age, except that he had an inquisitive mind, social sensitivity and aptitude for voracious reading and knowing new things. His diverse interests and accomplishments and faith in basic virtues motivated his life and shaped his action in whatever challenge he faced. Of these, none was stronger than his belief in the equality of man. And, that society must change only to survive and grow, and not be fixated on old values which have lost their relevance. "The world has changed, so must we", he says.

Smt. Yogmaya Devi : Mother

Dr. Bindeshwar Pathak was born on April 2, 1943 as the second son to Smt. Yogmaya Devi and Pandit Ramakant Pathak in Rampur Baghel village of district Vaishali, Bihar, into a traditional Brahmin family. His mother was central to his life and had enormous influence on his character. A pious housewife given to good old virtues and religious beliefs, she loved her second son very much, possibly because she saw in him a saviour of the family which had fallen on hard times. That was also because Bindeshwar, the boy, showed confidence and the bearing of a man who was sure of his future.

Pandit Ramakant Pathak : Father

The place where father practised medicine

Dr. Pathak, Smt. Amola Pathak, Madhubala (extreme left), Kumar Dilip and Kiranbala

His father was a respected leader of the community and a big spender (a habit that he passed on to his second son) given to performing social rituals. Both the parents were, however, firm in the belief that education alone would help the family get out of difficulty. Dr. Pathak's grandfather was an astrologer. "The more I live, the more I respect the teachings of my parents and maternal grandfather not only as ideals but also as practical guides to life. They gave me a life of love and compassion beyond my dreams." No wonder, what sets Dr. Pathak apart from others is less the quality of his mind than the warmth of his heart, although his life has always been surrounded by risk, drama, mystery and uncertainties.

Parents shaped his future

Dr. Pathak's childhood was spent in dignified poverty in a home in which his mother, a stern but amiable person, instilled in him the eternal truths that she held dear. His father infected him unconsciously with his endearing traits of forbearance and cheerfulness. A perfect marriage with Smt. Amola Pathak on July 2, 1965 did the rest. Madhubala was born to them in 1973 when the family was in the midst of struggle; with the coming of Kumar Dilip in 1975, the second child, the struggle was no less intense. And, when Kiranbala joined in 1977, the size of the family more than doubled. After marriage, Dr. Pathak had not enough money to buy things for his wife when she was to visit her father's place. The young Bindeshwar cried for the first time, not knowing his future.

Pandit Jainandan Jha, maternal grandfather (Nana). His liberal values had considerable influence on the life and mission of the Sulabh Founder

Dr. Pathak's maternal grandfather, Pandit Jainandan Jha, a Gandhian, was the role model for the young Bindeshwar who has inherited the latter's commitment to social service and the habit of doing things differently. His (Nana's) liberal values had considerable influence on Dr. Pathak's character. He, being a freedom fighter, did not accept untouchability in society and encouraged Harijans to visit his place and eat with him and others. Dr. Pathak's father being a doctor also had no special concern for conservative values. Hence, although the family was conservative, there was no special pressure to stick to old ways. Dr. Pathak also remembers Mr. R. Nath, a Bihar official, who told him, "Don't ever commit dishonesty and if ever you are lured into doing it, remember me." The Sulabh Founder never tires of quoting these lines to reiterate that integrity is key to public life, specially to a successful social reforms movement where the founder has to be a role model for others to follow.

The young Bindeshwar lived in his village for 18 years and studied in lower primary, primary, middle and high schools. In lower primary, he studied in the village school of his Nanaji who was also the chairman of the local civic board, Hazipur. In the 1950s, development works, including roads, education and health, used to be looked after by the board. As many as 16 years after B.A. from B.N. College, Patna, Dr. Pathak did M.A. and a series of other academic courses with distinction in many of them. This

The village school

was entirely because of his academic bent of mind and hunger for knowledge. This distinction in academic fields also helped him provide an intellectual context to the Sulabh Movement and how other reformers behaved in similar situation. No wonder, he has raised what was essentially toilet cleaning problem, to a civilisation crisis, comparing it to many other reforms also launched to end social injustice.

He did well at school, up to Class III, but somebody told his father that he should not study in the village of his Nana because of his unorthodox views. Hence, his father brought him to his own village. He did well in the secondary school examinations. While at school, he had to go to another village because his village had only lower primary school. While going to school every morning, he used to see a woman cleaning human excreta from a bucket toilet in the house of a landlord of Pohiyar village. Since the bucket toilet was near the road, it would often stink when he had to run to avoid the stench. Sometimes, he would see women carrying human excreta on the head. The passers-by also kept themselves away from scavengers. She was an untouchable scavenger who lived on the outskirts of the village in a broken hut in the midst of pigs, filth and squalor. Scavengers' children were not allowed to play with others. Growing up in a conservative family, he practised untouchability and avoided scavengers. But the memory still hurts.

A graduate boy

Village caste profile

Village Rampur Baghel had six major castes – Brahmin, Kshatriya, Yadava, Dusadh, Chamar and Dom. Brahmins were allowed to accept water only from Kshatriyas and Yadavas, not from others. Brahmins never used to accept cooked foods like rice and dal, even from Kshatriyas and Yadavas. Among the Shudras, there were three castes – Dusadh, Chamar and Dom. Dusadhs and Chamars were treated as impure castes. Dusadhs used to help in farming and tilling of land, cattle feeding etc. The Chamars used to throw away dead animals outside the village, skin them to make shoes and slippers for villagers. They also did farming. Dusadhs and Chamars were not treated as untouchables. The upper castes and backward castes would touch them on occasions when helping them to lift farm products but would not accept water from their hands. They were not allowed to draw water from the wells along with upper caste people or to visit the same temple. Hence, they had to make their own deities using earth and putting some vermilion on them.

There were two Dom families who were treated as untouchables. Nobody touched them. Nor were they allowed to draw water from

Smt. Amola Pathak in her village crop-field

any well of the village like those of Dusadh and Chamar castes. They were not even allowed to bathe in the village pond or offer prayers in the temple. Seeing their plight, Dr. Pathak's grandfather got a well dug exclusively for them. The Dom families were supposed to make utensils of bamboo like *soop and dagra* (a flat utensil to separate the grains from husk) for the villagers and provide fire for cremation of bodies on the banks of the Ganga. It is ironical that a person, who is treated as an untouchable becomes holier than Brahmin because he alone could give fire for cremation to light the pyre, or else the dead will 'not go to heaven'. This anomaly always intrigued the young Bindeshwar who, as a wayward child, refused to accept it.

Touching the untouchable

One day, an 'untouchable' Dom woman came to Bindeshwar's house to deliver utensils. As she was leaving, his grandmother started sprinkling Ganga water to purify the passage. Young Bindeshwar could not put up with such a cruel treatment to the woman at the hands of his grandmother. Apparently in protest, he touched the Dom woman after which the grandmother, with the help of some other boys, caught hold of Bindeshwar and made him swallow cow dung, cow urine and sand with Ganga water to de-contaminate him. That horrible trauma of childhood has always been in his memory along with the thought of how upper caste people humiliated the untouchables for the birth, in the choosing of which they had no say. He often narrates this event in his speeches. In those days, no school had toilets, either for boys or for girls. Hence, girls were not encouraged to go to school. In Rampur, his house also had no toilet. Dr. Pathak's house was built by his paternal grandfather in 1915, a large sprawling house having many rooms, a prayer room, a big courtyard with a well in the compound, but no toilet. His mother, sisters, aunts and grandmother would wake up early to go to the field in the darkness before sunrise. Some of them were even bitten by snakes. In summer, men had to go with umbrellas in the field to avoid being seen and also to avoid the scorching heat of the sun. In the rainy season when strong winds would blow away umbrellas, men were left almost naked, much to their embarrassment. In case

The village folk around the house

someone had diarrhoea, it was difficult to go to toilets many times a day, that too in summer, harsh winter or in the rainy season. Women were worst hit. They had to wait till sunset and, consequently, suffer from headache. No wonder, diseases caused by hookworm, roundworm, tapeworm were common in the village. This was the story of almost all villages. Even today, the rural picture has not changed much.

Future came unannounced

After doing his B.A. in Sociology from B.N. College in Patna, he was preparing to do M.A. from Sagar University, Madhya Pradesh, when an incident changed his life. He was standing at the railway station when two persons from the Bihar Gandhi Centenary Committee came to him and said, "If you become a lecturer after two years you will earn ₹ 450 per month but if you join the Committee, you will get a permanent post and big money. And you will also fulfil Gandhiji's dream of a scavenging-free India." Dr. Pathak followed their advice as he was earning only ₹ 5 a day as a teacher in a local school. But, there was no such post and Dr. Pathak had also missed the last date for admission. So, he worked with the committee for five months as a translator without pay. But the place made him aware of scavengers' problems and miseries. It was in 1969 that he developed the low-cost two-pit toilet system and made the first two Sulabh Shauchalayas at Arrah which triggered a revolution. And by 1974, Sulabh was recognised by the Bihar Government. The future has a way to come unannounced.

Dr. Pathak always remembers two incidents. One was the sight of a newly married girl being forced by her husband and in-laws to do scavenging. Dr. Pathak's protest, however, withered when asked challengingly if he would pay for living expenses. Scavenging was not a choice for them; it was due to poverty and traditional practice that forced her to take up scavenging against her will. The second incident was when a child in red clothes was attacked and gored by a bull but no one came to rescue and take him to hospital. The child was left to die on the road. Nobody saved him because he was an 'untouchable' son of a scavenger!

Dr. Pathak had seen and experienced all the three situations, defecation in the open, scavenging and untouchability, while he lived in the village. Little did he realise that one day he would have to address these problems which were the concern not only of his village and the country, but also of half the world. The practice of defecation in the open has been in existence right from the pre-Vedic to Vedic to Puranic periods followed by medieval and Mughal periods to British periods. The evil still persists in India although with much less horror. The factors responsible for this include tradition, absence of alternatives, lack of awareness, poverty etc. It is known now that exposed human excreta causes nearly 50 types of infections. As for scavenging all that can be said is that, it is a demeaning, degrading and humiliating work performed by a class of people called scavengers who carry excreta of others as head-load to make a meagre living.

Dr. Pathak had no ambition higher than finding a job because there was no money to buy food, nor many persons to lend it. Trudging in torn *khadi payjamas* and broken *chappals,* he did his graduation and started looking into the future. Until then, he had no thought of fame, name or power; he just wanted to become a teacher and live like all teachers did in respectable poverty. In true Brahmanical tradition, his appetite for knowledge has been insatiable. He did his advance studies, including doctorate, after he was married and became a father and at a time when the Sulabh Movement was in full swing. He simply shut himself off into a hostel room and prepared for examinations, secure in the belief that education alone would help him.

Debt of honour

He did not forget the days of his miseries when he worked as an errand boy at a tea stall in Patna. He kept all his friends and colleagues in comfort and looked after them and their families. He still remembers every man who may have done him any small favour and repays them many times over. He calls it debt of honour. His entire life is identified with miseries and redemption. He asks questions like a child and answers them like a philosopher. He is mystical, distant and lost in emotions, constantly in search of new frontiers. Alexander once said, "If I were not Alexander, I would have been a Diogenes" (a Greek *fakir* and philosopher). Dr. Pathak would have been a *fakir* if he were not the founder of the largest and the most powerful social movement of the second half of the century.

"I did not have even ₹ 25 to go and take a job when it was offered to me. Therefore, when somebody says he has no money, my past experiences come alive before me and I give away whatever I can lay my hands on. Experiences of suffering have been central to my life and work. And, probably, that is the source of the Sulabh Movement", says Dr. Pathak. The stories of his helplessness are depressing, no less than those of his latter-day achievements are uplifting.

Dr. Pathak travelled all over the country, visited and lived with scavengers in their *bastis,* studied their habits and social mores (doing his Ph.D. on scavenging), their history and geographical spread and eventually declared that scavengers were a special class united in their miseries and social degradation. "Let us save them from their squalid conditions and in doing so we will be redeeming the national conscience," Dr. Pathak said. Significantly, it was not a mere emotional outburst of the young Bindeshwar Pathak who by that time had fully equipped himself intellectually to find solutions to the problems. He knew that slogans alone would not help and, hence, developed a technology which has become a credible alternative to sewerage system and scavenging in India. Dr. Pathak observed after studying scriptures that scavenging has no religious sanction and, hence, those who practise untouchability commit a sin. Human excreta, instead of being thrown away, can be productively used in farms to raise productivity. And, he has successfully demonstrated that.

He sought to abolish scavenging not only out of sympathy for scavengers but also out of the belief that scavenging is a primitive, expensive and unhygienic practice which may create an explosive situation, in which case a highly dissatisfied group would turn lumpen and work to destroy the social system. The harmonisation of theory and practice distinguishes the Sulabh Sanitation Movement, which he launched to fight the evil of scavenging and untouchability. It is an indigenous concept based on experience and tested scientifically, combining in itself an appropriate technology and a demand for social morality. To put it simply, while other movements encountered problems and injustices in society, and failed to find solutions, Dr. Pathak identified the problems, developed a self-sustaining system, gave an appropriate technology and, finally, solved the problem. The Sulabh Founder never tires of telling how the conditions of scavengers had always pained him and once when he touched a scavenger, he was made to take cow dung and urine to purify his soul. This remained a lasting scar on his mind which finally made him work for abolition of scavenging in India.

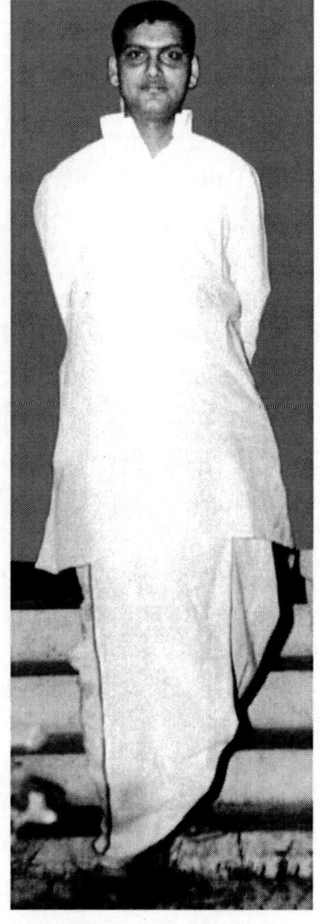

A homespun leader in making

THOMAS PAINE ALSO SAW A BOY KILLED AND NOBODY SAVED HIM

Thomas Paine

An another analogy, though far-fetched, is that of Thomas Paine (1737-1809), author, inventor, intellectual and one of the Founding Fathers of the United States. Paine became a passionate campaigner of natural justices after he saw a jeering crowd attacking, and finally beating a boy to death during his childhood in village, Thetford, Norfolk, England. Nobody saved the boy because he was black. Son of Joseph Paine, a Quaker who believes in the 'inner voice' of God and not in organised religion, including Christianity, Thomas Paine was so distressed by the death of the black boy that he adopted deism, which says that there is a Creator all right but he does not interfere in the working of the world.

Paine emigrated to the British American colonies in 1774 to participate in the American Revolution. His principal contributions were the powerful, widely read pamphlet *Common Sense* (1776), advocating colonial America's independence from the Kingdom of Great Britain, and *The American Crisis* (1776-1783), a pro-revolutionary pamphlet series. His writing of *Common Sense and The Age of Reason* was so influential in spurring on the Revolutionary War that John Adams reportedly said, "Without the pen of the author of Common Sense, the sword of Washington would have been raised in vain." In 1789 Paine was deeply involved in the early stages of the French Revolution. He wrote *The Rights of Man* (1791), in part a defence of the French Revolution. In December of 1793, he arrested and imprisoned in Paris, and then released in 1794.

In 1802, on President Jefferson's invitation, he returned to America where he died on June 8, 1809 paving the way for all revolutions that came after. It all began with the death of a black boy. The Sulabh Founder also saw a boy killed. Nobody saved him because he was a scavenger. Thus, started his campaigns for natural justice, which the Sulabh Movement symbolises. How strange that reformers are so similar and yet so different at once – in different ages and different countries and many oceans and climes apart.

"Man matures faster in poverty and war. Crisis tests the mettle of man and produces leaders who lead by example."
– Leo Tolstoy

CHAPTER 3

Long Journey Since Gandhi Centenary Year in Patna

It was struggle every step of the way

"As I speak here today, somewhere a scavenger must be physically cleaning toilets – hungry, unclean and hated; somewhere today, a scavenger mother, facing punishing poverty, still must be taking time off from toilet work to send her child to school, in the belief that this cruel world still has a place for her dreams. And, these thoughts haunt me even when I sleep." – Dr. Bindeshwar Pathak after accepting the 2009 Stockholm Water Prize in August 2009.

After completing graduation and wandering about for a while, young Bindeshwar Pathak joined the Bihar Gandhi Centenary Celebration Committee at Patna in 1968 when he was just 25 years of age, too young to think about serious things of life, nor about the gumption and bile of his age. Young, educated and jobless was a toxic mix which could produce a revolutionary but not a social reformer and serious social activist which the young boy grew to become later in life. It was the time when his family was caught between two systems of values – one which was not yet fully dead and another which was not yet fully born. The family had Gandhian followers, educated and honest good men and women wedded to old values and yet wanting a change without toppling the old social order, not knowing how to make the two opposite virtues combine to produce a society of their dream. Those were strange times when British values were set to vanish and Gandhian ethics of social change was not yet ready to take over. The transition produced a morally confused, materially poor and socially adrift barefoot generation. The young Pathak belonged to that split generation which left him alone to find his future in those turbulent times.

During his stay with the Bihar Gandhi Centenary Committee, Dr. Pathak was exposed to the miseries of the poor, especially of scavengers, which fuelled the flame already existing in his mind to change the social order. We know of great social reformers who wandered about without money, social standing and job in ancient time, but they were either saints, mendicants or wanderers who walked into the shadow of life, never again to see the light of the day. But of those who did make a mark, Dr. Pathak is the one, a chance career and earned success. And what a success at that!!

Soon after his joining the committee, it was realised by the members that no more befitting tribute could be paid to the Father of the Nation than launching a campaign to liberate scavengers from the demeaning work of physically cleaning and carrying human excreta and resettling them in other professions. Scavengers were dearest to Gandhiji who was so pained by their miseries that he wished to be born in the next birth as a scavenger to help them get out of miseries. True, it was an emotional burst but this resonated in the programmes launched by the Patna Committee which became a trend setter for the future national agenda.

Genesis of Sulabh Movement

The decisive moment came in Dr. Pathak's life when, on the suggestion of the then Bihar Chief Minister, Mr. Daroga Prasad Rai, and the Minister of Local Self-Government, Mr. Shatrughan Sharan Singh, he founded Sulabh Shauchalaya Sansthan in 1970 (now known as Sulabh International Social Service Organisation), a non-political organisation enjoying the support of all political parties and the public. The two leaders were of the opinion that social programmes could not be implemented by the government or by NGOs alone; both should work together in close cooperation to implement them. Dr. Pathak applied for a grant of ₹ 70,000 to run the newly-formed organisation. And, thereby hangs the Sulabh story.

Meanwhile, the government of Mr. Daroga Prasad Rai collapsed and his loan application was sent from the Local Self-Government to Planning and then to Finance, but to no avail. In 1971, Mr. Rameshwar Nath, an IAS officer, who had joined the Department of Local Self-Government, told Dr. Pathak that he had gone through his papers and felt that the Sulabh programme would make great impact in the country but he saw a danger in taking loan which would harm the credibility. He said the Finance Department would most likely object to grant. But when Dr. Pathak again applied for grant next year, the officer said he might get a grant of only ₹ 50,000 which would not make any impact. The officer suggested that instead of asking for grants, Dr. Pathak should take money for programme implementation and raise fund on his own. Thus, the government, instead of giving grant, started thinking of how to award work to Sulabh. But a decision in the matter was long delayed and Dr. Pathak, who was in need of funds, sold his land, wife's ornaments and also took loans from friends to run the organisation. This did not work. This period of his life was so depressing that at times he even thought of committing suicide. He slept on railway platforms and had to miss meals. Neither any grant nor any work was coming his way.

To make things work in 1973 Dr. Pathak persuaded a member of the Bihar Legislative Assembly, Mr. Bhagdeo Singh 'Yogi', to write a letter to the then Prime Minister of India, Mrs. Indira Gandhi, on the need for liberation of scavengers, requesting her to pay personal attention to the problem. Within a fortnight, the MLA received a reply from Mrs. Gandhi, stating that she was writing to the Chief Minister

PRIME MINISTER

No.234-PMO/73.

New Delhi,
April 5, 1973.

Dear Shri Singh,

I have your letter of the 17th March and am concerned to read that the State Government have not been able to utilise the Fourth Plan provision for Schemes designed to eliminate the odious practice of carrying night-soil on the head.

I am writing to the Chief Minister and asking him to give personal attention to this matter. I entirely agree with you that our Party should be active in this important social programme.

Yours sincerely,

Indira Gandhi

(Indira Gandhi)

Shri Bhagdeo Singh 'Yogi',
Member, Legislative Assembly,
21, Orthodox Chamber,
R Block, Patna-1.

Letter of late Mrs. Indira Gandhi to Mr. Bhagdeo Singh 'Yogi', former MLA, Bihar to give personal attention to the matter. Although the government took note of Mrs. Gandhi's letter, the issue again got lost in the cobweb of red tape. Thus, the problem remained unsolved.

Mrs. Indira Gandhi

How it all began

But suddenly, in August 1973, the future began to unfold itself. Dr. Pathak had gone to Arrah town to meet officers of other departments when he saw a name plate of Mr. R.K. Mishra, Executive Officer of the Arrah Municipality. He talked to the officer who asked him for the details of his programme to get government approval. Dr. Pathak told Mr. Mishra that the government had not given any direction in the matter to the local bodies. Mr. Mishra gave him ₹ 500 and asked him to construct two demonstration toilets in the office compound of the Arrah Municipality. When the Chairman of the Municipality, Mr. Ram Vilas Singh, saw the demonstration

Sulabh's first toilet came up at Arrah in Bihar (1973)

toilets, he was very impressed because being a freedom fighter, he was aware of the dream of Mahatma Gandhi to relieve scavengers from their dehumanising work. The Chairman agreed to the proposal of the Executive Officer to put up such toilets in Arrah town and to convert the existing bucket toilets in the town into Sulabh flush toilets. This was how it all began.

Dr. Pathak was alone when he started the work; he used to go door to door to motivate and educate the beneficiaries to get their bucket latrines converted into Sulabh toilets. Initially people were not ready to accept the new technology but finally one Councillor of the Arrah Municipality, Mr. Suresh Prasad Singh, came to his rescue and asked him to convert the bucket toilets of his house. After seeing the functioning of the Sulabh toilets in his house, his neighbours followed the example and, finally people of the town came in droves to set up Sulabh toilets. This was how the conversion of bucket latrine programme started in Bihar. The Executive Officer of the neighbouring town, Buxar, also asked Dr. Pathak to take up such projects.

In 1974, Sulabh took up the conversion work in Patna city. The Local Self-government Department, which was considering recognising Sulabh as a catalytic agent to work between government and beneficiaries, cleared the Sulabh proposal in April 1974 and the government sent a circular to all the local bodies to take the help of Sulabh in the conversion of bucket toilets and, thus, relieve scavengers. The programme later started throughout Bihar. This is how a small trickle turned into a torrent.

Later, during the Gandhi Centenary Year, the Government of India took up a special programme for converting dry toilets. Under this scheme, the householders were provided 25 per cent subsidy and 75 per cent loan recoverable in easy installments. The householders were also allowed to connect their service latrines to nearby public sewer, if there was any. The Ministry of Health suggested to the local bodies that no new buildings should be allowed to be built without flush latrines. In the areas where sewers had been laid, strict enforcement of law for compulsory connection of dry latrines in the existing houses to sewers should be launched and where sewers were not laid, a special drive should be launched for conversion of dry latrines into flush latrines or by connecting them to local septic tanks or leaching pits. This programme could not succeed because of lack of initiative by the people and the government. It was a concept that failed.

Angst and despair

This career choice was still not finally made by Dr. Pathak. While social service was the revered tradition in the family, Dr. Pathak was not inclined to accept it; he wanted to be a teacher. But after joining the Bihar Gandhi Centenary Committee, when he was exposed to the Gandhian ideology, opinion changed. And, he began to work for Gandhiji's campaign for the upliftment of Harijans. His work in the Centenary Committee involved extensive touring of villages throughout Bihar, during which he realised that the Gandhian philosophy would be of no avail until the campaign was accompanied by action-oriented programmes. He could sense that the untouchables were not impressed by exhortations; they wanted a change in their lives. Rhetoric for them had no meaning and, therefore, no appeal. He could see the hypocrisy of tall-talking do-gooders who indulged in mouthing fine phrases and dishing out populist promises while doing nothing.

It was about this time, he was transferred to scavengers' liberation cell where he saw for himself the pathetic condition of scavengers who cleaned and carried human excreta, often as head-load, generation after generation without any protest and with total resignation. This filled him with a strong desire to find out a viable mechanism for their liberation. Mahatma Gandhi wanted two things: one, that the scavengers' social status should be on a par with others and two, that there should be some scientific, safe and hygienic method of human waste disposal to replace manual scavenging when no one would be required to manually handle the human excreta of others to earn a living. This was the challenge which caused Dr. Pathak's concern and commitment to help scavengers get out of poverty.

The book that brought his Eureka moment

Meanwhile, the Bihar Government, at the instance of the Central Government, directed local bodies to get the bucket latrines converted into hand-flush latrines and connect them either to sewer lines or to leach pits. This was deemed as a tribute to Mahatma Gandhi. The directive could not make much headway on account of many reasons, the main reason being the absence of an affordable, acceptable and cost-effective technology. Imbued with the determination to find an appropriate alternative technology to replace manual scavenging, Dr. Pathak carried out an extensive research on the subject. He studied a large number of toilet designs which could possibly replace the manually cleaned bucket privies. Eventually, he came across a book titled *Excreta Disposal for Rural Areas and Small Communities*, by E.G. Wagner and J.N. Lanoix (WHO, Geneva, 1958) which stated with clarity and conclusive proof that "out of the heterogeneous mass of latrine designs produced the world over, the sanitary pit privy emerges as the most practical and universally applicable type." He got the clue to the riddle and developed a low-cost two-pit pour-flush water seal toilet system, popularly known as Sulabh Shauchalaya, which proved a viable and most effective alternative to replace the pit privies which required manual scavenging. The simple idea that struck him in the late seventies became a game-changer. This book brought his eureka moment. (A cry of joy when one finds something as Archimedes did). The Sulabh technology is more advantageous than the others that it has superseded. While the Bihar Government was interested in the large-scale conversion of service latrines into pour-flush toilets as a measure to eradicate manual scavenging, the local bodies had neither requisite technical knowledge nor the dedicated manpower base. The government was in a quandary because the money had been made available for the purpose and the public wanted the work to be executed soon. But the real problem was the absence of any organisation which could function as a coordinating agency. Sulabh Shauchalaya Sansthan, thus got a role to play.

Meanwhile, Sulabh's seminal work made the WHO, Government of India and UNICEF to convene a high-level seminar in Patna (May 25-27, 1978) to examine the Bihar experiment. The seminar recommended that "two-pit pour-flush water seal latrine with on-site excreta disposal system was the most appropriate low-cost technology to be introduced on a large scale in the urban areas because the system met the technical, social and cultural needs of the country". This recognition of the Sulabh technology and the work done in Bihar proved to be a milestone in the organisation's onward journey in making the country scavenging-free. Several state governments and Union Territories invited Sulabh to take up the conversion and construction work of Sulabh Shauchalayas. Sulabh's work encouraged the WHO, Government of India and UNICEF to convene yet another high-level seminar in Patna to again examine closely the Bihar experiment. Thus, the Sulabh technology was finally approved as a credible alternative to the sewerage system for universal use.

Work extension and whole town approach

Realising that the recognition of the Sulabh technology alone was not enough, the Sulabh Founder made an all-round effort to mobilise opinion for the formulation and implementation of a Central Government scheme to end manual scavenging. A breakthrough was made in March 1981 when a meeting was convened at Dr. Pathak's initiative with the then Minister of Works and Housing, Minister of Urban Development, Bihar and the Secretary and other senior officers of the Ministry of Home Affairs. It was decided that a comprehensive scheme should be introduced in the selected small and medium towns on the whole-town approach basis for conversion of dry latrines. The scavengers so liberated would be given alternative jobs. It was also agreed that the liberation of scavengers was one of the measures for the removal of untouchability under Sec. 15 A of the Protection of Civil Rights Act, 1955 because scavengers were the victims of the worst form of untouchability and the scheme could be taken up under the Home Ministry's Centrally-sponsored scheme of 'Machinery for Implementation of PCR Act'. The Bihar Government was asked to make comprehensive schemes for small and medium towns. These schemes were finally approved and Central assistance was released to the Bihar Government on the matching grant basis in respect of two towns, viz. Biharsharif and Purnia in March, 1981. Under the scheme 50 per cent of the total cost of conversion was given to the households as subsidy and the remaining 50 per cent as loan at nominal rate of interest recoverable in 10-12 years time. Next year in 1981-82, two more towns were taken up in Bihar with Central assistance. Later, the other states took up the scheme which worked very well.

Meanwhile, intervening in a debate in Parliament in 1983, Mrs. Indira Gandhi said, "The practice of carrying night soil as head-load was a disgrace which should be stopped as early as possible". Mrs. Gandhi, however, added that it was not possible to give any specific date by which this practice, prevalent in many parts of the country, could be ended. She said that the practice could not be banned unless alternative jobs were provided to the people employed in the work. She informed the House that as far as she was concerned, she had cleaned toilet herself while she was in Gandhiji's Ashram. These developments coming as they did one after another created social, political and administrative conditions in taking forward the Sulabh work in abolishing scavenging.

New schemes for old problems

The scheme, which was later transferred from the Ministry of Home Affairs to the newly created Ministry of Welfare in September 1985, worked very well and the response of the state governments was encouraging. There were, however, some inherent difficulties. The number of towns taken up in each state was limited to one or two every year due to lack of funds. Another problem was of coordination among the Department of Urban Development/ Municipal Administration and the department dealing with training and rehabilitation of scavengers in the state governments. The funding pattern of the scheme was also modified in 1989-90 on the recommendations of a Study Group constituted by the Committee of Secretaries under HUDCO.

The quantum of subsidy under the scheme was reduced from the existing 50 per cent of the total unit cost of conversion irrespective of the income of the beneficiary to 45 per cent in the case of the Economically Weaker Sections (EWS), 25 per cent for the Low-Income Groups (LIG) and no subsidy for other income groups like MIG and HIG. An element of beneficiary contribution was introduced for the first time – 5 per cent for EWS, 15 per cent for LIG and 25 per cent for MIG and HIG and the remaining amount as loan. In 1991, the scheme of liberation of scavengers was split into two parts. The component of conversion of dry latrines was transferred to the Ministry of Urban Development for implementation through HUDCO and the other component dealing with training and rehabilitation of liberated scavengers remained with the Ministry of Welfare.

The scheme suffered a setback after the change in the financial pattern and bifurcation into two parts, each handled by two different Ministries at the Centre without any machinery for proper co-ordination. Consequently, the pace of progress slowed down and hardly 19 lakhs of dry latrines had been converted into water-borne flush latrines in the country up to March, 2005. The reason for the slow progress was also inadequacy of funds and apathy of the state governments in selecting a reliable executing agency which could implement the scheme in right earnest instead of inviting tenders or getting the work done departmentally or entrusting it to petty contractors.

The National Scheme of Liberation and Rehabilitation of Scavengers, launched by the Ministry of Welfare in March 1991, carried the government's commitment to eliminate the practice of manual handling of night soil and filth by the end of the eighth Five-Year Plan. The main components of the scheme were: (a) time-bound programme for the identification of scavengers and their dependants; (b) training in identified trades; (c) rehabilitation in various trades and occupations; and (d) monitoring of the implementation of the scheme at various levels. The conceptual and structural deficiencies and the faulty implementation coupled with apathetic attitude of implementing agencies and large-scale leakages, had rendered the scheme ineffective. No wonder the scheme made only marginal impact on the socio-economic and working conditions of scavengers and their dependants.

Benefit-for-all schemes advocated

Dr. Pathak had pointed out to the government one basic lacuna in the scheme for the liberation and rehabilitation of scavengers and their dependants, which stipulated that the scheme would only cover the Scheduled Caste scavengers and was not open to non-Scheduled Caste scavengers. Dr. Pathak said in respect of subsidy, it was good to start from the bottom, but while building toilets the well-off people should not be left out. He persuaded the government to extend the benefit to the non-Scheduled Caste scavengers belonging to Muslim and Christian communities because they were equally the victims of institutionalised discriminations. The Government of India approved his suggestion and issued orders. Meanwhile, with the use of Sulabh's technology in over 15 lakh houses, dry toilets had been converted into Sulabh toilets and new toilets were constructed. And, thus, more than 2,00,000 scavengers had been freed from cleaning bucket privies and 640 towns had been made scavenging-free – a great success at that!

Thrust Areas

Sulabh had highlighted five thrust areas of work to realise Gandhiji's dream: (a) Liberation of scavengers, (b) their rehabilitation, (c) vocational training, (d) quality education for the children of scavengers, and (e) social upgradation. Sulabh thus sought to change the whole social structure through education, technology, persuasion and pressure and restore human dignity to the oppressed people, especially scavengers. It was realised that Sulabh's low-cost sanitation technology, which provided an alternative to manual scavenging, had to be backed up by social measures like providing alternative employment to the relieved scavengers to ensure its full impact on social condition of scavengers. Dr. Pathak thought that if this was not done, most scavengers might not like to give up their traditional occupation. He knew that by only freeing the scavengers, they might well be rendered jobless. Hence, if re-employment issue was not addressed properly, the liberated scavengers would go back to their old job. This, he thought, would nullify the gain.

The first priority was, therefore, to see that the liberated scavengers were not left jobless. Most of them were in the middle or advanced age groups and since they did not have skill for being absorbed elsewhere, the only alternative left was to get them employed in non-scavenging jobs within the municipalities/ municipal corporations. Dr. Pathak approached the municipal authorities in different cities and towns throughout the country and persuaded officials to employ the relieved scavengers in allied sanitation work like cleaning of roads. He pursued the matter at different levels and was eventually successful in making the concerned officials agreeable to this point. The scavengers, thus relieved, got non-scavenging jobs. He also thought that adequate care of the wards of scavengers had to be taken because in the absence of education and training, they might fall back upon the scavenging job.

The then President of India, Mr. R. Venkataraman, with Dr. Bindeshwar Pathak at Rashtrapati Bhavan in New Delhi on November 11, 1988. Dr. Pathak called on the President after his visit to the Nathdwara Temple along with the liberated scavengers

Training, education and rehabilitation

Dr. Pathak thought of setting up an institution which could enable them to acquire skills in certain selected vocations so that they could eventually join the mainstream of the national life. A vocational training centre for the liberated scavengers and their wards was thus started in Patna in 1985 by Sulabh with Central and state assistance. Under the scheme, training was imparted in nine trades, with a stipend of ₹ 350 to each of the trainees, and ₹ 250 for cost of training materials. This programme proved successful and 3,000 persons were trained. The programme continued for three years and provided jobs to hundreds of liberated scavengers. Later, Sulabh established training centres in New Delhi and Jambhol in Maharashtra. The centre in Delhi, set up in 1992, offered training in market-oriented trades like electrical, audio-equipment and television repairs, beauty care, driving, garment making, tailoring, typing,

Liberated scavengers in audience with the then Vice-President, Dr. Shankar Dayal Sharma, in New Delhi on November 5, 1988, after their visit to the Nathdwara Temple

computers etc. The programmes and results are evaluated by ITI staff and certificates are awarded by the Directorate of Training and Technical Education, NCT of Delhi. More than 10,000 wards of liberated scavengers have been given vocational training in these centres and settled in various trades and occupations. And, the Vocational Centre in Delhi has become a landmark success in Sulabh programme. *(More about it in later chapters).*

Breaking temple entry barrier

In his effort to provide a respectable social status to scavengers, Dr. Pathak persuaded the *Vedic* Brahmins to perform Hindu rituals for all those whom the priests had discarded. This was a very hard task to do. He held several meetings with Vedic Brahmins and argued with them to say that untouchability and the denial of human rights to scavengers did not have the sanction of the Vedas. He pleaded that the practice had to be discontinued at a time when the nation was talking about restoring dignity to the people of the low caste as part of the country's Constitutional commitment. While Dr. Pathak was arguing these points with pandits, a bizarre incident happened at the Nathdwara Temple in Udaipur, Rajasthan, where the priests refused to allow the temple entry to the Scheduled Castes. When the national media flashed the news, the then President of India, Mr. R. Venkataraman, offered to lead a group of Harijans to the temple

The then Prime Minister, Mr. Rajiv Gandhi, with sons and daughters of liberated scavengers who called on him on November 8, 1988, in New Delhi after their visit to the Nathdwara Temple

Social upgradation programme of scavengers implemented by Sulabh International: Mr. I. K. Gujral, former Prime Minister of India, adopting a scavenger family to bring it into the mainstream of society

and offer worship there. Dr. Pathak found the situation dangerous and thought that the forcible entry of the low-caste people in the temple would not solve the problem, but would further aggravate the situation. He thus arranged a meeting of Vedic Brahmins and pointed out to them that the practice of debarring temple entry to low-caste persons did not find favour with the religious ethos of Hinduism. His persuasions whittled down the resistance and Brahmins agreed to join 102 scavengers whom Dr. Pathak led to the Nathdwara Temple.

The group did not force the entry into the temple. Dr. Pathak's arguments with them clinched the issue, leading to the change of heart. Finally priests allowed them to enter the temple and offer prayers. His work symbolised the dismantling of discriminatory practices that fetter the Hindu religion. He attributed the success to arriving at a consensus rather than conflict. His visit to Nathdwara did neither spark off any controversy, nor did it create a situation of agitation or confrontation. Dr. Pathak also arranged community dinners when the Brahmins and scavengers took food together as a mark of social reconciliation.

Social mainstreaming and adoption programme

The Sulabh Founder said the removal of social disabilities of scavengers was not entirely a problem of money, technology or law; it was also a cultural and attitudinal problem deeply rooted in the minds of many Caste Hindus. If this mindset was not changed, the liberated scavengers will continue to be there as a class of untouchables subjected to a variety of discriminations. Sulabh's social adoption programme sought to link scavenger families to eminent people so that such families go up in the social ladder and they acquire self-confidence. Towards that end, Sulabh had persuaded a large number of dignitaries, including judges, eminent lawyers, politicians and other distinguished persons from all important walks of life to adopt one scavenger family each. This programme was a success. Sulabh's social adoption programme does not involve any legal obligation; the adopters are only required to befriend the adopted scavenger family, have nice social relations with its members, visit them at regular intervals, take food with them and occasionally invite them to social functions organised by the adopter's family. All these raised the social status of scavengers and helped them get into the mainstream of social life. While dealing with the rehabilitation of scavengers, Dr. Pathak came to know of the problems of manual scavenging in Alwar and with a view to having a first-hand knowledge, he visited the place where he met women who were engaged in manual scavenging. He promised to take them out of their dirty profession. And, thus, the Nai Disha training centre was set up.

Nai Disha — a novel experiment

Nai Disha, a vocational training centre in the Alwar district of Rajasthan, was set up in April 2003 with a distinct vision to abolish scavenging and train liberated scavengers. The rehabilitation of liberated women scavengers, after vocational training, is a model for other organisations. The idea behind the Alwar project was to take women scavengers out of their dirty occupation and bring them into the mainstream of society. That is why the vocational training centre was rightly named 'Nai Disha', a new paradigm. Having worked as manual scavengers for a greater part of their life, the liberated scavengers

The Nai Disha training centre at Alwar, Rajasthan

The liberated scavengers attending tailoring class

at the centre were learning skills which would help then get out of scavenging. A Nai Disha training module has been developed for the purpose; it has been divided into various segments such as food processing, cutting and tailoring, embroidery, beauty care and functional literacy. The centre holds regular medical check-ups to keep women healthy and also tell them the value of clean living. The decision regarding selection of courses is taken up by women scavengers themselves. Many women have been so far trained in food processing, beauty care, embroidery and cutting and tailoring. They are paid a monthly stipend of ₹ 3,700 so that they do not revert to their old profession of scavenging. In the first two years these women have not only learnt to interact with bank officials and sign on their cheques but also to market the products they produce on profit earning basis. The women who have undergone the training at the centre have acquired self-confidence.

Training schedule

The two-year training is followed by a one-year period of rehabilitation so that they get sufficient time for their economic empowerment. The trained women are of two categories. In the first category are those with leadership qualities and initiatives who can set up their own enterprise with the help of subsidies and loans available from the government. This will enable them to produce quality material and also to make necessary arrangements for their marketing. In the second category are those trainees who do not have the requisite leadership qualities. They can be brought under a cooperative society by providing all the facilities and assistance. Transforming the lives of these individuals was not an easy task. Initially, these women were not only least bothered about personal hygiene but their use of language, too, was far from polite. But the concerned professionals and functionaries at the centre were mentally prepared for it. Their patience and perseverance reaped results soon. They have instilled in them a sense of worth, to lead the rest of their life with dignity.

The social transformation brought about by the centre can be gauged by the fact that the same society that was averse even to touch a scavenger, today readily purchases products (even eatables) prepared by the former scavengers. Now these women have organised themselves into self-help groups and are availing of credit facilities from banks so that they can market their products effectively and sustain their life. Later, another batch of trainees was enrolled as some more women from Hazuri Gate expressed desire to come out of the profession of scavenging. These women were motivated to join Nai Disha with an ultimate goal to make themselves economically independent as this is the only means to eliminate the evil of scavenging from their social roots.

The initiative in imparting training to the liberated scavengers in market-oriented trades through vocational training centres has yielded laudable results. The liberated scavengers are now settled in dignified employment of trades and occupations. Their socio-economic status has been raised. They are now engaged in making their own products like garments, embroidery, pickles, papads etc. and sending them to all communities. This attitudinal change among the people towards them is remarkable, as at one point of time, when they were engaged in manual scavenging the people looked at them with contempt. But now they are using goods, articles, eatables prepared by them gladly and treat them at par with others. They have been brought into the mainstream of society.

Impressed with the success of the vocational training centre at Alwar, the Government of Rajasthan entrusted a project to Sulabh for training of 225 manual scavengers at Tonk. The project has since been successfully completed. 280 manual scavengers (245 females and 35 males), who were liberated from manual scavenging, have been rehabilitated. The Alwar and Tonk experiences have been replicated at Arrah in Bihar and Ghaziabad in Uttar Pradesh as will be seen from the following table:

	Centre	Female	Male	Total
Alwar	(Rajasthan)	115	-	115
Tonk	(Rajasthan)	245	35	280
Arrah	(Bihar)	27	22	49
Ghaziabad	(U.P.)	21	-	21
	Total	408	57	465

Liberated scavengers visit New York

The Nai Disha training model is a complete exercise in showing that liberation of scavengers was not enough; it was only the starting step. Equally important is to rehabilitate them in other professions so that they can stay out of scavenging and earn a good living. In order to showcase its success, seminars and meetings have been arranged. The liberated scavengers were also taken to the US on the UN invitation where they explained their problems and Sulabh's solutions to foreign dignitaries. World leaders and the Press widely welcomed the Sulabh scheme which is now being tried out on a larger scale elsewhere. *(For details access www.sulabhinternational.org).*

Liberated scavengers at the Statue of Liberty, New York

TOILET TALK AT NOTRE DAME UNIVERSITY

"You (students) have the abilities and talent to see and take advantage of the opportunities that will be present from an ever-changing world. And you have the Notre Dame values to make a difference, to make the world a better place. To motivate you, let me tell you a story about toilets!

"India is a country with many inspiring people. There is, of course, Mahatma Gandhi, the Father of the Nation. His teachings of tolerance really are the key to the success of democracy in India and he has influenced civil rights movements around the world including in the United States. There is Mother Teresa, who lived and worked in India although her legacy now touches the lives of children, women, and the poor all over the world. There is Rabindranath Tagore, the first non-European to win the Nobel Prize for Literature. But there are also many inspiring people, lesser known to the world, like Dr. Bindeshwar Pathak.

Timothy J. Roemer

"Dr. Pathak, although from a very high caste, knew at a very young age that there was nothing wrong with touching the untouchables. He has dedicated his life to restoring the human rights and providing dignity to scavengers, which is the bottom-rung caste in India responsible for cleaning up human waste. To do so, he used technology to develop a safe and environment-friendly toilet to replace pit latrines, reducing the need for scavenging and improving sanitation and hygiene for both rural and urban poor. He provided education to the children of scavengers, helping to break the never-ending family cycle of scavenging. He provided alternative economic opportunities so that women no longer have to clean toilets for the rest of their lives to provide for their families. All this has helped tackle a bigger problem – breaking down the caste system in India. As you leave Notre Dame today, I hope you will remember the story of Dr. Pathak."

– His Excellency Timothy J. Roemer, United States Ambassador to India, during the address at University of Notre Dame, Indiana, USA, May 21, 2011

"You (Dr. Pathak) have demonstrated through your actions the highest level of commitment to values and ideals shared by both the United States of America and India. Your life and work are an exceptional illustration of how one man, one person, can make a positive impact on the lives of millions."

– Timothy J. Roemer,
US Ambassador in India

CHAPTER 4

A Bridge Between Two Worlds, Old and New

Persuading people to protest and change

Dr. Bindeshwar Pathak is a natural gentleman whose private person and public persona are hard to distinguish; he wears his sincerity and innocence on his sleeves which are often more overwhelming than his arguments. He has created a Sulabh culture, marked by loyalty, dignity, trust and social responsibility. And, these set him apart from other leaders.

Dr. Bindeshwar Pathak is a man of many parts, often one independent of others, sometimes so clinically detached that one begins to wonder how the persona of the man is so different from the person. He is a born leader with commitment, dignity, gravitas, vision, power and skill to solve problems, reconcile opposite views and, thus win friends and influence people. He is a doting father, so fixated with his family values that he misses no marriage invitation (sometimes he travels long distances to participate in functions), a loving husband who, at times, seems to have no say in family matters, a good friend, inspiring leader and one of the tallest social leaders of our times who stands like a colossus in the midst of crises without flinch and blinking. In order to succeed, one has to have charisma, ambition, diligence, wisdom, experience, ruthless determination and also the courage to take risk. It is truer still if one is a social entrepreneur where the award is always a diminishing recompense to the risk and uncertainties.

He can do many things at the same time – discuss plans and projects, address meetings, check accounts, talk to a series of people in groups and individually and sing at the morning prayer; he is unflappable and a self-confessed optimist, always finding the glass half-full, and looking for the light at the end of the tunnel. He says, "We live in a time where the past is no guide to the future. Technology has opened out limitless possibilities virtually making history redundant." He is not a historian but knows history enough to talk about historical importunities. He quotes historians to say Greece, where democracy was first born, was also the place where philosophers defended slavery which was extensively practised by Romans and later all over the Arab world. The slavery in America is a legend which needs no retelling.

As a matter of fact, all ancient civilisations, including Assyrians, Egyptians, Indus and Mycenaean were built on slavery and exploitation. Cleopatra of Egypt used to bathe in the blood drawn from her slaves to keep her beautiful. The story has it that on seeing her nose, Caesar launched a thousand ships in the Mediterranean and conquered the entire northern Africa and gave that as a gift of love to Cleopatra. These stories may be apocryphal but slavery is an established fact of history. The caste system and the consequent untouchability is only a regional manifestation of the universal fact of slavery.

A great communicator

Dr. Pathak is a doer who enjoys doing things differently. He believes that his legacies will be written in his actions, not in words. "It will be written in the outcome of my work, and not in rhetorics. It will be visible in the smiles we put on the faces of the children of liberated scavengers and not by speeches I make", says the Sulabh Founder. Actually, India is a nation of entrepreneurs. In villages and small towns, the poor take risks. However, when the Mughals and the British came, the focus shifted to keeping us away from enterprise and we were reduced to tax-paying slaves. When the government becomes stronger, the chances of corruption and patronage become greater. In such a society, you will not see social entrepreneurship, which is all about using personal initiative, ability and optimism to create wealth, jobs and good life. Dr. Pathak never had official power or patronage. He worked alone during which he has developed the power of persuasion and the skill of communication, using his folksy wisdom and raw simplicity of a village boy, radiating innocence, sincerity and wearing disarming smile which wins friends. He uses universally understood, simple but powerful words and metaphors and radiates honesty, and commitment which are rare qualities in these times of cynicism, poverty, anger and the collapsing value system.

It is always refreshing to talk to him which is quite an experience, not because of his intellectual profundity and polemic skill but because of the simple facts of life very simply stated. Talking to him gives an out-of-the world feeling; his seductive manners work. We live in an age where the only constant is change. He is a man who readily trusts even those whom nobody else does. And, gets short-changed. But he never complains about it and continues to have social relation. He may be deeply aggrieved but never shows it. Even in his moments of anger, he only shows repentance more than aggression, and the desire to punish. He quotes Nietzsche to say, "Don't give power to those whose desire to punish is great. You can change a person more by persuasion and fellow feelings than by punishment." History is littered with examples when people and nations wanted to punish others by superior arms, money and deception and they all failed. Only Gandhiji succeeded. For that matter, Gandhiji will continue to guide the world forever, Dr. Pathak says.

A doer all the way

Dr. Pathak says education and technology are keys to the success of democracy and quotes the 2006 *Program for International Student Assessment* conducted by a consulting firm McKinsey in the US that measured the achievement gaps as manifest in applied learning and problem solving skills in 30 industrialised countries. The US ranked 25th out of the 30 in mathematics and 24th in science. "That put American average youth on a par with those from Portugal and the Slovak Republic, rather than with students in Canada, the Netherlands, Korea, and Australia," McKinsey has noted. "Which means that the longer American children are in school, the worse they perform compared to their international peers," the report says and adds that education alone will decide economic growth, social development and justice, health, and sanitation.

In sum, education will decide whether a nation will survive as a democracy, secure and safe, or not. Education is the deficit area in India, where the current literacy rate is 75 per cent (287 million illiterate in India, the largest in the world) of the population (2016). "To quote these figures is to despair," says Dr. Pathak. "There is also a lack of integrity in our thoughts and actions. We have seen ministers speaking on mobile phones and saying 'I don't believe in technology!' Another example is English medium schools. Every year, many scavenger women come and ask me for seats in Sulabh English Medium School. And, I am not able to meet their demand. They are ready to spend money also to get English education. The rich send their children to these schools, but we say English and computer are not good for the poor. It is a rich man's cheating and a source of social inequality.

We see greed, vanity and ego in public and social life. This is not about entrepreneurship; this is not about capitalism or socialism either, this is about the failure of good governance. We need to rein in our egos so that there is fairness, transparency and accountability. We need to live in harmony with the environment and society. The choice is not between capitalism and communism but about getting a right mix of both", Dr. Pathak says.

He has redefined good life

Dr. Pathak has redefined the idea of good life, central to which is

A LIFE FORGED OUT OF UNBORN DREAMS

Dr. Bindeshwar Pathak's life is all about power of dreams – to scale new heights and tread the land untrodden before. He has learned the ways of the world by direct experience which has unshackled his intellect to do things differently, always taking the risk. For that matter Sulabh was a gamble that did not fail. The romance of living life dangerously always fascinated him. A life of abstinence, virtue and commitment is his rich inheritance and to stick to them even while going through deep crises is the test of his character. His inventiveness, vision and ability to take people along are the sources of success.

He has always loved the ideas which he may have never known before academically, nor lived them in his daily life. It was like his falling in love with a song which he has never heard. He reads Gray's elegy; "The curfew tolls the knell of parting day – the ploughman homeward plods his weary way – leaving the world to darkness and to me." He is emotional and volatile – to be cold, calculative and scheming is alien to his nature. When under stress, he sings or hears somebody else sing for him. There is a lot of music in his life and rhythm in his living which sustain him in crisis. Dr. Pathak, for that matter, is an enigmatic man of many parts, at times one far too different from others – the one whose life is forged out of many dreams which he enjoys as they unfold themselves. He is not rich but famous.

sustainability. Human civilisation is heading for a crisis because of the hollow promises of perpetual progress, and economic expansion, quite ignoring the sustainable ecosystem solutions to our problems. This is the dominant cultural narrative which is called technological fundamentalism – the idea that improvement in technology would solve all problems. It will not. There are limits beyond which the ecosystem will not take growth and economic expansion – all of which are the consequences of natural sources, including earth, air, water, forests and other God-created sources on which depends human civilisation. Sulabh is a social movement of sustainability, taking care of the last man – Joe the Plumber – leaving the celebrities to take care of themselves. Dr. Pathak's major contribution, at the conceptual level, has been that he has brought a marginal idea, like toilet cleaning, to the mainstream and seeks to rebuild a new global order from the last man and stop our endless fascination for celebrities. For this to happen, the social narrative has to change. The Sulabh Movement is one such initiative.

India caught in trap of old values

Dr. Pathak says, "Indian society and culture have much to do about basic values. I am convinced that development is all about first developing a sense of basic values among people and finding leaders who stand for these values and can become role models. The ability of the leader to relate to the ground situation is important. This is fundamental to inclusive economic development. The moment we do this, I am convinced our growth rate will gallop. I don't consider land, capital and labour resources to be as important as values, skill, education and commitment. There are so many examples where nations have enormous natural endowments but they are poor. Take the case of Africa, it has all the natural endowments, manpower, rich land and forest and water. But, Africans are the poorest in the world. Take Japan, it has none of these but it is the second largest economy in the world, next only to the US." Sulabh is a wave of the future about which Dr. Pathak says, "Let the tide run free. The difference between a social reformer and a politician is the ability of the former to distinguish between the surface wave and the deep tide; between the wave of the moment and the wave of the future."

Dr. Pathak is a loner, although living in the midst of multitude. His attitude towards life, wealth and power is that of total resignation. He loves God and religion, but also listens to those who don't. His easy gestures make him look like a man next door, doing the daily household work like reaching children to school, buying vegetables and quarrelling with wife over broken cups. He punishes people by forgiving them. And, this hurts more than any other punishment. Dr. Pathak says, learning is the sign of a 'smart organisation', one that is continuously improving its internal processes. Learning is a high priority in Sulabh where 'learning networks' have been extensively spread out to ensure that new ideas and technologies don't go unattended. It is also the best way to avoid becoming complacent, acting as the best protection against making mistakes.

The Founder's special talent is in avoiding the traps that others fall into while exploiting the opportunities that arise from the mistakes other NGOs made, specially depending heavily on aid and assistance, in the effort at social reforms, where so many of the once mighty organisations have fallen. Sulabh's track record is impressive in improving things. What sets him apart from other leaders is also his focus on sanitation which, he says, is his religion. He combines an analytical mind with a real passion for change, always scanning the horizon for the next big thing. This intellectual restlessness resonates throughout his work and achievements.

When he was asked about the secret of his organisational success, Dr. Pathak said: "Trust; we give social workers big jobs and big responsibilities. Inevitably, they make mistakes, but we don't stop them and often they don't make mistakes again. They know I am watching them. Many organisations use confidential files to record errors. And, they use them to frighten workers into doing good work. It might work once but workers later discover that we do not want them to venture far enough from the beaten track and make mistake in the process. Consequently, there will be no new experiments, no test of new ideas, no learning of new things and no change. I don't want that to happen. If you reward good work and forgive bad work, the good will finally prevail over the bad. There is a case in point. A concern over trouble in the classroom led to research into the way teachers praise and blame students. It was found that all praise was for academic work and all blame was for bad behaviour. The teachers were told to praise good academic work and good behaviour both and to ignore the bad one. Within a few weeks, unruly behaviour almost disappeared. In a social organisation, your position never gives you the right to command; it only imposes on you the duty of living in a manner so that others can have confidence in your leadership. If the position is abused, and subordinates are ordered to follow the leader blindly and orders are given causing humiliation to them, the power centre will collapse, eventually. The price of greatness is responsibility and test of leadership is accountability. A leader is required to take care of followers which is possible only with humility and honesty and not by arrogance. Only this kind of leadership will bring the success at your doorstep."

A man in a hurry

He is sometimes criticised because he has called for the changes that propose to reduce power, status and influence of those who have profited from Old Order. He is a realist in means, but idealist in end. However, he is never devious, guileful, evasive, dissembling or ruthless. Even in most difficult periods of his career, he never ceased to be a good and cultured man. He condemns Brahminism, but radiates the Brahmanical virtues, like the habit of speaking truth, philanthropy, morning prayer, indifference to wealth and encouraging people to respect all religions which, he says, preach good things of life. Dr. Pathak is a man in a hurry who keeps shifting his furniture, offices and house which indicates that he is not at peace with himself, always seeking for the ultimate good. His success happened without driving ambition but with lots of hard work and good luck. Supported by good workers and a loving family, there is very little for him to do except doggedly march to his destiny. What keeps him going is the determination to succeed where others did not.

The Sulabh Founder has lived dangerously – always challenging customs, questioning values and interpreting religion differently, saying that the best of Hinduism is lost in rites, rituals, questionable beliefs and practices. However, he did not favour a new religion, but only a rebirth (renaissance) of the same. He is not a revolutionary but a reformer with passion for social justice. He has rediscovered Hinduism by putting it in right perspective if only to say that untouchability has no moral or religious legitimacy and those who practise it commit sacrilege. He matured faster in poverty crises. "There was no enemy to defeat but only friends and a lot of them – to win over to my thinking which is a tough job no less." He says that those who cannot deliver the goods, only blame the system, leaders or just bad weather.

A habitual spender

However, there are many angularities in his character also; at times he is impulsive, taking decisions in a hurry only to regret in leisure. He cannot say 'no' to people, many of whom take undue advantage of it. It seems, he enjoys being cheated, possibly in the belief that the cheat is only cheating himself. This is his temperamental problem which costs him not only money, time and embarrassment, but also sometimes structural problems in the system. He is a habitual spender, almost always spending beyond his resources. He has inherited this habit from his father who recklessly spent to push the family into poverty. His wife says that when she finds him depressed, she could guess that he has no money to give away. This was also his habit when he had borrowed from his friends or sold his wife's gold to help others in times of need. Taking tough decisions is also his problem even in the cases where wrong doing is proven beyond doubt. He believes that to be good is natural for man and if somebody is not so, let us find out the causes – poverty, bad company, bad habits or sheer obsession to destroy the system. In case of the latter, he is ruthless but in other cases he gives the benefit of the doubt to the concerned person. He allows mistakes to be committed freely. Otherwise, he says, people will tend to do what is easy, traditional and will not produce work that is innovative, ingenious, exciting and brilliant.

He stands tall in crisis

Dr. Pathak repeats the same mantra during his writings, speeches and debates; *"I need to get better,"* he would say. In the way, he has trained himself for competition; he sometimes looks as much a fighter as a social campaigner. Even before he entered public life, Dr. Pathak began improving his intellectual and organisational skills, and also his mental and emotional endurance which helped him stand alone monumentally in crises – personal and professional. In the process, he developed self-discipline.

He does not easily exult, despair or anger: to do so would be an indulgence, a distraction from his goals, he would say. Instead, he separates himself from the moment and assesses the man and situation. His man management skill is enormous – knowing most workers by their first names, the villages they belong to and their family. Nobody can cheat him in accounts though he cannot operate a computer; (he only purchases them) but his calculations are flawless because he has done mathematics in college. Since, mathematics is not only about numbers, it has brought discipline in his thinking and arguments which are well organised even when he is talking about metaphysics, religion and undefined human qualities. The Sulabh Founder is soft at heart but when his core values are hurt, he can be tough and unyielding, even to his very near and dear ones. Behind his sensitive exterior hides a tough man who can stand up and be counted. In his own ways, he stares sternly when the limit of his tolerance has reached. How else could he lead the movement amid controversies, criticisms and outright allegations, none of which did ever stick or blind his determination to keep pressing ahead undaunted!

Always open to new ideas

In case of India, we have people of different faiths whose religions and superstitions are also different. For instance, we had a Hindu woman as President, (Mrs. Pratibha Devisingh Patil); a Sikh as Prime Minister, (Dr. Manmohan Singh), a Dalit as Chief Justice of the Supreme Court (Mr. K.G. Balakrishnan) and till recently a Muslim as Vice-President, (Mr. Mohammad Hamid Ansari). And, the leader of the Congress party is a Christian (Mrs. Sonia Gandhi). India is a rainbow coalition of different faiths and beliefs but there is no conflict. The country is a mix of so many diverse streams, thought systems, castes and creeds. In the U.S., the first modern nation to legally separate church and the state, faith still plays a crucial role in public life. "Our secularism, for that matter, is more complete and complex than that of the Americans", says Dr. Pathak.

He loves to find common ground between religion and science and says, they are not mutually exclusive. To be a scientist, one has not necessarily to be godless. Faith defines at least approximately the areas of Creation where science is silent. One cannot live by science alone; faith keeps the world spinning, not the Copernican axis. Moral principles are the life support system. He quotes Immanuel Kant to say that there is established limitation of knowledge of the external world and argues, there are 'Categorical Imperatives', some fundamental moral codes which don't change. They are enduring and eternal. He says Immanuel Kant was never a theist but he believed in an absolute moral order. "And, I call it a divine dispensation". Being an absolutist, he says that there are some absolute values which don't change like goodness, compassion, sacrifice, love and affection. 'Relativism is a philosophical error'.

Dr. Pathak has high sense of right and wrong; when he feels he is not telling the absolute truth, he becomes tense and tries to find words to be ambivalent, shifting in his chair uncomfortably and drinking cups of tea. He cannot hide his feelings of despair, disgust and relief; all these primeval emotions come easily on his face. He says: "Life is all about walking between truth and untruth; one is not always a chooser but, in my case, my conscience does not let me sleep; sometimes, I feel like walking away from life's struggle. Money does not interest me beyond a point, but recognition of my social service and good work does." This may be his megalomania, but this drives him hard to achieve missions impossible.

People's participation

Dr. Pathak has made everybody involved in basic sanitation work, how high and important he or she may be in the organisation. This involves visiting toilets, supervising their cleanliness, talking to users and attending to their complaints and cleaning, if necessary. "This work should not be left to sweepers alone; all of us will have to do it. We lost freedom because of the occupation-based caste system under which only Kshatriyas would fight wars. And, when they became weak due to internal fighting for other reasons, the entire country lost freedom. India remained slave for centuries because of the caste system when the entire society, its people and resources were not mobilised to protect the country; rather, it was left to a group of people. Hence, every man should be a Rajput, Brahmin, Vaishya and

Shudra; every man and woman doing everything. This will mean the total involvement of society, not a section of it, in fighting war and making peace. It is like in a family where a man is father, husband, domestic help and baby-sitter, all rolled into one. In society also, his or her role should be like that of a family which is its building block. The fragmentation of Indian society is because of the occupation-based caste system, the like of which does not exist anywhere in the world. Sulabh seeks to correct this historical asymmetry", he says.

The efforts at social change are made through people's participation because scavenging is a historical distortion which cannot be settled by law alone. History has analogies. When the slaves were emancipated immediately after the Civil War in the US in the 1860s instead of rejoicing the freedom, they went up to the Yankee commanders and pleaded to be sent back to the cotton plantations. "Who will look after us? Who will feed us? Who will protect us? Who will beat us? And, who will love us?", they pleaded. No wonder, it took one hundred years and a Martin Luther King Jr. for slaves to eventually win back their civil rights and live independently. Martin Luther King Jr. was a Gandhian and, like Gandhiji, he was assassinated in 1968. No wonder, it took 100 years to give franchise to the Blacks by the 36th President, Lyndon B. Johnson, in 1964 after slavery was abolished by the 16th President, Abraham Lincoln, in 1864.

Like untouchability and the caste system, slavery was also intricately woven into the American way of life; both Blacks and Whites, had learnt to live with this inequality. Similarly, scavengers, over the centuries, have learnt to live with indignity and humiliation of cleaning and carrying somebody else's excreta. Many scavengers, liberated by Sulabh, returned to scavenging where their families, history, memories of childhood and youth lived on. Like American slaves, scavengers sought jobs and protection. Sulabh appeared on the scene to provide a strong leadership that has made a difference in their lives. And, after 40 years, scavengers are beginning to learn to live independently through a process set in by the Sulabh social upgradation, education, training and social mainstreaming programmes.

His life is a triumph of vision over reality

Albert Einstein says that as you move fast, time slows down. Sulabh cannot be riding on the fictional time machine, but the success of its attitude building campaign is opening out new possibilities as limitless as the sky which is there for the taking. What was fantasy till yesterday is becoming a reality today. It is true of science (like space travel) and truer still of social relationship (like liberation of scavengers) which is being re-interpreted to shed the ancient ways of living and thinking. This is the new wave, in the making of which Sulabh has a hand, however modest, however invisible. And, the Sulabh Founder is leading this campaign all the way. We know that wherever the pioneer goes, others follow because leadership makes the difference. Scavenging is beyond technology; it is also a question of leadership.

To be true, Dr. Pathak's life is a triumph of vision over reality; of hope over fear and of tomorrow over today. A life rich in achievements has blazed trails, rivalled only by those whose names are graven in stone. He has proved that in modern India, pedigree (Rajas, Maharajas, etc.) does not work; it is the performance all the way. How else could a village boy from Vaishali acquire global eminence? And, a very dazzling one at that. And, in times of crisis, he stands like a colossus – unmoved, unshaken and sometimes alone like Casablanca on the burning deck – in full majesty and defiance. He says with the Biblical ring, "Time is turning; which means you have to break old habits and barriers, abolish old order, define new social relationships, find new frontiers, dream new dreams and re-interpret history to create a new social order in which one man's excreta is not another man's head-load. Show me a hero and I will write a tragedy."

Charisma and charm mark his manner

Although charisma is a rare commodity and harder still to understand, it is an attribute of an ordinary man doing extraordinary work. The Sulabh Founder came from a disadvantaged background. Although his family was very respected and once very well off, it had fallen on bad times. The conservative traditions of a distinguished family were obstacles for any of its members to seek reform in the system, of which he was the product. But, this was also a priceless raw material to his charisma because he could tell people how a distinguished Brahmin could do enormous service to untouchables. His success and the consequent acclaim, added to the halo that he wears to theatrically demonstrate how the basic Hindu virtues, like compassion, love, justice and inter-faith tolerance, can be combined with the liberal views of modem India, symbolised in the constitutional pledge to ensure equal opportunity, social justice and equality before law. As a matter of fact, they are not mutually exclusive virtues, but only differently interpreted.

Dr. Pathak's high birth and low income also provided the contrary qualities of the Greek tragedy to which pathos is the central emotion. If a Harijan works to help Harijans (like Dr. B.R. Ambedkar), it is not much of news; there is something clannish about it. But, if a Brahmin violates the Brahmanical norm of *Chaturvarna* (four castes or Varnas) which has been a major source of oppression in India, and climbs down from his social pedestal to embrace excreta-carrying scavengers, his action is the stuff high dramas are made of. It creates mystique and a personal magic to his leadership, arousing popular loyalty, enthusiasm and a magnetic charm. This is what charisma is all about. Dr. Pathak's ability to empathise with scavengers only heightens his charismatic impact on people. Rajas and Maharajas looked tall because they stood on the shoulders of their forefathers and their glory. But when a jobless, wanderer boy becomes the tallest of them all, one begins to realise that something extraordinary has happened in history. He has made public service glamorous by bringing flamboyance and colour to sanitation which has been once considered a profanity to talk about.

He has been able to keep his bearing in the media glare after success and global recognition, not for once forgetting the central thrust of the movement – the last man, the scavenger. Dr. Pathak is a perfect blend of the man of action and the man of dreams who has captured the imagination of young generation *(midnight children)* and inspired them both by the manner of his life and success of his mission, creating the concept of *Shangrila,* the dream land of beauty and glory. He says that not everything is lost to us despite many problems, the most important of them being social apartheid. He approaches problems with reverence for the rich heritage built over thousands of years. Being a Brahmin by accident and a social revolutionary by choice, he has become a cult figure. His ultimate quest is for a scavenging-free society, not to make name and money, but to leave his footprints on the sands of time so that better and nobler people could reach the heights never reached before.

No level field in God's universe

Inequality is built into our genes, environment, education, social structure and in about everything that we have inherited or built ourselves. Yes, a civilised society provides equality of opportunity and rule of law. But it is a fact, that at least social degradation can be abolished to make life less painful for the underclass, including scavengers. By so arguing, he has brought a spiritual dimension and mystic splendour to the movement which also gives it a class character, artistry, majesty, ruthless efficiency, devastating force, consistency and the ultimate meaning to life. It is given to a very few persons to stay focused when one is criticised by society for doing hundreds of unconventional things. Toughness, as a matter of fact, is not physical but strength of character which

Dr. Pathak has shown by staying on course in the midst of protest, disapproval and criticism.

The Sulabh Founder is, however, by no means a perfect role model; he has all the weaknesses and strength of a common man but uncommon determination, steadfastness of aims, courage, drive and non-conformist views to make things happen. He is a pacifist who says that it was the peace movement, not nuclear deterrents, that ended the Cold War which produced no winner; rather, the US and the former USSR were left exhausted. His initial failures did not dissipate his resolve to succeed; he is never failing in staying power, always waiting to do things in peaceful ways, and differently. Seldom before has a man risen so far and so fast, making toilet central to his movement and philosophy. To be true, Dr. Pathak's future is rooted in his dreams when he is alone in his eminence. His friends say that while gazing at the stars, he should be watchful of the puddles on the roads. No wonder there is a mystical aura about him, also because he is a complex character – the more one tries to understand him, the more ununderstandable he becomes. His life has been very stormy and eventful. This is the stuff great careers are made of – at once awesome and fascinating.

> *"Life is at once factual and fictional, serious and satirical – it depends on what one makes out of these contradictions. Commoners live by the day while heroes do it for eternity."*
>
> *– Thomas Carlyle*

CHAPTER 5

Big Dreamer of Small Things: A Soft Man and Strong Leader

For whom unheard songs were still sweeter

Dr. Bindeshwar Pathak is a different man for different persons, an ordinary man next door, hard working social activist, a dreamer who sings, a campaigner, a Gandhian, an educationist, a speaker and a philanthropist. And, still the description is not complete. To sum it, he is a good man who helps people do small things in big ways and live well with others in peace and social harmony, specially scavengers. This is how he would like to be known.

Dr. Bindeshwar Pathak had multi-point entry in life; born into a traditional Brahmin family and in a village where Rajputs dominate; his father had plenty of land, most of which he sold out to meet family commitments and on rituals or marriages. There were no Brahmanical prejudices, fads and fetishes which make for discrimination of the caste-based social construct. There had been a family tradition of quest for knowledge which is Dr. Pathak's rich inheritance.

There was no toilet in Dr. Pathak's huge and sprawling house and women had to go out before sunrise and after dusk. This was the accepted social practice, so also the manual scavenging. He came in contact with liberal views during his stay with his Nana who was a social leader and Gandhian. There was, however, nothing to suggest in his formative years that he would break out of tradition and become a trailblazer in those times when life and values were frozen. And the worth of man was judged by his birth, feudal heritage or political influence, which was steadily changing the social landscape, especially in Bihar, which has been politically active, though poor and conservative.

Dr. Pathak was, however, not Brahmanical enough because he did not do what traditional Brahmins did, nor was he socially rebellious enough to openly challenge values and plead for a new social order. Life was like a piece of flotsam, swaying back and forth, with surging tide of time. He could speak Maithili, Bhojpuri, good Hindi, Bengali (though not fluently) and English which was the subject of his special interest. For that matter, he was a bit of chameleon or shape-shifter, a versatile man unlike a commoner with fixed views and frozen idealism. It was because of his different identities that he could appeal to a broad range of people from different backgrounds and professions.

Thus, well before he was firm on the way to his future career, he was wobbling all the way, in part seeking a job, and in part doing something about scavengers with whom he had lived in their colonies and seen their sufferings. He had the ability for doing a variety of things – teaching, his first choice, social reform that he could not define, reading and thinking hard, or drifting in fantasy, doing nothing. The more he read, the more it fired his imagination. Surely, he found there was more to life than leading a common life as a village teacher which he found unpoetical or making money or other common work which life is all about. No wonder, he was a restless youth seeking a new future which he could neither foresee nor define. Thus, emotionally he is given to intense oscillation of mood, at times sad, at times hopeful, but always restless.

Search for a future

When Dr. Pathak says his life and career is God-driven, he does not talk of his faith which is strong and firm, but about the uncertainties in life. Nothing was fixed, or pre-destined in life which was an open, drifting dream of some good things to happen some day somewhere. The innocence of a young man, born and raised in a dusty bowl of Bihar, was enormous, so also his audacity of hope to do something different, something extraordinary. Until he joined the Gandhi Centenary Celebration Committee in 1968, his life story was all about a drifter, dreamer, always remaining an outsider, but always winning acceptance in whatever new company he joined. Conciliation has been his way of life and the dominant feature of his social leadership. Dr. Pathak has read Voltaire and Thomas Paine carefully and would like to discuss *the Age of Reason* without compromising on his faith in God. He talks of *the Doctrine of Necessity* that the human mind is impelled to action or hold in rest by some power over which the mind itself has no control. In his philosophical mood, he would ask what the meaning of life is when death is the final destination. Why should one worry and work so hard when we know it will all end? Because God willed it so? Or, that we should continue to hunt will-o'-the-wisp? The more he thinks about these philosophical questions, the more withdrawn and sadder he becomes which one can see on his face. Dr. Pathak is a man of action, and not a philosopher, but he becomes philosophical which seems to be his Brahmanical quality that he disavows.

Thus, Dr. Pathak has always been winning, cool, intelligent and charming. He is not uncomfortable in the company of men from different professions and status and finds common areas to talk about, and is careful not to offend their sensibilities by his different, sometimes strong and abrasive opinion. However, he is not comfortable in the company of women; he does not know how to talk small things which women like to listen to like reaching children to school, rising prices, new fashion and fad, cinema or food. He cannot talk on any of these things without blushing like a teenager also because he has never done any of these things.

Mrs. Amola Pathak, being a caring and protective wife, never let her husband worry about their children and extended family, even in the days when life was hard. Even today, he does not know how the household is managed. He lives in reasonable comfort, but his tastes are local and Bihari; when abroad, he has the abundant supply of locally-made food items. He says high dinners and lunches always leave him hungry. He comes home and eats with his family again the food that his mother used to give him when he was a boy. He loves family and respects family values.

Dr. Pathak is a good story teller who reduces complex human relationship to folky narratives, telling things with ease and, thus, he relates himself to people very easily. He speaks fast and chips words; before addressing important meetings, he does rehearsal in eloquence, effect and manner, especially if he has to speak English. He says good life is lived in small ways, with happy family, good friends, and fair and just social order. And, to achieve these things, one does not have to fight battles, win elections, kill people or steal money. God has given most of these things free; one has only to reach out and take it. "I try to help people in small ways, celebrating and grieving with them, persuading and pressing them to change." Although a believer, he is also deeply committed to Nehruvian scientific temper. He talks about *the Age of Reason*, Renaissance and science and argues like an atheist, only to say that God and science can co-exist, if we know both of them intelligently. He does not like political jargon and empty words, but easy and direct way of communicating with people, leaving bigger things for bigger people to do.

Good man who is doing good work

In sum, the life story of the Sulabh Founder is that of a homespun boy who grew up to become honest, compassionate and good social leader committed to the rights of the poor and abolition of the caste system, which is a feudal construct and outgrowth of religious distortions. He is entirely a self-made man, a complex and paradoxical, and richly endowed human being, always fascinated with the dreams of a casteless society. His emotional conflict and impulsive decisions sometimes put him in embarrassment and loss but he has not ceased to make those mistakes again and again, knowing well it will hurt him. He seems to love his pain, sorrow and tragedy with purity of emotion and love for innocence. While talking to him, one can easily find out his unspoken sad thoughts into which he relapses even in the midst of celebrations. He cannot hide his emotion; he is not a dissembler, he cannot be. On meeting him, one never ceases to wonder how a very common next door man could become one of the tallest Indians of our times.

No wonder our sweetest songs tell of saddest thought. When a man is sad, he is at peace with himself and not when he is laughing. We never forget sad faces and never remember the laughing clowns. Monalisa's melancholy is celebrated all over the world. There is a lot of poetry in Dr. Pathak's life; he sings at meetings, mourns in dark and stares at things beyond silence of time and age. It is difficult to induce him to talk about the homely facts of his youth. It is a great piece of folly to attempt to make anything out of his early life. It can be all condensed into a simple sentence. Rather one will find an echo of Gray's Elegy in his life.

> The curfew tolls the knell of parting day,
> The lowing herd wind slowly o'er the lea,
> The plowman homeward plods his weary way,
> And leaves the world to darkness and to me.

A tough leader

However, behind his soft appearance there is a strong and determined man of action, ruthless in pursuit of his life's mission, ignoring the price he has to pay and the burden he has to carry. For that matter, he is stubborn and tenacious, never compromising on the basic values of life for which he had to take many tough decisions even in his family matters. He has the making of an inveterate fighter, a focused leader, uncaring about anything when he has to decide on social issues. He has the gambling instinct which is manifest while taking the decisions in which stakes are high. Once he has taken a decision, he is unyielding especially when he suspects that his core values are threatened. The Teflon quality of a strong leader comes to the surface when he is in the harm's way. He says: "Everything may fail, but I will not let my dreams fade away. I am a dreamer and Sulabh is my dream project. After all, I am a twice-born Brahmin; to remain poor is our tradition. But once I give

FEAR OF NEW IDEAS

"People fear new ideas because they threaten to bring about a change in social order which upset the ossified structure of which many are beneficiaries who are the rulers also. In that case there is a clash, sometimes resulting in civil war. But, technology has changed the terms of dialogue, giving greater power to the weak and dispossessed who seek equality with the strong and powerful. It may be recalled that most cases of violence have happened when a society shifts from one stage to another. It may be the end of the Bourbon in France, Czardom in Russia, Hapsburg in Austria or abolition of feudalism in India. New ideas, which spell out a change, are opposed. After all, what did they say new when I pleaded for scavengers' equal rights and their share in India's heritage? And, it took many laws and a massive social movement, like Sulabh, but still scavenging continues. I am telling the same story, again, again and again for more than 40 years and still counting but nothing seems to be happening because of the fear of new ideas. The truth is that the more we change Indian society the more it remains the same."

– Dr. Bindeshwar Pathak

up my conviction, nothing will be left of me to live for. I straddle the two worlds, one is old order, which I seek to change and the other is the new one which seems strange to me." He has fought long battles with the Press and leaders who sought to malign him but after the peace was restored, they became good friends.

Despite his diverse interests and many accomplishments, certain basic tenets have motivated his life and shaped his actions. Of these, none was stronger than his belief in "the sufficiency of reason for the care of human affairs." As a man of enlightenment, he believes in application of reason to social work and used the means by which mankind could obtain a more perfect society without violence to the system. From his commitment to reason flows his devotion to the rights of the poor, especially scavengers. His belief that knowledge is power inspired him to face the challenges of the established social order rationally. According to him, true leaders are those whose wisdom and fidelity don't desert them when times are hard. And, he is true to his conviction.

Leaders are visionaries who can see tomorrow and act today by putting a team to realise their dreams.

CHAPTER 6

A Leader Tested by Fire

A passion born out of a tragedy

Leaders think differently; they process information differently which leads to different ways of addressing problems. To be true, leadership is rooted in biology and re-enforced by culture. The Sulabh Founder, all his stormy career, has been tripping from one crisis to another which only strengthened his resolve to stand the test by fire. His success comes from commitment.

Dr. Bindeshwar Pathak has the making of a born leader. If he were not the Sulabh Founder, he would have been a pioneer in any other field of human endeavour. The defining qualities of a leader, like the ability to reconcile conflicting interests, inspire confidence and trust, and articulate views effectively, robust common sense, knowledge of people's habits, cultural preferences, folklore, compassion, taking people, along patriotism etc., are found in him in abundant measure. None of the movements before had a beginning as low as that of the toilet and about its cleaners, scavengers, the forgotten people lost in the mad race for growth. And, still harder for him was to mobilise mass support in a feudal society which has been built, layer upon layer, on social prejudices, caste system, untouchability and exploitation which are our inheritance from the past.

Dr. Pathak is marked out from other social reformers for his political, social and popular opinion mobilisation in the country and outside it, keeping the scavenger in the centre of the Sulabh Movement which is a syncretic initiative combining in its fold, education, social renewal, technology, justice and the empowerment of the weak and the disadvantaged section of society. He has, thus, forged a comprehensive social alliance of diverse and apparently opposite social groups in the understanding of the country's social problems by putting them in global context. He has, thus, broken the enduring stereotype of social reformers promoting reforms of only a section of people but not that of the whole society.

Dr. Pathak addressing at the International Water Week function in Singapore

All great revolutions had small beginnings

Dr. Pathak's leadership consists in breaking new ground, seeking new frontiers and reaching new heights if only to ensure just, clean and environmentally safe living conditions, achieving most of these objectives through a combination of technology, institutional innovations and new approach to old problems, including social injustice, human rights abuses and economic rehabilitation of the socially dispossessed and disenfranchised. His major innovative approach is his social mobilisation with toilet as the symbol of a new social order.

The focus of the French Revolution was 'Equality'; of the American Revolution the lowly tea and tax on it. (No taxation without representation); of the Civil Rights Movement was Rosa Parks' bus, out of which she was thrown out and which later became the campaign issue of Martin Luther King Jr. and for Gandhiji, it was the railway's all-White compartment in South Africa from which he was thrown out on the platform when he refused to accept the third class status for Indians. All great revolutions had small beginnings. In the case of Sulabh, it is a toilet which has been made a mascot of this social revolution. Toilet is the nucleus around which is woven the concept and dream of a scavenging-free society. Earlier, social reformers in India, including Buddha, Kabir, Sant Tukaram, Jyotiba Phule, Raja Rammohan Roy, Dayanand Saraswati, Vithal Panj Sindi, Thakkar Bapa and Gandhiji, were great leaders, who represented the hallowed values of humankind. However, big ideas are born only in historical context and few survive after the context has changed. Now, we have to find a new philosophy, new leaders to guide us. Sulabh foots the bill because it is forged out of many winning ideas whose time has come.

Value change with time

No social values remain unchanged. All social values and practices have context and they should be viewed in that context. For that matter, the Constitution of a country has the values of the generation which had written it and is not a timeless truth. The Indian Constitution is the most voluminous in the world with 444 articles in 22 parts, 12 schedules and 94 amendments, which bans untouchability and other social prejudices against which the saints and social reformers had fought. But those were the days of innocence. Now, we have to approach the same old problems in different ways. Today, technology has changed everything; the way we live our lives and manage our things. Equality has never been a primordial value; today it has become a constitutional value and human right. The revolution in idea was not a Western phenomenon, but it caught the imagination of the people all over the world. Dr. Bindeshwar Pathak is a product of that revolution in mind brought to India through media, education, technology and travel which have globalised the world.

Gunpowder, paper, printing press and compass – how ordinary and lowly things are they? Paper brought knowledge and preserved it also, compass helped Columbus discover America and later helped the British to conquer the world, gunpowder (a Chinese madness, at that!) gave a dangerous tool to the West after which half the world lost its life and liberty. For good or evil, technology has become a tool of social change. And, Dr. Pathak's still humbler technology of two-pit toilet is making new waves for social change *(Read about technology in a separate chapter).* Sulabh toilet is not only the place for morning visit or an artefact, but a mystique and a nucleus for social change.

Osmosis and change

Dr. Pathak says, while living through change, people are often stuck with their oldest belief and most durable source of security – religion. Technology has broken that gridlock, making man free to think anew. He has used technology to break *the cordon sanitaire* of the caste system, one half pure and one half polluted, freeing the scavenger, who is the last man in society. "If you lift society from the top, only the top will be lifted; lift the last man and the entire society will be lifted", he says. After all, the sense of justice is an evolved concept; it is not primordial. (For that matter man is also an evolved species, not created, says Charles Darwin). Dr. Pathak through his unremitting effort has made it socially accepted that scavengers' equality is also primordial; it cannot change to become negotiable. This debate is irrelevant in the West where it is already accepted as a given thing, but in the East, we have still to accept 'life, liberty and pursuit of happiness' as the manifest destiny of man. Caste in India is not race, a historic marker in US; it is worse. "Caste system, like racialism in the US, is our birthmark which has disfigured the face of this ancient country of ours where all great and glorious things have happened," says the Sulabh Founder.

He has brought about considerable social transformation through a sociological process of osmosis and change which has been a seamless make-over to new social order without causing violence to the existing system. He has provided the intellectual underpinning by an elaborate exercise through seminars, conferences, public meetings and media, putting paid the present notion that untouchability has the sanction of *the Vedas,* the original source of Hinduism. His effort has resulted in high caste Brahmins joining him in his crusade against scavenging. This social upgradation campaign has succeeded, which was evident when Dr. Pathak took scavengers to temples, including Nathdwara, where high priests welcomed scavengers and ate with them in community meals.

This social revolution could be possible only because Sulabh also popularised the two-pit toilet system which has been used in building toilets in homes. The people had nothing against scavengers, but they wanted their toilet cleaned up. Once the Sulabh technology was provided to them, scavenging disappeared from the town. The liberated scavengers have been trained in other skills. Now they are doing their own work. Sulabh's Nai Disha staff, however, keep a watch on them to ensure that they do not go back to scavenging where their friends and relatives may still be working.

Social acceptability

Now that social acceptability was largely restored, the problem was to train and find jobs for them. That is, however, a long-drawn process. Sulabh has provided financial support to them during the transitional period, after which many of them have become self-supporting. It may be noted that many were thrust into scavenging because of poverty. Although, this experiment is on the local basis, the government has taken initiatives to adopt Sulabh methodology and replicate it. While carrying out social and technological campaign, Dr. Pathak had full support of the media which highlighted the social degradation of scavengers and their poverty. The government and institutions also liberally supported him for social renewal and the result has been encouraging, much of which is evident in the declining number of scavengers and rising number of people adopting the Sulabh toilet technology.

Dr. Pathak has taken another step to prove that social action can be taken up by no-profit organisations which can serve the people and still make a good living. It is a major development in people's action programme because social work is best done by social organisations. The Sulabh model is now adopted by many social advocacy groups, working in various social service areas and they are doing well. Sulabh is a nucleus around which social movements have gathered a critical mass to grow by adopting its methodology, technology and intellectual sustenance. Dr. Pathak has also mobilised political support for social action. His initiative has been blessed by no less persons than the President of India, the Prime Minister and the Chief Ministers of the states. His leadership has also resulted in narrowing economic gaps, providing a comprehensive package for sanitation, and a model for peaceful social transformation, social mobility of scavengers, modern science-based English medium education for their children which has left considerable impact on the lives of scavengers who are beginning to see the light at the end of the tunnel.

To be true, his leadership is among the best things to happen in the first decade of the 21st century. There are many elegant theories of social and economic changes, none of which had, however, percolated down to the last man as a consequence of which social disparity and resentment grew with GDP. High growth has deepened the social division and widened the economic gap.

Dr. Pathak's quiet revolution has done to India what

Dr. Muhammad Yunus's Grameen Bank had done to Bangladesh although the focus is different. Dr. Pathak has also addressed the social problem while Dr. Yunus's movement has been against rural indebtedness. Sulabh has a lot of ideological content, social preferences and religious belief. But social developments take place in a context; movements in Bangladesh and the Sulabh Movement in India have the common objective of helping the poor, although their ways to go about it are different, so also the social and economic contexts.

Science and technology — the way of the future

Karl Marx has said, "the idea of the ruling class is the ruling idea of the day". Scavenging is the consequence of the social acceptance and religious sanction given by the ruling class to untouchability and discrimination. "This has to change not by confrontation, but by education, reforms, social entitlement and technology", says Dr. Pathak and adds that science and technology is the way of the future. Social science is all about combining technology and social reform if only to achieve ideology without which a social movement becomes a commercial enterprise.

Sulabh, however, does not seek Luddite solutions to social problems: that is, in order to combat joblessness destroy the factory, or in order to abolish untouchability, destroy the *touchables* or expropriate the expropriator as Marx has said. (The Luddite Movement was launched to oppose technology during the Industrial Revolution in the name of Ned Lud). Rather osmosis and change solution should be adopted, protesting social discrimination while encouraging change. Social dissenters have to be included in the Herbert Marcuse way because finally society is formed by consent and consensus and the government is based on force. "Change is inevitable and non-changing societies are dead", says the Sulabh Founder. He was taking about Alwar scavengers who visited New

York on the UN invitation and delegates also celebrated their redemption when they congregated at the Statue of Liberty to swear to work for the liberation of those still 'unfree', manually cleaning and carrying human waste and crushed under the social discrimination facing the vile instinct of exploiter.

From pariah to a redeemer

During the four decades of work, while promoting sanitation, liberating and rehabilitating scavengers and living with them, he has always been friendly with people calling him a 'toilet man' or *'Bhangi Raja'*, as Khushwant Singh once called him in his columns. Being a high-born Brahmin, his identity was manifest in his behaviour and that also gave him a persona which he could not live down despite working for scavengers. Dr. Pathak's family suffered embarrassment despite the fact that members of the family had modern outlook and were firmly set against social exclusion. But he carried the baggage all these years, always seeking redemption of scavengers with a measured success, and loud public support for the cause because of his good work, hallowed by Gandhiji's commitment, much of which was put in high focus.

He has been honoured by many national and international agencies for his commitment and technology, but the kind words of Prof. Rajmohan Gandhi, Gandhiji's grandson, about him are the dearest which he cherishes the most. "Meeting with him was like reliving the past which began unfolding itself as if I had been working with Gandhiji which he could not because he was only five years old when the country was left without him." Dr. Pathak says, "Man, in any case, is mortal, but his messages endure. Prof. Rajmohan Gandhi has re-interpreted his messages in a global perspective. Gandhiji spoke for all time and all mankind when he, bedrocked on the spiritual philosophy for the Kingdom of God, advocated the ultimate values of fairness and justice. He supported the doctrine of the world being one family and opposed commercialism of religion and godism, so also a doctrinaire approach to religion."

The Sulabh Founder is wedded to a cause which he has not been able to define fully yet. The rolling hills, distant drums and the vanishing horizons fascinate him, saying: "The far away hills are the greenest." He conceives of situations beyond the borders and far beyond his control, always working in the belief that we are living in extraordinary times when change in one country will produce change in the other. All bloody revolutions had failed to deliver stability, prosperity and good life to the people which are the objectives of all social movements. Being a communicator, he has enormous power of persuasion through raw and ruthless logic, or sheer scholarship. He concedes points peripherally only to preserve the core area of his faith and belief. If he loses in any argument and debate, he says with easy manners: "...but it is an error in right directions." His critics are disarmed and accept defeat in victory. How can you disagree with a person who says that the world should be clean and people healthy to live in a discrimination-free social order, at peace with itself?

Dr. Pathak says, the more time he spends among scavengers, the more convinced he becomes that scavenging is not created by scavengers. It is created by the system we have built, the institutions we have designed, the concepts we have formulated. Untouchability is an artificial, external imposition on the Indian society and since it is external, it can be removed. It is created by deficiencies in the institutions that we have built. For example, financial and social institutions refuse to provide financial services to nearly two-thirds of the world's population. For generations, they claimed that it could not be done, and everybody accepted that explanation. When a crisis is at its deepest, it can offer a huge opportunity. When things fall apart, that creates the opportunity to redesign, recast, and rebuild. We should not miss this opportunity to redesign our social and financial institutions. Let's convert them into inclusive institutions. Nobody should be refused access to financial services and social equality because it is vital for self-realisation of people.

A multi-dimensional man

Once we recognise this flaw in our social structure, solution becomes obvious. We can easily replace the one-dimensional person in economic theory with a multi-dimensional person – a person who has both selfish and selfless interests at the same time and immediately our picture of the society changes. We now see the need for two kinds of businesses, one for personal gain (profit maximisation), another dedicated to helping others. In one kind of business, the objective is to maximise economic gains for the owners, even if this leaves nothing for others, while in the other kind of social business, everything is for the benefit of others and nothing is for the owners, except the pleasure of serving humanity. Let us call this second kind of business, built on the selfless part of human nature, as 'social business'. This is what our economic theory has been lacking in. And, this is where social organisations become relevant, he says.

Identity problem

Dr. Pathak has redefined the role of social organisations to say that social service organisation which depends on philanthropy and government aid will finally end up facing charges of bad faith. Many great social organisations have phased out because they had no resources to support or, they lived on government dole and when the dole ended, so did the organisation. Sulabh is a self-sustainable organisation. It is this vision of Dr. Pathak which has made him financially self-supporting to pursue his social agenda on his own without waiting for help.

As the world grows smaller, it would be easier for human beings to recognise how similar we are, to understand that we, scavenger or non-scavenger, all basically want the same things, that we all hope for the chance to live out our lives with some measure of happiness and fulfilment for ourselves and our families. And yet, given the dizzying pace of globalisation, and the cultural levelling of modernity, it should come as no surprise that people fear the loss of what they cherish about their particular identities – their race, their tribe and, perhaps most powerfully, their religion and caste. In some places, this fear has led to conflict. At times, it even feels like we are moving backwards. "We do not have to live in an idealised world to reach for those ideals that will make it a better place. The non-violence practised by men like Gandhiji may not have been practical or possible in every circumstance, but the love that he preached – faith in human progress – must always be the North Star that guides us on our journey." We see it in nations that are torn asunder on tribal lines. In this shrinking world, social discrimination has no place.

Ideas move mountain

Winning leaders know that ideas are basic tools for shaping and motivating organisations. Leaders generate these ideas by constantly seeking new information, reflecting on their own experiences and searching for insights, not only into technology and human behaviour, but also into the larger world around them. "Arrogance is dangerous and harms an organisation. One's own ideas get enriched by other ideas, by philosophy and by thinking through the basic issues of life. In winning organisations, the source of the ideas is not what matters; it is the fact that the top leader embraces new ideas, spreads them throughout the organisation and encourages others also to have good and new ideas. In all the winning organisations, idea cascades through the ranks. Workers at each level draw on the central ideas. The fundamental quality of a good leader is to take new ideas to all levels and that will drive the organisation to success," says the Sulabh Founder.

The civil society will have to act. It is with the belief that law alone will not help that Dr. Pathak has launched the Sulabh civil rights movement which combines technology, law, *dharma,* education, sanitation, human rights, religion, social action, etc. to make it a comprehensive cover for social change when scavengers and non-scavengers can live together as equals and in peace. The Sulabh Movement does not produce winner or loser; it is a win-win game. Manual toilet cleaning will be over; new technology will do that. The disadvantaged and disempowered will be upgraded after education and training to help them make their own choices without robbing the rights of others, all without conflict but by slow movement from darkness to dawn. This is the Gandhism which is Sulabh's rich inheritance that defines its philosophy and work agenda.

Thus, Dr. Pathak's major social, economic and technological initiatives have halved, if not healed, the ugly racial wound left by India's history of caste system, and social segregation. He is the man who learns and organises. He is an instinctive leader who listens even to those who cannot speak; their tears, scarred faces and deep silence tell their stories more than any fiction writer can write. Dr. Pathak has the star quality of attracting people and leading them to greater effort and social recognition. It is a measure of the rarefied place in social change that has put Dr. Pathak among the tallest social reformers in India. His accomplishment, evident in the emancipation of scavengers and their rehabilitation, is among the many good works for which Sulabh will be remembered much after everything else is lost in the silence of time.

"My adversary has no name, no caste, no party – it is in the mind of man. And, that is where I want the change to happen."
– Dr. Bindeshwar Pathak

CHAPTER 7

A Social Reformer More by Chance than Choice

Sulabh, a keeper of Gandhian legacy

Martin Luther King Jr., Gandhiji and Dr. Pathak have one thing in common; they have been driven to social activism by chance, so also many other great social leaders for whom reform was an unintended consequence.

Writing in *Young India*, Gandhiji says, "Every good political movement passes through five stages: indifference, ridicule, abuse, repression and respect". This is also true of social movements which seek a radical departure from the accepted social construct like untouchability which has religious sanction. The caste system has not only created untouchability but exploitation of the poor and the weak. Dr. Pathak is not the first person to try to bring about social change. Many did before. But the Sulabh Founder has been more determined than most and the first to start his movement from toilet; the most unlikely place to launch any social movement. Also, he has been focused while passing through all the five stages in various ways to finally get national and global respect today. Successful people are no different except that they press along unmindful of failure. Dr. Pathak did just that – working longer hours and harder than most in the Gandhian way.

During the long haul of five decades, he had been associated with different kinds of people from different fields, admirers, hard workers or easy talkers and many others who make for this diverse Indian society. Many or most of them have left him midway, for one reason or the other, leaving him alone to fight the hardened social attitude. But he has no lament; on the contrary, he thanks them for having travelled with him so long. It was easy for him also to get out of this difficult life and live well, but his restless conscience never allowed him to do that, though his family, relatives and friends wanted him to leave scavengers alone and return to the Brahmanical fold. But he wondered what would happen to his commitment to scavengers and all the idealism that he imbibed in the Gandhi Centenary Celebration Committee!! The choice was clear for him – between his conscience and a good life.

The famous twosome

Diogenes, a Greek philosopher, was once sitting under a tree when a senior state official passed by him on his glittering horse. He stopped where the naked Diogenes was eating his gruel (coarse food) and said: "What are you doing, Diogenes?" "Why, I am eating this gruel," Diogenes answers. "You fool, if only you would learn to get along with the King, you wouldn't have to spend the rest of your life eating this miserable gruel". "My dear, Sir," answers Diogenes, "If only you would learn to eat this gruel, you wouldn't have to spend the rest of your life trying to get along with the King and speak the untruth for him". Dr. Pathak decided to speak the truth and without having to eat gruel.

Gandhiji also became Mahatma by chance

It may be interesting to note how Gandhiji became the Mahatma by chance as it happened with many other great men and great events. His protest movement had a background beginning at Kathiawar. The practice of law in Rajkot lost charm for Gandhiji. The 'petty politics' of Kathiawar – intrigue by prince against prince, sycophancy towards British or Indian political officers, and bribing the minions of these officers – also hurt Gandhiji. This was not the idyllic Kathiawar he had presented to the readers of *The Vegetarian*, an English newspaper. After Gandhiji returned to Rajkot from Kathiawar, again he was feeling depressed when a letter came from Dada Abdullah and Co, a Porbandar firm of Memon Muslims. The letter asked whether Gandhiji would be willing to go to South Africa, where the firm's head in South Africa, Abdullah Seth, did not know English, and his lawyers did not know Gujarati. Gandhiji knew both and, hence, his help would enable Abdullah to communicate with lawyers. He was promised a first class return fare and a sum of 105 pounds. Gandhiji promptly agreed, though fully realising that he was being asked to go not as a barrister but 'as a servant of the firm'. But he wanted somehow to leave India. He left for South Africa on April 19, 1893.

Turban issue and protest

On reaching Durban, Gandhiji met leading Indians (Muslims, Hindus, Christians and Parsees) and learnt of the racial prejudices they daily faced. Abdullah had asked Gandhiji to sit next to Abdullah's white attorney. After staring at Gandhiji, the magistrate asked him to remove his turban. Men like Abdullah could keep their turbans on because they were 'Arabs'. But an Indian like Gandhiji was expected to remove his headgear in a court. Gandhiji said, removing the turban was a humiliation, not a mark of courtesy.

Indian lawyers in the Bombay High Court did not take their turbans off. Refusing to remove it, Gandhiji left the Durban court. The next day the Natal Advertiser ran a story, headlined *'An Unwelcome Visitor'*, criticising Gandhiji for not taking off his turban. Gandhiji's reply appeared in the Advertiser on May 29, 1893, giving him 'an unexpected advertisement in South Africa' within days of arriving there. Though severely criticised by some for his 'temerity', he felt no remorse.

There are some historical events which produced unintended consequences: Gandhiji returned to India, his first political campaign was in Champaran, Bihar, where he demanded no more from the British rulers than to set up a committee to look into the distress of indigo cultivators. The demand was not accepted. Later, it snowballed into a mighty political movement to finally result in the end to the British rule.

The fact is that no social career is planned; it happens. It was Dr. Pathak's shock over the manifest injustice to scavengers that drove him to social activism more by accident than by choice. Gandhiji would never have opted for the work which he did until one day he was thrown out of a train compartment in South Africa meant for the Whites. Martin Luther King Jr. would never have launched a campaign against the white if Rosa Parks, a black passenger, would not have been thrown out of the bus in Montgomery, Alabama. Parisians would not have stormed Bastille if Queen Marie Antoinette would not have asked the hungry crowd to buy cake if bread was not available. "I would not have decided to fight for the untouchable if I had not seen a boy in red clothes being gored to death by a bull and nobody saved him because he was an untouchable. This drove me to combat the social prejudices", Dr. Pathak says. The hour had come, so also the man. Scavengers are the most wronged people in the world. It is not a social contract but sheer exploitation of the weak by the strong. Rousseau says, "Laws are useful to those who have property and power and harmful to those who have nothing." Scavengers have none beyond the toilet; their whole life revolves round it – from childhood to old age – till they die unsung and unknown. Democratic institutions don't help them either. They exist but they don't listen to their grievance despite law because they are not empowered in terms of property, knowledge or political influence. "The social change will not happen until our values are subjected to critical scrutiny and changed," says Dr. Pathak.

Gandhi clothes were policy statement

Gandhiji's *khadi* was not mere clothes; it was a policy statement, a symbol of attitude towards life which reflected the difference in those difficult times. Today's austerity drive is only the expansion of the Gandhian philosophy, and those who argue that travelling in exclusive classes works out cheaper than in train do not know how symbolism dominates life and policy of great persons. Several people still wonder why a well-dressed Bar-at-Law like Mr. M.K. Gandhi shed his western togs for a loincloth and acquired an obsession for *Khadi.* Prof. Rajmohan Gandhi writes in the portrait of his grandfather: "Gandhi's choice of simple, self-woven *khadi* at the time when the ruling class was seen to be an alien elite was a master-stroke – it brought him closer to the image of Indian icons like Kabir and even popular weaver poet like Thiruvalluvar".

Nehru too, though imbued with much more of the 'Saheb' image than Gandhiji, was clear on the importance of symbols like Indian clothes and was conscious of avoiding too much pomp and puffery as he went about his job. Lal Bahadur Shastri too, despite his brief tenure, made his mark when it came to symbols of being one with the masses. After two droughts in quick succession in the mid-sixties, his *'Jai Jawan, Jai Kisan'* cry exhorting people to skip one meal once a week in solidarity with those for whom life was not so good, struck a chord.

Ram Manohar Lohia (no Gandhian) and George Fernandes seemed to epitomise the 'common man' or 'equality' principle in the

The Father of the Nation

way they lived ('simple' and visibly so). In societies such as ours, one's life, one's deed, one's practice is the most effective medium of communication. "My life is my message", Gandhiji said. The general perception is that Gandhism is related to dress *(Khadi)*, manners and the lifestyle. This is not correct as these outward trappings and symbols do not constitute the essence of Gandhism. These are just exteriors to something which is fundamental and essential. For, Gandhism is a thought system which supports, among other things, peaceful way of solving problems, abolishing untouchability, women's empowerment, modern education, secularism, promoting small industry and a good and clean life.

Not everything has a price, specially Gandhism. Gandhiji practised austerity and lived a life of commitment to moral values, much of which was evident in his protest movement in South Africa where he re-enforced his moral position by reading Leo Tolstoy, Thoreau and other writers who had examined the moral dimension of political movement and adopted it with ascetic attitude to life, showing restraint and concern for the poor. He believed that no political movement would succeed if it morally failed and where people are starving. In order to identify himself with the poor, he discarded his English dresses and reduced himself to a saintly life and dressed like an ordinary Indian in South Africa (called coolie). He represented masses, their aspiration and hope. Gandhiji lived all his working life of 33 years in India as what Churchill called *"a fakir in sack cloth and ashes"*. His clothes became the symbol of protest all over the world. He went to London to meet the King during a round-table conference when newsmen asked him as to how he could stand the British cold in those scanty clothes, Gandhiji replied: "The King had enough clothes for both of us". Gandhiji's clothes attracted a worldwide attention with many British newspapers calling him English-speaking mendicant.

To be simpler still, if a Gandhian allows the areas around him to be dirty or he sees a scavenger cleaning excreta (Gandhiji wanted scavenging abolished), he is not a Gandhian. Gandhiji never asked his followers to become an ascetic or saint. A Gandhian is a *Karmayogi*, living very much in society, responding to social problems and attending to those with commitment. In this respect, Sulabh workers are Gandhians because they clean streets and toilets, plant trees, educate children of scavenger families, do campaigning for social cause and at the same time earn enough to live a good and clean life with family and friends. This is Gandhism for Sulabh which is the keeper of Gandhian legacy.

Between two wars

Gandhiji came back to India from South Africa in 1915, one year after the World War I had started, and was assassinated in 1948, three years after World War II ended. Between the two global wars and 33 years of his work in India, the world had become a morbid place. Many people were convinced that another global conflict would unleash forces of barbarism when decaying civilisation would be too powerless to resist and that the inevitable result would be the beginning of a new dark age. As the prospect of war drew closer, pessimism and defeatism were replaced with a grim determination to confront the manifest evil of Nazism. In the three years between the crises in Spain and Central Europe, British historian Richard Overy writes, "The balance between saving civilisation through peace and saving civilisation by war swung decisively in favour of war". When war eventually came, for many people it was almost an end of civilisation. This is the background of Gandhiji's work period. And, these were the chance elements which made Gandhiji a Mahatma. Those were very violent times (1915-48) when the world was bloodied and bruised in two global wars. There was not a single house in Europe which did not nourish the sick or mourn its dead. The continent had become a slaughterhouse twice in less than 20 years. The winners and losers both wanted peace to return and wounds to heal. This was the historical moment when Gandhiji appeared on the scene and, like Jesus, became a great healer of the sick and redeemer of the oppressed. If there were no Gandhiji, history would have produced one because he was a historical inevitability.

More than any other single person of his age, Gandhiji changed the character of politics by providing moral support to political resistance. He interpreted politics in moral term. His protest movement had moral underpinning which was largely talked about in the South African media. He also brought out his own publications, the *Harijan* and *Young India,* to tell his side of the stories and impress upon people that the movement was not all about politics but of social change. He opposed commercialism of religion, so also doctrinaire approach to religion. A man, however, is judged in a context and once the context changes, so does the assessment of the man.

My Mouth is Gagged

Reg. No. B 3092

HARIJAN

Editor: K. G. MASHRUWALA

VOL. IX, No. 32] AHMEDABAD—SUNDAY, AUGUST 23, 1942 [FIVE PICE

MAHADEV DESAI

On the 15th of August at about 8-30 P. M., Sevagram was informed over the phone by our Wardha friends that they heard over the radio the following communique of the Government of Bombay:

"The Government of Bombay regret to report the death, about 8-40 a. m., on Saturday, of Mr. Mahadev Desai, who was recently detained under the Defence of India Rules.

Mr. Desai was engaged in conversation with Col. Bhandari, I. M. S., Inspector-General of Prisons, and two of his fellow prisoners when he complained of giddiness. Col. Bhandari advised him to lie down and he found that his pulse was low and that he seemed cold. Dr. Sushila Nair who is detained in the same building was sent for and she arrived at once. As the Civil Surgeon could not immediately be found, another I. M. S. officer was summoned.

Injections were given to stimulate the action of the heart and everything else possible was done to keep up Mr. Desai's strength, but he died from heart failure only 20 minutes from the time when he first complained of feeling unwell."

Though the information was fairly detailed, the three or four persons who first got it were altogether unwilling to believe it, and pressed me not to break it immediately to Durgaben and Narayan (Mahadevbhai's wife and son respectively). Infructuous attempts were made to register trunk calls, and at last it was decided that while telegraphic confirmation should be sought from the Prison authorities, the news should be communicated to the family as it was. For a long time they refused to believe it. Both of them urged, "We are unable to feel the shock, which such news ought to give us. Hence, we feel that it must be false." Others concurred. I was alone to [illegible] otherwise. It was a difficult situation for us. Within a short time they were bound to be disillusioned. But should I say that this was wishful thinking? I kept silent and allowed them to express themselves.

At about 10-30 p. m. a condolence telegram was received from Bombay, followed shortly after by another from the Inspector General of Prisons, giving the bearest text "Regret Mr. Mahadev Desai died suddenly this morning of heart failure — Prisons."

The telegram was despatched at 10-5 P. M., and yet it does not say whether and how his body was disposed of subsequently. To the time of writing this, there is no further information, as indeed there is none about Gandhiji himself. But even before this confirmation had come, the usual mental process had gone on, and within a few minutes tears gushed out of their eyes involuntarily, and the mother and the son began to assure and comfort one another that though the information must be false, even if it were true, they should face it bravely,—Narayan urging, "Father has died at a time and in a manner which are most enviable, and which we shall always remain proud of."

Late Shri Mahadev Desai

He Did It

At the time when Mahadevbhai was, unknown to us, expiring at Poona, some of us at Wardha were considering the local and general situation, and contemplating to take some steps involving risk to our own lives. But not being used to take quick decisions, and still less to take action, we thought and ruminated over deadly non-violent methods of creating the force which will make India free. We thought and dispersed, not knowing that at the other end, Mahadevbhai had already done it and finished his part of the programme. A [illegible] amongst us remarked light-heartedly that it was not given to everyone to die gloriously.

Media support for his campaign

Media support was the foundation of his political career. While leaving South Africa, Gandhiji was given lots of gifts which he distributed among children or gave back to people despite the unwillingness of Kasturba who

Vol. II. JANUARY, 1919 No. 1

YOUNG INDIA

Published Monthly by the India Home Rule League of America
1400 Broadway, New York, N. Y.

India's Claim to Fiscal Autonomy
Woman's Position in India
India Facing Famine

To Members, Yearly $1.00 15c. a copy To Others, Yearly $1.50

wanted these to take back home. And, these small events were extensively reported in media to establish the fact that Gandhiji was the man of the masses. In the early stages, the circulation of the *Harijan* and *Young India* did not go beyond 40,000 and 30,000 copies, not enough to support the publication, but there used to be a veritable scramble for the copies of these journals because they set the trend of the time. According to journalist Arun Shourie, for a country of millions, these were no earth-shaking numbers. In 1925, Gandhiji was concerned that the circulation of *the Harijan* had dropped to 600 and that of *Young India* to 5,000. True, the Gujarati editions of his books sold a larger number of copies. Between 1927 and 1940, against the 6,000 copies of the English edition of his autobiography, 50,000 copies of the Gujarati edition found buyers.

Despite low circulation, the publications created political upset in England where the issue of exploitation in India was raised by Edmund Burke and other liberal leaders, including Harold Laski. It may be noted that this was not the media age. Those for whom Gandhiji agitated were mostly illiterate, hungry and poor masses. But Gandhiji defied all models in history before and since.

Gandhiji said that his humiliation in South Africa was the punishment for untouchability in India. During the Bengal famine in 1942, he again said this was the punishment for untouchability when Nehru wondered what had social problems to do with food shortage. (Prof. Amartya Sen says, the 1942 famine was not because of food shortage, but because of social entitlement). He was remorseful of untouchability and hence he has called it the reason for our problems, political and social.

Sulabh has inherited Gandhian legacy because Dr. Pathak's work started from the Bihar Gandhi Centenary Celebration. After being exposed to Gandhism in action, he wondered how best he could translate it into action, specially helping scavengers live a respectable life. But he was virtually groping in the dark. It was like two students, passing through the dense Sunderbans forests in Bangladesh, being asked to find out from the footprints the animals who travelled that way. The intelligent among them said, it was an elephant and also that the animal could not see from the left eye because its footprint was deeper on that side. The other student could not guess it because he wanted to see the whole animal. Similarly, Gandhism is more about guessing his 'footprints' by the greater application of mind than has been largely done by his followers who see Gandhism in *khadi* clothes and cap. But, his message was much beyond it – it was for the renewal of society, revisiting the feudal values and British imperial practices of governance and rediscovery of the moral foundation of society for it to endure and grow.

Dr. Pathak himself carried human excreta in Arrah (Bihar) along with manual scavengers to have the experience of their life which he seeks to change and the profession which he seeks to abolish

Gandhism being a comprehensive concept, Dr. Pathak decided to adopt only one segment,

A community meeting with manual scavengers advising them how to change and grow to live a better life.

abolishing scavenging, in which he saw the much larger possibility of social change. Hence, he translated Gandhism in a different way and set up a different intellectual discipline, *Gandhian in Action,* which is wholesome mix of Gandhian philosophy and his social action programmes in diverse fields. He had witnessed the humiliation and social degradation of scavengers being born into a Brahmin family. He had himself inherited many prejudices which became more hurtful when he was made to drink cow urine and dung after touching an untouchable (Dom). These social prejudices are deeper than they are apparent in our social relationship with them. They are treated with contempt and their only right to food was whatever was thrown from those whose toilets they clean. Untouchables had no land, no job except cleaning toilet and no life, or no future beyond their clusters of broken huts, living among pigs and dogs only to die young, unremembered and unsung.

No pandits would go to their huts to perform last rites because none is observed. Their names, if they have any, are also associated with hate words unlike those of upper castes like Raj Bahadur Singh or Pandit Vikram Chaturvedi. Their miseries are long stories, much like those written by Mrs. Strowe in *Uncle Tom's Cabin* which caused the Civil War in the US in 1865. But, not in India where these discrimination and prejudices are frozen and sanctified by religion or what passes for it. And, thus given a religious and social acceptability unlike in the US where slavery was a political expediency and not divine dispensation as the caste system in India has become.

Mahatma Gandhi and Dr. Bindeshwar Pathak have been separated by a generation or more. But they are like those of Jesus and St. Paul the Apostle, the preacher carried forward his message of peace, social justice and equality. When Gandhiji died, Dr. Pathak was a five-year-old child, hardly of school-going age, while Prof. Rajmohan Gandhi was a 12-year-old boy who saw his grandfather's body in Birla House. "I half expected him to stand up and start walking. Even on the train from Delhi that was taking to Triveni in Allahabad his ashes that I had assisted in collecting, I thought he might break out, whole and alive, from the pot containing the ashes. It was only when the vessel was emptied into the river waters that I accepted the end" (sic), says Prof. Rajmohan Gandhi. Since his death, Gandhiji had become a rallying point for revolutions. All those who protested against social injustice, invoked his name across many continents, oceans and seas and that worked wonders. Gandhiji spoke for all time and all mankind when he talked of the spiritual philosophy of the Kingdom of God and advocated for human culture as the ultimate value. In so doing, he supported the doctrine of *Advaita* of Aadi Shankaracharya as stated in *Upanishadic* philosophy.

> *"Religion without science is imperfect and science without religion is dangerous."*
> *– Albert Einstein*

CHAPTER 8

A Man of Faith and Good Conscience

Only morality can save the world

"Science is no substitute for God; science explores the mysteries of His creation and the scientists pray for the glory of the Lord of Heaven and Earth who has created this world, at once lovely and awesome."

– Dr. Bindeshwar Pathak

The sources of Dr. Bindeshwar Pathak's success are the sustained efforts and his firm faith in religion which he has re-interpreted to base it on universalism. True, rituals are the flab to remove, but he refuses to throw the baby along with the bath water. He has found time in his busy life to study religions, first to reject untouchablility, which has no religious sanction, and, second, to sustain his faith in hard work and human values. When reminded of Christian crusades, witch-hunt in medieval times, religion-based conflicts in the Balkans, massacre in Rwanda, Jews' persecution and honour killing, he says they are not religions but deviation or polities practised in the name of religion.

Dr. Pathak sees no incompatibility between religion and science. Earlier scientists and philosophers like Galileo, Newton, Descartes, Leibniz, Boyle, and John Ray were deeply religious men. For them, to explore the wonders of the world through science was the glory of God. Indian scientists were also great believers; they were simply seeking to understand the will of the mighty Creator who made the hills, mountains, rivers and this wonderful world with all its animate and inanimate things, sky, air, and planets working in a godly equilibrium.

Plato, four centuries before Christ, said the "ultimate truth is not reality but idea." Apostle St. John uses the Greek word 'logos' which means idea, mind or consciousness. Many philosophers, including Baruch Spinoza, have argued that consciousness is not just the noise that brains make but part of the fabric of the universe. Over the past 90 years or so, quantum physicists, including Niels Bohr and Erwin Schrodinger, have shown that the mind of the observer affects the outcome of experiments carried out on fundamental particles. "Finally, it is mind; it is idea", says Niels Bohr.

Consciousness is a burning topic in modern science, while Richard Dawkin's anti-God concept is crude materialism that belongs to the 19th century. Science, says Richard Dawkins, will lead us to omniscience (knowing everything). He tells us: "We know exactly how DNA works". This is untrue, absurd and dangerous. If it was true, there would be nothing new to find out; yet the nature each week reveals itself in many ways in which DNA is constantly changing. The truth is we are only at the beginning of finding out the mysteries of nature which God unveils but very slowly. The notion that science will tell everything is absurd, JS Mill said a century and a half ago; "We can never be sure that we haven't missed anything. We have no way of knowing what that might be. God is inscrutable."

Dr. Pathak says, "Morality alone can redeem humanity. Using science and technology without morality is dangerous. But don't forget the harm technology can cause, as in the case of weapons of war and the nuclear bomb. Throughout history, moral ideas have led to the worldwide search for justice, happiness and peace. This is more relevant in today's world, shaken by violence, inequalities and discriminations of gender, caste and ethnicity. What is needed is an idea that can inspire people's imagination, an idea that can change things for the better. If technological innovations were the only major instrument of social well-being, why would celebrities from the most advanced industrial nations periodically knock on the doors of Indian spiritual Gurus?". India has come to be celebrated as a land of soft power. Steve Jobs came to India looking for Karoli Baba, who was also a source of inspiration for Julia Roberts, another celebrity. Way back in the 1960s, rock superstars, the Beatles, came looking for peace and became Maharishi Mahesh Yogi's devotees. No society can function purely on technology. People will continue to search for spirituality and morally ennobling ideas. "Let there be no mistake, spirituality is no religion," says Dr. Pathak.

Science and religion: No contradictions in term

Now that capitalism is being redesigned in the West, manifest as it is in the *"Occupy Wall Street"* protest marches, economic meltdown and Eurozone crisis, God is being rediscovered to replace Adam Smith and Karl Marx who have failed to solve human problems. Scottish economist Adam Smith (1723-90), who fathered the concept of *'invisible hand'* (free market capitalism), thought of three per cent compound growth in global economy forever, quite ignoring the nature's ability to absorb and renew the high-tech exploitation of its resources. Karl Marx (1818-83) sought to destroy the unjust social structure and build a new egalitarian society based on the concept of "from each according to his abilities: to each according to his need". Both have failed to deliver on their concepts.

To be true, human civilisation is a continuing story of a search for new ways to live a life better than the Neanderthals did in the European caves, more than 50,000 years ago. The development of awesome technologies to exploit nature and destroy the world is the incidental consequences of this long search. Computing power has grown exponently, so has the human network. But the brain of Homo sapiens remains pretty much the same organ that evolved in the heads of African hunter-gatherers 200,000 years ago. And that brain has tendency to swing in the mood from greed to fear and from love to hate. Speaking at a conference in Ukraine in mid-September 2011, Apple founder Steve Jobs said, "The data equivalent to a total volume of information created from the beginning of human civilisation until 2003 can now be generated in just two weeks". But what avail these achievements if morality fails and man continues to behave like beast, killing the weak and defenceless people and destroying our lovely planets which no technology can recreate? Hence, the need for morality and God.

Science began with Vedas

Dr. Pathak says science began with *the Rig Veda,* written some 1500 years before Christ. Let us see what *the Rig Veda* says:

> *"In the beginning, there was no sky, and no heaven. What power was there? Who was that power? Was there an abyss of fathomless waters?*
>
> *We praise Thee with our thoughts, O God. We praise thee even as the sun praises Thee in the morning: may we find joy in being the servants. Keep us under thy protection. Forgive our sins and give us Thy love. God came after creation.*
> *God made the rivers to flow. They feel no weariness, they cease not from flowing. They fly swiftly like birds in the air. May the stream of my life flow into the river of righteousness. Loosen the bonds of sin that bind me. Let not the thread of my song be cut while I sing; and let not my work end before its fulfilment."*
>
> (Rig Veda II. 28)

Max Muller, German Indologist, was the first to translate the Vedas into English

This is *the Rig Veda,* the source of Hindusim. Where is superstition or caste system, untouchability or other kinds of absurdities which the latter-day pseo-pandits, supported by Western baiters of Hindusim, attribute to Hinduism to give a religious mandate for their birth-based advantages and entitlements? Max Muller (1823-1900), the German indologist who has translated *the Vedas*, said that *the Vedas* were the first books of science. "*The Vedas* predate science because in these books scientific enquiries were made about the world. The latter-day scientists continued what began with *the Vedas.*" This is the source of Hindusim, and not what is said in rituals, social discriminations and other *anti-Vedas* practices that have come to be associated with Hinduism if only to condemn it, says Dr. Pathak.

The Rig Veda was essentially the Aryan book, which said न सद्असि, न असद्असि (neither there is truth, nor untruth). The world came from nowhere; it was neither created nor born; it just happened. Varuna and Indra were Aryan gods. *The Vedas* never talked of God, but of human race. Shiva later emerged as God of common men – aboriginal tribals, Nagas and of other social groups. So, unlike handsome and well-dressed Indra and Varuna, Shiva had snake around the neck because Nagas worshipped snakes; He is known for phallic worship (Shivalinga) because it was widely prevalent in India and Europe also, according to British philosopher Bertrand Russell. Shiva was wild, but he had a family and a child and took indoxicants because it was widely prevalent, specially in Dravidian areas.

It was for this reason, we have Shiva and Parvati temples in all parts of the country starting from Kailash, up on the Himalayas. The Kamakshi Temple is dedicated to Kamakshi or Goddess Kamakhya, originally a deity of Guwahati, Assam. She is known as Parvati or consort of Lord Shiva, also called Shantadurga or Goddess of Peace. Another Kamakshi Temple is located in the historic city of Kanchipuram, near Chennai, and is popularly associated with Shankaracharya, one of the greatest Hindu Gurus. The Meenakshi Temple in Madurai, and the Akilandeswari Temple in Thiruvanaikaval near Tiruchirappalli in Tamil Nadu are also important centres of worship of Parvati as the mother Goddess. It is stated that Shiva's consort Sati took rebirth as Parvati in Kanyakumari in Tamil Nadu to marry Shiva again. But Shiva, while travelling from Kailash, reached late. Parvati said since Shiva was not in time to receive her, she would continue to be a girl child *(Kanya)*. Hence, the place is named as Kanyakumari. No God has so much fascination for Hindus of all castes, region, and belief than Shiva who is considered to be the uniter of India more than any other God or man.

Hinduism is as old as time

Hinduism is *Sanatana Dharma* (the eternal law), that sustains, upholds, and preserves the universe. Hinduism includes a wide spectrum of practices and prescriptions of daily morality based on the notion of *karma*, and *dharma.* Hinduism grants a great degree of freedom of belief and worship.

The word 'Hindu' is derived from the Sanskrit word 'Sindhu', the historic local appellation for the Indus river in the north-western part of India and is first mentioned in *the Rig Veda.* The word 'Hindu' was first used by Arab invaders and then went further west by the Arabic term *al-Hind,* referring to the land of the people who live across river Indus. The Persian term Hindu refers to all Indians. By the 13th century, *Hindustan* emerged as a popular alternative name of India, meaning the 'land of Hindus'.

Hinduism is syncretic which has diverse traditions and has no single founder. Among its direct roots is the historical Vedic religion of Iron Age. Hinduism is often called the oldest living religion or the oldest living major religion in the world. A large body of texts is classified as Hindu, divided into *Sruti* (revealed) and *Smriti* (remembered) texts. These texts discuss theology, philosophy and mythology, and provide information on the practice of *dharma.* Among these texts, *the Vedas* are the foremost in authority, importance and antiquity. Other major scriptures include the *Upanishads, Puranas* and the epics, the *Mahabharata* and the *Ramayana.* The *Bhagavad Gita* combines *Vedanta, Yoga,* and some *Samkhya* philosophy into its discussion of good conduct and life.

Dr. Pathak's concept of Hinduism is based on unity of human species or the concept that the world is a family (वसुधैव कुटुम्बकम) and the *Vedas*, the first code of moral life on the planet and from these flows his concept of universalism which inspires his philosophy for social change, of which the Sulabh Movement is the consequence.

Hinduism not a revealed religion

There is no such thing as Hinduism beyond being a territorial expression which indicates a set of faiths and beliefs which are timeless (सनातन) काफिले आते गए, हिंदुस्तान बसता गया (People came in droves from outside and Hindustan was formed as a country). Since the Central Asia and Middle East were arid or mountainous lands, there was no way to make a living. Hence, most conquerors, including the Mongols, came from these regions and settled in India to make Indian culture composite, multi-cultural and multi-lingual. No other countries, except the US, has absorbed so many people from different places in the world, so many cultures and languages from outside and assimilated them into a modern, growing nation that India has become today. This assimilation of different peoples, cultures and languages would not have been possible if Hinduism were not a tolerant religion. And, if there is nothing like Hinduism, how can there be Hindus, much less caste? Hence, the caste system is a pure concoction which has neither religious sanction, historical validity, nor moral legitimacy.

Hinduism is not a 'revealed' religion like Christianity, Islam or Judaism which have one messiah, one holy book and written rules of conduct. But Hinduism has an overwhelming sense of its own antiquity which began with time. Hinduism is secular and faith neutral. The study reveals that the ancient social order was not divinely ordained nor did it exist since the dawn of civilisation; social order was invented by humans for a social purpose. Any order made by humans can be unmade by humans. We have different ways of believing in God.

THEISM: It is the belief in one God that refers to His relationship to the universe. It conceives of God as omnipresent and active in the governance and organisation of the universe. Theism indicates the doctrine of monotheism which arose in the wake of the scientific revolution of the 17th century to contrast with the then emerging concept of deism that contended that God, though supreme, did not intervene in the governance of the world and could be known rationally but not via revelation. The term theism is derived from the Greek word 'theos', meaning 'god'. Theism can take forms such as deism, pantheism, and polytheism. The claim that the existence of any god is unknown is agnosticism, and can be compatible with theism and with atheism. The positive assertion of knowledge, either of the existence of gods or the absence of gods, can also be attributed to some theists and some atheists. Put simply, theism and atheism deal with belief, and agnosticism deals with absence of knowledge; they are not mutually exclusive as they deal with different domains.

ATHEISM: Atheism is the rejection of belief in the existence of deities. Atheism is the assertion of the position that there are no gods. Atheism is simply the absence of belief that any God exists. Atheism is contrasted with theism. Atheists tend to be skeptical of supernatural claims, citing a lack of empirical evidence. Atheists have offered various rationales for not believing in any god. These include the problem of evil and ineffectiveness of God. Other arguments for atheism range from the philosophical to the social to the historical. Although some atheists have adopted secular philosophies, there is no one ideology or set of behaviours to which all atheists adhere to. In Western culture, some atheists are frequently assumed to be irreligious, although other atheists are spiritual. Atheism also figures in certain religious and spiritual belief systems, such as Jainism, Buddhism, and neo-pagan movements. Jainism and some forms of Buddhism also do not advocate belief in gods.

DEISM: Deism says that supreme being exists but does not intervene in human affairs. Deists reject supernatural events such as prophecy and miracles. This idea is also known as theory, in which a God designs and builds the universe, but steps aside to let it run on its own. Deists believe in the existence of a god without any reliance on revealed religion, religious authority or holy books. Two main forms of deism currently exist: classical deism and modern deism.

Man of absolute values

Dr. Pathak believes in some absolute values, not relativism. He explains the existence of God in many ways. He says in all these cases, (theism, atheism, deism) existence of God is accepted or rejected. "How can you deny God until you have experience or fear of His existence? Accepting His being is intuitive and denial is contrived, intellectual hypocrisy". God is central to Dr. Pathak's life, conscience and good conduct which have become the defining features of the Sulabh Movement. To prove his point, Dr. Pathak says, despite all its world leader status and excellence in scientific research, far more people in America believe in the Devil than in Darwin as the 2007 poll has reported. Belief in hell and the devil was firm amongst 62 per cent of those surveyed in the US opinion poll. Darwin, and his evolution, natural selection, and the rest of it, clocked in with a poor 42 per cent. As many as 79 per cent believe in miracles, 75 per cent in heaven. Witches and UFOs (unidentified flying object) drew roughly the same score, with about a third of Americans believing in them. "The believers alone can be the custodians of conscience", he says.

> *"Nothing is possible without men but nothing is lasting without institution."*
>
> *– Robert Schuman, Architect of the European Union*

CHAPTER 9

Sulabh Founder is an Institution Builder

Work impact makes him a cult figure

We live in a media-driven world where news, information and opinions travel faster than they did ever before. When Lincoln was shot on April 14, 1885 at Ford's Theatre in Washington, it took one week for sailors and mariners to take the news across the Atlantic. When Ronald Reagan was shot and wounded on March 30, 1981, it did not take a minute to ring around the world which came almost to standstill. To be true, information network has globalised the world in an unspoken compact which has made people to compete or fall. Those who control the media control the minds of people where everything begins.

In fact, media has destroyed the British Empire more than the Second World War. The first Press set up in Calcutta, the then capital of India, exposed the British wrong doings. Hicky's *Bengal Gazette* (1780-82) set off the media wave to catch up later by other British writers and journalists. English writers, including George Orwell (born in Motihari in Bihar in 1903), Bombay-born Rudyard Kipling, Paul Scott, Christopher Sherwood and many others, not always admirers of India, conveyed our feelings to the British people invoking their native instinct for freedom in the best British tradition. Besides writers, English politicians and intellectuals like

Ernest Bevin and Harold Laski also conveyed our feelings to Britain. This promoted freedom.

The entire period from 1915, when Gandhiji came from South Africa, to 1947, was one of growth of the English language when it took root in India to finally emerge as a link language of entire South Asia. And, since then, the English language has powered the social and political movements in India. In spite of odds that it faced, one cannot but admire the way media has reached the remotest place to unearth facts and uncover the problems faced by the poor, the victimised, the faceless and the nameless ones aiming at awakening the conscience of society and helping the nation to develop and grow. Its independence can be attributed to the fact that it has refused to be suppressed and muzzled by authorities or bullying dominance of any ideology or any particular way of thinking. Free press is the hope of the free world.

No wonder, the Sulabh Movement which began in a dusty town of Arrah, Bihar, has become global wave to be discussed at national and international conferences and seminars. And, the sufferings of scavengers, have become a case of great human rights violation, greater than those atrocities in Darfur, Rwanda and civil disorders in other places, specially in Africa. Obviously the media has done the magic. Dr. Bindeshwar Pathak is a master of the media which has the uncanny skill to win over support in promoting the Sulabh campaign to liberate scavengers. He took this matter to the US and other centres of power, including the Pope at the Vatican, who has blessed him while he was honoured by the St. Assisi Award later. He has done it through institutions and in collaboration with various agencies, national and international. To be true, Dr. Pathak is a great institution builder.

In earlier times, social reformers and their followers campaigned and succeeded or failed alone. Martin Luther (1483-1546), the German Protestant theologian, succeeded because it was during that period when the printing press was invented in Germany by

Johannes Gutenberg. The protest message of Martin Luther rang around Europe and Christianity was split into two – Catholic and Protestant. We know the rest of the story. But, the Press sends news and information fast; it cannot change attitude and culture which needs social action and campaigning. For this to happen, Dr. Pathak has set up institutions and has collaboration and cooperation arrangement with national and international agencies. The following are some of the many such institutions, national and global arrangements to work together.

International Academy of Environmental Sanitation and Public Health

The Sulabh International Academy of Environmental Sanitation and Public Health (SIAES&PH), founded by Dr. Pathak in 1984, provides technical support to the parent organisation – Sulabh International Social Service Organisation. It was registered in the year 1993 under the Societies Registration Act XXI of 1860 and permission was given under the Foreign Contribution Regulation Act (FCRA) in 1997 by the Ministry of Home Affairs, Government of India. It is engaged in the development of new and sustainable technologies, their implementation, demonstration and dissemination of information for socio-economic reforms, training and consultancy in the fields of the environment, sanitation, water supply, sewerage, storm water drainage, low-cost on-site sanitation, cost-effective wastewater treatment, solid waste management, rain water harvesting and consultancy projects on sustainable technologies like biogas plants, duckweed-based wastewater treatment system and designs of pans and traps of toilets, bio-medical waste management, design of water supply, sewage and storm water drainage. It conducted training programmes for capacity building on sanitation for 14 African countries.

The academy has also trained about 100 *Sashastra Seema Bal*

(S.S.B.) personnel. There are almost regular visits of people for on-site training and demonstration purposes of these technologies. Students from several Indian as well as foreign universities come to the academy, where it provides such training to their requirements. The academy has a well-equipped laboratory for water, and air testing facilities. It had been one of the consultants approved by the Delhi Pollution Control Committee for designing appropriate treatment plants so as to save the Yamuna river from pollution due to liquid wastes from various industries.

SIAES&PH works to promote the larger mandate of acting as an international centre of holistic learning and education of all issues related to promotion of sanitation. The objective is to treat sanitation as a major field of education revitalising training programmes involving highly qualified sanitation experts, engineers, health professionals, scientists, social scientists, ecologists and scholars from all other related fields. The academy aims at bringing sanitation into sharp focus of academic activities and research nationally, regionally and globally. Towards this end an academy is being planned to be set up on an ambitious scale in a 44-acre plot in Gurgaon.

International Centre for Women and Child

The International Centre for Women and Child (ICWC), set up in 1994, is managed by women, providing the much-needed impetus to the holistic development of women and children by supporting various programmes which help preserve natural resources, promote education, encourage healthy lifestyle, stress civic involvement and work towards peace and understanding. It provides model programmes and projects encompassing major issues in the area of training and welfare and support services and awareness. The core areas of concern are counselling, child care, women health, adolescent health, education, vocational training, gender equity, water, sanitation, career pathways, and opportunities for better life for women and children. The centre works to provide a better world for the women and children in accordance with the spirit of the United Nations proclaimed Millennium Development Goals (MDGs), adopted at the Millennium Summit in 2000. Of these eight goals, six are directly related to women and children and the remaining two belong to the general category which concern the broad area of human development.

So far 670 women trainees have worked in different trades with an income of ₹ 300 to ₹ 2,200 per month. The organisation has completed the project sponsored by the National Commission for Women in the Mewat area, Haryana. The main objective of the public hearing was to bring to light the various issues of gender sensitisation and discrimination, violence against women, female foeticide, and the declining sex ratios, the burning question of the present scenario. Emphasising more on rural development the centre organised awareness camp on water rights funded by the National Legal Services Authority, and sensitised 3,000 rural women in Alwar and Mewat in 30 awareness camps on component of safe drinking water.

The organisation has developed 31 school sanitation clubs in Faridabad and built a resource group of 726 peer educators. It has sensitised J.J. Cluster of West Delhi under literacy campaign programme of AIDS funded by the Delhi State AIDS Control Society. The programmes organised in December 2008 and December 2009, covered a population of 1,500 in twelve camps in the J.J. Cluster of West Delhi. The organisation worked with the community dwellers to create awareness on HIV/AIDS and STD and HIV/AIDS-related services in Delhi among J.J. Cluster population and above all, to promote utilisation of available services under HIV/AIDS control programme. It is working for a cause in Tihar Jail for welfare of inmates. Tihar Jail authorities have given opportunities to inmates to run income-generating programmes.

Nai Disha centre for training

Sulabh has set up the Nai Disha centre as an innovative model for other organisations engaged in similar task. The centre has been established with the cooperation of specially enlightened women, belonging to the scavenging community in the vicinity. Nai Disha has vocational training centres at Alwar and Tonk districts of Rajasthan. At Alwar, Nai Disha was established in April 2003 with a batch of 28 women. Transforming the lives of 28 individuals was not an easy task. As per their interest, they have been trained in cutting, tailoring, embroidery, food processing, making papad, Jave (hand-made vermicelli) and handicraft. They are being paid a stipend of ₹ 3,700 per month. The social transformation brought about can be gauged by the incredible fact that the same communities which were averse even to touch a scavenger, today readily purchase these products.

An inside view of the Sulabh International Museum of Toilets

History of toilet in artefacts

The Sulabh International Museum of Toilets, established in 1992, is a unique project. It was set up to educate students about the historical trends in the development of toilets, to provide information to researchers about the design, materials and technologies adopted in the past and those in use in the contemporary world, to help policy-makers understand the efforts made by their predecessors in this field throughout the world, to help the manufacturers of toilet equipment and accessories in improving their products by functioning as a technological storehouse and to help sanitation experts learn from the past and solve problems in the sanitation sector. The museum has rare collections of facts, pictures and objects detailing the historic evolution of toilets from 2,500 BC to date.

The Toilet Museum provides a chronological account of developments relating to technology, toilet-related social customs, toilet etiquettes, prevailing sanitary conditions and legislative efforts of the respective times. It has an extensive display of privies, chamber pots, toilet furniture, bidets and water closets in use from 1145 AD to the modern times. It also has a rare collection of beautiful poems related to toilet. The museum displays artefacts of the Harappan settlers of India who were the first to use a toilet connected with a honey-comb of drains carrying out human excreta and stormwater. Other artefacts are about toilets in use in Egypt (2100 BC), Crete (1700 BC), Bahrain (1000 BC) and Rome 200 BC. The ancient Romans had a system of sewers. They built simple outhouses or latrines directly on the running streams pouring into the Tiber river. A toilet was discovered in the tomb of a Chinese king of the Western Han Dynasty that dates back to 206 BC.

Chamber pots were used during the Middle Ages. A breakthrough was possible in 1596 AD, when John Harington invented the first modern flush toilet in England. The first patent for the flushing toilet was issued to Alexander Cummings in 1775 AD. Later, several others came forward with fresh patents. The adoption of ceramic as new material in the second half of the 19th century brought freshness in the field. In the gallery, showing the modern period, one can see an African water-free composting toilet from South Africa and a portable eco-friendly tent toilet, a plastic mechanism from Canada. The museum has become a tourist destination; 3.2 million people have visited its website. About four thousand visitors come to the museum every year. A number of foreign Ambassadors, Governors, Swedish Prime Minister, Chief Ministers, M.Ps, senior executives and others have already visited the museum. Other visitors include medical students, nurses and sanitary workers.

International Institute of Health and Hygiene

International Institute of Health and Hygiene, launched in April, 1994, works to develop sanitation methods with health, hygiene,

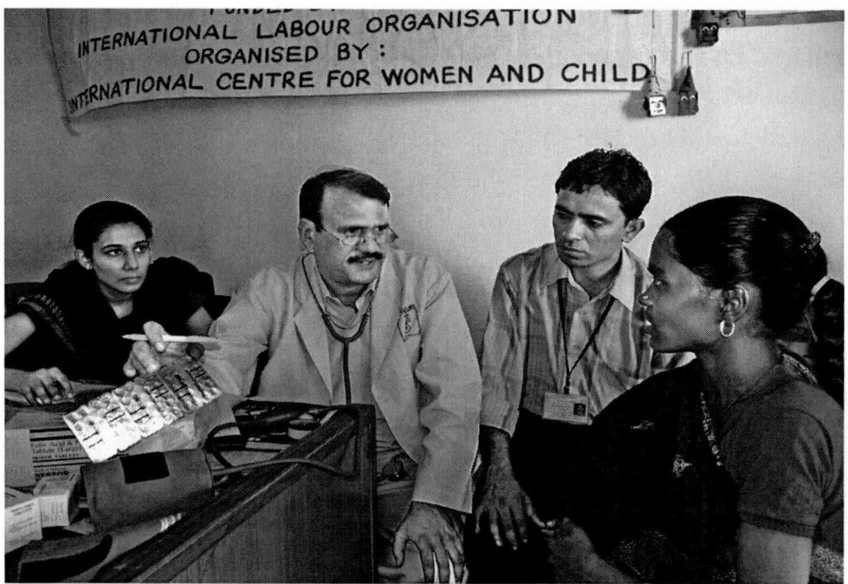

The International Institute of Health and Hygiene Centre, New Delhi, conducting an awareness programme

safe drinking water and community development programmes. There is impact of insanitation which is responsible for large number of diseases and death. The unit provides and suggests preventive, curative and rehabilitative measures to improve the health of the community. The organisation has completed various projects in collaboration with national and international agencies and state and Central governments. It has developed various models and modules regarding various components of health, hygiene, sanitation, safe drinking water and community development programme. It has trained about 12,099 women volunteers in urban and rural slums.

The organisation has developed an integrated approach of Sulabh Total Health Care Programme (STHCP). This is a totally new concept of health services, including safe disposal of various types of waste, safe drinking water and hygienic practices. It has also taken up a special programme for Pulse Polio, HIV/AIDS, Blood Donation and Population Stabilisation. In all, 30 Sulabh toilet complexes were set up in West Bengal. One thousand women were trained in creating awareness on HIV/AIDS. The current project is condom distribution at Sulabh toilet complexes through condom vending machine by Hindustan Latex Family Planning Promotion Ltd. The organisation has also developed Sulabh Water Filter System, which is cost-effective and can be used by poor people.

Women's empowerment organisation

The Sulabh Mahila Avom Bal Kalyan Sansthan, registered under the Societies Registration Act, 1860, is involved with issues related to women and children. It has been trying to empower young girls and women belonging to the poor and underprivileged sections of society at grassroots level, focusing on vocational training. The Sansthan is running three vocational training centres, which offer training in tailoring, embroidery, *mehendi* application and beautician's course and dress designing.

Certificates are given to the successful students after completion of their training. Some of the successful students have taken up jobs while others have started their own business. Surveys are conducted in slums and villages and women and young girls are motivated to take up these courses for self-improvement. While carrying out survey in urban villages in collaboration with the All-India Women's Education Fund Association (AIWEFA), the organisation has found that women face a lot of difficulties due to lack of toilet facility. Subsequently, a demonstration model of Sulabh toilet was built in the Vocational Training Centre at Pataudi village. This encouraged villagers and many of them constructed toilets in their houses. The students are encouraged to participate in cultural programmes organised by the Sansthan. In this way, they become interested in singing, dancing and acting. The central objective of the centre is to empower women in slums to find a role for themselves and help earn a living. The expansion and growth of the centre indicate its acceptance and success in its work.

Centre for Action Sociology

There are social scientists, often described as traditionalists, who view study of social relationship as the sole function of sociologists. There is, however, another school of social scientists, called Action Sociologists, who subscribe to the belief that apart from studying the various social processes and problems, action to remedy them is equally important. Such committed social scientists strive to bring desired changes in societal structure and functioning in order to make the society a better place to work and live in. These social scientists make an attempt to remove the inequalities from the society and help develop an equalitarian structure where everybody has an equal opportunity to develop as per his/her talent. Sulabh International Centre for Action Sociology (SICAS) subscribes to this view, both in terms of thought and action.

Dr. Pathak, who founded Sulabh International Social Service Organisation (SISSO) in 1970, also established SICAS in 1991 to plan and initiate action to help achieve the objectives of the movements through education, training, research and other similar activities, for the sustainable development of scavengers and other weaker sections of society. It has launched the programme of education, vocational training, slum welfare programmes and help in the formation of self-help groups, for their development. The approach is inclusive so that total personality of children of weaker sections is developed; it is demonstration also in the sense that it helps to test hypotheses and initiate process of sustainable change through action, a sociological process namely, conception, initiation, expansion and saturation with the help of activists of its various units, viz., Sulabh Public School, Sulabh Vocational Training Centre, Slum Children and Women Welfare Programme, Sulabh Social Integration Programme, Sulabh School Sanitation Club, Sulabh Research Division etc.

English medium school

In recent years, educational infrastructure in the country has expanded considerably and private schools have been set up which

Morning prayer at the Sulabh English Medium Public School

are managed on commercial lines. But very few children have access to quality education. For them Sulabh Public School was set up in Delhi in 1992. The school is recognised by the Directorate of Education and affiliated to CBSE up to the Secondary level. In several ways, this school is different from others. The school aims to prepare children from scavenging community and weaker sections of society for their all-round personality development so that they grow in a healthy environment. It brings quality education within the reach of boys and girls from scavenger households. It offers support facilities regularly and organises a wide range of co-curricular activities to promote social integration. This makes for a model to be replicated elsewhere. At present, 502 boys and girls are on the rolls of the school. Among them, 60 per cent are from scavenger households. They are provided free education, books, stationery, uniform and mid-day meal so that they may not drop out due to poverty.

Vocational training

The first Sulabh Vocational Training Centre was set up in Patna in 1985 and the next centre was opened in Delhi in 1992. The centre aims to provide development and training to boys and girls from the weaker sections of society, particularly Valmikis, so that they use their newly acquired talents to the fullest and achieve better economic and social adjustment. It offers training facilities in 10 trades: audio-visual repair, electrical equipment, computer, shorthand, typing, beauty care, fashion designing, cutting and sewing, tailoring, embroidery, and mobile repair. To cope with the demand, the centre functions in two shifts, forenoon and afternoon. Most of these trades are recognised by the appropriate authorities of the Delhi Government. The course contents and training methods follow the Industrial Training Institute pattern. More than 300 boys and girls are getting training every year. Considering the socio-economic

The Sulabh vocational training centre, New Delhi

liberalisation in the country, the demand for skill development is growing faster. The centre is gearing up for meeting this challenge. Cultural values, norms and traditions take time to change and require 'will' and initiative from one and all for such change. This necessitates modification of group attitudes and behaviour. With this view, Sulabh has evolved the modality of 'social upgradation' for enhancing their social status. This modality is direct and simple. It is purely voluntary and does not involve any legal obligation on the part of anyone. A conscientious citizen formally and publicly adopts the family of a scavenger. Subsequently, they interact closely and visit each other's home. They meet on social occasions and the adopting person tries to help the adopted family in getting jobs and solving their problems. Many conscientious citizens have adopted scavenger families in large numbers.

Slum children's welfare programme

Most of scavengers in urban areas live in slums. The brunt of the slum culture is borne by younger generation and they create deviant culture in the slums. They rarely go to school and the rate of absenteeism and 'dropoutism' is quite high. A few of them are also engaged in such low-paying work as rag-picking, domestic help and dish-washing in wayside kiosks, or simply live on the streets. Deprived of their childhood, they are exposed to several physical and social hazards. What is more surprising is the situation where the parents are not aware of the plight of their own children. Sulabh has launched a self-development programme for them. Its main thrusts are on education, personal hygiene, and environmental awareness.

These activities are organised during afternoon in the school campus. As is well known, literacy rate is low among women and pathetically low among those living in slum neighbourhoods. SICAS has taken a new initiative by starting the community-based programmes for women empowerment. It has used the community resources and launched the programme in West Delhi in 1997. The training is provided with family-centred approach for sustaining and empowering the poor families through non-formal education and sensitising them with local problems.

Sulabh has succeeded in making an impact on Indian and

Slum children at Sulabh School, New Delhi

global sanitation situation entirely because of its ability to organise people, experts, opinion makers, and set up institutions. Sulabh has floated a large number of global and regional networks, and collaboration arrangements which together have become a transmission belt to convey ideas and messages across the globe. Through information networking, conferences, seminars and visits all over the world, Dr. Bindeshwar Pathak has made a large number of personal friends and co-workers who have joined together to make a grand alliance to promote sanitation and clean environment, much of which was evident on the Earth Summit in Rio in 1992 and the MDG mega meeting in Johannesburg in 2002. At these conferences, time-bound targets were fixed with global consent to reduce greenhouse gases and to halve by 2015 the proportion of people without sustainable access to basic sanitation.

Global spread and acceptance

Sulabh's work has been evaluated by many international agencies, including UNDP, World Bank, UNICEF and WHO. Sulabh has tied up with many agencies for research and project work, including WHO, UNDP, ODA (Overseas Development Agency of the British Government), BORDA, (Bremen Overseas Research & Development Association), DANIDA (Danish International Development Agency), KFW (Krebitanstalt Fur Wiederaufbau, German Development Corporation), and EEC (European Economic Community). The Netherlands Government also funds low-cost sanitation projects in many states in India. Sulabh is working in the neighbouring countries like Nepal, Bhutan, China, Pakistan and Bangladesh. It has also taken up many programmes in collaboration with the UN Centre for Human Settlement, Nairobi; and the International Water and Sanitation Centre, Loughborough University of Technology, (UK), and through the Water Engineering and Development Centre (WEDC). Sulabh is also closely working in collaboration with other agencies like NBO, CBRI, HUDCO, Ministries of Social Justice and Empowerment, Urban Development and Rural Development, Government of India, All-India Institute of Hygiene and Public Health, Calcutta, etc.

Consultancy services

Dr. Pathak has worked as a Consultant on a number of World Bank – assisted projects, either independently or in collaboration with Engineering Service (India) Pvt. Ltd. (ESI). Some projects pertain to the collection of data and information on the status of rural water supply and sanitation development in seven states of India, laying down criteria and guidelines for selecting villages and districts to be included in the Integrated Rural Water Supply and Environmental Sanitation Project in Uttar Pradesh, identification of low-cost sanitation alternative for Chennai city, and low-cost sanitation for the Thiruvananthapuram Sewerage and Sanitation Improvement Project. Sulabh is engaged in consultancy in collaboration with ESI on: (1) Low-Cost Sanitation under Environmental Sanitation Programme in Chennai and the adjacent urban areas; (2) Low-Cost Sanitation in Kozhikode Sanitation Planning Area; and (3) Community Awareness, Environment and Health Education Studies in Chennai. Dr. Pathak has taken the initiative in persuading the Government of India to take up Centrally-Sponsored Schemes for the Liberation and Rehabilitation of Scavengers with the twin objectives of conversion of dry latrines into sanitary toilets and liberation and rehabilitation of scavengers.

This is the story in brief about the NGOs delivering social services at the doorsteps. However, Sulabh has transcended these barriers to spread all over the country and abroad, doing a variety of services, including setting up and maintaining toilets, opening schools, and training centres, developing technologies, campaigning for social change and abolition of social prejudices, including untouchability.

Sulabh has many NGOs directly affiliated with it, although with their independent status. There are trained people from many countries in Africa and Asia to promote sanitation. A total of 47 officials and entrepreneurs from 14 African countries (namely Ethiopia, Mozambique, Uganda, Cameroon, Burkina Faso, Kenya, Nigeria, Senegal, Ghana, Zambia, Tanzania, Cote d' Ivorie, Mali and Rwanda) were provided practical training in sanitation technology for capacity building in 2005 and 2006. And, its services have been recognised nationally and internationally.

Information centre

Working with the Union Ministry of Environment and Forests, Dr. Pathak also established the Sulabh Environmental Information System (ENVIS) centre to gather and disseminate environmental information related to hygiene, sanitation, and sewage treatment system and technology for enhancing, supporting, facilitating and bringing under one umbrella the huge data bank on the aforementioned subject area for the benefit of a diverse group of people ranging from students, policy-makers, researchers and academicians to industries and institutions even at international level. The Sulabh ENVIS centre is actively involved in:

- Developing and expanding the online data base, especially the publication and distribution of E-Newsletter.
- An online query-response system to respond to national and international queries on sanitation and related topics.
- Preparation of training write-ups, CDs and publication of important technology issues in national and international journals.
- Surveys and data collection from urban slums and rural areas for collection of primary data on hygiene and sanitation.

- Developing an educational research programme in the shape of documentary films.

Sulabh Sanitation Mission Foundation

This is the centre of social, educational and career promotion foundation which funds empowerment programmes. It also takes up scavengers' social upgradation programmes with extensive network in states to do this work. Its volunteers visit scavengers and other social groups of disadvantaged people and help and advise them about their career choices and how to go about managing work and life if only to get out of the poverty trap.

"Sulabh is an amazing story of hope, change and progress."

– Timothy J. Roemer,
US Ambassador in India

CHAPTER 10

A Synthesis of Gandhism and Social Democracy

Old thought systems re-invented

Dr. Bindeshwar Pathak held no office, wore no cap, rode no lal batti *(red siren) car and addressed no mass meeting; he held nothing nobler than the humble broom in one hand, and the Gandhian book in another. That changed the way people think and clean places. The romance of the Sulabh Movement lies not in what it has achieved but what it promises. Dr. Pathak symbolises social change without conflict. This is the Sulabh philosophy which is a synthesis of decades of experience in social democratic discourse on ideas, changing internal and external social dynamics and reappraisal of thought systems by revisiting them to find their relevance today. However, Gandhism is central to the Sulabh philosophy, the only addition being technology.*

When the Sulabh Movement was launched in 1970, there was no clear ideological profile, apart from those of Gandhism which is neither a doctrine nor a regimented thought system for violent social change. It was a moral enterprise, the central focus being on Independence, without violence, or major social upset. The Congress, for that matter, has always been an umbrella organisation where the Muslim League and the Hindu Mahasabha, rightists, leftists and a variety of other parties on the political spectrum found adequate articulation of their views. The Independence movement was not violent and those who pleaded violence had to leave the party and later constituted fringe groups after the Independence in 1947.

In sum, Gandhism is a collection of inspirations, principles, beliefs and ideals of Mahatma Gandhi which he preached and practised in his lifetime. It is a body of ideas that describes his vision and his life work. The term 'Gandhism' also encompasses what Gandhiji's actions meant to people around the world, and how they used them for guidance in building their own future. Talking about 'Gandhism', Gandhiji had said, "There is no such thing as Gandhism, and I do not want to leave any sect after me. I do not claim to have originated any new principle or doctrine. I have simply tried in my own ways to apply the eternal truths to our daily life and problems. The opinions I have formed and the conclusions I have arrived at are not final. I may change them tomorrow. I have nothing new to teach the world." Truth and non-violence are as old as the hills, he said. Among the cardinal Gandhian principles is *Satyagraha* which is formed by two Sanskrit words *Satya* (truth) and *Agraha* (holding firmly to). The term meant Gandhiji's commitment to non-violence, human freedom, equality and justice which arose from his personal examination and not out of any doctrine like communism and capitalism.

When Gandhiji returned to India in the middle of the World War I, he said, it would be wrong to demand equal rights for Indians in the Empire, and yet not contribute to British defence in the war. However, by the time of the advance of the Japanese in the World War II, Gandhiji had given up notions of fighting alongside the British and argued for non-violence instead. Gandhiji developed a way of life by his constant 'experimenting with truth' – a phrase that formed the sub-title to his autobiography. He was prepared to learn through trial and error, often admitting to mistakes and changing his behaviour accordingly. This was particularly notable when Gandhiji stopped the nationwide civil resistance in 1922 after the Chauri Chaura incident. He would forsake political independence for truth, believing that Indians should not become murderers and commit the very evils they were accusing the British of perpetrating in India.

Non–violence remains central to Gandhism

The concept of non-violence *(Ahimsa)* and non-resistance has a long history in Indian thought and had many revivals in Hindu, Buddhist, Jain and Christian contexts. Gandhiji explains his philosophy and way of life in his autobiography, *The Story of My Experiments With Truth.* He says, "What difference does it make to the dead, the orphans, and the homeless, whether the mad destruction is wrought under the name of totalitarianism or the holy name of liberty and democracy?"
"An eye for an eye makes the whole world blind".
"It has always been easier to destroy than to create".
"There are many causes that I am prepared to die for but no causes that I am prepared to kill for".

Gandhiji's deep commitment and belief in non-violent civil disobedience as a way to oppose tyranny, oppression and injustice have inspired many subsequent political figures, including Martin Luther King Jr., Julius Nyerere of Tanzania, Nelson Mandela and Steve Biko of South Africa, Lech Walesa of Poland and Aung San Suu Kyi of Myanmar. Gandhiji's work in South Africa between 1910 and 1915, for the rights of Indian residents oppressed by the racist white minority, inspired the African National Congress (ANC). From the 1950s, the ANC organised non-violent civil disobedience akin to the campaign advanced by the Indian National Congress during the 1920s and 1940s. ANC activists braved the sticks and bullets of the police, water-hoses, teargas and dogs to protest against tyranny, racism and oppression in South Africa. Many, especially Mandela, languished for decades in jail, while the world outside was divided on the continuance of apartheid. Steve Biko, the most vocal adherent to non-violent civil resistance, was allegedly murdered in 1977 by agents of the apartheid regime.

Martin Luther King Jr., a Civil Rights leader of America

Martin Luther King Jr., a young Christian preacher and leader of the American Civil Rights Movement seeking the liberation of African Americans from racial segregation in the American South, and also from economic and social injustice and political disenfranchisement, travelled to India in 1962 to meet Jawaharlal Nehru. The two discussed Gandhiji's teachings, and the methodology of organising peaceful resistance. The graphic imagery of black protesters being hounded by police, beaten and brutalised, evoked admiration for King and the protesters across America and the world, and precipitated the 1964 Civil Rights Act. The Non-violent Solidarity Movement of Lech Walesa of Poland overthrew a Soviet-backed communist government after two decades of peaceful resistance and strikes in 1989, marking the beginning of the downfall of the Soviet Communist Empire.

Scavenging is anti-Gandhian

Gandhism means condemning of untouchability and scavenging in society; it means condemning the victimisation of women and coerced conversions to Islam and Christianity in the same breath. Gandhism has respect for people and not for power. "No institution or individual is infallible, save God", Gandhiji said and believed that all humans are susceptible to sinful actions and behaviour, and the worst of dictators were essentially the same despite the difference in their lives, beliefs and actions. Despite this, he held firmly that humans had no right to punish each other. He believed punishment to be the responsibility of God. Gandhism was the synthesis of many thought systems but Gandhiji was most influenced by social democracy which is also the core philosophy of the Indian Constitution. India was the first country in the modern era to decolonise itself, a feat achieved after a sustained campaign of self-assertion that lasted from 1905 to 1947. Over that period, a combination of political reasonableness, sharp criticism and massive mobilisation made the British leave India without major violence.

The Gandhian culture of non-violence is the heritage of the Sulabh Movement except that the latter has technological underpinning while the former has none. Going farther into the past in search of the roots of the Sulabh Movement, it will be interesting to give an ideological context to the Sulabh story. It is also because no social movement as comprehensive as Sulabh can be born out of nowhere – it is only a continuation of the trends already in existence.

Gandhism is rooted in social democracy

Gandhism is rooted in the long tradition of social democracy, a dominant concept, first born as a political doctrine in Sweden in late 19th century. The social democratic movement came into being after a split in the socialist movement which marked parting of ways between those who insisted on political revolution as a pre-condition for the achievement of socialist goals and those who maintained that a gradual or evolutionary path to socialism was both possible and desirable. Many related movements, including pacifism, anarchism, and syndicalism, arose at the same time and from the same source. These ideologies were often promulgated by individuals who split from the pre-existing socialist movement, and held a variety of different objections to Marxism. One of the key founders of contemporary social democracy was Eduard Bernstein, a proponent of reformist socialism and a revisionist of Marxism. Bernstein had originally been a Marxist and had held close association with Karl Marx and Friedrich Engels, but he saw flaws in Marxian thinking and began such criticism when he investigated and challenged the Marxian materialist theory of history. Bernstein criticised Marxism's concept of *'irreconcilable class conflicts'* and Marxism's hostility to liberalism. Bernstein refuted Marx's position on liberalism by claiming that liberal democrats and social democrats held common grounds that could be utilised to create a 'socialist republic'.

Eduard Bernstein and his gradualism

On the issue of class conflict, Bernstein believed that economic disparities between the bourgeoisie and the proletariat would gradually be eliminated through reforms and economic redistribution programmes. Bernstein rejected the Marxian principle of dictatorship of the proletariat, claiming that gradualist democratic reforms will improve the rights of the working class. Furthermore, he believed that class cooperation was a preferable course to achieve socialism, rather than class conflict. On the issue of class conflict and responding to the Marxian principle of dictatorship of the proletariat, Bernstein said, "It is dangerous to destroy civil society which takes hundreds of years to build. Social democracy does not want to break up civil society and make all its members proletarians (poor) together; rather, it ceaselessly works to raise the worker in the social position of a proletarian to that of a citizen and, thus, make citizenship universal. It does not want to replace civil society with a proletarian society but a capitalist order of society with a socialist one."

Bernstein urged social democrats to be committed to a long-term agenda of transforming the capitalist economy to a socialist economy rather than a sudden upheaval of capitalism, saying: "Social democracy should neither expect nor desire the imminent collapse of the existing economic system... What social democracy should be doing, and doing for a long time to come, is to organise the working class politically, train it for democracy, and fight for any and all reforms in the state which are designed to raise the working class and make the state more democratic."

Third way of change without conflict

However, since the 1980s, there has been a perception that social democracy has been on the retreat in the Western world, particularly in English-speaking countries where social democratic values are arguably not as firmly rooted in local law and culture as elsewhere. In recent years, a number of historically social democratic parties and governments have moved away from some traditional elements of social democracy by endorsing the Third Way ideals and thus supporting both the privatisation of certain state-controlled industries and services and the reduction of regulation of the market. The adoption of the Third Way ideology by many social democrats has proved divisive within the broader social democratic community. Traditional social democrats argue that the Third Way ideology has caused the movement to become too centrist, and that even the movement may be becoming centre-right. In general, apparent reversals in policy have encountered significant opposition among party members and core voters; many of the latter have claimed that their leaders have betrayed the principles of social democracy.

The Third Way represents a re-alignment of the values of social democracy to the realities of the modern world: traditional social democracy thrived during the prevailing international climate of the post-war Bretton Woods consensus, which collapsed in the 1970s. It has also become difficult for political parties in the developed world to win elections on a distinctively left-wing platform, now that electorates are increasingly middle class and consumerists. Thus, socialism ceased to be attractive. The development of new social democratic policies in this environment is the subject of wide-ranging debate within the left and centre-left. A number of political think-tanks, such as Policy Network and Wiardi Beckman Stichting, have been active in facilitating and promoting this debate.

Gradualism is also the Sulabh way

After this complex argument, it becomes clear that Gandhism, like most other thought systems, was neither new nor very innovative. This principle had already been stated in many political philosophies, among which social democracy was most prominent. Social democrats say: (1) It is not necessary to adopt violence to change society. (2) Rather, it should be a process of gradualism. (3) Instead of destroying the rich (bourgeoisie), upgrade the proletariat (poor). (4) To do these, persuasion, pressure, education and empowerment should be used as weapons, instead of coercion. (5) There is nothing (as Marx said) like 'irreconcilable class conflict'. All conflicts can be solved by non-violent method. (6) It is easier to destroy than to create (which Gandhiji used literally in his message to the British Government during the World War II). (7) Hence, there is a Third Way – the first being the bourgeoisie (rich) rule and the second the Marxian theology of proletarian tyranny which seeks to exterminate the rich.

The Third Way seeks to do neither; it seeks to merge the social divisions and work for social reconciliation through social democracy which is neither capitalism nor communism, but a combination of both. Industries should be run by private people and social services by the government, which is the representative of the people. There should be social control on public sources. This is what Gandhiji said and this is what the Sulabh Movement seeks to work out on ground in practical ways. These basic tenets of social democracy are also part of the Gandhian philosophy which the Sulabh Founder, a Gandhian in different ways, has followed.

Sulabh philosophy is revival of old values

The Sulabh Movement has rich Gandhian legacy so also of social democracy and, hence, like Gandhism, it is not a thought system of a fixed body of dogmas and practices that one should swear by. It has the tradition of ideas shaped by long years of theoretical debate and practical realities. The collection of these ideas, values and dreams has been packaged into Sulabh philosophy, which is far too different from dogmas-bound doctrine. For that matter, the Sulabh philosophy is a synthesis of decades of experience of social democratic discussion on changing internal and external conditions and re-appraisal of thought systems by revisiting them to find their relevance today. However, Gandhism is central to the Sulabh philosophy, the only addition being technology.

Understanding the role of technology and its impact on economic, social, political, and cultural conditions is crucial to understanding society because technology is the impetus for social change. The telegraph, telephone, internet and information technology have brought about changes which no war or revolution could do before. Technology has created new political philosophies, thought systems and has established new social relations. Technology has changed our values, our age-old perception and world view. In sum, technology has produced the modern world. Sulabh has used technology to abolish scavenging and change their lives. Dr. Pathak says that expansion of social services, including education, old-age security, women's empowerment, social equality, health care, child care and economic protection, should be taken care of by the state. However, this could be possible only if there was strong economy and high growth. Hence, he says, there has to be private investment. For that matter, production of wealth should be left in private hands and the government's role should be restricted to social welfare. This is what social democrats said, so did Gandhiji and so does the Founder of the Sulabh Movement. "There are many things in the world, including water, air, forest and land, which have value more than any price can reflect. They should not be privatised. People are different; if the requirement that everyone should have the chance to freely shape his/her life is a serious one, then we must naturally accept that the choices will be different. From this perspective, sameness, the requirement for everyone to fit into the same mould becomes the enemy of equality because it means that those who do not fit into the given mould are forced to adapt to it and are thereby deprived of the opportunity to control their own lives. Equality demands diversity and variation. In some central aspects, however, the demand for equality is precisely about sameness: everyone has the same value as an individual, and the same right to grow and develop as a person", says Dr. Pathak.

Everyone is a member of society and everyone's living conditions are affected by the surrounding society. It is from these similarities that the demand for equality – the same opportunities to control one's life and the same opportunities to influence one's society is defined. Many different factors create inequalities in society. Economic structures or class structures create inequalities depending on position in working life. Social patterns, which make different demands and offer different opportunities to men and women create inequality between the genders. Discrimination against people who are seen as different because of ethnic background, disability or sexual orientation creates unequal chances in life for those being discriminated against. "And, these cannot be addressed by force alone but also by conciliation", the Sulabh Founder says.

"I do not feel obliged to believe that the same God who has endowed us with sense, reason and intellect has intended us not to use them."
– Galileo

CHAPTER 11

Dr. Pathak's World View: Trusteeship Idea Revived

The days of revolutions are now over

Dr. Bindeshwar Pathak, who has formed his world view after extensive tour of the world and deep study of world's leading thought systems, remains unconvinced about the Western analysis of class structure and says Gandhism, which is eclectic and syncretic both, is the only solution to the problems of our troubled times. Although technology has changed the world beyond belief, the core values remain the same. "Man wants to be equal, free and make his own choices the primitive human passions that have not changed," says Dr. Pathak.

Dr. Bindeshwar Pathak is a cosmopolitan both by birth and upbringing, never claiming to hold the dike alone, as if beyond him there will be deluge; his work is the continuation of the Gandhian reforms and ideology. His foreign visits have broadened his world view to never become clueless in the world of various thought systems and choices. However, he says there is a time for everything, even for social injustice to end. He quotes Otto Bismarck, the German Chancellor, who created the modern Germany out of what was a tiny Prussia: "The statesman can only wait and listen until he hears the footsteps of God, resounding through events; then he must jump up and grasp the hem of His coat and justice and truth will prevail in the world".

Social activists used liberalism to enforce the rights of civil society and justify civil disobedience. Dr. Pathak has adopted this formulation to provide an intellectual background for the Sulabh Movement. John Locke formulated the classic expression of liberalism which inspired the writers of the American Constitution and Gandhiji quoted Locke to empower the weak and poor. The Sulabh Founder also does it although with greater emphasis on the welfare of the scavenger who, he says, is the face of social injustices, inhumanity and all that is wrong and skewed in a democratic polity.

Dr. Pathak's world view is as complicated as his life and work are mystical. He refuses to avow by any straightjacket political philosophy or theory, saying that human behaviour is too complex, unpredictable to be treated as a commodity to be traded in market or measured in economic indices. Man can be at once sublime and cruel, miser and extravagant, soft and tough. We have the stories of men being great killers like Hannibal, Attila, Huns and Hitler, and saviours like Jesus, Buddha, Florence Nightingale, Gandhiji and St. Francis of Assisi, Italy, who opted to suffer so that others could live well. So, how can one say with certainty about the complex human behaviour and put it in any political, philosophical ism or social theory. "So any claim to have the knowledge of human mind and behaviour is hollow," says Dr. Pathak. However, he refers to various political thought systems and discusses them with enthusiasm without saying anything beyond calling himself a Gandhian which is an umbrella concept, not doctrine.

Thoreau and Gandhi

Dr. Pathak has reinterpreted the philosophy of Gandhian civil disobedience to say that civil disobedience is often undertaken in obedience to what is perceived as a higher moral law. The term also implies an open, usually public act, risking and often inviting state action, in order to arouse public awareness or to exert pressure on the civil authority. It is allied to the strategy of non-violent (or passive) resistance, in which the superior force of the government is confronted. It is also used for purpose of social change. The term civil disobedience was coined by Henry David Thoreau in his essay *"On the Duty of Civil Disobedience"* (1849). While accepting the necessity of government, (but endorsing the motto "That government is best which governs least"), Thoreau did not accept the necessity of acceding to its unjust or immoral actions. It is our duty, he argues, to take some action and expose and overturn the wrong and to preserve our own moral integrity. Thoreau himself was briefly jailed when he refused to pay a poll tax because the U.S. government permitted slavery and was seeking to extend it in the Mexican War of 1846-48.

The two most notable and successful heirs to Thoreau's notion were Mahatma Gandhi and Martin Luther King Jr., but the tactic of non-violent direct action has also been employed, for example, in South Africa in defiance of apartheid laws and in the United States by anti-abortion protesters. Gandhiji called it Satyagraha (from the Sanskrit for 'truth' and 'persistence') and mobilised masses of people in a 30-year campaign of non-cooperation with British rule in the country. King was inspired by his Christian faith and Gandhiji's example, and under his leadership, the American civil rights movement adopted a strategy of non-violent confrontation and civil disobedience aimed at exposing the evils of southern discrimination and segregation. The tactic sought to appeal to white men's conscience by meeting violence and hatred with humility and love, and to pressure the U.S. government to intervene with federal power and federal law. Gandhiji had made it into a political philosophy which is followed all over the world, latest being in Egypt, and Tunisia where autocratic rulers were made to step down following peaceful demonstration. The Gandhi idea is now making waves in societies where social injustice exists.

Class is an artificial social construct

The terms caste and class, denoting social divisions and inequalities, are based on heredity, or other distinctions, and they should be abolished, says Dr. Pathak. Social stratification is almost as old as human society, including the caste system. The Industrial Revolution had brought about significant changes in the social order, giving rise to prosperous entrepreneurs and a large urban workforce that began to be seen in terms of 'classes' of people, defined according to their economic function and their relation to the system of production. However, caste is another story. (*See other chapter on caste*).

Although he did not invent the concept, French socialist Claude-Henri Saint-Simon was among the first thinkers to analyse social divisions in the light of industrialisation. The theory of class is associated primarily with Marx and Engels, who declared in The Communist Manifesto (1848), that "the history of all hitherto existing society is the history of class struggles." They saw economic relations specifically, ownership and non-ownership of property as the defining feature of social structures and group identity. In this analysis, various human societies have always been divided into hostile groups while under capitalism, they are reduced to two: the bourgeoisie, or owning class, and the proletariat, or working class. (The French term *bourgeois* denotes the middle class merchants and professionals whose incomes and social status place them between the aristocracy of wealth or title, on the one hand, and labourers and the poor, on the other). Under capitalism class divisions foster class consciousness, an awareness of common interests which fuels class conflict and ultimately leads to socialist revolution. Like Gandhiji, Dr. Pathak does not accept this analysis.

Power of spirit

The Marxist class analysis has also been challenged by many, including Max Weber, whose concept of class was broader and more flexible than Marx's. For example, he emphasises divisions within classes, distinguishes between the owning and commercial classes, and stresses inequality of life chances as the crucial determinant of class divisions. Weber also argues that social status stems not only from class but also from status and power, neither of them necessarily deriving from one's economic situation. The claim by Marx was also challenged by Yugoslavian Vice-President Milovan Djilas and others. Marxism was practised in the former Soviet Union for 70 years and failed for all to see.

But Hegel saw human consciousness (or 'spirit') as the motive force in history, creating social and material circumstances. Marx believed just opposite, "Consciousness does not determine life; life determines consciousness." He and Engels wrote in The German Ideology, that economic circumstances – the relations of production, through which nature is transformed into material goods by human labour – determine social organisation, which in turn shapes our ideas, relationships, and identities. The exploitative relations that characterise capitalist production, Marx contended, generate class conflict between workers and owners that will inevitably produce a revolutionary upheaval in which capitalism is replaced by socialism, a synthesis that achieves workers' aspirations to control the fruits of their labour while retaining the structure of the state, which will ultimately 'wither away' under full communism. This did not happen. The state, instead of withering away, became stronger and the principal source of social exploitation and authoritarianism.

Not suitable for us, says Sulabh Founder

Dr. Pathak says the Marxian social construct dividing the society between owner and labourer may be suitable for the industrialised West and not for India or other Asian countries where societies had been organised along caste, religion, tribal loyalty or feudal social order. We had never seen the Industrial Revolution as the West. Ours had been pastoral and agricultural societies organised along different value systems and beliefs. Hence, Marxism is entirely a Western concept, right or wrong. We have our indigenous values and belief of which Gandhism presents the reformed and changed face. "This is what I also accept", says Dr. Pathak.

The American ideals of equality, justice and freedom and the rising incomes of unionised labour in the post-war 20th century have also prompted resistance to the use of class as a descriptive concept, despite great inequalities in wealth and income in the United States today. There is, however, broad agreement that economic circumstance is not the sole factor in determining class divisions in modern society. Racism, for example, may play a more crucial role, as the continued existence of a large African-American underclass attests. These are the landmark ideological divides which work as reference points in philosophical discourse which Dr. Pathak has studied and differed with focus on Gandhism.

Charles Darwin and his natural selection

Charles Darwin, yet another man of controversy, was an English naturalist, whose theory of evolution through natural selection, revolutionised biological science and had a profound impact on the world. Darwin's ideas were based in part on the data he collected on his round-the-world voyage with HMS Beagle in 1831-36, especially the observations he made of the variations between related species on the Galapagos Islands. By 1837, he had formulated the conclusion, which he termed 'descent with modification', that species change, or 'evolve', over time through the appearance of new traits that slowly modify ancestral forms until their descendants are distinctly different. To the question 'how do new traits emerge?' Darwin first offered the explanation that individuals' acquired characteristics emerge randomly within populations, which are the part of evolutionary process.

According to this theory of natural selection, 'preferred traits' – those that give an individual the best chance of survival and procreation – are propagated and become characteristics of descendant species, while harmful traits are bred out of the population. Darwin's theory created a volcanic theological controversy (one that continues today), which escalated with the publication in 1871 of *The Descent of Man,* a work that explicitly placed humanity on the evolutionary chain. The theory was hailed, however, by many of his fellow scientists. The major theoretical problem Darwin faced, and which he was never able to overcome, was his inability to satisfactorily explain the origin of new traits and the mechanism of hereditary changes. Ironically, the answer, the genetic principle of inheritance was established by Gregor Mendel in 1865 but ignored by the scientific community until the early 20th century.

Thomas Jefferson and slavery

Dr. Pathak quotes Charles Darwin (1809-82) and Karl Marx (1818-83), contemporary thinkers, only to say that of all the sources of class conflict, genetic or economic or caste have never had any justification. The caste system has neither genetic nor economic reason to exist. It is purely an artificial social construct which evolved through thousands of years of despotic rule of kings and conquerors or both. He says there cannot be any philosophical or theoretical defence for the caste system. Hence, it can be abolished straightaway without causing any social upset. "I am concerned about the social structure because its distortion has created the scavenging system which I seek to abolish through social reform and technology", says Dr. Pathak without taking a position on the views expressed by Marx and Darwin, stating "they are pure intellectuals while I am a social activist."

A very amazing case is about Thomas Jefferson who wrote the American Constitution to send the message of "the right to life, liberty and pursuit of happiness". Jefferson, the greatest upholder of freedom, had slaves and possibly he believed in the Darwinian theory of selection while talking about American slaves. Jefferson's views on slavery were coloured by the prejudices of the gentry class and shaped by his general political philosophy. Although he regarded the institution of slavery in America as a 'hideous evil', Jefferson was ambivalent over the exact status of Blacks within the human community. When he saw his ideal classical republic threatened by limitations on the expansion of slavery, he joined the extreme anti-abolitionists in advocating the extension of slavery into the West.

The only way that Jefferson could reasonably reconcile slavery with his ideal polity of independent, educated, and active citizens was to question the equal human status of Blacks and Whites. In his Notes on the State of Virginia, Jefferson cited the popular 'scientific' 18th century evidence that Blacks were a distinct race between apes and men, and he based their inferior status on the deficiencies in the human faculties of reason and imagination. However, when comparing American black slaves with the white slaves of Greek and Roman antiquity, Jefferson found the ancient slaves excelling in art and science, lending support to his argument that the 'Blacks' inferiority was attributable to their native abilities rather than to their enslaved condition.

Roman slaves too excelled, in science, insomuch as to be usually employed as tutors to their masters' children. Epictetus, Terence, and Phoedrus were slaves. But still, they were so employed despite the belief that Blacks were inherently inferior to Whites, and possibly even a distinct race separate from humans. Jefferson expressed 'doubts' over the attitude of the gentry that after liberation from slavery, the Blacks might prove themselves equal to Whites in all human abilities.

Dr. Pathak disagrees with this view about which Jefferson himself was in doubt when he said in 1788, "I wish I am wrong. But nobody can wish more ardently than I do that slavery should be abolished because slavery is a moral degradation without any defence for this inhuman practice". The Sulabh Founder says caste is no slavery. People of all castes in India are of the same genetic and racial group, treated differently for different historical reasons; far too different for the ones Darwin or Jefferson talked about in their theories.

Dr. Pathak is closest to liberalism

Dr. Pathak, by his liberal education and family influence, is very clearly a liberal thinker although he does not totally agree to its Western interpretation. Liberalism is social, and economic doctrine that in its classic construction emphasises individual freedom, limited government, gradual social progress, and in its modern incarnation favours state involvement in social welfare and economic policy while upholding personal liberty. The term has the same root as 'liberty' and implies freedom of conscience and action. Liberalism developed in the early 19th century as the ideology of the middle class of merchants and entrepreneurs. It had its intellectual basis in the political philosophy of John Locke, the enlightenment faith in human progress and rationalism, the economic theories of Adam Smith, and the utilitarianism of Jeremy Bentham and John Stuart Mill. Locke's republicanism and other liberal ideals played a significant part in the founding of the American republic. Gandhiji, Nehru and most contemporary leaders supported this thought with some changes. So does Dr. Pathak.

The 19th century liberals advocated religious tolerance, individualism, and self-reliance, sought moderate political and social reforms (in England, the voting 'right' was extended only to male property holders, not women or those without property), and viewed poverty as a moral failing. Liberal policies have been historically identified in England with the Liberal Party and in the United States with the Democratic Party, both of which were formed in the 1830s. In the 1930s, President Franklin Roosevelt redefined the term 'liberalism' to describe his New Deal programmes, calling it "a changed concept of the duty and responsibility of government toward economic life." In this interpretation of liberalism, government is seen as the guarantor of individual rights and freedoms through the regulation of economic and social policy to check the excess of capitalism and provide a 'safety net' against poverty.

The 20th century brand of political liberalism is sometimes labelled 'neo-liberalism.' That term is also applied to economic policies for developing countries that emphasise free markets and free trade, as opposed to economic planning and protection of domestic industries. In international relations, the term refers to policies that favour reliance on international institutions, rather than on the traditional tools of power politics, to address global problems. Gandhiji quoted liberalism to reject the caste system and the exploitation of the poor.

Liberalism used in different context

A little more about it will be in order because this term, liberalism, is widely used in different contexts and with different consequences. Roman Catholics stress social and political action on behalf of the poor and oppressed. Originating in Latin America, it grew out of a Marxist-influenced analysis that attributed chronic urban and rural poverty to oligarchical institutions and capitalist economic exploitation, and faulted the church for condoning that system instead of taking the side of its victims. Liberalism theory has also inspired social change movements throughout the world. For example, in Korea, Minjung (poor people) theology uses indigenous folktales to teach self-liberation. In the United States, black theology reads the Bible in terms of African-American experience and preaches emancipation from racism and white cultural dominance. In Indian context, liberalism is used for fair treatment to all, specially the poor, freedom of speech, conscience and setting up a just society. And none of these can be denied by any political party or social organisation, also because it is a very respectable and flexible term. Dr. Pathak uses liberalism to condemn caste system and support scavengers' right to be free.

Dr. Pathak's world view is based on Gandhism

Gandhiji was author of the philosophy and practice of *Satyagraha*, or constructive non-violent resistance to oppression. His thinking drew from a diversity of sources, including *the Bible* and *the Bhagavad Gita*, as well as more recent works such as Thoreau's '*Civil Disobedience*' and, above all, from Tolstoy's philosophy of universal love and passive resistance to evil. Gandhiji lived for two decades in South Africa, where he developed his philosophy of non-violent direct action in a series of campaigns to end discrimination and for the Indian independence from the British rule. Gandhiji saw no distinction between the social and spiritual, the personal and political.

He believed that life is part of the controlling essence of the universe, which he called *Satya* ('truth'); we are all literally one and must therefore love each other as fully as we do ourselves. Central to this belief was the ancient principle of *Ahimsa*, non-injury to and respect for living being. Both, Gandhiji's activist strategy and his religious philosophy embraced three principal concepts: *Satyagraha*, *Swaraj* (self-rule), implying national independence and personal self-control, and *Swadeshi* ('one's own land'), the development of self-sufficient local economies at the village level. The Swadeshi movement, symbolised by the act of spinning, which Gandhiji himself did every day, encouraged the wearing of homespun cotton clothing (*khadi*) and the boycott of British-manufactured cloth. His advocacy of *Hind Swaraj*, (or home rule), urged the strengthening of Indian identity in opposition to colonial culture and called for a government rooted in indigenous values and traditions.

For Gandhiji, non-violent resistance was hardly passive, but an active confrontation of 'brute force' with 'soul force' that not merely disrupted colonial rule but also appealed to the essential humanity of the oppressor. *Satyagraha*, a decisive factor in achieving Indian independence in 1947, was pursued over many years by a variety of means, including mass marches and demonstrations, civil disobedience, boycotts, and hunger strikes. Gandhiji himself practised an ascetic way of life, encouraged community cooperation and communal living (he considered private property a violation of the oneness of humanity), and strove for tolerance among antagonistic social groups. He vainly tried to prevent the partition of India and challenged the caste system, calling the outcaste untouchables 'Harijans'. Dr. Pathak mentions these names and their thoughts only to outline the broad spectrum of thinking from Marx, on the one hand, and Gandhiji on the other. They had their own ways of explaining human relationship and social structure. "Gandhism is a combination of human values, social equity and fairness. To be true, all these help me in my objective to achieve the redemption of scavengers and other depressed classes, and that is my philosophy. Gandhism is one on which hinges the Sulabh Movement for social change". This is the world view of Dr. Pathak.

NOTE:

Dr. Pathak has formed his world view after extensive tour of most parts of the world with Europe and America becoming his virtual stomping ground. He had attended various global meetings on invitations, including the Rio de Janeiro Earth Summit in 1992, Bali Climate Change Conference in 2007, Johannesburg Sustainable Summit in 2002, Copenhagen Social Development Conference 1995; Global Collaborative Council Meeting for Water Supply and Sanitation, Oslo, 1991; Water Supply and Sanitation Collaborative Council Meeting at Rabat, Morocco, 1993; World Summit for Social Development, Copenhagen, 1995; Water Supply & Sanitation Collaborative Council, Manila, 1997; World Toilet Summit, Singapore, 2001; World Summit on Sustainable Development, (Earth – II) Johannesburg, 2002; World Toilet Summit, Seoul, 2002; Third World Water Forum, Kyoto, 2003; Conference organised by the Water Supply and Sanitation Collaborative Council, Geneva, 2003. He himself organised the World Toilet Summit in New Delhi in 2007.

Besides these, he had been invited by the official agencies from 14 countries in Africa, and by the agencies in Pakistan and China to study sanitation, environmental and human rights problems. He has been on various panels constituted by the Government of India and state governments to finalise policy profiles and co-opt them in the development plans. He was invited by the Cambridge University in January, 2011 to address the intellectuals and show how the Sulabh concept of social change could be made relevant to different social conditions.

> *"Small steps somewhere turn into giant stride*
> *for mankind everywhere."*
>
> *– John F. Kennedy*

CHAPTER 12

Sulabh Movement Forged Out of a Million Dreams

Areas of major initiatives and achievements

Dr. Bindeshwar Pathak has reached out to the scavenger, the 'untouchable', who are seldom reached by anyone after Mahatma Gandhi whose legacy is the rich inheritance of the Sulabh Movement. To address scavengers' problems, Sulabh goes international to appeal for a rethink on social relationships which alone will bring smile where there were tears and hope where there was despair. By doing so, Dr. Pathak seeks to rewrite the destiny of the scavenger, crushed and unseen, and help him rise and carve out space not only for himself but for others also, similarly marginalised for whom the new dawn is still to break on the horizon.

Some ages are defined by war and conflict; other by industrial growth and yet another by baby boom and some ages are, however, defined by their epidemics. In 1347, rats and fleas, stirred up by Tartar traders cutting caravan routes through Central Asia, brought bubonic plague to Sicily. In the span of two years, Black Death, which spread from China, killed up to 30 million people in Europe in the 14th century. It is estimated that between one-third and one-half of the British population was affected by it. In 1520, Cortes army carried smallpox to Mexico wiping out half the native population. In 1918, a virulent strain of flu swept through troops in the trenches of France. By the time it was over, 21 million men and women died, more than those killed in the World War I.

Descartes died of pneumonia in Stockholm; Kant died of dehydration in his village Konigsberg where he spent all his life to become one of the greatest philosophers of all time (categorical imperative); Alexander died of malaria; Pompey lost to Caesar on the bank of the Rubicon river because he could not mobilise his army which got bad stomach because of poor sanitation; David Livingstone, a British missionary on the holy mission to civilise (read conquer) Africa, had to come back to London to die of malaria unmourned and unsung. The story is not complete: adequate sanitation decides happiness, success and failure, war and peace. Only clean societies grow.

The post-Independence India had many achievements to its credit, but many social asymmetries, distortions and injustices still persist that have undermined our claim to be a civilised society. Fifty years down the road, poverty and human deprivation in India is hard to accept. Nearly 38 per cent of Indians lives below poverty line* (officially this figure is 28 per cent). We have 10 per cent more poor people today than there were in 1947, twice as many illiterate, hungry and marginalised people – barely existing and excluded from the mainstream of economy entirely because of population which grew from 350 million to 1,170 million plus now and it is growing. Our children get less protein and fewer calories than their grandparents did at the same age. More than half a million children under the age of 5 years die of diarrhoea and other illness due to dirty water and lack of access to sanitation.

*The number of illiterate persons still exceeds 304 million making India the country with the highest number of illiterate persons in the world.** Two-thirds of the total number of illiterates in India are women. The country has the maximum number of school dropouts. In sum, every third illiterate in the world is an Indian. In its report,

---

* *Suresh Tendulkar*

** *Mid-term Appraisal–Eleventh Five-Year Plan, 2007-2012*

State of the World's Children - 1999, UNICEF has other disquieting things to say about India. Though committed to achieve the UN-declared goal of making primary education free to all, the country at present allocates just 3.7 per cent of its GNP on education.

In course of Dr. Pathak's research work, the idea came to his mind about maintaining public toilets out of the money collected from users. He thought that these two concepts together – conversion of dry latrines into Sulabh Shauchalayas and the pay-and-use public toilet system – would go a long way in improving personal hygiene, community health and economic well-being of the poor, specially scavengers and they did that beyond all expectations. Thus, Sulabh started doing the conversion initially in six states of Andhra Pradesh, Bihar, Madhya Pradesh, Orissa, Uttar Pradesh and West Bengal. Later, it expanded to more states and, finally, to all over the country. Sulabh designs (with certain modifications) have also been adopted by the UNDP (World Bank) and other national and international agencies. This was the expansion phase of the Sulabh Sanitation Movement.

It may be recalled that the small beginning of the movement was made at Arrah, a small dusty town in north Bihar, where the first meeting of the Sansthan was held in a hut. It was attended by seven persons who laid out broad outlines of policies and philosophy of the mission, hardly knowing that the small one-time effort at social service would become a pan-India movement, enclosing within its fold almost the entire area between Kashmir and Kanyakumari. A 'baby' born in a hut finally became a colossus – the largest self-supporting organisation set up to render social service to the poor. It does not get any aid or assistance from any national or international agency because it asks for none, but generates its own resources to run the organisation and promotes the ideals of the movement by setting up its own delivery system and implementing its own work agenda.

No dramatic start

However, the origin and growth of the Sulabh Sanitation Movement was neither as momentous as the fall of apple in Newton's courtyard, nor as fortuitous as the sight of a dead man that turned Prince Siddhartha into Gautam Buddha who enlightened the world. To be true, Sulabh was born more by accident than design. A young boy was searching for a job and he became one of the tallest social leaders of our time. But, who knows what the future holds for us? Gandhiji wanted only a seat in an all-White railway compartment in South Africa and he was thrown out of that Pietermaritzburg railway station (now named after Gandhi) and, the British lost the Indian

SULABH OBJECTIVES IN BRIEF

- To liberate and rehabilitate scavengers.
- Their social upgradation.
- Promote indigenous technologies.
- Harness non-conventional energy sources from human waste and save fuel and forests.
- To educate people not to defecate in the open and prevent environmental pollution.
- Procure manure from Sulabh toilets and use it to raise farm productivity.
- Motivate people to get bucket privies converted into Sulabh toilets and set up toilets in their houses.
- Building community toilets with bathing, washing, and urinal facilities on pay-and-use basis at public places.
- Promote vocational training and primary health care.
- Create new jobs by training change-agents for integrated rural development.
- Promote consultancy, research and development in technical and social fields.
- Promote awareness through mass communication.

empire. Napoleon just asked 24 francs from his girlfriend, Disrae to buy uniform and with that he went to Paris from Corsica and captured the entire Europe. Lincoln's life's dream was to travel from his log cabin in Kentucky to walk along the Potomac river in Washington DC where he finally lived and died as President of the United States. Newton was a shy indoor man living alone with his cat, but when he decided to sit out in his apple orchard, the world was never the same. Great achievements are sometimes difficult to explain; they are governed by the Laws of Unintended Consequences. The Sulabh Sanitation Movement is no exception.

Areas of major initiatives

Institutions are created to carry on missions, faith and ideas. Christianity is a faith and Church is an institution. Buddhism, Jainism, Hinduism, Marxism, Capitalism etc. are missions or faith and they have separate organisations to carry out their objectives. Institutions are built with bricks and mortars which age and decline with time. But faith and ideas don't. The Marxist State in the former Soviet Union declined and fell into the dustbin of history, but Marxism remains a dominant concept even today. The *Mahabharata* is about 5,000-year-old story, philosophy, faith and ideas but this book continues to be the source of Indian culture. Ideas are enduring, permanent and indestructible and remain in the air when everything else is lost and forgotten.

Sulabh International Social Service Organisation is the leading non-profit making outfit, working to promote sanitation and prevent environmental pollution which are critical components to a healthy and productive society. The growing population and the consequent strain on shrinking resources have produced slums, violence, houselessness and human miseries which are evident among the people living on the edge. The growing urbanisation has also caused serious shortages of houses, forcing people to live in shanty colonies without toilet facilities. Beginning from a small town in Bihar, Sulabh now works virtually all over the country with the help of a large workforce of over 60,000 committed social volunteers, including administrators, management experts, engineers, architects, sociologists, scientists, media persons, etc. Similarly, the Sulabh Sanitation Movement is a mission and Sulabh International Social Service Organisation is an institution to implement its programmes and objectives. Since Sulabh objectives are many, needing different kinds of approach, different kinds of allied organisations have been set up, with experts heading them. However, there is a co-ordination at the apex level to ensure that their working is congruent with objectives.

The Sulabh Movement being a combination of 'hardware' (technology) and 'software' (education, etc.) components, engineers and social scientists work together, firm in the belief that technology only facilitates change; working as a means to provide good life and create a just social order. But, its role has to be finally integrated with the holistic objectives. Hence, the complex – although well-defined concept of the Sulabh Movement – is evident in the institutional spread of Sulabh International which is the country's largest pan-India network. It is, therefore, necessary to know the comprehensive institutional spread to fully comprehend the 'mission and faith' of the Sulabh Sanitation Movement.

It is now an established fact that most diseases are caused by bad sanitation. People build houses but not toilets, indicating skewed attitudinal and cultural preferences. Official agencies are sinners no less. They also do not lay sufficient stress on sanitation, most specially toilet facilities in buildings. The snag in sanitation programmes is also technological. The sewerage system is very costly and, hence, not sustainable. There is neither enough water in rivers to carry city effluent, nor enough money to set up sewage treatment plants. Even France has been able to treat only 40 per cent of the Paris sewage; the remaining waste flows into the Seine river, untreated.

Liberation of scavengers

Sulabh aims at restoring human rights and dignity to scavengers, their social integration, and poverty alleviation, on the one hand, and prevention of environmental pollution and promotion of sanitation, health and hygiene, on the other. During the last 47 years, Sulabh has succeeded in liberating a large number of scavengers from the demeaning practice of physically cleaning and carrying human waste, rehabilitating them in other professions, setting up 1.5 million scavenging-free pour-flush toilets with bathing facilities. The Point 11A in the Government of India's 20-Point Programme of 1986 relates to 'Justice to Scheduled Castes and Scheduled Tribes'. This clause was inserted in the 20-Point Programme by the then Prime Minister, Mr. Rajiv Gandhi, on the persuasion of the Sulabh Founder. Under this programme, large-scale toilet conversion and construction project was launched in 1986 when cholera broke out in Delhi. Later, this plan was expanded into a national plan of sanitation and health to cover the entire country.

Indigenous technology

In India, out of about 7,935 towns (2011 census) only about 929 are sewer-based and that, too, partially. It is estimated that only 34 per cent of the urban population has sewerage connections and only about 33 per cent has a household toilet connected to sewer or on-site disposal. There are 269 Sewerage Treatment Plants (STP) all over the country. The remaining 302 Class I cities, 467 Class II towns and 26 other towns are having sewage generation but there are no sewage treatment facilities. As per the Central Pollution Control Board (CPCB) estimate of 2005, major cities in India generate an estimated 38,254.82 million litres per day (MLD) sewage. However, the sewage treatment capacity is only 11,786 MLD (32 per cent) and as such only 13.5 per cent of the sewage is treated. The cost of construction and maintenance of sewerage is prohibitive. The septic tanks have found favour with only 38 per cent of urban population because its vent pipes emit foul odour and pollute the air. Moreover, cleaning septic tanks periodically needs the services of scavengers. *(Source: 2011 Census).* The two-pit pour-flush toilet that Dr. Pathak had developed requires no manual handling of human waste. It has a specially designed pan with a steep slope, a trap and a water seal. The space of about 2 sq. metres is enough for its construction. The water seal prevents foul gases from leaking out of the pit. This cost-effective toilet requires 1 to 1.5 litre of water for flushing, instead of 10-15 litres needed in the conventional systems. The biggest advantage of the Sulabh toilet system in the Indian context is the fact that it does not require the services of scavengers. It is the safest low-cost on-site human waste disposal system invented so far. The Sulabh technology has been found to be a viable alternative to sewerage and septic tank systems. *(Read details in technology chapter).*

Pay-and-use toilet system

Between 1970 and 1974, the growth of the organisation was linear – a steady progression from one stage to another, beginning with Dr. Pathak's experience in the Valmiki Liberation Cell, study of scavengers' problem and finding out a technology which is the lever of change. The movement was limited to these. It did not go to the people's door steps until 1974 when the Sulabh Founder introduced the system of operating and maintaining the pay-and-use community toilets with bathing, washing and urinal facilities along with round-the-clock attendants' service and availability of water and electricity. It benefited a large number of people who began to see a change in their lives by becoming partners in the sanitation campaign. These toilet complexes are being used by a large floating population, mostly in slums, and by pavement dwellers, rickshaw pullers, physically handicapped, commuters and tourists. Sulabh toilet complexes came to be accepted by the people and admired by authorities for their cleanliness and good management. About 8,500 community toilets and baths have already been set up. The facilities of household individual toilets and public toilets are now being used by about 20 million people every day. Bharat Ratna late Mr. J.R.D. Tata was so impressed with the system that he not only himself sponsored a new Sulabh toilet complex in Mumbai, but proudly inaugurated it if only to highlight the need for public toilets.

The Sulabh Founder, however, discovered that liberation and training alone was not enough to abolish scavenging and rehabilitate scavengers. Stressing the need for a change in the attitude of the people who should accept scavengers as their equals, on October 2, 1990 Sulabh organised rallies to highlight the need to end untouchability which Gandhiji sought to do. In 1993, a novel programme was launched for the social upgradation of scavenger families. Under this programme, the elite of society were requested to have social relations with scavengers to enable them live a dignified life as equals in the society. So far 10,000 scavenger families have been socially upgraded and brought into the social mainstream. It was with these objectives that Sulabh International Centre for Action Sociology (SICAS) was set up in 1991. For the benefit of the masses, Sulabh began bringing out literature on the Sulabh Sanitation Movement in 15 major languages of the country. Dr. Pathak has himself written a number of books. Prominent among them are: *Road to Freedom, A Study of Directed Change, A Simple Idea that Worked and Eradication of Scavenging and Environmental Sanitation in India.*

Swachch Bharat Mission

The Hon'ble Prime Minister, Shri Narendra Modi, launched Swachch Bharat Mission on October 2, 2014 to fulfil Mahatma Gandhiji's vision of a Clean India by his 150th birth anniversary in 2019 and had advocated that without freedom from filth, India cannot become a great nation. It is a national mission to make India's streets, roads and infrastructure clean by 2019. The central component of the mission is construction of toilets. Besides constructing toilets in every school immediately, it plans to construct 12 crore toilets in the rural areas. The aim is to provide every household with a toilet and thus eliminate open defecation by conversion of insanitary toilets into pour-flush toilets and eradication of manual scavenging. No doubt Dr. Pathak, along with Sulabh, which has a formidable expertise and track record in this area, is playing an important role in the mission. Sulabh has adopted many villages like Harmithila in Haryana making them free from open defecation. Here, Sulabh has built 18,737 individual household toilets and several toilets in schools under the Corporate Social Responsibility (CSR) programme.

Sulabh Water Treatment Plant

Besides developing a technology of purifying drinking water long back in 1974 at Patna, Sulabh has installed water treatment plants at six sites in West Bengal, viz., Madhusudankati in North 24 Pargana, Murshidabad, Mayapur in Nadia Suvasgram and Chaksultan in West Medinipur. Raw water is drawn from the river Ganga in Mayapur and Murshidabad while in Madhusudankati, it is taken from a local pond. In Haridaspur, Chaksultan and Mirzapur (West Medinipur), it is taken from a well. After its treatment at the plants, the water becomes pure and safe for drinking. Sulabh is bottling this water which is available for 50 paisa per litre.

Apart from supplying safe drinking water, Sulabh is also treating people suffering from arsenic poisoning at the health centre adjacent to the Water Treatment Plant at the Sulabh Campus in New Delhi. Purified water is available at ₹ 1 per litre at the Sulabh Water ATM.

Housekeeping and cleaning

Sulabh has also been entrusted with the work of maintenance and housekeeping services in government and public/private sector organisations and hospitals in the country. Notable among them are the President's Estate, the Vice President's Secretariat, National Technical Research Organisation, a division of P.M's office and a number of ministries such as the Ministry of Defence (South Block), Ministry of Rural Development, Krishi Bhawan, Ministry of Telecommunication, Sanchar Bhawan etc. Sulabh is also providing housekeeping services at AIIMS, Ram Manohar Lohia Hospital, Safdarjung Hospital, Lady Hardinge Medical College and other hospitals. The total number of units where Sulabh is engaged in housekeeping and maintenance works in the country is 429 which include 223 offices and 88 hospitals.

Programmes in slums

Slum growth is ubiquitous in most developing countries. Urban areas in India share this problem, with a difference. Most of the Scheduled Castes, including scavengers, live in slums and the children are worst hit. They symbolise social drift. Many among them are close to coming in conflict with law. For them, Sulabh has launched a self-development programme. Its main thrusts are on education and training, personal hygiene and environmental awareness. These activities are held during afternoons. They are brought to the Sulabh School and given training in a variety of job skills. Sulabh has made special arrangements for educating the children who work for their parents, and young girls who cannot be taken in any school, or those who have no money to spend on education. Literacy among women is low and still lower among those living in slums. Keeping this in view, SICAS has started a community-based literacy programme. Drawing upon the community resources as well as its own existing resources, it launched the programme in 1997, in Delhi. Space and a few volunteers were provided by the community. The centre provides the services of Sulabh volunteers and teaching material, including books, stationery, black-boards, etc. Not only women and girls learn alphabets but they are also exposed to functional literacy. Frequently, they participate in social functions and workshops. A large number of housewives benefit from this programme.

R&D work

In order to keep abreast of the changing social realities, SICAS has all along attached great importance to social research. For this, it has provided adequate in-house facilities, including word processing, computer for data analysis, etc. It invites outside specialists to do evaluation and research studies. It also collaborates with national and international agencies. Main research areas have been the problems of the weaker sections of society, social intervention strategies, processes of change and development and the manner in which these percolate to the grassroots. Grants-in-aid are being given to many of the courses offered by the Sulabh Vocational Training Centre by the Ministry of Human Resources Development, Government of India. Most training courses offered by the Sulabh Vocational Training Centre are recognised by the Directorate of Training and Technical Education, Government of National Capital Territory of Delhi.

The growth of the Sulabh Sanitation Movement was in three stages – one was setting out policies and priorities after its birth in 1970; the second was developing technologies and methodologies and the final stage, (which is still continuing) is the search of knowledge, spreading its message across the countries and beyond. The Sulabh International Institute of Technical Research and Training (SIITRAT) was launched in 1993 to do technical research and development. Techno-economic issues relating to low-cost sanitation and biotechnology are studied by SIITRAT experts to make them cost-effective and efficient. Investigations are going on for optimum utilisation to recycle the other wastes such as aquatic and terrestrial weeds, agricultural wastes, certain organic industrial wastes, etc. for producing bio-energy.

Many R&D projects have been taken up in collaboration with various national, and international agencies. Sulabh has also a tie-up with the British Council to train teachers on environmental and sanitation programmes. The teachers will finally transfer knowledge to students to ensure a clean environment. Sulabh is the first to generate biogas from human excreta collected and it relieves villagers of the trouble of bringing firewood for cooking purposes, makes kitchen free of smoke and also helps save forests. Schoolchildren are periodically taken round Sulabh toilet complexes along with teachers to create sanitation awareness and inform them about the Sulabh technology and biogas system. SIITRAT looks after the biogas generation.

Education on environment

The Ministry of Environment and Forests, through the National River Conservation Directorate (NRCD) has sponsored the Yamuna Cleaning Programme through education, awareness and campaign. Sulabh International Institute of Rural Development (SIIRD) is an implementing agency. Under the project, education on Yamuna cleaning and the environment was started in four western towns of Mathura, Vrindavan, Agra and Etawah. Under the project, the participatory development programme known as 'Better School: Better Living' was also launched. The highlight of the project was organising groups of local motivators through the orientation training of 400 teachers. As many as 800 students have been trained to work as change-agents who participate in the National River Conservation Programme.

Why Sulabh matters

Sulabh plays an important part in identifying ways and means of solving common social problems through people's participation in self-sustaining project. Sulabh has demonstrated that people themselves, and not the government alone, can solve the problems and the NGOs should play the role of a catalyst in making it happen. Specially, women's major problems are lack of education and skewed social structure which is set against them in gender bias. Women hold key to the success of any development programme; they can bring about lasting changes in the family and society. Sulabh's strategy is to ensure full participation of women in rural programmes by discouraging the prejudices flowing from casteism, religious radicalism and untouchability which have also been the sources of backwardness and poverty. Sulabh combats these by organising the poor in cooperation with others for creating an equitable and just social order. It is called Sulabh synergy.

Community participation has been central to the Sulabh Movement which has laid special emphasis on health education and creating awareness about sanitation and environment. It has set up primary health care centres at community toilets. As a result of this, considerable awareness has been created about the importance of personal hygiene and sanitation. It has helped in bringing about a change in social values and hygiene habits of the urban poor and helped them adopt cleanliness and sanitation as parts of their daily routine. In fact, Sulabh works to turn development process into a people's movement with the people themselves becoming agents of change. Its innovative approach provides sustainable environmental sanitation strategy to change the habits and attitudes of the people. This approach has helped in building the capacity of the community and usher in a new self-sustaining sanitation order in society. Literacy, specially of women, is the major ideological foundation of the Sulabh Movement, which is a knowledge and technology-based movement which seeks to change social norms and preferences by education, campaign, persuasion and pressure.

Sulabh has been working with various national and international agencies, important among them are: the Central Ministry of Works and Housing and other Ministries, including the Planning Commission, the Delhi Government, as many as 25 state governments, and the Government of Bhutan. These collaborations are in different areas, largely sanitation-related, including the Ganga Acton Plan. International agencies include UNICEF, UNDP and agencies in China and Pakistan. No wonder, Sulabh activities are recorded in various citations and media reports, both at home and abroad. Many eminent persons from all over the world have visited its various activity centres and recorded their appreciation. Dr. Pathak has been invited by different countries to seek his advice on low-cost sanitation. What started as a small voluntary group of seven persons has snowballed into a mighty movement. At the time of its birth, nobody could set the course of action for the movement which later kept on changing as it moved along. And quite predictably so because Dr. Pathak discovered that abolishing scavenging was not a matter of money, technology, education or social upgradation alone. But the whole lot of these and other social co-efficients constitute a diverse society like India. No wonder, farther the Sulabh moved, the more complex and distant receded the solution to the problem of abolition of scavenging in India.

Sulabh's success should be measured by its knowledge and radical ideas. Knowledge is the perceived value of a society while idea is the response to a problem. When we mix ideas with knowledge, we get capabilities to promote inter-group social relationship across divergent disciplines and perspectives. Norms are "unwritten and unstated, mutual understandings on what is appropriate behaviour under given sets of conditions". In a society, customs are norms. How do norms differ from rules and laws? Authorities enforce laws and social pressure enforces norms.

Violation of a law may not result in social disapproval, but violation of norms does. Norms are the community's view of an action or behaviour. Prohibited action can be *mala in se* or *male prohibita. Mala in se* means inherently evil. *Mala prohibita* means they are illegal only because the rules say so. This is the ideological perspective of Sulabh and for that matter this movement is different from any social movement launched in India so far.

Sulabh is an NGO whose work has been successful and has had a great impact as it works in cooperation with the government. It has both sanction and widespread acceptance, nationally and internationally. The impact of the work of Sulabh is visible in micro and macro achievements. Apart from restoring social dignity and improving health, the Sulabh toilets have in-built mechanism that reduces greenhouse effect. Gases produced during decomposition of excreta in the pit do not escape into the atmosphere, rather they are absorbed in the soil. Thus, it prevents global warming and improves the environment.

> *"We can move the world, we can touch the sky*
> *We can climb the highest mountains, spread and fly*
> *We can learn to grab our dreams and hopes*
> *We can move the world."*
>
> *– Joe Crone*

CHAPTER 13

Global Perspective to Sulabh Movement

The swimmer matters or the tide?

In Greek mythology, Icarus was the son of Daldalus who escaped from Crete, using the wings of wax made by his father. He thought he could now soar too close to the sun. And when he did that, his wings of wax melted away and he fell. Success produces overreaching ambition among heroes which proves their undoing like that of Icarus. Dr. Bindeshwar Pathak has never allowed arrogance to overtake his performance. But, like all other leaders, his work also has a context, Indian and global. Let us see how!

Historian Paul Kennedy, author of *The Rise and the Fall of Great Powers,* says, crises produce generals, fighters, reformers and leaders who make history. Abraham Lincoln had Civil War, Roosevelt had World War II which also produced Churchill; Napoleon had the French Revolution, Washington had the American War of Independence, Gandhiji had Boer War and India's Independence struggle, to name only a few leaders who were born out of crises that tested their commitments and moral strength. Earlier, Thomas Carlyle, quoting Hitler, Stalin and Roosevelt, says, "Heroes take control over the competing forces within a society. Hopes and fears of people take the form of ideas, and later ossified into ideologies, formulas or isms which heroes master and convert them into effective heroic human action. Delusion of one man is insanity and delusion of many is ideology. Heroes have influenced thought systems". In his book, *On Heroes, Hero-Worship and the Heroic in History,* he compared different types of heroes, including Oliver Cromwell, Odin and William Shakespeare, and analyse their roles in context of their times.

For Carlyle, the hero was similar to Aristotle's 'Magnanimous' man, a person who has flourished in the fullest sense. However, for Carlyle, unlike Aristotle, the world was filled with contradictions with which the hero had to deal. All heroes will be flawed. Their heroism lay in their creative energy in the face of these difficulties, not in their moral perfection. To sneer at such a person for their moral failings is the comfort of the weak. Carlyle called this 'valetism', from the expression 'no man is a hero to his valet'. However, Carlyle lost much of his moral authority when he defended slavery and said it was necessary to keep order and make lazy Negroes work. This and Carlyle's support for the British repressive measures in Jamaica, further alienated him from his old liberal allies like Stuart Mill Emerson. Carlyle also made a favourable impression on some slaveholders in the U.S. Carlyle's dislike for democracy and his belief in charismatic leadership was unsurprisingly appealing to Adolf Hitler who was reading Carlyle's biography of Frederick during his last days in 1945.

Marx opposes Carlyle

Interestingly, the most important challenge to Carlyle's great hero theory came from his fellow Victorian, anti-idealist philosopher-historian and political economist, Karl Marx. In the opening paragraphs of his classic, *The Eighteenth Brumaire,* he says, "Men make their own history, but they do not make it as they please; they do not make it under self-selected circumstances, but under circumstances existing already, given and transmitted from the past." Churchill's accomplishments were staggering; but he could not alter the larger tides of history, and he had to make his policies within the limits he had inherited. Hence, it is widely agreed that men 'make' history only under circumstances existing already, given and transmitted from the past. Present is product of the past. So, the long-standing academic dispute as to who makes history, the leader (swimmer) or the circumstances (tide) that produce leaders remains unresolved. It is the chicken and egg conundrum whether the leader created the circumstances or the circumstances produced leader?

Sources of conflict in post-war world

In many newly independent nations, ethnic diversity led to disagreements and, in some cases, to civil war. To win independence, nationalist leaders had promised peasants and urban workers economic improvements and political rights. Following independence, these same leaders found it impossible to follow through on their assurances. There were not sufficient resources to provide the promised improvements. Failure to reach unrealistic goals led to rivalries among ethnic groups that threatened to disrupt the political processes completely. As they attempted to maintain their governments, leaders neglected other serious social and economic problems.

POPULATION BOOM: Most Western-educated leaders anticipated the most formidable barrier to rapid economic development which was extraordinary population growth. Importation of new food crops from the Americas, infrastructure that cut down on regional famines and the end of localised war – all contributed to population growth in Asia and Africa as death rates declined. Medical improvements that cut into the mortality rates from tropical diseases also stimulated population increases. Population surges continued from Independence almost to the present in many parts of Asia and all of Africa. Lacking industrialisation to provide employment and to produce consumer goods, newly independent nations could not cope with increasing numbers of people. They also found it difficult to import food and raw materials from

BAAY BOOM – TIMELINE

1805

1bn. Just a few years after Thomas Malthus predicted the demise of humans by overpopulation and famine, the 1 billionth child was born.

Thomas R. Malthus (1766-1834)

1900

1.65bn. The dawn of 20th century marked the beginning of a 100-year baby boom. The current population explosion is happening in Asia while in 1900s, the US recorded the fastest population growth.

1927

2bn. In the interim between the two world wars, the Western world, and in particular the United States, experienced an era of prosperity and kept fuelling the population boom.

1959

3bn. It took more than a century for the population to grow from 1 billion people to 2 billion people, but later it took just 32 years to add another billion.

1974

4bn. It took only 15 years for another billion – the time between billions was getting shorter.

1987

5bn. When the world population hit the 5-bn mark, some demographers said that the globe could not support even that many people. However, it did not happen.

1999

6bn. Developed economies were still booming, but the population explosion has changed hands from Western countries to Asia.

2011

7bn. The 7th bn child was reportedly born in India on October 31, 2011.

outside to supplement indigenous resources. Although birth control programmes have been introduced in the Third World, there has been resistance rooted in traditional culture to their use. Thus, more people are demanding more from the same sources. That being not possible, resentment grew.

CROWDED CITIES: Massive internal migration to urban areas was one of the most common experiences of the post-colonial period in Africa and Asia. Lacking industrialisation, the cities offered little in the way of employment, resulting in the construction of extensive slums. Masses of urban poor have proved to be politically volatile. In many Asian and African nations, cities are parasitic, dependent on imports of food from the countryside or abroad. Without factories, the cities provide little in return. Overpopulation in rural areas has depleted soils, led to deforestation, and destroyed tropical ecosystems. Despite having small industrial sectors, pollution in developing nations tends to be a significant problem. Exports of raw materials and food products (what economists define as primary products) in exchange for capital continued to result in economic dependency. With the exception of petroleum exporting nations, African and Asian countries have fared poorly in global markets. African and Asian leaders blame poverty on neo-

HOW MANY ARE SEVEN BILLION PEOPLE?

If everyone on Earth joined hands to form a human chain, it would stretch about 7 million kilometres. The chain would circle the Earth at the equator about 175 times, stretch to the Moon and back about nine times, and reach about one-fifth of the way to Mars when it's at its closest point to Earth. Although, there are more than double the number of people living in the world today than 50 years ago, the foodgrain production has kept pace with growing demand. Today, there is more food available per capita than 50 years ago. However, the baby boom will begin to hurt the humankind if it does not find an equilibrium between man's demand and the nature's ability to meet it. That point has reached now.

colonialism. Corruption, inequities of wealth and the failure of basic social and economic reforms have also contributed to the slow pace of development.

Different leaders adopted different approaches to social reform and economic progress. Programmes have rarely been able to raise standards of living for the majority. Some solutions to problems have created new dilemmas. Kwame Nkrumah's career as leader of Ghana was indicative of the lack of success enjoyed by those nationalists who retreated to authoritarian forms of government. After promising reforms, Nkrumah discovered that he was unable to deliver. Leftist, Nkrumah lost support from the West. He also faced dissent from rival ethnic groups. Finally, cocoa, Ghana's primary export product, fell in value on world markets. As his development failed, Nkrumah became increasingly dictatorial. He sought to engender mass support by references to African forms of culture and socialism. Nkrumah attempted to establish a cult of personality and successfully made himself an object of veneration in Ghana. When he left the country for a diplomatic mission in 1966, a military coup ousted him. He died in exile. It was one of the many cases in the Third World where leaders failed the people.

SOCIAL REVOLUTIONS: Asian and African armies were often more resistant to social change. Because commanders were anti-communist, they also attracted support from the West and thus they became repressive. At their worst, military commanders, such as those in Uganda, Burma, and Zaire, sought to enrich themselves rather than introduce social reforms. Too often, scarce economic resources were devoted to military hardware rather than development. Gamal Abdul Nasser of Egypt was an exception. He took power after a military coup in 1952 as part of the Free Officers Movement. By 1954, all political parties were abolished. Nasser used dictatorial powers to force through radical social and economic reforms. He ordered the redistribution of land to peasants, provided free education, subsidised food prices and created employment.

Nasser also limited foreign investment and nationalised some foreign properties. In 1956, he was able to force the British to leave the Canal Zone. Despite good intentions, Nasser's development schemes often foundered through corruption, lack of adequate capitalisation, and poor government planning. The Aswan Dam project, the cornerstone of economic development in Nasser's Egypt, actually had more negative than positive results. Rising population wiped out development gains. An attempted aggressive foreign policy, which had generally poor results, also drained money from development schemes.

THE INDIAN SOCIALISM: India began the process of development with a stronger industrial base and stronger infrastructure than did Egypt. India also possessed a larger middle class in proportion to its total population than any other Asian or African nation. Despite tremendous ethnic and religious diversity, India has been able to preserve both its unity and a democratic Constitution. The Congress party has been able to retain its political dominance without repressing the Opposition. Under Jawaharlal Nehru, the Indian government pushed state planning in some sectors but continued to welcome foreign investment and capitalism. Both industrial and agricultural productivity has expanded, and India has a major high-tech sector. Despite greater development than elsewhere, India also suffered from massive population growth and limited resources. Many Indians continue to live in abject poverty. Social reforms have been slow, leaving the poor with little perceived benefits from economic development.

APARTHEID: By the 1970s, South Africa was the largest area still dominated by a white minority. After the 1940s, white political control was consolidated under the Nationalist Party and its institutionalised policy of racism, apartheid. In 1960, the Nationalists won Independence from Britain. Apartheid completely separated Whites from other groups. Whites monopolised the economy, the educational system, and politics. The government restricted black linguistic groups to homelands within South Africa. To maintain apartheid, the government developed into a police state funded from the mineral wealth of the nation. The government declared illegal black political organisations, such as the African National Congress. The regime imprisoned Nelson Mandela and Walter Sisulu, ANC leaders, and killed others. South Africa promoted ethnic differences among the black community in order to lessen the possibility of joint action against apartheid. As resistance mounted, the government became increasingly repressive. In the 1980s, a global boycott of South Africa began to force a softening of the government's attitudes. Moderate Afrikaner leaders such as F.W. De Klerk pressed for reforms. Following the release of Nelson Mandela in 1990, the government began to negotiate with black groups to provide political rights for the majority of South African citizens. Elections in 1994 brought an end to apartheid. Despite fears, the transition of power to the ANC was without violence. Problems remain in South Africa. Ethnic rivalries among Blacks periodically result in violence. White supremacists still seek to undermine the concept of majority rule.

A global view of new world

Despite a large number of countries becoming free, more people came in a different kind of imperialism. Former British Prime Minister Tony Blair made a messianic speech to the Labour Party's annual conference at Brighton in April, 2010 and talked of the need to 're-order this world around us'. The impending war to overthrow and replace the Taliban regime in Afghanistan, he suggested, was not the first step in the direction of such a 're-ordering'; nor would it be the last. Already there had been successful interventions against other 'rogue' governments: the Milosevic regime in Serbia and the 'murderous group of gangsters' who had attempted to seize power in Sierra Leone. "And I tell you," Mr. Blair declared, "if a Rwanda happened again as it did in 1993, when a million people were slaughtered in cold blood, we would have a moral duty to act there also."

The cases of Kosovo and Sierra Leone were plainly to be understood as models of what could be achieved. This is the kind of argument which Rudyard Kipling made while talking about the 'white man's' burden after which half the world lost their freedom to the West. Mr. Blair defined the new role of the West and said, "Justice consists not only in punishing the guilty but justice is to bring the values of democracy and freedom to people round the world. The starving, the wretched, the dispossessed, the ignorant, those living in want and squalor from the deserts of Northern Africa to the slums of Gaza, to the mountain ranges of Afghanistan – they too are our cause." Mr. Blair added, "The weak still need the strong and the strong still need an orderly world. A world in which the efficient and well-governed export stability and liberty to the weak and people which is open for investment and growth – all of this seems eminently desirable." This is the face of new world order in which social injustice is embedded in the system and against which reform from within and not war from outside will help.

After colonies were freed, new kinds of problems came up. Colonial powers left their colonies but continued to have their supporters as the rulers who reflected the Western values and lifestyle more than the internal poverty of the people exploited by their colonial masters. As many as 54 assorted countries joined the Commonwealth which ensures the continuity of British traditions and the English language. This has many advantages also but the disadvantages were also many, chief among them was the alienation of ordinary person from the Anglophile rulers, as a consequence of which social systems developed skews and distortions and social reform movements sprang up. Many leaders came up to occupy centre stage. Dr. Pathak represents one such social movement which is continuation of Gandhian initiatives to give a fair deal to the poor, specially scavengers.

Global background to Sulabh work

Dr. Pathak has therefore inherited this global background, it can be argued, to become a product of history which he seeks to change. Untouchability, of which scavenging is the consequence, was the pre-existing circumstance. Many leaders, including Gandhiji, worked to abolish it, so does Dr. Pathak. So where does his leadership fit in? Nowhere. The historians seek to find an analogy between widely different and separated events to find a model which is not universal. This does not happen. The coming of the post-modern age has upset all paradigms and new conditions have been created in the post-war world which the baby boomer generation, of which Dr. Pathak is one, is struggling to address in different ways, using technology and through democratic method.

For instance, Lincoln fought the Civil War to abolish slavery, a condition which he had inherited and not created. Churchill fought the global war which had started already and Gandhiji fought for Independence which he had never launched. They all had well-defined enemies and a cause and, they became crusaders. But that is not the case with Dr. Pathak. In the circumstances that existed already, untouchability and scavenging were abolished by law and education and social justice were made part of the Constitution, democracy is in full bloom and good health, with people making and unmaking government, without revolt as in Thailand now, and a series of affirmative actions, like reservation, are in place to help the disadvantaged people. So, where is the cause for Dr. Pathak to become a crusader? Where is the enemy to kill or empire to defend? To understand these, one has to analyse the post-war condition in the world. The globalisation has produced strange kinds of forces which have created skewed social order against which there is a constant fight and Dr. Pathak is that kind of fighter. He has to reform the social deformities which have survived democracy, social action and law. Untouchability, women's disempowerments, and other social injustice are there to see. For that matter, he is in the leadership league of Martin Luther King Jr. and Nelson Mandela, both of whom worked to end the injustices which had already been abolished by law and yet they existed. Hence, they had to launch movements within law and democratic social order. In America, for instance, the Civil Rights Act was passed in 1957 and later the Voting Rights Bill. But racial discrimination existed and Dr. Martin Luther King Jr. had to launch the Civil Rights Movement and had to die for it. In South Africa also, apartheid was ended in 1948 by de Klark but continued until Mandela was released from jail in 1991. And, Bantuland, where Bantu-speaking people were cluttered together, was abolished.

New world order after global war

These distantly related events happening across many continents and generations have to be examined together to find the background to the Sulabh Movement and the role of its founder, Dr. Bindeshwar Pathak. After the British Empire ended and the poor and subject nations of Africa and Asia were made free to manage their own affairs, a piquant situation arose in these countries many of which ended up facing internal civil wars, right from Rwanda to Sudan, Kenya, Somalia, and to Ethiopia and practically all over Africa which was under the control of colonial powers, including British, Dutch, German, French and Dutch all of which had colonies which supplied them with slaves, minerals, timbers and raw material and supported their prosperity. New weapons developed in the West were supplied to the warring factions in these countries including the infamous Maxim guns, invented by an American in a London underground basement which alone conquered the entire Africa within months. Now, who do we blame for political instability, poverty and war? Naturally not colonial powers because they have left them free. The fact is that the most difficult challenges in the Third World occurred after the colonisers had withdrawn from colonies. Divisions along ethnic groups, dependent economies, growing debt, cultural dependence on the West, and widespread social unrest made the progress of newly independent nations painful and trying. Leaders adopted various strategies to resolve these problems.

Dr. Pathak is of baby boomer generation

To be true Dr. Bindeshwar Pathak is of post-war baby boomer generation though he was born in 1943. Between 1945 and 1950, the entire British Empire vanished, so also other colonies of the world. The empires ended but not imperialism. In the post-war world, fruits of growth were very unevenly distributed, resulting in political fragmentation and social discontent. On the eve of the World War I, imperialism had reduced the number of independent countries in the world to 59. But since the advent of decolonisation, there have been sustained increases in the number of free nations. In 1946, there were 74 independent countries; in 1950, it was 89. By 1995, the number was 192, with the two biggest increases coming in the 1960s (mainly Africa, where 25 new states were formed between 1960 and 1964) and the 1990s (mainly Eastern Europe, as the Soviet Empire disintegrated). No fewer than 58 of today's states have populations less than 2.5 million; 35 have less than 500,000 inhabitants. Small countries are often formed as a result of civil war within an earlier multi-ethnic polity – the most common form of conflict since 1945.

The fragmentation of states and its attendant economic costs have been among the principal sources of instability in the post-war world and social injustices and distortion. That produced new kinds of leaders; some wanted to unite their countries as in India while others wanted to separate as in the Balkan. Nelson Mandela was the product of post-war imperialism because of apartheid.

Dr. Pathak's role should be judged against this global context of social injustice, untouchability, and disempowerment. He has no enemy to fight against unlike the conquerors and killers of the past. The distortion is in the system, which is historical, like apartheid in Africa, and racialism in the US. Dr. Pathak's role should be examined in that historical context. So also that of the Sulabh Social Movement, which is an internal initiative to address the social problems and prejudices. Like Moses who took his people out of Egypt towards the Promised Land, Dr. Pathak has led the disadvantaged and disempowered people out of despair to a new life of hope and promise. Leadership comes effortlessly to him and always. Changing minds, however, takes time. There has to be a tipping point; some external intervention, like education, reform, and technology. Social transformation began in a big way after the coming on the scene of Mahatma Gandhi, though it was started earlier with the teaching of English (see separate chapter). The technological change, demographic transformation and its evolving consequences for cultural and religious beliefs were the roots of social change. The rise of Gandhiji to supreme power was an admirable outcome to liberal and progressive forces. Dr. Pathak, as a young boy, saw this happening which had very visible impact on his life. "Every man has his own ambition. I have no other so great as that of being respected by fellow men for my good work that is worthy of their esteem", says Dr. Pathak.

Thus, a great career emerged from scavengers' colony – an amazing story at that!!

"A day will come when war will seem absurd... when the only fields of battle will be markets opening to trade and minds opening to ideas."
– Victor Hugo (1802-85)

CHAPTER 14

The Ideas that Define Sulabh Movement

A new synergy for mass social action

The Sulabh Movement is a synergy of ideas, ideology, social justice, education, empiricism and technology. Social movements were launched before but they did not achieve the critical mass until all the six ingredients were blended into a social 'reactor' to produce explosive agents for change. The syncretic solution provided by Dr. Bindeshwar Pathak is his major contribution to social transformation at the conceptual level. For that matter, the Sulabh Movement is the first modern social initiative for change in the latter half of the last century. The rest is detail.

Synergy consists in coordinating various disciplines – technologies, sociology, politics, economics and tradition besides religious orthodoxy which is a major source of untouchability, of which scavenging is the worst consequence. They are the 'idea areas' where a new approach has to be adopted by combining all of them in a right mix and pursue it vigorously, while campaigning to produce social impact. Dr. Pathak has studied all these areas of knowledge to be finally combined in the fine-tuned 'ideas package' in the Sulabh Movement.

Ideas produce social change; Rousseau produced the French Revolution, John Locke produced the American War of

Independence, Adam Smith produced Capitalism, Marx gave us Communism, Nietzsche produced wars and Gandhiji produced peace – the list is unending. In every age, people had different views on social structure and as the context changed, so did interpretations of right and wrong, justice and injustice, and also relationship between man and man. Ideas are not information but a vision that starts off debate, stimulate thoughts, produce movements and fundamentally change the ways we think about the world and live our lives. Albert Einstein, Vivekanand, Rawls and Keynes, for instance, changed the world view. Marx says man's relationship with the means of production determines social and political systems. Freud says, 'Explore your mind to understand emotions and behaviour.' These were ideas which enabled us to explain our behaviour and make attempts to answer the daunting questions in our extraordinary times.

Information and ideas

Information was once a source of ideas, but today we are inundated with useless information which don't produce ideas, but methodology, technology, new inventions and other things of comforts. Information is just about knowing things like the daily weather, political events, crime stories and police action. Information has money value. Hence, we know more than we have ever known, but we think about it less. Courtesy internet, we seem to have immediate access to anything that anyone could ever want to know. In the past, we sought not just to know the world but to truly think about it, which is the primary function of ideas. What the future portends is more and more information but none of them will be big idea but only useless information for the chattering class thronging clubs, social gatherings and seminars, which pass for intellectuals. Today, we avoid ideas and love information because knowing gives money, jobs and keeps us connected to our friends and employers.

Ideas don't. However, ideas have a life forever while nothing is older than yesterday's newspaper. To be true, we are living in a post-idea world – a world in which the big ideas that can't instantly produce profit are considered of little value. No wonder fewer people are thinking big.

The Sulabh Founder says that one man's excreta cannot be another man's head-load. This is an idea, not information which raises the basic question of social justice. This is not a human rights question, nor entirely of social discrimination, which has a long history of protest movements, beginning from Spartacus in Roman times, Magna Carta (1215), Chartist Movement (1838), Satyagraha (1915-47), Civil Rights Movement (1950-60), French Revolution (1789), October Revolution (1917), Communist Revolution (1989) and Spring Revolution in the Arab world (2011) and many more.

As a matter of fact, we have a million mutinies taking place all over the world everyday, caused by twitter, interface, You Tube, and other means of instant information which have reduced the world to the veritable size of a village. But, none of these has touched the life of scavengers which is the focus of the Sulabh Movement.

By saying that scavenging is more than a human rights question, Dr. Pathak points out to skewed political decision because of systematic flaws. He talks about the principle of localisation which is founded on the realisation that 'one size does not fit all.' Where there could be universal principles, there is not likely to be a single package of these principles with universal applicability. The packaging must be done by local communities. The principle of lateralisation requires that lateral links be deliberately designed across boundaries, so that people coordinate laterally, rather than expecting a power above them to compel them to coordinate. Ostrom's research describes ways to achieve lateral coordination without an overbearing coordinator above. Such lateral coordination is obtained by communities of shared interests and processes for collaborative decision making. The third principle is learning based on 'systems thinking'. Systems thinking is an orientation that has been killed by overspecialisation. Experts live in 'conceptually gated communities'. They know a lot about a little and understand little about the whole. Processes for understanding systems must be applied to enable us to solve global problems that have been created by our fragmented views of reality.

Dr. Pathak also talks about the principle of listening. Experts must listen to each other. But most of all, experts must listen to the real people. They must understand the language of real people. A line from Woody Allen's *Midnight in Paris* explains it very well. Adriana, the French woman, says to Pinder, the American writer, "That's the problem with you writers. You are full of words. But I am more emotional." This is India's challenge of governance. People are saying, "That's the problem with you economists and planners. You are full of numbers. You don't understand our emotions – our hopes and fears. How can we trust you to create a better world for us?" Therefore, we must build processes for listening. It is not easy in a vast country in which people have varied perceptions and interests, and may not want to listen to each other. But only by listening to many perspectives can we understand the whole system. This is an idea, new to the social thought system.

All idea movements have bypassed them; rather, scavengers' miseries and humiliation never attracted the attention of revolutionary leaders. Scavengers have been treated as chattel (a personal possession like sheep) to be shifted around from one toilet to another. This was also because their problems did not fit into the stereotype of caste, colour, religion, political persuasion or economic status. They suffered at the far end of life, beyond all great ideas, revolutions, or high social thought systems which have found mention in agenda for social change. It is because scavenging is not entirely a poverty problem nor of human rights violation or social discrimination, much less of political injustice, but all rolled into one.

An idea movement

Sulabh is more of an idea than social activism for the following reasons: Dr. Pathak floated the idea of inclusive growth to build a new social order without demolishing the old. He is concerned about liberating scavengers as much as retaining the prestige of non-scavengers, including Brahmins, Kshatriyas and other upper castes. Unlike the Tamilian Movement, which virtually drove Brahmins out of South, Sulabh seeks inclusion, not exclusion, or entitlement to bring about social change. The Sulabh Founder has put the history of scavengers in a different perspective. He says scavenging never existed in Vedic times, nor is there in any religious sanction to practise it; it is a distortion in Hinduism as was in Christianity in whose name the Inquisition was practised when heretics were burnt alive. The suicide bombers, Crusades, Israeli-Palestinian wars, Serb-Croat-Muslim massacres, persecution of Jews as 'Christ-killers', Northern Ireland Catholic Protestant conflict, honour killings, evangelists fleecing gullible believers of their money ('God wants you to give till it hurts'), public beheadings of blasphemers, and flogging of female for the crime of showing an inch of her skin were all practised in the name of religion. But not one of them was Hinduism which is pacifist, and tolerant. However, the practice of casteism and untouchability is as cruel as any of the above and scavenging is the product of the caste biases made worse.

Technology as change agent

Technologies have produced new ideas. It was true well before the social media was conceived by Mark Zuckerberg. Globalisation of ideas is marked by human rights concern, liberalism and democracy. Ideas have been produced in all ages all over the world. For instance, what is common between the bullock-cart and a car? Yes, both of them move, except that one moves faster than the other. But both the contraptions are products of ideas. What separates them is the number of ideas that have coalesced to shape their final form. A car is the product of a much larger conglomeration of ideas than a bullock-cart. The ideas of transport of getting from one point to another are revolutionised by the car. So, in this paradigm, high technology is product of higher density of ideas which come from the network of globalised thinking. But globalisation excludes as much as it includes. Millions are left out of the process, millions do not benefit from globalisation and millions more are damaged by its asymmetric applications. It is the coalescing of various ideas in the context of social change that has produced the Sulabh Movement.

Dr. Pathak has highlighted the use of technology as a fulcrum for social change. Slavery was abolished in America not entirely because of Civil War but also because of a technology which replaced slave labour in plantation fields. Romans deployed slaves to man warships but use of technology ended it. The crucifixion of Spartacus, Roman slave and gladiator, is still fresh in our mind. But technology also produced war and massacre at unimaginable scales. Very clearly, big technologies have created more problems than they have solved. For this reason, Dr. Pathak has advocated use of small, affordable, and culturally appropriate technologies. The Sulabh two-pit pour-flush technology has acquired international endorsement because of its appropriateness (Read: *'Small is Beautiful'* by E.F. Schumacher). This is the consequence of Dr. Pathak's view of technologies being used for social change.

Today, only one-third of the country's households are connected with sewers. If the entire country gets fully sewered, our rivers will be choked; stinking and causing any number of diseases which is hard to foresee now. This happened in London in 1858 when the Thames was frozen into a mighty excreta cake resulting in 'great stink' that threatened the life in the city and stopped Parliament from functioning. Still earlier, the insanitation caused cholera and bubonic plague in the West (1347-50) which threatened the Western civilisation. However, the West had small population and abundant water supply to flush out the excreta, and enough money to set up sewage treatment plants later. We have none. Hence, the two-pit, on-site waste disposal Sulabh toilet system is the only answer to avert this civilisational crisis.

The Sulabh toilet system was born more as an idea than a technology – the idea to dispose human waste on site and turn it into organic fertiliser to raise farm productivity, instead of taking it into the water area, treated or untreated, polluting it, and endangering the marine life.

Dr. Pathak has done his Ph.D on scavenging to give a historical perspective to the problem; he brings out publications (including *Sulabh India*) to promote the idea of a scavenging-free India, first mooted by Mahatma Gandhi who wanted a scavenging girl made the first Governor-General of India. These and many other disciplines of learning have been combined into a synergy to be finally known 'Sulabh Idea' which is a package to end untouchability and establish a just social order. India's growth from the 'basket case' to a booming economy took place between 1991 and now when the country has become among the fastest growing economies of the world. Still scavenging continues when a man has to carry somebody else's excreta to make a living. Why? It is because of the 'idea gap' in planning, as a result of which the poorest and weakest have been left out of the loop to suffer poverty and social degradation.

Education as empowerment

The third major Sulabh idea is the use of education, social upgradation and mainstreaming over a period to narrow social divide more than entitlement. For any boy who has no money for education, health or anything else, the state should provide. This is affirmative action, not entitlement. Society should grow together and not in parts. Dr. Pathak says, "growth is not a zero-sum game, when somebody's gain will be somebody's loss. Future will belong to those who narrow the gap and not deepen it". That the social divisions have been politicised is a sad and ominous development of our times.

Dr. Pathak has laid special emphasis on women's empowerment and quotes Mao Zedong to say that "women hold up half the sky". Educate a boy, and you educate a man; and educate a girl, and you educate a family. Greek culture travelled to Rome through their women who educated Roman children and told them of the virtue of good living. No wonder, Greek culture became Greco-Roman culture – all because of their women. "Woman", Sulabh Founder says, "is the symbol of civilisation. If women are educated and stay healthy, your future is safe and secure. Hence, Sulabh has special programmes for women's education, training and scholarship. Scavenger women are the central focus of the Sulabh Movement."

Civil society re-invented

The fourth idea is about civil society organisations. Dr. Pathak says non-government organisations (NGOs) should be self-sustaining; they should not depend on government aid for their survival. India has world's largest number of NGOs (over a million) managed by intellectuals, senior officials, writers, advocates and eminent people from all walks of life, representing various professions from bee-keeping to global peace mission. If most of them are not in good health it is because of the fact that they heavily depend on government assistance. Sulabh is a model NGO which does not take government aid or any other assistance from any Indian or foreign agencies of which many offers had been made. It takes up social welfare projects like sanitation, education and awareness, and takes service charges and owns up full responsibility for the projects for long years.

These and other Sulabh ideas are neither revolutionary nor new but Dr. Pathak has coalesced them into a critical mass which has produced a huge social movement. Atoms, for instance, are flying around us as particles which can neither be seen nor divided. But, once they are put in nuclear reactor, they produce explosion. Dr. Pathak has put these flying ideas into the Sulabh reactor which has become the Sulabh Movement. The Sulabh ideas are its identity more than the Sulabh system.

Perspective to social change

Social changes happen in a context, involving human behaviour and its consequences. This context provides, what Malcolm Gladwell calls, the tipping point, or a trigger, which leads to critical mass. After crises come solutions when we reframe the way we think about the world, and establish new social relationships because we are powerfully influenced by our surrounding which is our immediate context. If we want change to happen, we have to change the surrounding as a context. And, to get the context, first we must have the bedrock belief that change is possible – that people can transform their behaviour or belief in the face of the right kind of pressure or persuasion. Once we have the bedrock belief and right context, we can be sure that change will happen.

For that, says Malcolm Gladwell, three things are necessary, the connector, maven (experts), and media. And, these are governed by the 'Law of the Few' – that you don't need many leaders, but only a few committed persons with tightly focused, targeted commitment who have willingness to go a bridge too far to achieve the objectives. Which does not mean that the three will have to make sacrifices in a heroic mould of riding horses in shining armours like Spanish conquistador. No, they will be ordinary men and women who will take up social projects while looking after their families, doing jobs and leading a normal social life.

And, still they can be great change-makers, making a difference in the ways we live our lives and determine social relationships. They are 'special ordinary people', doing extraordinary work. These special people hold much social power by sheer commitment and passion for good work. Simply by finding and reaching these few special people, we can shape the course of social movement. In the end, when tipping point (or trigger) is achieved, the power of intelligent group action will produce change.

Human behaviour is highly volatile and complex and to change it is beyond science or law. However, with the slight push at the right place, it can be tipped. In case of crisis, it is easier to influence human behaviour, say in war, when people unite and fight it. But when life is normal and social structure is stable but still unjust and skewed, how do you go about it? Here, a variety of ways have to be found to give a context to change that one seeks to bring about.

For that matter every social development has a context. *The Gita* had the *Mahabharata, Gone with the Wind* had American Civil war, Nelson Mandela had apartheid, and Gandhiji had the British Empire as context. Similarly, the Sulabh Movement has scavenging and also Dr. Bindeshwar Pathak joining the Gandhi Birth Centenary Committee where he was exposed to the problems of scavengers.

Democracy is an idea more than a system of governance. Its institutions grow more from local history, culture and geography than on Madison, Mill and Tocqueville. But, today, we have only information, not idea or vision. Ideas live forever while nothing is older than the yesterday's newspaper. Sulabh, for that matter, is a vision which has produced a social movement. There had been many initiatives in the past to help scavengers, but Dr. Pathak is the only person who has turned it into a movement because he has a larger vision than any conceived before.

How Sulabh movement is different from others

There had been many initiatives in the past to help scavengers but none of them became a movement. The social movement is a group action focused on specific social issues, carrying out mass action for social change. Social movement is possible through education and increased mobility of labour due to the industrialisation and urbanisation of 19th century societies. Freedom of expression, education and relative economic independence are also responsible for a number of social movements. However, many social movements of the last hundred years grew up, like the Mau Mau in Kenya, to oppose Western colonialism. Either way, social movements have been and continue to be closely connected with democratic political systems. Over the past 200 years, they have become part of a popular and global expression of dissent and reform. Social movements often utilise technology and the internet to mobilise people globally. However, the government action or those of a few good well-meaning individuals without mass supports, is not a social movement which is almost always conducted outside the government administrative fold.

There were idealistic ideas like Gandhiji's plea to make a young scavenger girl Governor-General of India, or half measures like social entitlements or job reservation by the government. Not one of them was adequate to address the scavenging problem holistically. Dr. Pathak is the only thinker and social activist who has provided a link between Gandhiji's idealism and Locke's empiricism. No wonder, Dr. Pathak is able to turn an ideal into a mass movement in the promotion of which he has devoted all his life. Dr. Pathak, a voracious reader and profound thinker of vintage values and scientific reason, tested his idealism, at the toilet level. He has set up schools, training centres, social upgradation programmes and travelled with scavengers to temples and to the US if only to test how his idealism worked out in practice.

Historical coincidence

Dr. Bindeshwar Pathak was in the right place at the right time when he changed people's thinking in ways not many could do before. A young Brahmin boy searching for a job missed a train and found his future. It was on the railway platform that he was told about a job in the Bihar Gandhi Centenary Celebration Committee (1968-69) where the man met his moment. During the stay with the committee and after, he was exposed to the miseries of scavengers, lived in their *bastis* and saw a boy gored to death by a bull who was not saved just because he was an untouchable from a scavenger family. Add to it the other events, including the one when he had to swallow cow dung because he had touched a Dom (untouchable) and the context of the Sulabh story is complete. After all, Dr. Pathak was not alone to watch the boy gored to death or experience untouchability. We all experience untouchability everyday. But he alone reacted; it is because he has the making to become the change agent. The fertile and sensitive mind of the young Bindeshwar was already filled with new ideas and strong passion to change things and the scavenger boy provided a trigger, a tipping point only to make a choice which he did when he founded the Sulabh Shauchalaya Sansthan in 1970. What follows is what this book is all about. The context led to trigger a change, and thus, a great social movement was born. These accumulated experiences of human miseries and the consequence of hurt conscience, turned him into a quiet rebel at 27, refusing to be trapped in dogmas and face the consequence of other people's thinking which is orthodox, unfair and inhuman.

He also refused to be drowned in the social rituals of caste system and other discriminatory social practices and wrongs writ large on the faces of scavengers. Out of this fantasy was born the Sulabh Sanitation Movement in an Arrah toilet to later become a global symbol of sanitation, human rights protection and social renewal. His success is the result of a combination of low-cost technology, leadership quality, Gandhian commitment and a flair to think differently in a broader perspective of universalism, connecting the dots to retain social cohesiveness. In doing these, he is clearly ahead of his time.

Dr. Bindeshwar Pathak has also given an intellectual and technological context to the sanitation movement which has been already existing, good or bad, by relating it to wider consequences, like productivity, health, happiness and everything else. This again was not new; for, scientist like Dr. Feachem of the London School of Health and Tropical Medicine had said that of the many pollutants, excreta contaminates most. But this was the scientific analysis. Dr. Pathak has given a context by taking the argument further to say that individual initiative alone will not do; community will have to move in a major way. So much so that the matter reached the Millennium Development Goal (MDG) meeting in Johannesburg in 2002 where sanitation became the Target 10 of Goal 7.

Growing together

The bottom line of the argument is that the entire society will have to grow together, though not equally but less unequally, in order to live above the poverty benchmark, or what is called the middle class. The entire rich western countries consist of two classes, a small group of very rich people and the middle class.

There is no poor class because of social safety net and entitlements network. The income is less unevenly distributed. This kind of change in social perception is the intellectual context which Dr. Pathak has provided to sanitation which is the single most important co-efficient of growth, more important than building bombs, supercomputers or landing on the moon. And which is possible if only we change the way we think and stop dividing people as touchable and untouchable. There is just about accepting equal social status and staying clean, healthy and happy which is the sole objective of all political systems, all religions, and philosophies. It all begins with cleanliness which is the source of change, economic growth and human happiness. This is the context of Dr. Pathak's movement.

Going it alone

In simpler terms, a reformer or scientist could go it alone, but not now when technology has changed everything including the way we look at life and its many complicated problems, none of which can be addressed alone. According to a popular story, Michael Faraday was asked after his lecture on electricity, "What use is electricity without electromagnetism?" He replied, "What is the use of a new-born baby?"

This was when the first electric bulb was lit. The Sulabh idea package is a new model, which can be expanded, refined and redone as the time passes, and our turbulent present lapses into past. Sulabh toilets will vanish and 'Sulabh ideas' will endure much after we are lost in the silence of time.

Social reforms, like frontier research, come from young maverick. Steve Jobs (iPad, iPod Guru) was born (like ex-German Chancellor Willy Brandt) outside marriage and never got his college degree. He was never qualified as engineer or computer designer. He had lived with an Indian Guru in an Ashram and wanted to become a monk. But he became the 'inventor of the future', as is said about him. Einstein was a clerk in a patent office in Bern, Switzerland, and later a watch-maker. His $e = mc^2$ equation is world's most famous equation which suggests that tiny amount of mass can be converted into huge energy. Thus, atomic bomb was born. Socrates, Prophet Mohammad, and Guru Nanak Devji could never read and write. Vivekanand (though educated at Presidency College, Calcutta), Martin Luther, Gandhiji or Tolstoy never made names in academic fields to be known as great scholars.

They were young mavericks, who would think differently to make a mark in history. Nor is Dr. Pathak. He was educated at B.N. College and Patna University, no Oxford, or Ivy League institutions. He was a jobless wanderer whose life's only ambition was to become a teacher. He has now become one of the tallest change-makers of our times.

All great ideas had begun as heresies only to become accepted ways of life after they had succeeded. To think of toilet as a place to start a movement was crazy but now toilet has become a mascot of social reform and modernity.

CHAPTER 15

Sulabh Seeks to Change Mindset and Attitude

Toilet is where Sulabh reforms begin

Sulabh works at two levels; first, it is intellectually engaged with the problems of change and, second, to develop technologies to deliver it and, it has succeeded in both. For, a stable social structure is built not on exploitation, victory or defeat, but on reconciliation and truth.

It is easier to win a war than to change attitude. Most wars, since Alexander, were fought not over land, money or slaves; they were manifestation of egocentricity that one race or country is superior to others in strength, racial purity or ethnicity. Hence, it has the right to rule over others. The World War I, for instance, was fought for the expansion of Austria-Hungary empire; in the World War II, Germans wanted to establish the purity of their Aryan blood over others, especially the Jews. The local civil conflicts such as in Rwanda, Somalia, Congo, Kosovo, Darfur, Liberia, Sierra-Leone and Sri Lanka, to quote only the recent ones, were over ethnicity. In Rwanda and Hutus, a tribe killed close to 800,000 Tutsis, another local tribe, in a genocide.

This is the attitude which is born in the minds of men and this is where the change has to happen. There have been wars to prevent wars and, in consequence, more violence, hunger and social instability. This is the law of unintended consequences. A movement seeks to change that attitude without violence; and, this is the provenance of all social movements in the world; name any and you will find this common source. The Sulabh Movement is of that league; technology is only its facilitator. Sulabh is an intellectual movement conceived in the European tradition as mentioned by Paul Johnson in his book 'Intellectuals'. The writings of some of them like Karl Marx, Friedrich Nietzche, Jean-Jacques Rousseau, Leo Tolstoy, Jean-Paul Sartre and Bertrand Russell had a profound and lasting effect on generations of Europeans and Americans. India also produced intellectuals but their impact on Indian society has been only marginal. Why?

This is India's 21st century challenge. Mindsets and institutions are not easy to change. But change we must to realise our aspirations for a more inclusive society. New processes must be invented. Sixty years ago, our far seeing Constitution created political democracy. Now, there is a growing recognition of human rights that go beyond the political right to vote, to economic and social rights too – to livelihoods, education, health and dignity. Movements for obtaining such rights are being turbo charged by the power of information unleashed by India's Right to Information laws and enabled by 21st century communication technologies. The centre can no longer control. Now, we must shape "plans by the people for the people". For inclusive growth, we must listen to people.

Whenever a reformer or group of reformers use software, including campaigning, persuasion, social pressure, technology and education, to reform a thought process among a section of people, it is termed a social movement or social reform. Such leaders are called social reformers. Consider the brilliant examples of Raja Rammohan Roy's abolition of child marriage and *Sati*, women`s emancipation through education driven by Maharshi Karve, or any number of other successful social reformers with worthy initiatives to match and many others. But when a section of people makes its government answerable, whether local or national, it is a political movement. Take an example of the movement, led by Mahatma Gandhi, which demanded end to colonialism; Why can't we be allowed to govern ourselves? Or, for that matter, consider Nelson Mandela's anti-apartheid movement in South Africa, Lech Walesa's call for democracy in Poland, the Dalai Lama's decades of engagement with China (until he gave up his role as the political head of the Tibetans to usher in democracy), Aung San Suu Kyi`s struggle in Myanmar and, the Middle East`s 'Jasmine' revolution or Spring Revolution in North Africa. They have been political movements though with considerable social content.

All these movements have been people's movements. But specifically, as they have made their governments answerable, they have a distinct political flavour. It applies as well to the one India is currently witnessing: the government is being questioned by citizens on its lack of urgency in framing a strong anti-corruption Bill. Any movement directed to focus on rendering service to others – where the seeker chooses to pay or not for services so rendered, but willingly and happily seeks such service – is also spiritual in content. All real dharma Gurus, for example, who strive for the well-being of their followers, are engaged in enhancing and elevating the spiritual content in them. Social movements have this content.

We know the religion has nothing to do with spirituality. It is at best a vehicle, if one chooses to mount it, available as an option. Religion, per se, can be safely parked aside. A spiritual person may not be religious and a religious person need not be spiritual. In an anti-corruption or anti-scavenging movement, the spirit and energies of the people are directed towards a common cause: that of improving the living conditions of others which can lead to an improved quality of life for all. Such a movement has great spiritual merit and the content of social reform.

There is enough reason for any person true to his chosen spiritual path to not shy away from politics, but to actively engage with the political process on a continual basis. As a corollary, anyone in political service ought to be connected spiritually with himself to render such service. A great disservice would be done if each were to stay clear of the other. The Mahatma said, "My brand of politics is based on truth, ethics and non-violence. It (politics) is an inextricable part of me." This recalls Aristotle who in his wisdom told us, "A truly ethical life can only be lived by someone who participates in politics."

One can assign two reasons for the failure of our intellectuals to change society. One is that most of them wrote in English which barely two per cent of educated Indians could read and comprehend. The masses never got to know about them. The second, and the more important factor in isolating intellectuals has been the fact that the vast majority of our countrymen look up to their Gurus or godmen for guidance, and not to intellectuals, because they speak their language. It is an oral and not written communication. Gurus have mass followings but their learning is limited to churning out accepted religious concepts unaffected by occidental learning. Most of their *Pravachans* (preachings) are accompanied by hymns singing and at times dancing in ecstasy. Their congregations return to their homes happy and at peace with themselves because they do not have to wrestle with new ideas. That is why caste discriminations persist, foeticide is widely practised and population continues to grow at a suicidal rate. Our Gurus never deal with such social problems.

In India, great social movements were also led by many great leaders, intellectuals and thinkers, including Raja Rammohan Roy (Brahmo Samaj), Dayananda Saraswati (Arya Samaj), Annie Besant (Theosophical Society), Gokhale, Tilak, Aurobindo and M. N. Roy. But excepting those with political objectives, they had limited impact which was because they could not communicate in understandable ways. Hence, Dr. Pathak found out a different and novel medium of social reform that is a toilet which is not only a Sulabh mascot of sanitation but also of a social change, abolishing scavenging, rehabilitating scavengers and empowering women.

There have been different slogans for different reformers. For Rammohan Roy, it was the *Sati system;* for Gandhiji it was *Charkha* (spinning wheel), and different focus areas for different reformers. For Dr. Pathak, it is a toilet which symbolises his mission and commitment to social reform which he communicates in local languages and in different ways. No wonder Sulabh has a pan-India spread unlike any other movements before. Dr. Pathak also provided technologies and other ways of doing things without violence and social upset. Technology has provided a cutting edge to the Sulabh Movement which is marked by mass mobilisation, direct approach to people in order to rebuild relationships with the poor, speaking their language, singing their songs at their doorsteps.

Managing dissent

For a movement or a country to be moving and not caught in a state of stasis, the leader will have to manage dissent and contradictions and this is what Dr. Bindeshwar Pathak has been doing all these four decades and his success is largely because of this. For, neither a country, nor a movement crumbles because of external forces but because of stresses in its internal fault lines which deepen the conflicts if not resolved without producing losers or winners. These contributions cannot be managed by force. Democracy is a win-win game in which nobody loses, not even those who have actually lost their argument, interest or social status because the loser's claim is also integrated in the victor's agenda. Both winners and losers celebrate the victory of democracy based on reconciliation.

Osmosis and change

Jawaharlal Nehru, the pioneer of social change, said that the stable social system is not built on winning or losing but on reconciliation and consensus. Sardar Patel abolished princely estates but saw to it that princes were not made orphans; they were given allowances, made Governors and were allowed to retain much of their regal paraphernalia. This illusion had official patronage. This was the case when the *zamindari* was abolished. Nehru gave jobs to the zamindars' staff, and gave money and compensation spread for over 40 years. While giving these, Nehru told Parliament that during the one generation of official protection, princes' children and their grandchildren would learn to live a common man's life, forgetting their past. In sociology, this is called the process of osmosis and change.

If a rat is put in a jar and warm water is poured in, the rat will jump out violently; but if the warm water is dripped over a time, the rat will learn to live in warm water and absorb the change without violence and they have, which is evident in the members of the former royal families taking to different jobs and even politics, loudly supporting the Nehruvian policy which had deprived them of their kingdoms. This was a unique case in history.

Philosophy of reconciliation

The same philosophy of social reconciliation and consensus is true of any social movement, very specially of Sulabh which is a metaphor for reconciling conflicting interests and viewpoints through debate, campaigning, pressure and persuasion. No wonder the Brahmins and priests who earlier did not allow scavengers to enter the Nathdwara temple in Jaipur not only relented later but had meal with them and openly accepted them as equals. In case of the Alwar project (under which scavengers were taken to the UN and honoured by the President of India and other senior leaders), those persons whose toilets the liberated scavengers previously cleaned and who did not touch them, again celebrated their redemption and had food together. This was the case of exploiters and exploited closing ranks and living in harmony without conflict. This is the

Nehruvian concept of rebuilding relationship and repairing the fault lines in the social architecture. Which is what Sulabh does, staying outside power and without official patronage.

Origin of most revolutions

If Norman Borlaug would have been born two centuries earlier to produce a technology for hybrid Mexican variety of wheat, there would have been no French Revolution which was sparked off after Queen Marie Antoinette said: "If they (people) have no bread, ask them to eat cake". There was neither bread nor cake and Bastille Fort was attacked on July 14, 1789, setting off a revolution after which the world was never the same again. So is technology. Now with a scavenging-free technology, Dr. Pathak was pretty sure that demand for scavenging would be cut off and supply would dry up and scavengers as a separate group would cease to exist. He set up Sulabh Shauchalaya Sansthan (later Sulabh International) in 1970 in Patna. The Sulabh Movement was, thus, officially born.

The problem, however, did not end with technology. As the movement marched ahead, taking into its sweep town after town, state after state, Dr. Pathak discovered that liberation of scavengers from the demeaning practice of manually cleaning excrement was only one part of the much larger problem. The other problems, no less important, were their rehabilitation and social upgradation which involved extensive training and education. Changes don't take place in isolation; change in one area leads to changes in other. Therefore, the problems have to be solved holistically. Sulabh started schemes to do that, involving more people and more agencies than thought he would do. This is the Sulabh policy of osmosis and change.

All social reform movements are attempts to achieve a synthesis between opposite ideas. In the case of Sulabh, technology has added a new dimension to the issue, working as a facilitator to end scavenging. The Sulabh philosophy is a combination of the ideas of Mahatma Gandhi and Dr. Ambedkar, both being great leaders, thinkers and political campaigners.

Sulabh, however, seeks to change the mindset and attitude of people through education and empowerment and not politics which cannot be a basis for a permanent solution to the civilisational crisis, manifest in caste conflict in India, and the consequent threat to our social cohesiveness. For conflict, like war, first begins in the mind and there it has to be defeated before it spills over in the open.

> *"The greatest glory in living lies not in never falling, but in rising every time we fall."*
>
> *– Nelson Mandela*

CHAPTER 16

World's Civil Rights Movements that Inspired the Founder

In the recorded human history, the US Civil Rights Movement is most momentous and critical in social mobilisation against discrimination outside the governmental system. This is mother of all social movements in the world. Apartheid is another, marked by Nelson Mandela remaining in jail for 27 years. There had been many more civil movements in the West that are part of history.

The social transformation in the US that began in the 1960s with the Civil Rights Act and the Voting Rights Act, as well as changes in immigration rules, is extraordinary. The technological leaps forward of the late 1980s and 1990s shrank distance and broke physical and mind-space barriers in ways that are plainly visible in everyday life even as their profound impact on society is being studied and analysed. But rapid demographic transformation and its consequences for cultural beliefs may be at the root of schisms that have opened up in America's socio-cultural terrain. A rise to supreme power of someone like Mr. Obama is an admirable outcome for liberals and progressives. It can, however, appear alarming to others.

Demographers predict that by the middle of this century Whites in America will become a minority. In the biggest state, California, they are already so. The Irish faced discrimination in the 19th century, the East Europeans in the early 20th century and the Jews when they first came. But they have all merged into the American mainstream while retaining certain distinctive cultural characteristics and practices. America has always been changing and it is changing faster in new President Donald Trump's time from January 20, 2017.

In the last decade of the 19th century in the United States, racially discriminatory laws and racial violence aimed at African Americans began to mushroom. Elected, appointed, or hired government authorities began to permit discrimination, specially in the states of Texas, Louisiana, Mississippi, Alabama, Georgia, Florida, South Carolina, North Carolina, Virginia, Arkansas, Tennessee, Oklahoma, and Kansas. There were four permitted acts of discrimination against African Americans. They included racial segregation – upheld by the United States Supreme Court decision in Plessy v. Ferguson in 1896 – which was legally mandated by southern states and nationwide at the local level of government, voter suppression or disfranchisement in the southern states, denial of economic opportunity or resources nationwide, and private acts of violence and mass racial violence aimed at African Americans unhindered or encouraged by government authorities. Although racial discrimination was present nationwide, the combination of law, public and private acts of discrimination, marginal economic opportunity, and violence directed towards African Americans in the southern states became known as Jim Crow.

The civil rights movements were struggles by African Americans from the mid-1950s to late 1960s to achieve civil rights equal to those of Whites, including equal opportunity in employment, housing, and education, as well as the right to vote, the right of equal access to public facilities, and the right to be free of racial discrimination. No social or political movement of the 20th century has had so much profound effect on the legal and political institutions of the United States. This movement sought to restore to African Americans the rights of citizenship guaranteed by the 14th and 15th amendments, which had been eroded by segregationist Jim Crow laws in the South.

It had fundamentally altered relations between the federal government and the states, as the federal government was forced many times to enforce its laws and protect the rights of African American citizens. The civil rights movements also spurred the re-emergence of the judiciary, including the Supreme Court, in its role as protector of individual liberties against majority power. In addition, as the Reverend Martin Luther King, Jr., and other leaders of the movement had predicted, the movement prompted gains not only for African Americans but also for women, persons with disabilities, and many others.

The civil rights movements have been called the Second Reconstruction, referring to the Reconstruction imposed upon the South following its loss in the Civil War. During this period, the 14th Amendment (1868) – granting equal protection of the laws – and 15th Amendment (1870) – giving the right to vote to all males regardless of race – were ratified, and troops from the North occupied

ALL SOCIAL MOVEMENTS HAVE CIVIL RIGHTS ORIGIN

American black revolution started not for property or seat reservation but to protest against the depraved practice of a black woman, Rosa Parks, being forced to endure the humiliation of standing up and giving seat on a bus to a white person in Alabama. Martin Luther King Jr. was 16 years of age when he started the movement and was 39 years when he was assassinated. His message, "I have a dream", met its moment when Barack Obama, a Black with roots in Africa, became President of America in 2009. The Civil Rights Act was passed in the US as late as in 1964, a full 100 years after Lincoln fought a Civil War (1861-65) for it. Gandhiji also wanted to travel in the first class compartment for which he had paid but he was thrown out by the South African police. All social revolutions have civil rights origins.

the South from 1865 to 1877 to enforce the abolition of slavery. However, with the end of Reconstruction in 1877, southern Whites again took control of the South, passing a variety of laws that discriminated on the basis of race. These were called Jim Crow laws, or the Black Codes, which segregated Whites from Blacks in education, housing, and the use of public and private facilities such as restaurants, trains, and rest rooms; they also denied Blacks the right to vote, to move freely, and to marry Whites. Many other prejudicial and discriminatory practices were committed as well, from routine denial of the right to a fair trial to outright murder through lynching. These laws and practices were realities of US life well into the 20th century.

Organised efforts by African Americans to gain their civil rights began well before the official civil rights movement got under way. By 1909, Blacks and Whites together had formed the National Association for the Advancement of Coloured People (NAACP), which became a leading organisation in the cause of civil rights for African Americans. From its beginning, the NAACP and its attorneys challenged many discriminatory laws in court, but it was not until after World War II that a widespread movement for civil rights gathered force.

Mrs. Rosa Parks and her bus travel

The war itself contributed to the origins of the movement. When African Americans who had fought for their country returned home, they could not accept being treated as second class citizens. The movement's first major legal victory came in 1954, when the NAACP won Brown v. Board of Education of Topeka, Kansas, in which the Supreme Court struck down laws segregating white and black children into different public elementary schools. Another catalysing event occurred on December 1, 1955, when Rosa Parks, an African American woman, was arrested after she refused to give up her seat to a white man on a Montgomery (Alabama) bus. The law required African Americans to sit in the back of city buses and to give up their seats to Whites should the white section of the bus become full. The city's black residents, long tired of the indignities of segregation that they were forced to suffer, began a boycott of city buses. They recruited Martin Luther King, Jr., a 27-year-old preacher, to head the Montgomery Improvement Association, the group organising the boycott. The African Americans of Montgomery held out for nearly a year despite violence – including the bombing of King's home – directed at them by angry Whites. This violence was repugnant to many Whites and actually increased support for the civil rights movement among them. The boycott finally achieved its goal on November 13, 1956, when the Supreme Court, declared Montgomery's bus segregation law unconstitutional. By December 1956, the city was forced to desegregate its buses.

The Montgomery bus boycott gained significant media attention for the civil rights cause, and it brought King to the fore as a leader. King would go on to head the Southern Christian Leadership Conference (SCLC), which was formed in 1957, and to guide the civil rights movement itself. The boycott also marked the end of reliance on litigation as the major tactic for gaining civil rights for African Americans. From now on the movement would also engage in non-violent direct action, a technique of civil disobedience that had been used before by pacifists, by labour movements, and by Gandhiji in the struggle to secure India's freedom from Great Britain.

Gandhian model of civil disobedience

Non-violent methods had been used by African Americans since the 1940s, when the Congress of Racial Equality (CORE) – a group of Blacks and Whites that formed in 1942 to lobby for equal civil rights for all – organised non-violent direct action to protest racial discrimination. King described his own view of non-violent protest in his 1958 book, *Stride Toward Freedom.* This type of protest worked in part by seeking to create a sense of moral shame in the opponent.

Both the non-violence of the Civil Rights Movement and the power of the federal government over the states were tested as African–Americans sought to make use of the rights that had been confirmed by the Supreme Court. For example, segregationist Whites, including the Alabama Legislature, refused to recognise the rulings of the federal judiciary regarding school desegregation. Some Whites formed citizens' councils to combat desegregation, and the Ku Klux Klan and other reactionary Whites began a campaign of terrorism, including bombings and murders, intended to intimidate African Americans into giving up their cause.

A significant state-federal confrontation took place in 1957 at Little Rock, Arkansas's Central High School, when angry mobs of Whites attacked nine black students attempting to enroll for classes. President Dwight D. Eisenhower had to send in troops to enforce the Supreme Court's decision in Brown confirming the right of the students to attend the school. In 1962, when James Meredith attempted to enroll at the University of Mississippi, President John F. Kennedy also sent in federal military troops to uphold desegregation.

The SCLC, which under King's leadership had become one of the most important civil rights organisations in the country, in turn, spawned another influential group, the Student Non-Violent Coordinating Committee (SNCC, popularly called Snick). In 1960, this group, which was made up of both Blacks and Whites, became a major player in the civil rights struggle. SNCC attracted youths who were often dissatisfied with what they saw as the unnecessarily moderate goals and methods of the NAACP and the SCLC. SNCC members later led voting registration and education efforts throughout the South, often at great personal risk. Eventually, it planted the seed of factionalism in the civil rights movement, as it became increasingly radical and alienated from the mainstream of the movement as represented by King.

King played an influential role in 'sit-ins', another form of non-violent direct action employed in the civil rights movements. These demonstrations often focused upon the 'Whites only' lunch counters across the South. Armed only with a strict code of conduct that forbade them to hit back their opponents, the demonstrators endured jeers, spitting, and blows by angry Whites. One tactic associated with this strategy was the 'jail-in' – also called 'jail, no bail' – in which hundreds of people, many of them underage youths, arrived in waves at segregated lunch counters, were arrested for trespassing, and proceeded to overcrowd local jails. 'Jail-ins' bogged down local governments and drew national attention to the cause. In the North, activists responded by picketing businesses, including the Woolworth chain of stores, that operated segregated lunch counters in the South. The right to participate in sit-ins was upheld by the Supreme Court decisions.

The Freedom Rides were a type of non-violent direct action designed to oppose segregation in interstate buses and bus stations. They were inspired in part by the 1960 Supreme Court decision which outlawed racial segregation in bus terminals and other places of public accommodation related to interstate transportation. Organised by CORE in 1961, the Freedom Rides were undertaken by six Whites and seven Blacks who rode two interstate buses from Washington, D.C., to New Orleans. Along the way, the riders deliberately violated segregation policies on the buses and in bus terminal rest rooms, waiting areas, and restaurants. White mobs beat Freedom Riders of both races savagely at different stops in the Deep South and in Alabama, one of the buses was firebombed.

'I have a dream' speech by Martin Luther King Jr.

On August 28, 1963, the civil rights movement reached a high point of public visibility when it held the march on Washington. Hundreds of thousands of people – an estimated 20 to 30 per cent of them Whites – gathered in front of the Lincoln Memorial in Washington, D.C., to urge Congress and the federal government to support desegregation and voting rights. On this occasion, King gave his famous 'I Have a Dream' speech. The following summer, civil rights activists in Mississippi organised another highly publicised event, Freedom Summer, a campaign to bring one thousand students, both Whites and Blacks, into the South to teach and organise voter registration. Many civil rights groups provided backing for this movement.

Throughout this period of non-violent protest, the civil rights movement continued to suffer the effects of white violence. Medgar Evers, an NAACP leader, who was organising a black boycott in Jackson, was shot and killed outside his home in 1963. Three participants in Freedom Summer – James Chaney, an African American, and Andrew Goodman and Michael Schwerner, both Whites – were killed in Mississippi in June 1964. Events such as these murders outraged many in the nation and solidified popular support for the civil rights cause.

In 1964, Congress passed one of the most significant pieces of civil rights legislation ever proposed, the Civil Rights Act of 1964. This Act made Congress more of an equal partner with the Supreme Court in establishing civil rights. The Act outlawed discrimination in all places of public accommodation, including restaurants and lunch counters, motels and hotels, gas stations, theaters, and sports arenas. It also allowed the Department of Justice to bring suit in order to achieve desegregation in public schools. The following year, Congress passed another important piece of legislation, the Voting Rights Act of 1965. This Act outlawed the voting qualifications, including literacy tests, that Whites had used to keep African Americans away from voting. It also gave the federal government oversight powers regarding changes in state voting laws. These laws together with federal actions showed that the civil rights movement had the backing of the powers of the federal government, and that no amount of resistance, however violent, by white southerners would impede the cause.

Urban riots mark change in method

By the mid-1960s, the nature of the civil rights movement began to change. African Americans, who had been united in their support of activities such as the Montgomery bus boycott, began to diverge in their views over what political action should be taken to improve their situation. Different groups within the movement increasingly expressed their dissatisfaction with each other. More radical groups, including the black Muslims and black power proponents, voiced discontent with the limited goals of the civil rights movement and its advocacy of non-violence.

Many of the new African American radicals called for black separatism or nationalism – that is, separation from white society rather than integration with it. Not content merely to seek civil equality, they began to press for social and economic equality. They also questioned the usefulness of non-violence and no longer sought to include Whites in the movement. SNCC, for example, became an all-black organisation in 1966. The arguments of the African American radicals were punctuated by urban riots such as those in the Watts section of Los Angeles in 1965. By the late 1960s, African Americans still suffered from many disadvantages, including poverty rates that were much higher than those among Whites and physical health that was much worse. Racially motivated violence persisted as well, as seen in the assassination of King by a white man in 1968.

Despite these problems, the civil rights movement had forever changed the face of US law and politics. It had led to legislation that gave greater protection to the rights of minorities. It had also greatly changed the role of the judiciary in the US government, as the Supreme Court had become more active in its defence of individual rights, often in response to litigation and demonstrations initiated by those in the movement. In this respect, the court and the civil rights movement had great influence on each other, with each reacting to and encouraging the efforts of the other. Likewise, the federal government had, even if hesitatingly, enforced the rights of a persecuted minority in the face of vigorous opposition from the southern states.

New kind of movements

Sulabh is a new kind of social movement which seeks to explain the new trends that came in the mid-1960s that mark a departure from the conventional social movement paradigm. The new social movements are consequences of the post-industrial economy because it concentrates not entirely on economic issues but on less materialistic qualities of life, like social justice, women's empowerment, ecology and peace movements. Many of these new movements emphasise social change, identity, lifestyle and culture, rather than pushing for public policy or for economic changes. Unlike pressure groups that have a formal organisation, the new movements are loosely organised with extensive social network of supporters unlike say of the Communist party which is a parallel government. It is also called the neo-civil society organisation because, by definition, civil society is the citizen groups, working outside government. However, the definition is more conceptual than specific.

The new social movements are, however, always non-government citizen groups, pressure and advocacy outfits, objective specific and non-violent. Many such social movements, including Orange Revolution in Ukraine, and Tulip Revolution in Kyrgyzstan, and Solidarity Movement in Poland later seized political power. In all countries and continents, there have been a number of such civil society movements which had considerable impact on the lives of the people. The Sulabh Movement is one new social movement which has pan-India impact and has also global imprints on global sanitation and human rights.

In simpler terms, Sulabh is a search for scavengers' new identity and ways how the scavengers, who still manually clean and carry human excreta, should rebuild their lives after redemption and what civil society and government should do to mainstream them in social life. It is not enough to pass laws and launch fancy schemes which seldom go beyond becoming media events. What would be scavengers' identity in terms of caste, profession, religion, customs, value and social status? Just like all the king's soldiers and all the king's men could not put Humpty Dumpty together again, it is unlikely that redefining the scavengers' identity will rebuild their devastated lives. But the country cannot cry out in despair either like the 11th century Danish King Canute who said: "Let all men know how empty and worthless is the power of kings on whose command these unruly waves don't roll back." This may be a hilarious analogy, but it is true that the government is quite incapable of bringing about social reforms which civil society alone can do. Scholars have talked about identity as an "aggregation of affiliations and associations" but they do not guide us through the welter of intellectual and moral formulas about reconstructing the social order. One would also like men and women of eminence to tell people about the identity of scavenger whom Gandhiji wanted to make the first Governor-General of India. In these amoral times, we seem to have forgotten the values which have sustained us through our history of 5,000 years and beyond.

Dr. Bindeshwar Pathak says: "I have been working for the past 40 years to help scavengers get out of the unclean and degrading profession and live a dignified and clean life like anyone of us and thus create a scavenger-free society of Gandhiji's dream. But, the faster I run to achieve the zero-scavenging society the farther it recedes to become a holy grail. I seek the moral and intellectual guidance how do we go about from here and achieve the redemption of scavengers." For that matter, Sulabh is a philosophical question which has to be answered in moral terms, also because other entitlements, which are many, remain on paper. Let us have profile of some such movements in Africa and Latin America.

LANDLESS PEOPLE'S MOVEMENT: The Landless People's Movement (LPM) is an independent social movement made up of the poor and landless in South Africa. It represents rural people and people living in shack settlements in cities. The nature of the Landless People's Movement is one that seeks to redefine the fundamental interactions and social relations in society. The interactions run deep and relate to basic human processes with nature and life in general. It identifies the sources of land dispossession as historical inequalities and economic policies. The LPM boycotts parliamentary elections. On July 24, 2001, provincial representatives of the local landless formations met with regional organisations to list their grievances and collectively seek change in order to relieve their struggles. Increasing neo-liberal pressure and the negative consequences of increasingly strict monetary policies towards the poor majority of South Africa have created the context from which the movement arose. An additional contributor to the struggle has been the political favouring of the economically prosperous. Reconstruction of economic policies and actions have left the poor fighting large, organised, common interest alliances that have already established agendas on their constructed political platforms. What resulted was a quasi-welfare state built upon social policies to prevent economic fall-out. For the poor who remain marginalised, the social services provided by the policies prove useless or limited since they are costly.

ABAHLALI BASEMJONDOLO: Abahlali base Mjondolo (AbM) is a shack-dwellers' movement in South Africa. The movement grew out of a road blockade organised from the Kennedy Road shack settlement in the city of Durban in early 2005 and now also operates in the cities of Pietermaritzburg and in Cape Town. It is the largest shack dweller's organisation in South Africa and campaigns to improve the living conditions of poor people and to democratise society from below. The movement refuses party politics and boycotts elections. The key strategy is to try 'to recreate Commons' from below by trying to create a series of linked communes. According to the *The Times,* the movement "has shaken the political landscape of South Africa." According to Professor Peter Vale, Abahlali base Mjondolo is "along with the campaign, the most effective grouping in South African civil society."

WESTERN CAPE ANTI-EVICTION CAMPAIGN: The Western Cape Anti-Eviction Campaign is a popular movement made up of poor and oppressed communities in Cape Town, South Africa. It was formed in November 2000 with the aim of fighting evictions, water cut-offs and poor health services, obtaining free electricity, securing decent housing, and opposing police brutality. It has been able to successfully mobilise against the recent xenophobic attacks in the areas where it is strong. The movement is the oldest of the first generation of the so-called 'new social movements' to spring up after the end of apartheid and is known for its direct action style militancy, its refusal of all forms of vanguardism, including NGO (Non-Governmental Organisations) authoritarianism and its networked or hydra-style mode of organisation.

ZAPATISTA ARMY OF NATIONAL LIBERATION: The Zapatista Army of National Liberation is a revolutionary group based in Chiapas, the southernmost state of Mexico. Chiapas is one of the richest states in Mexico but suffers from massive inequality and poverty. Since 1994, they have been at war 'against the Mexican state,' though this war has been primarily non-violent and defensive against military, paramilitary, and corporate incursions on their territory. Their social base is mostly rural indigenous people but they have some supporters in urban areas as well at international level.

Their ideology combines libertarian socialism, libertarian municipalism, and indigenous Mayan political thought. They align themselves with the wider anti-globalisation, anti-neoliberal social movement and seek indigenous control over their local resources, especially land. *The New York Times* called the Zapatista movement the first 'post-modern' revolution: an armed revolutionary group that has abstained from using their weapons since their 1994 uprising and was countered by the superior military might of the Mexican army. The Zapatistas quickly adopted a new strategy by trying to garner the support of Mexican and international socialist societies. They try to achieve this by using the Internet to disseminate their statements and to enlist the support of NGOs and solidarity groups. Awareness of the Zapatista Movement has also been raised due to support from bands such as Rage Against the Machine, Garotos Podres, Leftöver Crack, Brujeria, Anti-Flag, Immortal Technique, Manu Chao and Active Member.

LANDLESS WORKERS' MOVEMENT: Landless Workers' Movement (Portuguese: Movimento dos Trabalhadores Rurais Sem Terra - MST) is a social movement in Brazil; it is the largest in Latin America, with an estimated 1.5 million landless members organised in 23 out of Brazil's 26 states. The MST states it carries out land reform in a country mired by unjust land distribution. It organises landless and impoverished farmers to realise their civil rights. The MST fights for access to land on behalf of the dispossessed. They demand for the restoration of a social contract that provides a sustainable way of life for the poor living in rural areas. In Brazil, 1.6 per cent of the landowners control roughly half (46.8 per cent) of the land on which crops could be grown. Just three per cent of the population owns two-thirds of all arable lands. The MST claims land occupations are rooted in the Constitution of Brazil of 1988, by interpreting a passage which states that land should serve a 'larger social function'. These are only the sample narratives of some of the many social movements that had marked the post-war social developments after the collapse of empire and growth of new social awareness all over the world.

Former colonies have built their institutions on the model of their colonial masters; no wonder, most of them are struggling with the consequences of their choice.

CHAPTER 17

Middle Class Behind Most Social Movements

Challenge of blending tradition with change

The Indian social movements had been led by middle class English-speaking professionals, including lawyers, journalists, doctors, landed class and some businessmen who sought to promote Western values and way of life without demolishing Indian traditions. No wonder, today we have British legal, political, educational, and administrative systems much after the rulers have gone. And, we are beginning to see great virtues in the legacies which the Britishers left behind in a huff, not knowing their dated systems will become great Indian heritage.

Most social movements in the world have been launched by the middle class, variously defined as the educated people with income enough to buy houses, provide education, and buy consumer goods. This is a very explosive class which runs political parties, fights elections, takes crucial decisions, leads movements and brings other social changes. These are the people who are scientists, professors, middle-order businessmen, law makers and other professionals, always remaining in high profile. Conversely, the 'high class', or super rich people are too busy retaining their class distinction, privileges and wealth to worry about social and political issues. The 'low class' (the poor) are multitude who live by the day, constantly struggling to keep the head above water. Their life is everyday's struggle.

The 'low class' people are too famished to speak out their opinion nor they have education to understand issues and protest against injustice. Their bodies are just stitched together in a fragile frame which lives by the day. However, they fight war, revolution, and face the consequences, dying in millions. Their bodies are not counted, nor do they make for the tragedy. These people are traded like chattel, paid to fight, and kill people against whom they have no complaint, nor do they know cause of the fight. Those who died on the Western Front, Normandy Coast, in Berlin, France and Flanders, never knew what those fights were all about. They were cannon fodder who died so that the disputes, caused by the middle or upper class, could be settled. All social and economic ideologies, including communism, socialism and liberalism, were born in the name of the common people, who never benefited, always remaining at the far end of life – poor, unwashed, uneducated, and struggling. Once you broadly accept this analysis, the history of social movements will become easier to understand.

The Indian social movements were launched by the middle class often in the name of the poor. But, there is a special feature of India's social movements, beginning from the last century. They all had their leaders who were English-educated professional middle class people who had great stake in preserving the British legacies, including their language, institutions, habits and social values. This was true from Rammohan Roy to Independence struggle leaders, including Gandhiji, Nehru, Patel, Subash Bose, and Swami Vivekanand who were products of the English thought system which most of them upheld even after Britishers have left the country.

Pavan K. Varma, a brilliant writer and scholar, is among the many distinguished scholars who have given a perspective to India's social movements, telling us how we have lost our culture, language, tradition and everything else to become a British clone. No wonder today, Indian society is divided between English-speaking and non-English speaking classes. Those who speak English have jobs, money, status and everything else, but those who don't, have to struggle below the poverty line. English, says Varma, has caused social exclusion. One may disagree with him, as I do, but this is the brutal fact and a thoughtful analysis much of which is quoted in this chapter.

Anglicised class

This English-centric structure was seen in social movement also. For instance, Madan Mohan Malaviya, founder of the Hindu Mahasabha, was an English-educated person who launched the Hindu revivalist movement in the 19th century. The prime movers of the Hindu social renaissance were motivated by the noble intention to cleanse the religious and social institutions of corruption and distortions that had crept into them over the centuries. And in doing so, the leaders also sought to gain 'respectability' in the eyes of the British to be better able to absorb the new ideas of science and rationalism of which the West was the harbinger. The most important of such movements were the Brahmo Samaj and the Arya Samaj. Rammohan Roy, who founded the Brahmo Samaj in 1830, was himself a great protagonist of English education. The Arya Samaj was less anglicised but even in its militant assertion of *the Vedas* as the sole repository of wisdom and authority, its leaders sought to win the 'respect' of the West by emulating 'the ideological and the organisational characteristics of Christianity.'

Unlike other colonial powers such as France, Spain, Portugal and Holland, Britain followed a liberal policy of giving English-educated Indians access to high positions in the British administration. It was essential to have the knowledge of Persian to get a job in the Mughal courts, and it was also necessary to know Latin and Greek to get admission in Oxford in olden times. But it was necessary to know English to get employed by the British administrations. English was also a passport to get jobs and avail of positions dominated by British barristers. But soon a second tier of Indian lawyers, called pleaders (or *Vakils*,) emerged, many of whom found both money and recognition by mastering the judicial intricacies of Privy Council pronouncements. "The volume of litigation was rising sharply owing to the new property relations which the British Government had established after 1857, and there was a great flow of legal briefs from the rural districts to the courts in the city", says Pavan K. Varma.

Search for identity

The members of the emerging Indian middle class of the 19th century did not feel a sense of humiliation in collaborating with the British. Indeed, they were appreciative of the West's civilisational values and envious of its material achievements. They sought social acceptance within the imperial framework and copied the British lifestyle. However, they did feel the occasional sense of resentment at the British flaunting their racial superiority and felt hurt when the British overtly persisted in keeping a distance and separateness from natives. Compartments in trains were reserved for Englishmen, and however anglicised an Indian might have been in deportment and demeanour, he was rarely allowed entry. It may be recalled that Gandhiji had paid for his first class ticket, but was thrown out of the 'White-only' railway coach. And, this insult sowed the seed of the Indian freedom movement.

Motilal Nehru was a case in point. His early education was confined entirely to Persian and Arabic at home; his adolescence was moulded by the Kashmiri Pandit traditions. He began learning English only in his teens. He never distinguished himself in his studies and, in fact, never completed his graduation. However, he did exceptionally well in the High Court Vakils' examinations. As a young lawyer, Motilal made no secret of his rejection of many elements of his own heritage. He did not look to the revival of ancient times. He disliked many old social customs and caste. On his return from Europe, he refused to perform *Prayaschit* (purification) ceremony which created quite an uproar in the conservative Kashmiri community. His rejection of Indian orthodoxy endeared him to British rulers that helped him earn a lot of money.

Indian National Congress

Allan Octavian Hume (1829-1912)

The launching of the Indian National Congress in 1885 by an Englishman, Hume, should be studied in this context. Allan Octavian Hume (1829-1912) was a civil servant, political reformer and amateur ornithologist in British India. A notable ornithologist, Hume has also been called "the Father of Indian Ornithology." The Hume Congress became, for the first time, an all-India platform to speak out the opinions of Indians. Yet, it was essentially an upper and middle-class affair that did not seek to challenge the British rule but only to create a forum which could facilitate a dialogue with the British on such matters as the Indian participation in the legislative councils and the progressive Indianisation of the civil services and the army. The method to achieve these goals was to be within the framework of the law, through constitutional agitation and through petitions and appeals. Jawaharlal Nehru has written about this phase with candour in his autobiography. He says, "My politics had been that of my class, the bourgeoisie." Indeed, politics then was that of the middle class. The moderate represented the upper middle class who had prospered under British rule and wanted no change which might endanger their position and interests. They had close relations with the British Government and the land-owning class. The extremist represented the lower middle class as fringe groups which had neither money, nor support nor party. Only people's sympathy and their commitments. Lawyers were the most prominent group, so also the landed gentry. Though some journalists and educationists constituted the leadership of the Congress, its support base was largely confined to the middle and lower middle classes in cities and towns. The content and style of the meetings of the Congress was of a piece with the social background and motivations of the participants. Nehru attended the Bankipore session of the Congress in 1912 and wrote, "It was very much an English-knowing upper class affair where morning coats and well-pressed trousers were greatly in evidence. Essentially, it was a social gathering with no political excitement or tension."

The Gandhian movement

The political emergence of Gandhiji in 1920 gave, for the first time, a mass character to the national movement. He influenced the middle class and changed the character of the national politics. The Swadeshi Movement was launched in 1903 with emphasis on popular festivals and melas such as the Ganapati and Shivaji festivals but also had impact on the lower middle class in cities. The Home Rule League Movement, led by Annie Besant, had also acquired popularity, largely among the educated. The phase of revolutionary terrorism, from 1908 to 1918, was no doubt contributory to the growth of nationalist feeling, but this too was essentially a middle and lower middle class movement and had spent itself out for want of a mass base or money. It was Gandhiji's personal lifestyle, his identification with the poorest and the deprived, and the Indian ethos he conjured up combined to win popularity for him. And, the freedom movement, for the first time got popular base which was more than evident during the non-cooperation movements in the

1920s and 1930s and in the Quit India Movement of 1942. It was equally identifiable in the support Gandhiji received of the *Charkha* and *Swadeshi* movements and for his policies of socio-economic reforms.

The city-based, educated, middle class leadership of the Congress was aware of the goals of the freedom struggle and its own critical role in that process. The masses, particularly after the advent of Gandhiji, were enthused by the concept of freedom from the British. But within this broad area of congruence, the motivations that inspired the masses, and their perceptions of events and leaders, were often at considerable variance with the grand and heroic version commonly accepted of Indian nationalism. This distinction between elite nationalism and the hinterland culture is brought out, for instance, in Shahid Amin's study of Gandhiji's visit to Gorakhpur in 1921. For the common workers and peasants of Gorakhpur district, Gandhiji was perceived as an *avatar* whose *Darshan* was an elevating end in itself and who could, in the tradition of Mahatmas, even perform miracles. To see the Mahatma in person and become his devotees were the only roles assigned to them, while it was for the urban intelligentsia and full-time party activists to convert this groundswell of popular feeling into an organised social movement.

Idea that changed world

Gandhiji's most revolutionary idea was of non-violence, an instrument of action linked to a larger philosophical vision which espoused the most unwavering conviction. It captured the imagination of the Indian people and left the British groping for an effective response. It gave to the Indian freedom movement a moral high ground that had become its defining characteristic. However, this strategy which succeeded in throwing out the world's most powerful colonial power was not the most effective one in bringing about enduring changes in India. This is not to say that both

Gandhiji and his political heir, Nehru, did not seek to change the social fabric they did. Yet, non-cooperation against the British turned out to be the only moral persuasion against the vested India interests blocking the desired change internally. And moral persuasion alone does not bring about social change. Law, education, empowerment and power do.

Gandhiji brought about the participation of the masses in the freedom struggle; but he did not seek to dislodge the middle and upper-class leadership of the Congress. His way was to try and transform, through moral pressure, the relations within the existing social structure but he did not wish to change the structure itself. His path-breaking struggle for the uplift of the Harijans has to be seen from this reference point; it is this same approach which renders explicable his concept of the rich holding their wealth as trustees for the poor. It is also argued by Pavan K. Varma that Gandhiji was an astute politician. "His goal was the freedom of India and the end of the British rule; uncontrolled social turmoil could have become a hindrance to the achievement of that goal. But, given his consistent emphasis on the definition of freedom being more than merely the absence of the British, it did not appear entirely plausible. The truth is that Gandhiji was a reformer, not a revolutionary." There are many societies which have benefited from revolutionary changes, and there are others which have not. Gandhiji's approach to social change, profoundly moving in its moral sensitivity, to the conditions of the less privileged, and containing within itself the potential for far-reaching social metamorphosis, did little violence to the entrenched upper and middle class leadership of the Congress. No wonder, despite high moral content, Gandhiji could hardly do much to bring about social change in his lifetime.

The Britishers were always far more comfortable in dealing with the English-knowing, urban-centric middle class Congress than with the poor masses who were both impoverished and illiterate and were hardly in a position to be interlocutors. As a colonial power, the primary aim of the British was the perpetuation of their rule and not improving the living conditions of the people. After the revolt of 1857, they had shifted their patronage away from the Muslim feudal nobility to mercantile classes. Later, they had good relation with the Congress leadership to approach the common problem. The Congress leaders were people in British mould who spoke English and were well-versed in the niceties of British constitutional history. As a conservative colonial power and because of its history of constitutional evolution, the British had an abhorrence of uncontrolled social turbulence. The memories of the carnage of 1857 could never be obliterated from their minds. This dread was equally shared by the middle class Indians, who, while believing in the liberal doctrines of the West, wanted a change at a pace they could control. Constitutional protest, marked by the occasional radical agitations, always non-violent and always led by English-speaking people, was an acceptable strategy of political agitation and it worked towards desired goals without the social upheaval that could erode middle class centre over politics.

Sulabh synthesis, a new trend

Although not complete, this is, however, the broad background of the social movements in India in the 19th century, all led by English-speaking moderate leaders of political, social and religious groups who wanted slow, gradual and peaceful change, retaining the British values without rejecting the Indian traditions. Since, one cannot make omelette without breaking eggs, the British values could not be promoted without rejecting Indian rituals, cant, caste system and feudal habits. Many social movements were launched to synthesise East and West, combining both in the manner as to retain the best of the two and give a distinctive Indian character. Sulabh is one such movement, with the only difference that it has used technology as a fulcrum of social change, besides pressure, persuasion, and moral suasion, which Gandhiji wanted, and education and empowerment which Dr. B.R. Ambedkar worked all his life to promote. Dr. Bindeshwar Pathak, Sulabh Founder says, "The truth does not reveal itself in black and white but in various shades of grey. We have to study them in full spectrum and its accumulated light and colour will define India's pluralistic, multi-cultural and multi-ethnic social fabric which I seek to repair without damaging the basic structure." It is neither East nor West but the unity of species and, thereby hangs the story of the Sulabh Movement.

> *"Keep your faith, the new dawn is nigh."*
> *– Martin Luther King Jr.*

CHAPTER 18

Some Social Movements and Reformers' Profiles

Sulabh provides critical historical link

In the early twenties, the condition of scavengers remained deplorable and they continued to suffer both socially and economically. They were treated as the lowest in the caste hierarchy. The Indian National Congress was there but its main objective was only winning freedom. It felt that by diverting the attention of the people to social reforms, it may harm the national cause. But, it did not when Gandhiji first took up scavengers' cause.

India has been virtually in a state of stasis during a thousand years or more with kings and killers changing hands without major impact on the lives of the people who lived as they always did, in endogamous or local groups practising rituals. Their lives were nasty, brutish and short. The invasion of Muslims after 14th century had only marginal impact because their influence was largely confined to city centres. But things changed enormously after the coming of the British in India.

Earlier in the late 19th century, there were many social reformers in India who sought to change the social order without violence. Prominent among them were: Jyotiba Phule, Sahu Maharaj, Dr. B.R. Ambedkar in Maharashtra, Periyar E.V. Ramaswami Naicker in Tamil Nadu, Narayana Guru, Dr. Palpu, Kumaran Asan, K. Ayyappan and Ayyankali in Kerala, Bhagya Reddy Verma in Andhra, Mangoo Ram and Chhotu Ram in Punjab, Achutanand and Ram Charan in Uttar Pradesh, Hari Chandra Thakur, Guru Chanda and Jogendranath Mandal in Bengal, and Sonadhar Senapathy in Assam. Among other great social reformers Raja Rammohan Roy, Dayanand Saraswati (Arya Samaj), Swami Vivekanand, Annie Besant (Theosophical Society), Dadabhai Naoroji, and Surendranath Bannerjee were moderate social reformers while Gopal Krishna Gokhale was liberal. Tilak, Bipin Pal and Aurobindo Ghose were extremists in their views. M.N. Roy was radical humanist who led Communist movement in India. The rest is the story of modern India.

E.V. Ramaswami Naicker
(1879-1973)

It was Basaveshwara, the Chief Minister of Mysore, who launched a social movement for the first time in the 12th century against the absolute domination of Brahmins and the traditional sanctions favouring inequality based on birth. So long as Basaveshwara remained in power, the movement spread successfully but after his differences with the ruler, the movement suffered a setback. The pioneering efforts in this respect were made by Raja Rammohan Roy. He did not launch any movement directly for the uplift of the untouchables but his ideas of individual liberty, social justice and universalism provided a background for the future ideological struggle.

The Brahmo Samaj, established by him, revived human values, provided a platform for safeguard against exploitation and encouraged social workers and reformers to fight for the just rights of the suffering people. The Brahmo Samaj was a social reform movement; its rationalism, its universalism, its conception of the religion of humanity and its ideal of synthesis of the East and the West prepared the intellectual foundations for future national movement. Thus, Brahmo Samaj helped in the promotion of a rational outlook in general, which definitely acted as an inspiring force in the arousal of ideas advocating restoration of just rights to the downtrodden sections of the society.

Dayanand Saraswati

Dayanand Saraswati

Similarly, the ideals and thoughts of Dayanand Saraswati (1824-83) and his action-oriented efforts in the form of Arya Samaj, also occupy a meaningful place in the movement for the emancipation of the poor. It is a fact that the hereditary system of occupation and birth-oriented status in traditional Indian society formed the basis for the rigid caste hierarchy and permitted the exploitation of untouchables in the name of sacred sanction and customary obligations. Swami Dayanand Saraswati opposed the birth-based occupational hierarchy and championed the cause of recognising personal and individual worth. He did not challenge the sacred scriptures, but reinterpreted the religious sanctions in a rational way. He favoured *Varnashrama Dharma* but gave a new explanation which served as the foundation for the development of the progressive ideas of social liberty and distributive social justice. Mahatma Gandhi wrote, "Among the many rich legacies that Swami Dayanand left to us, his unequivocal pronouncement against untouchability is undoubtedly one".

In addition to the movements of Brahmo Samaj and Arya Samaj under the patronage of Raja Rammohan Roy and Swami Dayanand

Saraswati the ideas and struggles of Devendra Nath Thakur (1817-1905), Keshav Chandra Sen (1838-1884), Ishwar Chand Vidyasagar, Annie Besant (1847-1933), Bhagwan Das (1869-1959), Rabindra Nath Tagore (1861-1941) and Swami Vivekanand (1863-1902) worked as dynamic force in developing social awakening in respect of the emanicipation of the downtrodden people, in general and the untouchables, in particular. Their emphasis on equality and equal opportunity and their attack on hereditary system of occupational classes and status differentiation helped break the rigidity of caste system and promote social and occupational mobility.

Bhagwan Das, for example, advocated 'equitability' as the basis for the division of labour and presented an organic social philosophy in which the four classes – Brahmins, Kshatriyas, Vaishyas and Shudras – would be organised in guilds (*srenis*) presided over by a holy man chosen from all the four classes on the basis of knowledge and experience.

Swami Vivekanand

In the same way, Swami Vivekanand rejected the Brahmanical doctrine of *Adhikarvada*; on the other hand he pleaded for spiritual equality and declared that all are equal. The exclusion of the Shudras from the benefit of *Vedic* knowledge was condemned by him. He advocated the breaking of all the bondages opposed to the ideals of equality and democratic spiritualism. He wanted the uplift of the untouchables or the masses, and observed, "Thus you will confer greater blessing on

Swami Vivekanand

the masses, unshackle their bondage and uplift the whole nation". Swami Vivekanand regarded the improvement in the lot of the masses or downtrodden as inevitable. The social idealism was definitely a heavy blow to the traditional concept of *Adhikarvada* and the unjust rigidity in caste hierarchy of the traditional society. As stated earlier, the political consideration and immediate objectives deferred the Indian National Congress plan to launch a fight against untouchability. Hence, nothing concrete could be done by the Congress till 1917, when Mahatma Gandhi took over its leadership.

Sri Narayana Guru

One important movement was started in Kerala by Sri Narayana Guru (1854-1928). He established the SNDP Yogam in 1903 with his gospel, 'one caste, one religion, one God'. This organisation had two important programmes; one was to uplift the *Ezhavas*, a depressed caste group of Kerala as part of the Yogam. Narayana Guru started a number of schools and colleges throughout Kerala. Secondly, he built a number of temples and simplified rituals regarding worship, marriage and funerals. The temple entry programmes undertaken by some of the *Ezhava* leaders, in association with the Nayar Service Society, finally led to the temple entry proclamation in 1936. Sir C. P. Ramaswamy Iyer, the Dewan of the Travancore State, felt the need for consolidating the Hindus and building up the unity of the Hindus of the state as a countermove against the growing power and influence of the Christians. The Vykom Satyagraha was a movement

Sri Narayana Guru

started to restore social privileges to the untouchables in Kerala. It was a very important event in the state from the point of view of social reform. The Satyagarha was started in 1924 and its objective was to open the temple streets for the untouchables.

Acharya Vinoba Bhave

After Gandhiji, it was Acharya Vinoba Bhave who led the Bhoodan Movement for the distribution of land among the landless people, particularly the Scheduled Castes and Scheduled Tribes. The rich landowning class was persuaded by Vinoba Bhave to donate their surplus land for distribution among the landless peasants. This movements proved to be very successful and thousands of acres of land were distributed. Vinoba Bhave while in Gandhiji's Sabarmati Ashram in the early twenties took to scavenging as a part of Ashram disciplines just to bring about a revoluntary change in the attitude of the people. Even Kasturba could not tolerate that pious and learned Brahmins like Vinoba and Balkoba (Vinobajee's brother) could take to scavenging. They were both helping her in the kitchen. She complained to Gandhiji and requested him to ask them to stop this dirty job. But Gandhiji stood firmly by Vinoba and Balkoba saying that it should have occurred to him to start this work. Vinobaji took to it as part of spiritual Sadhna, trying to be one with the lowest of the low in society. While staying at Pavnar Ashram in the thirties, Vinobaji used to visit a neighbouring village to do scavenging and insisted on calling himself '*Bhangi*' of the village.

Acharya Vinoba Bhave

Harijan Sewak Sangh

In 1932, the All-India Untouchability League was formed under Gandhiji's inspiration. This was later called the Harijan Sevak Sangh and it soon engaged itself in propaganda against untouchability and for getting open for Harijans' use, roads, temples, Dharmashalas, public ghats and schools. Gandhiji started a special column in *The Harijan* naming temples, schools, wells, etc. which were thrown open to them. Various movements launched in different parts of the country were concerned with different groups of untouchables. But, none of them was concerned with the '*Bhangis*'. It was Gandhiji, who first paid attention to the pathetic condition of the '*Bhangis*'. As stated above, the seed of innovative ideas against untouchability was sown in the heart and mind of Gandhiji while he was still a child. One of the leading disciples of Gandhiji in the cause of *Bhangi Mukti* was Appa Saheb Patwardhan. He was very much impressed by Gandhiji's approach and joined Sabarmati Ashram in 1919. He evinced keen interest in the *Bhangi Mukti* programme and struggled throughout his life for this cause.

Hindu reform movements

The Hindu reform movements were launched to introduce regeneration and reform to Hinduism. Although these movements are very individual in their exact philosophies they generally stress the spiritual, secular and logical and scientific aspects of the Vedic traditions, creating a form that is egalitarian and does not discriminate based on Jati (caste or sub-caste), gender, or race. Thus, most modern

Sri Aurobindo

Hindu reform movements advocate a return to ancient, egalitarian forms of Hinduism, and view the aspects of modern Hinduism, such as discrimination and the caste system, as being corrupt results from colonialism and foreign influence. Active Hindu communities were to be found in all parts of the world. In particular, countries of the former Soviet Union and Poland have thriving Hindu communities due to the missionary work of the Hare Krishnas.

There are groups in India that are actively engaged in getting women and those from socially disadvantaged *Jatis* to become priests of *Vedic* ritual. One of the foremost movements in breaking the caste system and educating the downtrodden was the Lingayat Movement spearheaded by Basavanna in the 12th century in Anubhava Mantapa in Kalyani of Karnataka. The less accessible *Vedas* were rejected and parallel *Vachanas* were compiled.

The new movements look up to Swami Vivekanand, Rabindranath Tagore, Ramana Maharshi, Sri Aurobindo (for his Integral Yoga), A.C. Bhaktivedanta Swami Prabhupada (founder of the modern Hare Krishna Movement), Swami Sivananda, Swami Rama Tirtha, Narayana Guru, Paramhansa Yogananda, and Anandamurti for inspiration. More recently, the works of Maharishi Mahesh Yogi, Sathya Sai Baba, Shirdi Sai Baba, Swami Muktananda, Swami Chinmayananda, Maharishi Dayananda Saraswati, Sri Sri Ravi Shankar, and Mata Amritanandamayi have inspired millions to create new centres of spiritual development. In the intellectual field, the writings of Ananda Coomaraswamy, Ram Swarup, Stephen Knapp, Sita Ram Goel, Subhash Kak and David Frawley have been influential.

Hinduism and the West

In social work, Mahatma Gandhi, Vinoba Bhave, Baba Amte and Anandamurti have been most important. Sunderlal Bahuguna created the Chipko Movement for the preservation of forest lands according to the Hindu ecological ideas. The Rashtriya Swayamsevak Sangh (RSS) was founded by Keshav Baliram Hedgewar in 1925. The goal was to unite Hindus, make them rise over their caste differences and work to achieve a Hindu Rashtra; the ideology of the Sangh, closely associated with political Hinduism, came to be known as Hindutva. In Indonesia, several movements favour a return to Hinduism in Java, Sumatra, Kalimantan, and Sulawesi. Balinese Hinduism, known as Agama Hindu Dharma, has witnessed great resurgence in recent years. Shri Prabhat Ranjan Sarkar (founder of Ananda Marga) initiated a new renaissance in the Indian world of Samgeet.

Since the counterculture revolution of the 1960s, there have been an increasing number of Western devotees of various Hindu lineages and practices. These have come about not only through the Hare Krishnas, but also through the universalist teachings of such Hindu figures as Sri Ramakrishna, and the Yoga teachings of B.K.S. Iyengar. The growing number of Indian immigrants relocating into the West, and the subsequent building of Hindu temples to meet the spiritual needs of these newly established Hindu communities, have also resulted in Westerners having ready access to traditional teachings. Many Western converts were introduced to Hinduism after attending the Western temples and then embracing the tradition. There can also be no doubt that the fitness revolution's ecstatic love affair with Yoga in the 1990s has helped spur on new interest in the teachings of Hinduism in the West. More and more texts are being written by Western-born Hindu converts specifically for a new Western audience, the vast bulk of which have little to no experience with Sanskrit which renders traditional literature all but useless. Some of the more notable instructional texts are the Shaivistic teaching series of the Western-born Satguru Sivaya Subramuniyaswami's Himalayan Academy, which includes a book on how to convert to Hinduism.

Reformers' profiles

The ancient thinkers and religious leaders set the trend for reforms in Hinduism. Prominent among them were:

Buddha (5th century BC): He talked of change of heart through four Noble Truths – suffering can be ended by right view, right intention, right speech and right livelihood to eventually arrive at Nirvana.

Lord Buddha

Mahavira (599-527): He also believed that enlightenment can be achieved by giving up worldly possessions and by adopting total non-violence. He founded Jainism.

Kabir (15th century): Born Muslim, he preached for blending of religions and oneness of soul. Sufism was for ascetic living and good behaviour. He was a weaver by profession.

Ravidas: He was also a sponsor of the Bhakti Movement. Meerabai, Rajput princess, was among his followers.

Guru Nanak Devji (15th century): He founded a new faith, Sikhism. He was also the product of the Bhakti Movement. He pleaded for universal religion based on justice and rejected rites and rituals.

Siddha (Tamil Saint): He said, caste is one and God is one. He equated love with God; he rejected prejudices of all types.

Baswa: A Brahmin by birth, born in Karnataka. He launched Virashaiva Movement (or followers of Shiva). It was also a branch of the Bhakti Movement. He boycotted cultural transformation. He sought social reform by changing the social system.

Varakari Movement in Maharashtra (13 to 17th century): It was also the product of the Bhakti Movement; produced saint poet Namdev (a tailor by profession). Chokha was a saint in that tradition like Kabir and Ravi Das.

Tukaram (17th century): He was the brightest star in the Varakari Movement. He was a grocer by profession – a poet and saint. Among his followers was Mahatma Phule.

Mahatma Jyotirao Phule

Mahatma Jyotirao Phule (1827-1890): He protested against social injustice. Kabir, Ravi Das, Dadu and Nanak worked in tandem also at different times. He worked for liberation of caste victims. His was primarily a Maharashtrian movement against Brahmanical social order. He set up Satyashodhak Samaj which had become a rallying cry against casteism and discrimination in Maharashtra. Phule, Periyar (in Tamil Nadu) and Dr. Ambedkar were on the frontal fight against caste domination.

Gandhiji (1869-1948): He believed in change of heart, right means and non-violence at all cost. He was the first to use non-violence; Gandhiji has become a phenomenon, the world has not seen since Jesus Christ. Remove Gandhi and the history of world will become a story of bloodletting, conspiracy, massacre and disaster.

Dr. B.R. Ambedkar (1891-1956): A Dalit, great social reformer, scholar and legal expert. He made India's Constitution and left imprints on how we govern society and state.

Tamil Movement: This movement was slightly different from other social movements. It was to promote Dravidian culture and end Aryan (or Brahmin) domination. It was essentially a non-

Brahmanical movement. Today, Tamil Nadu politics is influenced by that concept.

Rammohan Roy and Brahmo Samaj

Raja Rammohan Roy

Rammohan Roy (1772-1833) was the father of the Hindu reform movement of the 19th century. He represented the new spirit of India with its thrust on science and rationalism, reform, and broad humanism. But though he had a passionate love for reform he yet had a critical regard for the past and disinclination for revolt. Rammohan, who was born in an orthodox Brahmin family, was at an early age placed in charge of a Maulavi to learn Persian, since knowledge of Persian was then essential for attaining success and social status. After he had learnt Persian at the age of nine he was sent to Patna to study Arabic. He soon became familiar with the works of Sufi poets and thus became critical of idolatry and polytheism. At the age of fourteen he went to Banaras (Varanasi) to learn Sanskrit. Knowledge of Sanskrit enabled him to study *the Vedanta* and the *Upanishads*. Such study made him still more critical of idolatry.

A stormy career

Returning home from Benaras, Rammohan wrote a book condemning idolatry. This led to a rupture between him and his conservative father. He then left home and went as far as Tibet where he studied Buddhism. But the crude form in which the tenets of Buddhism were taught repelled him and he criticised them. This antagonised the Lamas who threatened him with physical violence. Rammohan was saved by a kind-hearted lady. He was touched and was deeply grateful for this, and, throughout his life, he was a great believer in the emancipation of women. Rammohan's father had by this time relented and sent emissaries to get him back. Rammohan returned, was reconciled with his father, but renewed his attacks on idolatry and orthodox Brahmins. Soon thereafter his elder brother died and his widow immolated herself on the funeral pyre. Rammohan was greatly distressed and decided to start a crusade against the cruel practice of *Sati.*

Long before he acquired any knowledge of English, Rammohan, mainly as a result of his studies in Patna, a lively centre of Islamic thought, had developed certain ideas about religious reform. Had he not come into contact with European thought, he might have become a religious reformer in the manner of Nanak or Kabir. In 1796 he began learning English. He also studied *the Upanishads* and *the Vedanta Sutras* in Sanskrit and *the Old and New Testaments* in the original Hebrew and Greek. He published some translations of the *Upanishads* and a book entitled *Precepts of Jesus, the Guide to Peace and Happiness* which contained not so much a message for his own countrymen as an answer to the Christian missionaries. He rejected the doctrine of the divinity of Jesus but was much impressed by his ethical teachings. His arguments against the Doctrine of Trinity were so convincing that he converted to Unitarianism the Scotch missionary with whom he had entered into a joint venture to translate *the New Testament* into Bengali. He had many Christian missionary friends but spurned the attempts of some of them to convert him to Christianity.

Roy was a civil servant in British India

Rammohan had been a distinguished administrator in the Bengal Civil Service. His success as an administrator and an assured income from landed property enabled him to retire from service at the age of forty-two, to settle down in Calcutta and to devote himself completely to spiritual, social, and political matters. During the last years of his life he went to England to plead the cause of the powerless Emperor of Delhi, who had conferred on him the title of 'Raja'. He reached England after a hazardous journey which lasted a year and a half. In crossing 'the black waters' to go to England he defied one of the prevalent taboos of the Hindu society.

In England he spoke before the Committee of Parliament about the ways and means of improving the working of the Government of India. There he also came into contact with Jeremy Bentham who hailed him as his great friend, and wrote to him in a letter, "Your works are made known to me by a book in which I read a style which but for the name of a Hindu, I should certainly have ascribed to the pen of a highly educated and instructed Englishman". In England, Rammohan was honoured as an unofficial ambassador of India. He died in Bristol in 1833. Rammohan had to wage a war on two fronts – against the Christian missionaries and against the orthodox Hindus. He sought to defend Hinduism by reinterpreting it as also by purifying it. He did not reject the spirit of modern Europe nor did he succumb to it. Rammohan inveighed against the inequities of the caste system. He was convinced that the divisions and sub-divisions of caste deprived the people of political feeling and that the multitude of religious rites and ceremonies and the laws of purification prevented them from undertaking any difficult enterprise. He said that some change in the religion of his countrymen was necessary "at least for the sake of their political advantage and social comfort."

William Bentinck and Sati

In 1818 Rammohan began his celebrated crusade for the abolition of *Sati* and in 1829 Lord William Bentinck, the Governor-General, rendered *Sati* illegal. In cooperating with foreign rulers to enact socially progressive legislation Rammohan was the forerunner of

Lord William Bentinck

later social reformers such as Ranade and Gokhale. Originally Rammohan had only hatred for the English, but after considerable social intercourse with them, he came to the conclusion that English rule, though foreign, would for some time be favourable to the progress of Indians as it would facilitate the growth of liberal religious thought and social reform movements. In 1821, Rammohan founded a Bengali journal, *the Samvad Kaumudi,* and he agitated against the Press Regulations of 1823. In a memo to the Supreme Court he and his colleagues maintained that a free Press was necessary as much for the sake of the rulers as of the ruled. For in the absence of a free Press popular discontent festered underground and excited rebellion. As a result of efforts like these the Press was freed by Sir Charles Metcalfe in 1835.

Universalist Church

Along with the traditional Hindu lineages that are opening their doors to Westerners, there are also many non-traditional spiritualities that are also embracing the beliefs and practices of Hinduism to varying extents. The Unitarian Universalist Church often makes room in their schedule to host events tied to Hindu holidays and celebrations, during which non-Hindus can learn more about the tradition and begin to take part in the observances. There are also several Neopagan and Wiccan traditions, such as SHARANYA, which teach traditional Shakta Tantra within a Western, Wicca-influenced context.

German Indologist Axel Michaels in his 1998 book about Hinduism distinguished founding, proselytising religions, 'Guruism' as religious groups originating in India, but also widespread in the West, founded by charismatic persons with a corpus of esoteric writings of Gurus predominantly in English: Maharishi Mahesh Yogi and Transcendental Meditation, Sathya Sai Baba and the Sathya Sai Organisation, Bhaktivedanta Swami Prabhupada and ISKCON, Guru Maharaj Ji and the Divine Light Mission, Rajneesh Chandra Mohan and the Sannyasi Movement in Poona, etc. These founding, proselytising religions, 'guruism' are, according to the book, one of the three sub-groups of founded religions of Hinduism, the other two being sectarian religions and syncretically founded religions. The founded religions in turn are, according to the book, one of the three Hindu religions that comprise Hinduism.

Hinduism has been evolving over many centuries. "But, the more we change, the more we remain the same. How else can we explain the continuing practice of manual scavenging which would not have persisted for so long, if these reforms had succeeded," says Dr. Pathak. The Sulabh Movement seeks to fill the historical gaps in these movements which concentrated largely on preaching. They did not provide alternatives which Sulabh does by acting out what is practised, using technology, education, campaigning and a variety of modern gadgets as agents of change. These were not available to earlier social movements, though great and noble they were. But, all social movements happen in a context, and when the context changes, so do the profile of the movements. Sulabh, for that matter, is a critical link in the long chain of social reforms, beginning from Buddha to Gandhiji. This is how it was so desired by history.

Theosophical Society and Annie Besant

Theosophy is a religious system that tries to realise God through meditation. The Theosophical Society was started first in New York in 1875. In India, the Theosophical Society was founded by Madame Blavatsky, a Russian, and Colonel Olcott, an American, stimulated the spirit of cultural nationalism among Indians. Both founders of the Theosophical Society repudiated Christianity. In a letter to Dayananda in February 1878, Olcott said that the Theosophists "have openly proclaimed themselves enemies of the Christian religion". Both Blavatsky and Olcott were converted to Buddhism. Blavatsky told Annie Besant, the most important propagator of Theosophy in India, that she embraced Buddhism because she wanted to show that "a religion of the East was better than the religion of the West". Olcott spoke about the majesty of eastern scriptures and appealed to the patriotic Indians to uphold the religion of their forefathers. He lamented that in schools and colleges, Indian students were not taught their native religion, and he also pleaded for the revival of Sanskrit learning and of the ancient philosophy, drama, music, and literature of the Hindus.

Annie Besant had an interesting past. In Britain she had been a free thinker along with Charles Bradlaugh and a Fabian Socialist along with Bernard Shaw. Besant always upheld enthusiastically whatever cause she believed in and however unpopular the cause might be. Besant had a pious Victorian girlhood and in 1867 she married an Anglican clergyman. But it was a clear case of mismatch. Besant found no outlet for her intellectual and spiritual energies in the humdrum life of Reverend Frank Besant, and she separated from him when she was 25.

Annie Besant supported Malthus

Later, Annie Besant became involved in a sensational case with the republication of a book by Dr. Charles Knowlton, a follower of Malthus, who pleaded that married people should limit their families. The book had been sold for many years without attracting much attention but later a bookseller sold the book by adding to it some indecent pictures. He was prosecuted and convicted. It was at this stage that Bradlaugh and Besant decided to republish the book to vindicate the right of free thought, though they did not agree with all that was contained therein. Many world leaders, including Giuseppe Garibaldi (1807-82), who united Italy, acclaimed this, and the law took its course. Bradlaugh and Besant were arrested and tried. The Chief Justice summed up strongly for an acquittal, but the jury found the accused guilty. This verdict was, however, eventually quashed. After coming to India, Besant translated *the Bhagavad Gita* into English and became a pillar of Hindu revivalism. She, however, condemned early marriage and forced widowhood. She was also associated with the founding of the Central Hindu College at Banaras in 1898.

These are some samples of reforms, none of which were, however, as comprehensive, global, secular views and as widely disseminated without any religious component, national or social bias as Sulabh. This is, however, not to suggest that they did not do enough to help reform society. They did a lot and all of them were great men and women, although born in different times, age and had to face different social challenges. Hence, they had different world view, which cannot be compared with the movements launched in media-dominated post-War world of the last century, when the Sulabh Movement was born amid Gandhian views and social values, the benchmarks to assess the role of Dr. Bindeshwar Pathak, its Founder.

Reforms in British period

The coming of the British from the farther west affected Indian life and polity. Much that is vital in modern Indian culture is either a response to or a reaction against western civilisation. They are syncretic. The new culture of the West kindled the liberal forces in India. The first spark of Indian liberalism was lighted by Rammohan Roy. Rammohan gave a public dinner in Calcutta in 1820 when the Spanish got a Constitution. It has been said that the Western contact gave India modern political ideals, that India owes her nationalistic and democratic spirit to the European literature of nationalism. Such a claim is clearly exaggerated, but it cannot be gainsaid that the Western influence in India has been considerable.

Jawaharlal Nehru

Jawaharlal Nehru, speaking in the Constituent Assembly in May 1949, said that as a result of the British rule for more than a century, many developments took place which were bad and against which Indians struggled but there were also many other positive developments. "Here I am an example of contacts with British culture, speaking in this Honourable House in the English language. We are functioning here under certain rules and regulations for which the model has been the British Constitution."

In the 19th century, Western civilisation had an irresistible appeal for educated Indians. In 1941, a few months before his death, Tagore described how in his youth the English-educated Indians were eloquent with declamations of Burke, Shakespeare's drama and Byron's poetry and how they were inspired by liberalism of the 19th century English politics, when educated Indians hoped that the victor would himself pave the path for the freedom of the vanquished. But this romantic vision of the chivalrous West did not last long, and Tagore expressed his disillusionment in *the Crisis of Civilisation,* where, after referring to the ruins of the proud civilisation of the West, he said that "the new dawn will come from this horizon, from the East where the sun rises."

Sulabh sets new model

Sulabh has not conformed to any template; it has gone its own way, setting up a new work model, combining best and honest business practices with social services. For instance, Sulabh does projects at a 15 per cent premium as service charge and takes up the responsibility to keep it in state of good repair for a period, ranging from 10 to 30 years. It is not like building a road and giving repair bills next year. This is a good business practice of accountability and spending the surplus from projects on social services like education, campaigning, research and other social work, not on giving dividends. For that matter Dr. Bindeshwar Pathak has re-invented the role of NGO making it an agent of social change, working without government help or assistance from any quarter. Sulabh is an exception, not the norm.

Far too different from others, Dr. Pathak's Gandhism has no political content; it is a vision of an entirely justice-based social order to ensure equal opportunity and empowerment of the disenfranchised people through education, training, social mainstreaming in non-violent ways and without upsetting the existing social order but through a process, what he calls, osmosis and change.

The Sulabh philosophy is scientific, pragmatic, syncretic and a synthesis of all these. Dr. Pathak's philosophy is ideology-neutral. He talks of a 'multi-dimensional man'. Dr. Pathak says, "Man's character is too complex to be fitted into an ideological template. Hence, man can be too good and too bad at the same time. Nazi killers, including Himmler and Goebbels, were philosophy students at Berlin University. Hence, the only valid philosophy is Kantian humanism which will remain true for all time and to all societies. Political ideologies are only different methods of production and how best to maximise profit, in public or private sector. They are no response to social discrimination and injustice. Politics without ideology can end up becoming a mere accounting exercise".

What one finds intriguing is how the neoclassicism and social welfare can be conflated to produce the growth in India. Neoclassicism constitutes a revival of classical theory of capitalism, an economic system characterised by private ownership of property and capital investment to the exclusion of the poor who are reduced to becoming lifeless objects working for the rich. This is a dangerous doctrine that produced imperialism, mercantilism and colonialism in protest of which communism, a still more damaging system, was born in Manchester. The rest is the known story.

India lives by ideals and commitment

In India, we live by our ideals, social commitment and family roots and not by money alone. That the Indian government has combined growth with social concerns to produce an Indian equivalent of GDP growth is a new experiment. In that case, it is necessary to make the social system inclusive and ideology-based with social justice at the centre of the framework for social development. Dr. Pathak developed modes of critical thinking. His analyses here exemplify Hegelian and Marxian dialectical philosophy both in his relentless critique of existing modes of what he considers uncritical thought and in his working out of the categories of critical and dialectical thinking in social and economic development.

Since sociology, as an independent science, was not established before the 19th century, the theory of society up to that time was an integral part of philosophy or of those sciences the conceptual structure of which was to a large extent based upon specific philosophical doctrines. This intrinsic connection between philosophy and the theory of society formulates the pattern of most theories of social change in the ancient world, in the middle ages, and on the commencement of modern times. One decisive result is the emphasis on the fact that social change cannot be interpreted within a particular social science, but must be understood within the social and natural totality of human life. This conception uses, to a large extent, psychological factors in the theories of social change. However, the derivation of social and political concepts from the 'psyche' of man is not a psychological method in the modern sense but rather involves the negation of psychology as a special science.

Sulabh philosophy based on justice

The Sulabh philosophy is a dialectical logic in the Marxian tradition – thesis, antithesis and synthesis. The caste system is thesis (a given fact); the revolt against it (rise of the Dalit movement) is antithesis and the Sulabh philosophy of reconciliation between the two is synthesis. Dr. Pathak says that it is true that there had been oppression, injustice and discrimination in society, with the victims of the skewed system. And, truer still is the fact that the oppressed should be adequately compensated and be given a chance to rise and be equal with others through a process of education, reforms and by creating greater opportunities for them to grow. This change has to be brought about through non-violent methods and national consensus. And, not by revolution and bloodshed. These are the postulates of the Sulabh philosophy.

The Sulabh philosophy is a way of life which lays out how one can live a virtuous and good life in family while doing social service. Dr. Pathak is a Gandhian in action and not in appearance. Gandhiji prescribed austere code of life to render social service. For Sulabh workers, it is not necessary to do all that, only to be good to the neighbour, help the poor, and serve society in hundred different ways. Gandhiji's life was his message but a Sulabh worker lives as he likes while doing Gandhian work. He does not necessarily have to wear *khadi* and spin the wheel to establish a Gandhian social order.

The Sulabh philosophy is a combination of money, social work and prestige. Money is necessary for living and supporting the family, while social work gives prestige and money both. The three things are not mutually exclusive; rather, they are complementary. Here, it differs from the Gandhian philosophy which wants followers to do social work without money. As long as Gandhiji was alive and his followers were in positions of power, the concept of selfless and unpaid social service worked, but later it did not. The movements like the Harijan Sevak Sangh, Sarvodaya, the Arya Samaj and many others phased out because they were not sustainable. Those who launched these peacetime agitations to change things were noble persons inspired by lofty ideas and commitment. But these alone could not go very far; for one needs money to buy food and raise family. Sulabh has combined social service with livelihood to make the movement sustainable and expand the areas of participation by ordinary people doing extraordinary work in creating a new society out of the old.

Middle path

The Sulabh code of conduct prescribes middle path, living a good but disciplined life in the family while serving society. The 'middle path' is a combination of a healthy existence with social commitment. "It is between Lord Buddha and Raja Janak; the former left the world to become a *Sanyasi* and found new ways to salvation while the latter lived the life of a king but with total detachment to pleasure and pain."

Dr. Pathak says the greatest philosophy consists in the constant knowledge of the inevitability of death. Once people realise it adequately, much of evil things will vanish. India is, as a matter of fact, going through a learning process in respect of strengthening civil society organisations through a process of creating a collection culture to ensure a change in the feudal mindset.

Power is central to the Sulabh philosophy – the power of knowledge, persuasion and the power to make things happen through application of science and technology, political decision and social pressure. Power is often associated with coercion and use of force to influence the behaviour of people. It is not true because this situation cannot always endure. Gandhiji, Martin Luther, Newton, Confucius and so also many other social reformers, scientists and pacifist movement (like Greenpeace) leaders enjoyed enormous power to change social behaviour more than any conquerors ever had. It is necessary to acquire the power of this kind to make any movement succeed, not by coercion.

"Every action has an equal and opposite reaction."
– Isaac Newton

CHAPTER 19

Dialectics of Social Change: Opposites Lead to Synthesis

The Sulabh theory of social intervention

"Caste has killed public spirit; it has destroyed the sense of public charity and has made public opinion impossible to emerge. Virtue has become caste-ridden and morality has become caste-bound."
– B.R. Ambedkar, in 'the Annihilation of Caste, 1936.'

The word 'dialectic' originated in Ancient Greece, and was made popular by Plato-Socratic dialogues. Dialectic is rooted in the ordinary practice of a dialogue between two people who hold different ideas and wish to persuade each other. The presupposition of a dialectical argument is that the participants, even if they do not agree, share at least some meanings and principles of inference. Different forms of dialectical reason have emerged in the East and in the West. Among the classical Greek thinkers, the meanings of dialectic ranged from a technique of refutation in debate, through a method for systematic evaluation of definitions, to the investigation and classification of the relationships between specific and general concepts. From the time of the Stoic philosophers until the end of the Middle Ages, dialectic was more or less closely identified with the discipline of formal logic.

Theoretically, dialectic is based around three basic metaphysical concepts: everything is transient and finite, existing in the medium of time; everything is made out of opposing forces (contradictions) and gradual changes lead to a point, where one force overcomes the other and change moves in spirals (or helices), not circles and, finally, opposite forces are synthesised. In Plato's and Socrates' dialogues, the latter attempts to examine someone's beliefs, or premises by which we all reason and argue. Socrates typically argues by cross-examining his interlocutors' claims and premises in order to draw out a contradiction or inconsistency among them. According to Plato, the rational detection of error amounts to finding the proof of the antithesis.

Eastern forms of dialectic

Indian debate on an intra- and inter-*dharmic* dialectic was a spectator sport in the court. The king himself was often the judge at these debates, and loss to an opponent could have sometimes serious consequences. It was a bloody sport at times. To cite an example, Eaivite Ñanasambandar Nayanar, a Tamil scholar, defeated in a debate the Jain Acharyas in Madurai in the court of the Pandya King, Maravarman Avaniúûlamani (620-645). This debate is said to have resulted in the impalement (killing with sharp weapons) of 8,000 Jains, an event still celebrated in the Meenakshi Temple of Madurai. Usually, the results were, however, not so drastic; they could mean formal recognition by the defeated side of the superiority of the winning party, forced conversions, or, as in the case of the Council of Lhasa, which was conducted by Indians, banishment of the losers.

In Brahminism, certain dialectical elements can be found in the idea of the three eternal and simultaneously occurring phases of creation (Brahma), maintenance of order (Vishnu) and destruction or disorder (Shiva). This is the Hindu dialectic as also discussed by Hegel and Engels, while writing on chaos theory. Hindu philosophers however, say that the relationship between the gods Vishnu and Shiva is not antagonism between good and evil, but the dynamic and developmental relationship of harmony and discord dialectic.

In *the Vedas,* which date from around 1500 BC, are hymns to the gods, but as Hegel also points out, Eastern religions are very philosophical in character. The gods have less of a personal character and are more akin to general concepts and symbols. We find these elements of dialectics in Hinduism as Engels has explained. The deities of *the Vedas* may be fruitfully engaged as manifestations of the ultimate truth, *dharma.*

Buddhist dialectic and change

Buddhism has also developed sophisticated and institutionalised traditions of dialectics. Nalanda University is an example. The historical development and clarification of Buddhist doctrine and polemics through dialectics and formal debate is documented. The Buddhist doctrine was contested in a highly consistent and logical way in the 2nd century by Nagarjuna, whose rationalism became the basis for the development of one stream of Buddhist logic. The logic of Buddhism was later developed by other notable thinkers such as Dignaga and Dharmakirti. Protracted dialectic is evident throughout the traditions of Madhyamaka, Yogacara and Tantric Buddhism. Trisong Detsen, and later Je Tsongkhapa, championed the value of dialectic and debate in Tibet. Since Buddhism is neutral to God, it is all about dialectic.

This detailed description on dialectic has been made if only to give a perspective to the Sulabh thought system which is central to the Sulabh social reform movement. Dr. Pathak says, the division of Indian society along caste, community, ethnic or regional lines has been a part of the social evolution which is found all over the world. Kant and Hegal talked of dialectic to explain the philosophical concept by deconstructing an idea into different parts and reconstructing them again by joining them on the common ground. This kind of method has been in Hindu philosophy well before them.

While analysing social structure and its movement over

thousands of years, Dr. Pathak says, there has been inherent strength in the Indian social system which has become irrelevant today when we have a highly organised social structure based on science and technology. Earlier, it was not and hence, people organised their lives in groups and professions which later became castes. We have to change the system not through violence but social intervention, education and entitlement. To carry out this work, he has founded an intellectual discipline called Action Sociology which means social action to ensure economic and social growth, poverty reduction (read elimination of scavenging); education to all, specially women; population control; environmental sanitation; modernisation of society etc.

In a democratic society, like India, there cannot be one set of standards in the legal system (equality before law) and politics (every adult has a vote) and another set of standards in the free market economic system in which the poor have no social choice but to perish in an unequal globalisation race. "The cost benefit concept has no moral construct; it is a sheer exploitation perpetuated by capitalist economists. For a fair and just society to grow, there has to be a social intervention to change the unjust system." Dr. Pathak quotes Newton's First Law: Every material body persists in its state of rest or of uniform motion in a straight line if (and only if) it is not compelled by any external force to change that state.

"Free play of market forces will lead to chaos"

Dr. Pathak says, the roots of the current global crisis lie in the interplay of several developments that have fundamentally transformed the finance capitalism that existed in 1929. This is because of lack of social intervention. Traditionally banks were careful to lend only to trusted clients, and carried the debt on their books. They bore the risk. Now there is securitisation. Lenders pool the loans and resell them as asset-backed securities. These securities are then repackaged, leveraged, trenched and resold many times over. A second related development is the emergence of highly sophisticated derivative products. Especially important among these today are the credit default swaps (CDSs). Taken together, asset-backed securities and derivatives widely spread the risk, but they also breed complacency towards risk. The selling and reselling of risk also lays the foundation for quick contagion. This all happened because in the capitalism, social intervention is not accepted. It is a free for all. Consequently, the crisis which was triggered off in New York has become the global phenomenon.

Dr. Pathak says, a scavenger or a *Harijan* or a landlord will remain the same until there is social intervention to change the state of inertia. The *laissez-faire* negates this truism and goes back to the Darwin's theory of the survival of the fittest which could be true in the evolution of living species but not while setting up a social system which has to be based on justice and equality. The Action Sociology provides a conceptual basis for social action to bring about change. Marx also said, "We know history but the question is how to change it." Likewise, it can be said that we know source of social injustices in India, but the question is how to change it. The state itself seeks to change things but not always for the common good. People, for instance, were driven to wars without knowing their enemies. In the book, *All Quiet on the Western Front*, the hero (a soldier in the trench) says, "I do not know my enemy, a German, whom I killed, but I know my girlfriend whom I love. Murder no more – Oh! Lord, stop this carnage. I want to go home and meet my ailing parents and my sweet girl. I don't want to kill anymore."

What dictators did was state (not social) intervention which brought about miseries to humankind. For, the state is based on force and violence, and not on morality and ethics. For this reason, Dr. Pathak says that social (read NGO) intervention is necessary to set up a just social order. The Sulabh Movement is a social intervention where the people seek to change themselves on their own and not by the state. The Sulabh Movement combines in itself Newton's First Law, Max Weber's thought on social change and Buddha's philosophy *(that all human behaviour must have ethical basis)* to set up a composite social order when the people will 'act and be acted upon' both in the process of change.

Democracy will prevail only in just society

"State can change the system but it cannot change the mindset. The world is infinitely varied and constantly changing. We have also to change or perish," says Dr. Pathak. He says that religious orthodoxy, caste system and feudalism are the main hurdles to change. Science and mathematics-based education, free trade, social mobility, industrialisation, media and liberal political ideologies alone can change them. Law will not be of much help. The chaos in Indian society is largely because of the change that is taking place in society. The feudal and casteist mindset which determines our preferences, is threatened with change. Hence, the people who benefit from this old order resist it. Add to it, the uncontrollable growth in population, and the story of social chaos in India will be complete.

The refusal to change leads to social unrest which may also cause massive migration of people as in Rwanda, Congo, and Horn of Africa where people just walked and walked to fill the road, edge to edge, when only soft and weary whisper of feet was heard. The people used last scrap of energy just to keep moving in total silence. It was a sudden return of more than 450,000 Rwandan refugees from camps in Tanzania to their home country after the brutal upheavals in 1994 and 1995. Forced out of Tanzania, the refugees left the huge camps and started walking again to nowhere. Something like this will happen everywhere if uncontrolled population growth and migration to cities are not taken care of by social and state intervention. Behind the stable appearance of much of the world, the same kinds of numbers could be moving quietly at airports, seaports, railway stations, along forested borders, and even where steel and barbed wires make barriers that seem impenetrable, thousands upon thousands of people are on their way to somewhere new.

They don't make much noise, but they change the world. Some 60 million Europeans left home after the last World War. Some 15 million Hindus, Sikhs, and Muslims were swept up in a tumultuous exchange of citizens between India and Pakistan after partition of the subcontinent in 1947. The US was populated by convicts, persecuted and migrating people who fled violence and war. This monumental misery happens in the countries that don't change. "Therefore, change, we must", says Dr. Pathak, and Action Sociology tells you how.

City life demolishes old values

The growth of urban concentrations is a relatively recent phenomenon, dating back only about 150 years, although the world's first cities date back more than 5,000 years. Urbanisation has had a major effect on the social structures of industrial societies, affecting not only where people live but how they live, and urban sociology has emerged as a distinct area of study which affects the status of an individual's social position, or the esteem in which he or she is held by others in society. Formal social status is attached to a particular social position, occupation, role, or office. Informal social status is based on an individual's own personal talents, skills, or personality. Both within and between occupations or social positions there is a status hierarchy. Accompanying high status are usually status symbols, such as insignia of office or an expensive car, etc. Sociologists distinguish between ascribed status, which is bestowed by others, and achieved status, which is the result of one's own efforts. An IAS officer or a minister enjoys 'ascribed status' and a social leader, scholar or a thinker has 'acquired status'. The former has power enforceable by police while the latter has influence 'enforceable' by consent. Status is seen as a key influence on human behaviour, on the way people evaluate themselves and others.

Dr. Pathak says, Indian society is stereotyped (from Greek term meaning fixed impression) having one-sided, irrational, and preconceived idea about a particular group or society. It is based on prejudices rather than facts, and, by repetition, stereotypes become fixed in people's minds which become resistant to change or to factual evidence to the contrary and, intolerant to dissent. Stereotypes can prove dangerous when used to justify persecution and discrimination. Some sociologists believe that stereotyping reflects a power structure in which one group in society uses labelling to keep another group in its inferior place. The concept is true of all societies but truer of India where the so-called upper castes produce a series of arguments, religious and secular, to defend discrimination and prejudices, quoting (*Manusmriti*) and misquoting (*Vedas* etc.) books of religion.

Gandhiji was among many who promoted this cultural perception. He belonged to a fairly rich family, and had studied law in London but he lived a life of poverty. And, this culture of poverty, real or simulated, had enormous impact on our economic activities. Max Weber had said that culture and religion have enormous impact on the development of economic system. In case of India, it is truer. In the caste system religion, however, had given sanction to economic pursuit including *Banias*, a trader caste, who produced goods and Dalits who provided service to keep society move on.

The Sociology of Hinduism and Buddhism was Weber's major work on the sociology of religion. In this work, he deals with the structure of Indian society, with the orthodox doctrines of Hinduism and the heterodox doctrines of Buddhism, with modifications brought by the influence of popular religiosity, and finally with the impact of religious beliefs on the secular ethic of Indian society. The ancient Indian social system was shaped by the concept of caste. It directly linked religious belief and the segregation of society into status groups. Weber describes the caste system, consisting of the

Brahmins (priests), the Kshatriyas (warriors), the Vaishyas (merchants) and the Shudras (labourers). Then he describes the spread of the caste system in India due to conquests, the marginalisation of certain tribes and the sub-division of castes. Weber pays special attention to Brahmins and analyses why they occupied the highest place in Indian society for so many centuries. With regard to the concept of *dharma* he concludes that the Indian ethical pluralism is very different both from the universal ethic of Confucianism and Christianity. He notes that the caste system prevented the development of urban status groups.

Weber and Hinduism's world view

Weber analyses the Hindu religious beliefs, including asceticism and the Hindu world view, the Brahmin orthodox doctrines, the rise and fall of Buddhism in India, the Hindu restoration, and the evolution of the Guru. Weber asks the question whether religion had any influence upon economic activities and how it impacted economic conduct. He says, the traditional caste system, supported by the religion, slowed economic development; in other words, the 'spirit' of the caste system militated against an indigenous development of capitalism and expansion of economic activities. Thus, Weber also agrees that India's poverty is because of the caste-based social structure and social exclusion.

Max Weber

Weber notes that the beliefs tended to interpret the meaning of life as a mystical experience, while the intellectuals tend to be apolitical in their orientation, and that the social world was fundamentally divided between the educated, whose lives are oriented towards the exemplary conduct of a wise man, and the uneducated masses who remain caught in their misplaced belief and believed in magic. In Asia, no messianic prophecy appeared that could have given "plan and meaning to the everyday life of educated and uneducated alike." He argues that it was the messianic prophecies in the countries of the Near East, as distinguished from the prophecy of the Asiatic mainland, that prevented Western countries from following the paths of China and India, and his next work, *Ancient Judaism* was an attempt to prove this theory.

Weber has explained the 'combination of circumstances' which resulted in the early differences between Oriental and Occidental religiosity. It is especially visible when the inner worldly asceticism developed by Western Christianity is contrasted with mystical contemplation of the kind developed in India. Weber noted that some aspects of Christianity sought to conquer and change the world, rather than withdraw from its imperfections. This fundamental characteristic of Christianity (when compared to Far Eastern religions) stems originally from ancient Jewish prophecy. Anyone who is heir to the traditions of modern European civilisation will approach the problems of universal history with a set of questions, which to him appear both inevitable and legitimate. These questions will turn on the combination of circumstances which has brought about the cultural phenomena that are uniquely Western and that have at the same time a universal cultural significance.

Breakdown of consensus

The Sulabh Founder uses the term 'alienation' not in Kantian term of categorical imperative, but he uses it in the Marxian sense to describe the poor conditions of the disadvantaged people as 'estranged and alienated.' It is a flawed social construct and not categorical imperative, as Immanuel Kant had said. Dr. Pathak associates alienation with anomie, a state created by a breakdown of the commonly agreed standards of behaviour and social morality. This term is used by sociologists to indicate a situation where the order is critically threatened by social discrimination. By development, Dr. Pathak does not mean only economic development, but also the human resource development which, he says, alone will empower the poor whose inclusion in the social development is necessary to ensure that growth benefits all. This empowerment will also enable the poor to move up and down the social scale. The extent and range of social mobility will help abolish or reduce the impact of the caste system which, Dr. Pathak says, is the source of all evils. The caste system in India and the feudalism of medieval Europe are the examples of closed societies where very little social mobility takes place. The class system of the Western industrial societies is relatively open and flexible. Individual social mobility occurs through education, marriage, talent and so on. The group mobility occurs through occupational structures caused by new technological and economic development.

Values are variable determined by time

Dr. Pathak quotes a variety of opinions, from sociologists and economists to say that all concepts are relevant only to their time. But, the principles of Action Sociology are valid forever, also because they are not doctrinaire, or fixed. These principles change with times; the only fixed thing about them is the target – the poorest among the poor. No theory should be considered socially valid until they are actionable – to be applied effectively and appropriately. The need for Action Sociologist arose because most sociologists have become theory-bound and, thus, socially irrelevant. In truth, sociology has been reduced to only a discussion point or a 'pass subject' for weak students in colleges and universities because it has no applied value which Action Sociology seeks to produce. Dr. Pathak agrees with Prof. Amartya Sen to say that Buddha was the greatest of all Indian thinkers, social reformers, economists and sages. The sight of an ill person, an old man reduced by age and the dead man being carried to cremation ground set Buddha asking himself: What kind of life is it? And, from this flows modern economics, says Prof. Sen.

Civilisational question

It is feared that India will fossilise if it does not change. The only conceptual category permitting this thinking is civilisation. Recently turned into a dirty word, civilisation conjures images of 'clashes', all the more terrifying because they bear the force of history – experiences which have accumulated over a time to form an unchanging culture. However, civilisations are not static. The concept has an older pedigree dating to Toynbee and Spengler. Later Benjamin Nelson injected a dose of dynamism into civilisational analysis with his idea of inter-civilisational encounters. Indians are uncommonly gifted as a cultural group to take on new ideas and adapt to them without upsetting social structure.

To be true, modern India needs to be understood in terms of civilisation because the development of our state is complex. In Europe, the state came first which coerced peoples into a sense of national identity. It was the opposite in India where our ancestors developed a sense of Indianness and then a state came and managed it. Such developments are hard to explain in terms of East-West divide; they only become explicable if we abandon the East-West divide theory and recognise the modern sensibilities of Indian traditions and how they came about during the time civilisation was evolving over many centuries. A civilisational approach to Indian history will answer many questions on how India is traditional and modern at once.

The Hindu society is a synthesis of many thought systems, religions, ethnicity, caste groups and other contradictions. The syncretic nature of Indian society has produced flexibility and created a culture of tolerance, much of which is manifest in

Hinduism which is a combination of many streams of thoughts and beliefs, combined in an umbrella concept and culture called Hinduism. A Hindu may be theist, deist, atheist or agnostic; he may or may not believe in one of the many thousands of gods and religious books. And, his identity as a Hindu will remain unchallenged. Hinduism is, thus, a product of the dialectic process of change through many centuries. And, it is still changing.

East-West divide

Much of the continuities in Indian cultural life is ignored by the flawed concept of East-West, tradition and modernity divide which the westernised intellectuals use to comprehend the world. Those who are modern are Western; others are Eastern. The dualistic approach assumes that while Mumbai and Delhi might be the East's oases of modernity, it is the West that is modern. Tradition remains synonymous with backwardness and resistance to change while modernity conjures up images of a liberal, enlightened West, supporters of progress, and everything else. This argument confuses technological progress in the West with its being modern in a social and political sense also.

Prof. Sen rejects the 'received wisdom' and says, if India is a non-modern and traditional nation how does the Indian state manage its diversity so well? How a sense of unity has prevailed in a land that is larger than Europe? He says, it is a part of a historical continuum that makes modern Indians inheritors of traditions, spread over centuries and enriched by the mixing of diverse sets of peoples. These traditions accommodated the Mughals, the British and, more recently, permitted Indians to harness globalisation. It would appear that Indian tradition is a repository of some very modern ideas such as plasticity, flexibility and adaptability. Indian experience short-circuits imported notions of modernity and tradition as invented in Europe.

If the mindless growth mania is not restrained,
there can be civilisational collapse caused by deforestation,
desertification, drought, famine and the consequent social disorder.
This is what Gandhiji, Schumacher and Dr. Pathak say,
though in different ways.

CHAPTER 20

Dr. Pathak is a Third Generation Gandhian

Gandhi, Fritz Schumacher and Sulabh

Although born three decades apart in different countries, raised in entirely different social, political and academic environments, Fritz Schumacher and Dr. Bindeshwar Pathak have many things in common. Both favour greater human involvement in social and economic development by adopting intermediate technologies with "a human face" and, thus, end social exclusion and poverty; both seek restraint on limitless expansion of human needs to ensure that nature's resources and world's endowments are used not more than they can be renewed and replenished. And, thus, avert a civilisational collapse which, cannot be averted until we change.

Dr. Bindeshwar Pathak is a third generation Gandhian who has revisited Gandhism in order to put it into practice in modern and scientific ways. The first-generation Gandhians were those who worked with Gandhiji during the freedom struggle against the British, staying outside power and living in poverty. Their lives were legends of sacrifice and self-denial, and they suffered in myriad ways so that the people of India could be free. They were the builders of the free India who will always be remembered with respect and nostalgia.

The second generation Gandhians fought elections and captured power after Gandhiji's death in 1948 and remained in power until about 1977 after which power started shifting out of the Congress hand following the defeat of Mrs. Indira Gandhi. The second generation Gandhians had stabilised the political system and set the country firmly on democratic path. This was also the year when the Left Front Government took over in West Bengal with Mr. Jyoti Basu whose 23 years in power (1977-2000) created a national record. The non-Congress governments also took power in many states.

The third generation Gandhians re-invented Gandhism and re-interpreted it to relate it to the welfare of the poor and the deprived section of society and also seek freedom and fair deal for them, prominent foreigners among them being Martin Luther King Jr., Aung San Suu Kyi, Nelson Mandela, E.F. Schumacher and Jeffrey Sachs. In this period, Gandhism became a global slogan and nothing was left of the first generation Gandhism when Gandhism was identified by their dress, and austere living, like Vinoba Bhave and a whole lot of Gandhians, who were also members of non-Congress parties, like Acharya Kripalani, Jayaprakash Narayan and Dr. Rammanohar Lohia who practised Gandhism while criticising Gandhiji. But none of these Gandhian ideas survived the second generation and the Gandhians of the third generation promoted Gandhism locally and globally relating Gandhiji to human rights, democracy, economic development from the bottom (*Antyodaya*), non-violent social and political change.

Global Gandhi

Alexander Dubcek of Czechoslovakia rallied his countrymen under a Gandhian slogan to protest Soviet occupation and became President in 1969. Mandela is the greatest Gandhian of all times and Nobel Laureate Aung San Suu Kyi is a symbol of Gandhian peaceful resistance. The latest still is the Occupy Wall Street Movement in protest against social injustice in America where, as Jeffrey Sachs says, one per cent population owns 25 per cent of the country's wealth.

Among the third generation Gandhians

Nelson Mandela (South Africa) | **Aung San Suu Kyi** (Myanmar) | **Alexander Dubcek** (Czech Republic) | **E.F. Fritz Schumacher** (Born in Germany) | **Dr. Bindeshwar Pathak** (India)

Gandhiji has been remembered all over New York in 2011 during the Occupy Wall Street Movement as a patron saint, inspiring non-violent protest. (The demonstrators even named a lane after him.) Then he emerged at the Metropolitan Opera as the Star of Philip Glass's opera Satyagraha. But, is it worth asking what would Gandhiji do in the world today? Occupy Wall Street was at once political theatre, counter-cultural commune, and recruiting agent for progressive causes. Gandhiji would have admired the community spirit in Zuccotti Park, in New York but if he were at the protests, he would have suggested some modifications.

First, Gandhiji always rejected the division between the 99 per cent and the one per cent. Gandhiji did not believe in enemies: He worked on the premise that solutions emerged only from cooperation. This truth is often lost in discussions of his political tactics of non-cooperation and civil disobedience. Non-cooperation is best understood as an invitation to cooperate. 'We are the 100 per cent' may not make for a dramatic slogan, but from Gandhiji's perspective, it is the only way to achieve true and lasting change in society.

Social change in Gandhian way

Gandhiji said social transformation required significant responsibility on the part of each of us. The world is not a static system or an unalterable one. Society exists in a certain way when we enter it, but it is our actions or our inactions that maintain the status quo, make things worse, or transform them for the better. Gandhiji explained this most pointedly when he declared that the British Empire existed because Indians had let it exist. He would say the same thing about the drastic income inequality in America today: it is here because Americans collectively allow it to be here. They are to be blamed, their thinking and philosophy.

Pointing fingers and assigning blame is easy – it can even be helpful. Protesting to the extent that both help us think through the current state of our society, and they contribute to a common cause of uplift and improvement. But they are most meaningful when they set the stage for constructive social action, through which we might begin to mend the world. This is exactly what Dr. Pathak says when he re-affirms that in order to end scavenging you don't have to blame those, who benefited from their services. "Like Gandhiji, I don't believe in enmity. For social change, the entire society has to work together. Even social entitlements should be treated as an affirmative action and not an act of hostility against non-reserved people", says Dr. Pathak. This is the thinking of the third generation Gandhian. Gandhiji's technique of passive resistance – *Satyagraha* – has also been seen in action across West Asia and North Africa, where people have been protesting peacefully in front of heavily armed soldiers. Though many of them were carrying portraits of the leftist guerilla leader Che Guevara, their method was unmistakably Gandhian. "Today, the ideas of Gandhi are more important than his personality. It is the only alternative way of civilisational dialogue. The uprising in Egypt, the economic breakdown in the West and the environmental disaster at Fukushima are a reminder of what Gandhi had warned," says Feroz Abbas Khan, the National Award-winning director of *'Gandhi, My Father'*.

Back in 1931, the jobless workers of Lancashire could probably see and appreciate Gandhiji's vision. So did George Orwell who refused to call him a saint. "Regarded simply as a politician, and compared with the other leading political figures of our time, how sweet a smell he has managed to leave behind," wrote Orwell in his essay one year after Gandhiji's assassination. The sweet smell still hangs in the air even as the experiment with Gandhism continues by the third generation Gandhians.

The New York Times correspondent Thomas L. Friedman and the author of *'The World is Flat'* writes (November 7, 2011): "Gandhism is relived every day in India. Vijay Pratap Singh Aditya, the CEO of Ekgaon, has built a software program that offers illiterate farmers a voice or text advisory program that tells them when the best time to plant their crops is how to mix their fertilisers and pesticides, and how much water to add each day. K. Chandrasekhar, the CEO of Forus Health, has his focus on avoidable blindness among the rural poor. A quarter of the world's blind people, some 12 million, are in India, and more than 80 per cent of those are blind as a result of lack of basic eye care in rural areas. So Forus has invented a single, portable, intelligent, non-invasive, eye pre-screening device that can identify all five major ailments. They are the Gandhian innovations of the third generation that will make India a dominant nation of the world."

Gandhism is not quasi-biblical revelation but the end-result of long experience in struggle and the result of historical evolution combined together by Mahatma Gandhi while putting these ideas into practical use during the freedom struggle. It is self-evidently wrong to argue that any idea, however universal, will be relevant forever. Nor can the Gandhism as was practised by the first generation Gandhians. Ideas and institutions change, so has Gandhism. Sulabh is the birth of third generation Gandhism of which Dr. Pathak is an eminent practitioner.

Gandhism in the third generation has, thus, become a potent force of social change, specially now when communism and socialism both have failed to deliver on social justice which Scottish economist Adam Smith (1723-90) and German emigre

Jew Karl Marx (1818-83) had abundantly promised. In sum, the third generation Gandhians all over the world have been social campaigners, not political leaders, with different global perspectives while talking of Gandhism. This was the true manifestation of Gandhian philosophy which has changed society more than any political power system could do.

Sulabh is Gandhi's second coming

Among such Gandhians is Dr. Bindeshwar Pathak who has acted out Gandhian ideals in practice, combining it with technology, sanitation, and ethics by putting them to social services. Far too different from others, Dr. Pathak's Gandhism has no political content; it is a vision of a justice-based social order to ensure equal opportunity and empowerment of the disenfranchised people through education, training, social mainstreaming in non-violent ways and without upsetting the existing social order but through a process, which he calls, osmosis and change.

Gandhiji, Fritz Schumacher and Dr. Bindeshwar have one thing in common – they want a restraint on human consumption, not essentially for any spiritual reason but because the limitless growth is not sustainable. Adam Smith conceived of three per cent global compound growth forever. But in 1804, the world's population was one billion which has become seven billion today who consume the natural resources which have not expanded while the number of consumers have increased sevenfold. In simpler term, today seven persons are using the same

Gandhiji at a mass rally

resources what one person did in 1804 – land, water, forest, air and biospheres – the main sources of production which have not expanded; rather they are depleting. In which case, until equilibrium is established between man's growing demands and the nature's shrinking ability to meet them, there will be a civilisational collapse. And, this is what we see today in the climate change, drought, flood, civil unrest, food riots, (Ethiopia, Somalia, Congo) and much other resources-related social unrest. Climate change is also closely related to sanitation which is central to human civilisation.

Fritz Schumacher was not talking of metaphysics when he said in his revolutionary book, *Small is Beautiful,* that "cleanliness is an absolute value itself." Cleanliness is important not because the absence of it causes diseases, bad health, low productivity and stink, nor can it be argued that to wash is uneconomical because it costs money and produces nothing except cleanliness. Economists have divided the whole spectrum of human behaviour into production and consumption. When one buys food, vegetable, furniture, a house or a cinema ticket, one consumes. And, if goods are produced by use of land, labour and capital, they are products. For economists, love, hate, good living, good reading, beauty, caring, sharing, compassion, music and all other good things of life have no economic value because they don't show on the economic scale.

But, real life cannot be classified in these two simplistic categories. When Adam was driven out of Heaven into the Garden of Eden, he was given a 'tree of knowledge' which was not a product but a thing of beauty and cleanliness which will last forever unlike the product which perishes. Fritz Schumacher has called it an economics of permanence because all goods are produced by sources which are limited while cleanliness and beauty are divine and limitless.

In this context, Schumacher has talked of meta-economics (beyond economics). This is a seminal concept, relating the economic growth to natural resources. "To be able to find wisdom, one has to liberate oneself from greed and envy. The core of wisdom is permanence which is yet another way to live at peace with nature and in the divine dispensation which nobody has the right to destroy because nobody has created it," says the German philosopher.

Metaeconomics

Growth takes place within the nature's resources and world's endowments. Development does not start with products; it starts with people, their education, discipline and affordable technologies without which the resources will remain untapped, latent and without use. Oil, for instance, was under the ground since time immemorial until it was discovered in the early 1930s which has revolutionised transportation and everything else. There are countries, including Japan, which are prosperous without resources, including oil, and also the countries which have plenty of resources but they are poor, like the countries in Africa. (or back home, Orissa and Jharkhand).

Sustainable growth is Gandhian

Technology is application of knowledge to the practical aims of human life for changing or manipulating the environment. Technology includes use of materials, tools, techniques and sources of power to make life easier or more pleasant and work more productive. Whereas science is concerned with how and why things happen, technology makes things happen. Technology accelerated the Industrial Revolution and the substitution of machines for animal and human labour. Accelerated technological development has also had costs, in terms of air and water pollution and other harmful environmental effects.

However, the problem with technology is that it does not recognise any limit in terms of size, speed or violence. It is not self-balancing or sustainable, a term which is used to suggest the 'wise' use of technology. It is the use of just enough resource which can renew itself because the lifestyle, which is based on limitless expansion of demand far beyond the capacity of finite resources and limited world's endowment, will harm the world beyond redemption. The idea of unlimited economic growth (until everybody has everything) is to be studied in the context of basic resources available for use and the capacity of the environment to cope with the waste (including greenhouse gases such as carbon dioxide). The greenhouse effect is trapping of the sun's heat in the earth's lower atmosphere due to the greater exposure of the atmosphere to visible radiation from the Sun than to infrared radiation coming from the planet's surface.

Gandhiji said, "The Earth has enough for our needs but not for our greed." This was the view shared by John Maynard Keynes, an economist who provided a solution to the European inflation in the 1930s. He condemned 'frenzy of greed' and the powerful human drive for selfishness. "When I see humans recklessly damaging the environment for unsustainable growth, I reach for my Bible to pray that the deluge may not happen again," he said.

Seven billionth baby born

Baby Nargis Yadav, born on October 31, 2011, in Dauraha village on the outskirts of Lucknow, was officially declared in India to be the seven billionth citizen of the world. For the world that Nargis has been born into is in a real sense a very different planet from that in which her counterparts in the more materially advanced countries had their births. Our common globe has long been divided into at least three different planets: the developed First World, the developing Second World and the

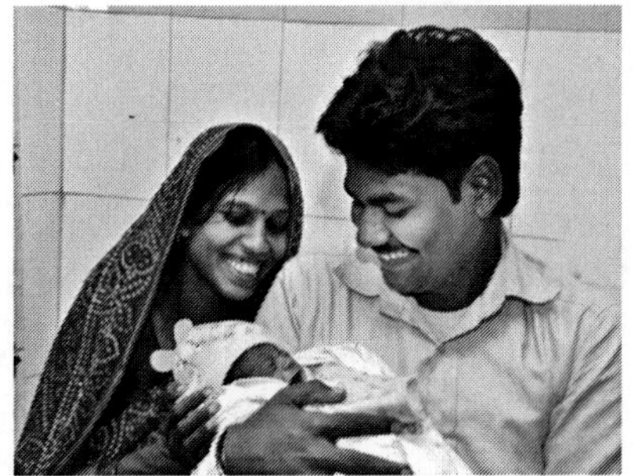

Parents fondling the world's seven billionth baby girl, Nargis, born in a Lucknow suburb on October 31, 2011

underdeveloped Third World. There may even be Fourth and Fifth Worlds, represented by communities so marginalised by mainstream populations that they barely, if at all, register on the radar of our consciousness.

The differentiation of the Earth into separate planets, separate Worlds with separate numbers assigned to them – First, Second, Third etc – is best illustrated by the case of the US, which is the leader and role model of the so-called First World. With a population of some 312 million people, it is the world's third most populous country, after China and India whose populations are 1.3 billion and 1.2 billion respectively. In terms of population size, China and India are obviously way ahead of the US; in terms of the consumption of resources, however, India and China, and other residents of the Second and Third Worlds, are just as obviously way, way behind.

Americans constitute about 5 per cent of the global population but consume 24 per cent of the world's energy. One American is said to consume as much energy as six Mexicans, 13 Chinese, 31 Indians, 128 Bangladeshis, 307 Tanzanians and 370 Ethiopians. With seven billion people and still growing, the world is getting dangerously overcrowded with the increasing inequalities in accessing the world's non-renewable resources. The problem is not population growth alone; the problem is – and long has been – the plundering of the Earth's resources to benefit the First World at the expense of the other, lesser Worlds which are seen as colonised planets to be exploited for their natural wealth, which includes the wealth of their growing markets with their capacity to absorb goods and services produced by the First World. The only non-depleting – in fact, ever increasing – resource that Earth has is its population, its people and the human potential they represent.

According to eminent columnist Jug Suraiya, at the time of Buddha, the global population was under 100 million; when Christ was born it was 170 million; when Newton discovered gravity it was 545 million. Statistically speaking, with its population of seven billion, the Earth today has the human potential to produce many Buddhas, many Christs, many Newtons, and many Shakespeares. All of whom will remain unknown and unrecognised because they are born as children of the lesser Worlds, lesser in terms of access to nutrition, health care, education and the most basic of civic amenities, including drinking water and sanitation.

The inequality and the consequent poverty perpetuate themselves. To avert this situation, Schumacher had advocated technologies 'with humane face.' He also developed the concept of intermediate technologies, specially for the developing countries. (He was the chairman-founder of the Intermediate Technology Group which was an extension on the Luddite Movement launched in the UK during 1811-16 to oppose new technologies which created joblessness, Great Plague, insanitation and city slums (Ned Ludd was hanged along with many of his supporters).

Gandhiji has said the poor of the world cannot be helped by mass production but only by production by the masses. The system of mass production, based on sophisticated, high energy and capital-intensive technology, presupposes that we are all rich and our environmental resources are limitless. But, the system of production by the masses mobilises the priceless resources which are possessed by human beings – their clever brains and skilful hands. The technology of mass production is inherently violent, ecologically damaging, self-defeating in terms of non-renewable resources and stultifying for human beings. The technology of production by the masses, making use of the best of modern knowledge and experience, is compatible with the laws of ecology, gentle in its use of scarce resources, and designed to serve man instead of making him the servant of machines. "I have named it intermediate technology to signify that it is vastly superior to the primitive technology of bygone ages but at the same time much simpler, cheaper, and freer than the super-technology of the rich. One can also call it self-help technology, or people's technology – technology which everybody can acquire and which is not reserved only for the rich and powerful," says Schumacher.

To find such technology is, however, not easy. It is more difficult to be direct and simple than to be sophisticated and complex. Any engineer or researcher can increase complexity; but it takes a real insight to make things simple, affordable, and appropriate. This does not come easily to people who are alienated from the ground realities, productive work and from the self-balancing system of nature. Any activity which fails to recognise a self-limiting principle of nature is dangerous. In the developing countries, poverty is the greatest limitation.

A man who can see tomorrow

To be true, Dr. Pathak is the man who could see tomorrow with incredible prescient view of the future; he could see things before they happen, not by divine gift, magic or logical deduction but by a study of processes of change in a crusted and traditional society like India's which is structured on centuries of social prejudices. As a sociologist, he could also know why other movements failed. For instance, Dr. Pathak could foresee that abolition of manual scavenging, however cruel and inhuman, would not be possible without a viable alternative to it. And, thus, came Sulabh two-pit technology which immediately became socially and culturally acceptable. Dr. Pathak's assumption is that as long as there is a demand, there will be supply; technology will cut off the demand and the supply of scavengers will dry up. And, it did, as is evident in the diminishing number of manual scavengers.

Slavery in America was necessitated because slaves were needed to grow cotton in the South. If there were a technology to grow cotton, slavery would not have been necessary at all. And, when technology was found, slavery ended and the US founded a country, Liberia, in 1822 on the western coast of Africa to rehabilitate the American slaves. And most of those who did not go to Liberia were settled in the marshy land of the Mississippi delta, many of whom died in the Katrina cyclone in July, 2005. They are the third or fourth generations of American slaves who have lost their home and country (Slavery was abolished in Morocco as late as in 1970 when this backward country found a technology. Americans abolished it in 1864). Women's liberation in Europe became possible also only because of technology. Invention of pressure cooker, dishwashing machine, and other domestic gadgets left enough time for women to come out in streets and demand liberation which came but not before the first quarter of the last century (In Switzerland, the most advanced country, women got vote as late as in 1971.)

Sulabh is a new social construct in Gandhian image

Dr. Pathak, like Schumacher, is an avid reader of history and through analysis of historical process, he has concluded that untouchability has lasted far too long to be acceptable now. And, this primitive practice cannot stand the impact of Western ideals of liberalism, equality and democracy – the concepts which mark out the new age from the old. Dr. Pathak never tires of telling that the Bourbons of France and the tsars of Russia would have stood the impact of revolutions in their countries if they had accepted the dominant ideas of their times. In any case, social prejudices and values also have time-limit after which they go out of practice. Kingship, feudalism, slavery, women's serfdom, zamindari system, communism and capitalism had their days. Now, they are lost in the silence of history. Sulabh sets up a social model, inclusive and free from prejudices, and based on modern education of science, mathematics and reasoning. Like Voltaire, Dr. Pathak says, anything that cannot be rationally proved does not exist. Anything which is immoral cannot be legal.

We live in an extraordinary time where none of these old ideas and practices are acceptable. The tired old world does not interest us; we suffer from fatigue syndrome. Ours is the world of ideas. And, ideas are changed, finessed and rejected. Change is the only unchanging truth of life. Dr. Pathak's slogan is 'change and win.' To be ahead of new ideas is the only way to survive and grow. He says this is the world of winners not losers. It is no new discovery, but that he has initiated a movement to bring about change at the grassroots level is his major contribution to the social dynamics of our times. The Sulabh strategy has been of social aggregation (not segregation) which unites people of all persuasions on a comprehensive human relationship basis and not on professional and economic groups. This is sought to be done by persuading the distinguished persons, notables, grandees and known faces to associate themselves with Sulabh.

The Sulabh Founder and Schumacher believe in meta-economics, peaceful change, use of intermediate technologies and empowering the poor to abolish poverty. Both believe in the Gandhian philosophy of 'production by masses and not mass production;' both say that Buddha was the greatest thinker of all times who said everyone should plant a tree in a year; both support Buddha's slogan 'Grow with nature, the best is yet to be' and oppose the dictatorship of economics, dividing human life into consumption and production. They say that infinite growth of material consumption in a finite world is an impossibility and that man, not technology, is central to the divine dispensation in which alone life is worth living. They interpret human behaviour differently to be relevant for all times to come.

Fear of global collapse

Sanitation is a measure of growth and happiness and there are no quick fixes for good sanitation; it involves changing of attitude, re-prioritising growth items, new laws and new technology. Sanitation is very closely related to the environment and if we don't preserve the environment, it may lead to global collapse. Dylan Evans of the University of West England writes: “It is possible that global civilisation might collapse within our lifetime or that of our children’s. Until recently, such an idea was the preserve of lunatics and cults. However, an increasing number of intelligent and credible people have been warning that global collapse is a genuine possibility. And many of them are sober scientists, including Lord May, David King and Jared Diamond – people not given to exaggeration or drama.” Among the causes are climate change, resource depletion and population explosion. Many of these dangers are interrelated, with one tending to exacerbate the others. Overuse of resources, for instance, leads to biodegradation which, in turn, will lead to a series of consequences. And, finally, to collapse.

Many societies – from the Maya in Mexico to the Polynesians of Easter Island – had collapsed in the past, because of the very same dangers that threaten us today. As scientist Diamond explains in his book, *Collapse,* the Mayans destroyed one of their principal resources – trees – and this triggered a series of problems such as soil erosion, decrease in usable farmland, and drought. The growing population that drove this overexploitation of resources was, thus, faced with a diminishing amount of food, which led to increasing migration and bloody civil war.

The collapse of the civilisation on Easter Island (near West Chile) followed a similar pattern, with deforestation leading to other ecological problems and civil war. Unlike these dead societies, our civilisation is global. On the positive side, globalisation means that when one part of the world gets into trouble, it can appeal to the rest of the world for help as in tsunami cyclone. Neither the Mayans nor the inhabitants of Easter Island had this luxury because they were isolated civilisations. On the negative side, globalisation means that when one part of the world gets into trouble, the trouble can quickly be exported to other parts. If modern civilisation collapses, it will happen everywhere. Everyone now stands or falls together.

Global collapse would probably still follow the same basic pattern as a local collapse but on a greater scale. With the Mayans, the trouble began in one region but engulfed the whole civilisation. Today, as climate change makes some areas less hospitable than others, increasing numbers of people will move to the more habitable areas. The increasing population will make them less habitable and lead to further migration in a domino effect. Huge movements of people and capital will put the international financial system under strain and may cause it to give way. In his book *The Future of Money,* Belgian economist Bernard Lietaer argues that the global monetary system is already unstable. Financial crises have certainly grown in scale and frequency over the past decade. The South-East Asian crisis of 1994 was followed by the Russian crash of 1998 and the Brazilian crisis of 1999. This is another example of the way globalisation can exacerbate rather than minimise the risk of total collapse.

Yet another planet needed for China and India!

Schumacher and Dr. Pathak's views are confirmed by the Washington-based Worldwatch Institute's *'State of the World Report-2006'* which says that the Earth lacks the energy, arable land and water to enable populous and fast-growing China and India to attain Western levels of resource consumption.

The Worldwatch Institute says booming China and India, once sleepy backwaters in the world economy, are becoming not only economic powers, but "planetary powers that are shaping the global biosphere" and affecting world economic policies. The economic miracles in China and India masked severe air and water pollution crises in those countries, while demand for resources spurred surging worldwide oil and commodity prices. "The world's ecological capacity is simply insufficient to satisfy the ambitions of China, India, Japan, Europe and the US as well as the aspirations of the rest of the world in a sustainable way," says the 244-page report. If China and India, each with more than a billion people, were to match by 2030 the per capita use of resources of Japan, "together they would require a full planet Earth to meet their needs," it says. Per capita oil consumption in China and India is, respectively, one-fifteenth and one-thirtieth that of the US. To attain half of US consumption levels would cause the two countries to use 100 million barrels per day, more than 2005's total daily world consumption of 85 million barrels, it says.

Sketching a similar trajectory for grain consumption, the report says that, with their shrinking and environmentally stressed farmland, China and India will buy more grain abroad, driving up prices for consumers. The report says, the United States, with 4.5 per cent of the world's population consuming a vastly outsized share of world resources, needs to embrace China and India as decision-makers in global efforts to pursue sustainable energy.

However, this will not be the end of the world. The collapse of modern civilisation would entail the deaths of billions of people but not the end of the human race. Some Mayans survived the collapse by abandoning their cities and retreating into the jungle, where they continue to live to this day. In the same way, some of us would survive the end of the industrial age by reverting to a pre-industrial lifestyle. The enormity of such a scenario makes it hard to imagine the extent of destruction and loss. It is human nature to assume that the world will carry on much as it has been. But it is worth remembering that in the years preceding the collapse of their civilisation, the Mayans too were convinced that their world would last forever. But, it did not.

But what has sanitation to do with global collapse? Yes, it has; sanitation is a generic term which includes trees, land, water, flora and fauna and their interrelationship in clean and healthy manners. A study of all these is also part of sanitation. And, that is the area of Sulabh study. And, in this context, Schumacher's little book and

Dr. Pathak's movement become relevant. Both advise growth mania to be restrained. For instance, if the rest of the world has to have the American level of consumption, we have to find one more planet. Since, that is not possible, we have to learn to live at peace with nature. That is what Schumacher and Dr. Pathak advise us to do so that the human race may last forever.

Dr. Pathak is a Schumacher of India and a Gandhiji reborn. The technologies he has invented for sanitation have a humane face, peaceful and renew the nature's resources and make them sustainable. The Sulabh Movement leads to economic growth as well as meta-economics.

> *"At the social level of providing a common medium of communication in India, the English language has succeeded. English is no threat to Hindi; both can grow together."*
>
> *– Jawaharlal Nehru*

CHAPTER 21

The English Language and Social Reforms

It paved the way for Indian renaissance

The British rule, for all its fault, did more good than is often understood and always denied with lots of justification. The British slave trade cannot be disclaimed anymore than the Irish potato famine and Amritsar massacre. Or, Churchill's hubris of wanting to erase out Gandhiji from history. However, when Nehru decided to adopt English as interstate language of communication, a right choice was made. Knowledge of English is an enabling tool to larger choices in life.

The Sulabh Founder, Dr. Bindeshwar Pathak, sought ways to reach his message across the globe and found that, along with Indian languages, he should also encourage English which has become the most widely spoken language in the world. His search has a historical context. The media caused the Arab uprising in 2011 which overthrew despots. Similar things happened during the Reformation, nearly 500 years ago, when Martin Luther and his allies took the new media of their day – pamphlets, folksongs and paintings – and circulated them through social networks to promote their message of religious reform. Thus, the media split Christianity into two – Catholics and Protestants.

From Martin Luther to Sulabh

The start of the Reformation is usually dated to Luther's nailing of his '95 Theses' on the Power and Efficacy of Indulgences' to the church door in Wittenberg on October 31, 1517. The '95 Theses' were propositions written in Latin that he wished to discuss, in the academic custom of the day, in an open debate at the university. Luther, then an obscure theologian was outraged by the behaviour of Johann Tetzel, a Dominican friar, who was selling indulgences to raise money to fund the pet project of his boss, Pope Leo X – the Reconstruction of St. Peter's Basilica in Rome.

The media environment, that Luther had shown himself so adept at managing, had much in common with today's online ecosystem of blogs, social networks and discussion threads. It was a decentralised system whose participants took care of distribution, deciding collectively which messages to amplify through sharing and recommendation. Modern media theorists refer to participants in such systems as a 'networked public', rather than an 'audience', since they do more than just consume information. Luther would pass the text of a new pamphlet to a friendly printer (no money changed hands) and then wait for it to ripple through the network of printing centres across Germany.

Dr. Pathak knew that the media alone could take his movement across the people. Hence, he also encouraged use of English. The social media are not unprecedented; rather, they are the continuation of a long tradition. Modern digital networks may be able to do it more quickly, but even 500 years ago the sharing of media used to play a supporting role in precipitating a revolution. Today's social media systems do not just connect us to each other; they also link us to the past. Dr. Pathak knew that the media alone could take his idea across to become a global movement today. Hence, he has encouraged the use of the English language, though he never studied in any English medium school, nor had he any English upbringing. He is a home-grown movement leader but good at the English language.

Language is the reflection of a civilisation. It is the medium through which people formulate and express their ideas. To be true, the evolution of a language mirrors the development of society. If there is any language that symbolised ancient India, it was Sanskrit. Today, we tend to think of Sanskrit as a static language, mainly for religious ceremonies, rather like Latin is used in Roman Catholic countries of Europe. However, in ancient times, Sanskrit was a vibrant language, used for activities ranging from poetry and drama to science, philosophy, law and mathematics. It was successful because over the centuries, it underwent enormous changes in order to accommodate evolving intellectual and social requirements.

Sanskrit was part of a continuum of mutually intelligible dialects. Sanskrit was merely the formal end of the spectrum, also used for legal, academic and administrative purposes, besides being the medium of formal religion and high literature. At the other end of the spectrum were various Prakrits spoken in everyday life. Their very names tell the story – Sanskrit literally means cultured or perfected while Prakrit means natural. Sanskrit was not an isolated and ring-fenced tongue but was a part of a larger milieu.

Sanskrit was constantly evolving. The ancient Sanskrit of *the Rig Veda* (compiled in the third millennium BC) was in many ways closer to ancient Iranian rather than to the language of the epics, *the Ramayana* and *the Mahabharata* (probably composed between 1000 and 800 BC). In turn, the language and vocabulary of the great epics are very different from those used by Kalidasa during the Gupta empire of the 3rd to 5th century AD. Throughout these centuries, Sanskrit happily absorbed new words and usages from other languages, including ancient Dravidian, Munda and probably even Greek. Many Sanskrit words, appearing in modern Dravidian languages including Tamil, are probably ancient Tamil words. In fact, the Sanskrit language had been evolving in so many directions that from time to time it had to be standardised by grammarians like

Panini in the 5th century BC and Patanjali in the 2nd century BC.

Unfortunately, over the centuries, the guardians of the language became increasingly preoccupied with the purity of form and vocabulary. More and more grammars were written and the rules became an end in themselves. The language stopped absorbing new words and ideas. Eventually Sanskrit was killed by overregulation. Contrast this with the fate of the unregulated Prakrit dialects that continue to thrive today as modern Indian languages like Hindi, Gujarati, Marathi, Assamese, and Bengali. Clearly internal over-regulation proved to be far more deadly than foreign domination. Sanskrit reflected the ideas of medieval India.

Unfortunately, the intellectual and political leaders of medieval India became increasingly obsessed with regulating everything. There were rules for castes, rules about food, rules for professions, rules for religious rituals, rules for crossing the seas, and rules about auspicious time. Rules, rules, rules. Some of these rules have ancient origins but they increasingly became obsessive. Consequently, India closed off its mind and regulated itself into centuries of decline. The Muslim rule only added additional layers of rules. This was the milieu in place when the British embarked on their conquest of India. This over regulation created the caste system which was a critical reason for the defeat almost in all battles fought since Kalinga in Ashoka times. It was only in the early 19th century that this web of social and intellectual regulation began to relax. But then the country was already in the iron grip of the British control.

The reawakening

The Portuguese were the first Europeans to establish trading posts in India. They were followed by many other Europeans – the Dutch, the French, the Danish and the British. However, till the mid-18th century, these were no more that tiny enclaves. This changed after the British East India Company conquered Bengal in the Battle of

Plassey in 1757. However, the British may have conquered India for their own commercial or imperial purposes but they did have a very positive long-term impact on India's 'wounded civilisation' by introducing India to modern institutions and science through the English language. Most importantly, they created an environment in which a number of remarkable individuals were able to set about unshackling the Indian mind and relaxing social control.

A language of traders

English came to India with European ships, and for much of the 17th and 18th centuries, it was seen mainly as a port language, a tongue spoken among merchants. In fact, English was just one part of '*Firangi*', a pidgin tongue, Indians used to communicate with foreign traders which was a blend of Hindustani, Portuguese, French, Dutch and English. For a long time, few people used English exclusively, and even as the East India Company expanded its power across India, company officials kept Portuguese dictionaries and Persian translators by their side to help them communicate.

One reason, the East India Company did not force the English language in India was, as the historian Nicholas Ostler has noted, Britain's loss of a major colony in the Americas. In India, this loss was felt especially great. Lord Cornwallis, Governor-General of Bengal (1786 to 1793), had arrived in India after his defeat by the Americans, having surrendered to George Washington at Yorktown in 1781 after which Britain was convinced that would result in the collapse of its empire. It was, therefore, especially wary about bringing English to India, and one Governor-General remarked that educating Indians in English would result in the British getting kicked out in three months. This became true later because most freedom fighters, including Gandhiji, Nehru, Patel, and Subhash Chandra Bose had first class English education in England which had also become the meeting ground of Indian leaders.

English used as change agent

Perhaps the most important of these early reformers were Rammohan Roy and Ishwar Chandra Vidyasagar, both Bengalis who lived in the first half of the 19th century. By this time, the glories of ancient India were almost forgotten. If the great works of Aryabhatta, Charaka and the Vedic philosophers were not entirely lost, it was because they were learned by rote generation after generation by the families, mostly in Maharashtra, many of whom did not know the meaning of the epics. They did it without award or money and without knowing their meaning. The disintegration of the Mughal empire left the country in chaos during the 18th century when Rammohan Roy and Vidyasagar set about reconstructing the Indian civilisation from ashes.

Rammohan Roy was fluent in several languages, including Bengali, Hindi, Arabic, Persian and Sanskrit but he realised that a true renaissance would only be possible if the country was provided with a means to access the new ideas emanating from the West. Therefore, he fought for the introduction of English in Indian schools and for the teaching of 'modern' subjects like human anatomy and mathematics.

The importance of the English language in reawakening India cannot be overstated. The language played a very important role in not just opening the country to new ideas but in the rediscovery of its past. For the first time since the decline of Sanskrit, did educated Indians have a common language to talk to each other on intellectual matters. It may be noted that the English language played a critical role in freedom struggle also. Liberal ideas also came to India through this language.

Vidyasagar was one of the first products of the new approach to learning. He came to Calcutta (now Kolkata) from a remote village to study at the newly opened Sanskrit College in 1829. Over the next few years, he taught himself the ancient Sanskrit texts as well as English and Hindi. Having imbibed the spirit of renaissance, he made major contributions in areas ranging from women's rights and education to Indian language publications. He set up schools for girls and helped found Calcutta University, the subcontinent's first modern university, in 1857.

Rammohan Roy and Ishwar Chandra Vidyasagar were followed by a series of brilliant reformers including Dadabhai Naoroji, Gazulu Chetty, Madhav Ranade and Swami Vivekanand. They all were the products of the new education system and lived in the 'British' cities of Madras, Calcutta and Bombay. The old 'Indian' cities of Delhi, Hyderabad and Lucknow produced few reformers. Most importantly, these 19th century reformers were all very conscious of the need of a wider civilisational reawakening. Over the next century, their idea of cultural modernisation led the Independence movement. Note that throughout this period, the country's intellectual leadership continued to emphasise the need for innovation and cultural openness. Rammohan Roy's intellectual successor, Nobel laureate Rabindranath Tagore, wrote this famous poem in his Gitanjali collection published in 1913:

Where the Mind is Without Fear

Where the mind is without fear and the head is held high;
Where knowledge is free;
Where the world has not been broken up into fragments by narrow domestic walls;
Where words come out from the depth of truth;
Where tireless striving stretches its arms towards perfection;
Where the clear stream of reason has not lost its way into the dreary desert sand of dead habit;
Where the mind is led forward by thee into

Rabindranath Tagore – an icon of the Indian culture and civilisation

ever-widening thought and action–
Into that heaven of freedom, my Father,
let my country awake.

English education was the catalyst

The introduction of English education changed the whole cultural life of India. The joint activities of David Hare and Raja Rammohan Roy resulted in the foundation of the Hindu College in 1817. The object of the college was to impart education to the sons of respectable Indians in English and in Indian languages, and also in the literature and sciences of Europe. A year later a zealous trio of Baptist missionaries – Carey, Marshman and Ward – founded the Serampore College for propagating Christianity. In 1830, another college was started by Alexander Duff. These private enterprises soon attracted the government's attention. A government proclamation was issued in 1844 which opened up prospects of profitable employment for those who succeeded at an examination which involved an acquaintance with the works of Bacon, Johnson, Milton, Shakespeare, and others. *Pari passu* with this educational movement there appeared, as its offshoot, journals and clubs on the English model. *The Gyananneshi* (the pursuer of knowledge) was published by Dakshinaranjan Majumdar and Rasik Krishna Mullick, two Hindu College students of Henry Derozio.

English triggered social reforms

While Raja Rammohan Roy was spreading education through the English language, he was distressed to find in 1823 that the government had decided to found a new college for Sanskrit studies to impart such knowledge as was already current in India. Such schools, he felt, could only load the minds of the youth with grammatical niceties and metaphysical distinctions of no practical use. The pupils there would acquire what was known two thousand years ago "with the addition of vain and empty subtleties since then produced by speculative men". Raja Rammohan Roy pointed out that Sanskrit was a difficult language and that almost a lifetime was necessary for acquiring its knowledge. He said: "In 1834 when Thomas Babington Macaulay became the President of the Committee of Public Instruction, it was divided between anglicists and orientalists. The anglicists wanted to train a class of clerks and others who would become loyal government servants and docile executants of the English will. The orientalists, on the other hand, feared that the spread of English education would offend the sensibilities of the Indian upper classes and may even lead to resistance".

Sanskrit scholar welcomed English

The orientalists were partly Brahminised and they could hardly be expected to help in an attempt to Westernise the Brahmins. One conspicuous exception to this was Ishwar Chandra Vidyasagar (1820-91) who became the Principal of the Sanskrit College in 1851. Though Vidyasagar was a Sanskrit scholar he, like Raja Rammohan Roy, welcomed English education, saying, "That *the Vedanta* and *Sankhya* are false systems of philosophy is no more a matter of dispute. These systems, false as they are, command reverence from the Hindus. While teaching these in the Sanskrit course, we should oppose them by sound philosophy in the English course to counteract their influence."

Macaulay, who arrived from England when he was only thirty-four, had little knowledge of the Indian languages but he unhesitatingly decided in favour of the anglicists. In his *"Minute on Education",* while supporting the anglicists, he used many of the arguments and even some of the phraseology of Raja Rammohan Roy. "I have no knowledge", he stated, "of either Sanskrit or Arabic.

But it is no exaggeration to say that all the historical information which has been collected from all the books written in the Sanskrit language is less valuable than what may be found in the most paltry abridgements used at preparatory schools in England… How, then, stands the case... We must teach them some foreign language." As a result of this minute the anglicists had their way. "Thereafter the wave of Western learning was poured into the old bottle of Hinduism which went into the heads of young Bengal", wrote Earl of Ronaldshay, once Governor of Bengal, in *Heart of Aryavarta.* No wonder protest writings first began in Bengal.

Macaulay sought to produce British clones

Macaulay, who was largely responsible for the introduction of English education in India, sought to train a class of persons who would be "Indian in blood and colour, but English in taste, opinion, words and intellect". It was also his hope that the introduction of English education would result in the destruction of Hinduism and their large-scale conversion to Christianity. "It is my firm belief", he wrote, "that if our plans of education are followed up, there will not be a single idolater among the respectable classes of Bengal thirty years hence. And this will be done without efforts to proselytise; without the smallest interference with religious liberty but merely by the natural operation of knowledge and reflection".

Such was also the hope of Sir Charles Trevelyan, a member of the Committee of Public Instruction and brother-in-law of Macaulay. Trevelyan believed that the introduction of Western education would "shake Hinduism and Mohammedanism to their centre and firmly establish our language and learning and ultimately our religion in India". As a result of British rule, India suffered a long process of exploitation, but India also came into contact with the scientific and industrial West. Europe had its scientific lamps ablaze when it came to India. "We must light up torches at its wick", said Rabindranath

Tagore. Similarly, Nehru welcomed science for "its capacity to transform an economy of scarcity into one of abundance", and for countering the forces of superstition and tradition.

Imperial approach

"We must at present do our best to form a class of persons, Indian in blood and colour, but English in taste, in opinions, in morals, and in intellect." With these words, spoken in 1835, Lord Macaulay crystallised an imperial approach to the English language that unfortunately continues to work to its detriment today. The old resentments about English being the language of the ruling classes, the old accusations about it being an imposition that dilutes our cultural ethos, continue to be political currency.

No wonder we have some leaders proposing a ban on English in Indian schools. But there is a disconnect between the section of the political class that denigrates English, and the aspirations of India's burgeoning middle class and the poor. Such English-baiting politicians are playing to a constituency that is diminishing by the day. The English language is both an aspirational ideal and a practical tool that propels economic empowerment. The people have realised this even if some politicians have not.

Little wonder that English medium schools have proliferated in slums and rural areas, or that politicians who have no compunctions about employing the rhetoric of linguistic chauvinism send their children to English medium schools. West Bengal tried to cut back on English in schools two decades ago but had to backtrack when the move was seen as contributing to the state's backwardness. Meanwhile, China is moving ahead with comprehensive initiatives to teach English to Chinese children from a young age in an attempt to win a greater share of the outsourcing pie.

The idea that English education fosters elitism has been an influential one. But the way to deal with this is not by restricting the number of English speakers even more. The elite has the means to get access to English, come what may. Locking the underprivileged out would be tantamount to reinforcing their lack of privilege. Let's build on what most of us acknowledge that knowledge of English can provide access to better jobs, or even raise one's income in one's present occupation. The poor save in order to send their wards to schools that teach English. Implicit in this is an intuitive recognition that knowledge of English can offer an escape route from poverty.

None of this is, however, to suggest that local languages should be ignored. Our richest cultural expressions can continue to be in these languages, and our educational institutions should do all they can to facilitate this. But there's no reason why multiple languages can't co-exist. Indeed, they have done so since time immemorial in this country. English is just a practical skill, a tool of empowerment which will help everyone access the world of commerce and opportunity.

Gokhale also supported English teaching

English education was associated with English rule, but later when the nationalist movement developed and English rule was sought to be liberalised by the moderates, they yet continued to welcome such education. In December 1903, Gokhale, a moderate leader said, "In the present circumstances of India all Western education is valuable and useful". In 1913 Pandit Bishan Narayan Dhar, another moderate leader said, "Books like Lecky's *History of Rationalism and European Morals,* Guizot's *History of Civilisation,* Maine's *Ancient Law, Spencer's*

Gopal Krishna Gokhale

Study of Sociology, Mill's *Liberty and Representative Government,* Sir Alfred Lyell's *Asiatic Studies,* Morley's *Compromise,* Bagehot's *Physics and Politics, and* Seeley's *Expansion of England Lectures in Political Science* ought to form part of every undergraduate's private studies." And one of the major criticisms by the moderates of the prevailing system of education was that it paid insufficient attention to instruction in Western science and technology.

Even the extremists, who were not as enthusiastic for Western education as the moderates, and who were interested in establishing a system of national education, did not want to banish Western science and culture altogether from national schools. The object of the National Council of Education, which was started in Bengal during the pre-Partition days, was to impart education on national lines and exclusively under national control, attaching special importance to the country's literature, history, and philosophy, but "designed to incorporate in the best oriental ideals of life and thought the best assailable ideals of the West".

Reaction to English teaching in India

Lala Lajpat Rai also denounced those who believed that national education could only be based on a total rejection of modern Western thought. Indians, he said, could not completely replace modern medicine and surgery by old Indian medical methods and allow thousands to die in order that they might remain truly national; in military matters, it would have been disastrous for Indians to rely for their defence on the bows and arrows, swords and spears, and to refuse to learn the modern science of arms; in economics, they would remain ignorant if they only studied the old *Arthashastras* and

Lala Lajpat Rai

neglected the newer and fuller *Arthashastras* written by European thinkers; in law they would be taking a retrograde step if they took the laws of Manu, Narada, and Apastamba as their guides and rejected all the laws of modern India which were more in harmony with the spirit of the times.

In the early days of English education, Western ideas had the romance of the new thing and their introduction demolished everything old. Westernism demanded of its votaries that they should ignore the civilisation of their own country. The more the admiration for everything Western, the more vehement was the denunciation of everything Eastern. But the borrowed culture of the West was only half assimilated. Students in the college halls of Calcutta and Bombay openly derided the faith of the ancient sages but were inwardly uneasy. There was an intellectual conversion to Western doctrines but without a foundation of faith. No wonder, criticism of Indian religions created opposition. The indiscriminate attacks of some Christian missionaries on Indian way of life and thought brought about a return to Vedantism. The attacks were so outrageous that in the first decade of the 19th century the then Governor-General (Lord Minto) ordered confiscation of Christian propaganda leaflets on the ground that without arguments of any kind they were filled with hell fire and still better fire against a whole race of men merely for believing in the religion which they were taught by their fathers and mothers and the truth of which, it is impossible, it should have entered into their minds to doubt. In these circumstances a plea was made by Raja Rammohan Roy for the Advaita philosophy which rejected idolatry, caste, and superstitions. Rammohan brought from the ancient storehouse of Hindu thought new weapons to meet the challenge posed by the thought of the 18th century and early 19th century Europe. And he, instead of repudiating the claims of the unseen in the determination of the truth, sought to blend the experiences of the religious and spiritual life of India with the message of social democracy of the French Revolution.

Dalit and English language

Meanwhile, the English language was gaining support from the Dalit community. For the Dalits, English was a language exempt from the restrictive conventions of Indian literature, which was imbued with the traditions of caste and untouchability. Hindu texts were ambiguous at best on the question of education and literacy for the lower castes. At worst, they were outright discriminatory. *The Manusmriti* (Law of Manu), the authoritative Hindu text on India's caste system, said that "molten lead is to be poured into the ears of the low-born" who dare to hear the recital of the written word. As a result, like many of the early Indian reformers, Dalit leaders viewed English as emancipator, free to the smudgy fingerprints of Hindu discrimination and the stigma of 'untouchable' traditions. Dr. B.R. Ambedkar is quoted where he said, "English is the lioness' milk; those who drink will roar like a lion". The Dalits also came to support English as a language that enabled communication across linguistic regions, giving the low castes a 'nationwide solidarity', and enabling their voices to be heard in the public sphere. In the Dalit Movement for social rights, English is playing a unifying role among various castes spread all over the country.

In 2010 the Dalit activist, Chandra Bhan Prasad, started a private school and built a temple dedicated to a new deity, 'Dalit Goddess English'. His supposition was that Dalits, being socially and educationally excluded, should learn English so as to advance. The bronze image of 'Dalit Goddess English' held a pen in one hand and books in the other, and the mantra chanted at her dedication ceremony was 'A-B-C-D'. Prasad believed that only by deifying the English language via the goddess would he be able to persuade low-caste parents to send their children to the new school.

In South India, however, protests erupted in 1965 across Tamil Nadu against the imminent shift to Hindi as the official language. Rallies took place all over South India, and South Indian cabinet ministers threatened to resign unless English was retained. Riots broke out in Tamil Nadu, people burnt effigies of the 'Hindu demoness' and students and members of the Dravida Munnetra Kazhagam (DMK) immolated themselves across the state. Police opened fire on rioting crowds, killing 300 people. In the Legislative Assembly, DMK members made fiery speeches threatening secession. At the same time, pro-Hindi organisations such as the Jan Sangh launched a violent agitation in favour of abolishing English not only in official use but also in shop and street signs and on number plates. The government had thought Hindi would be 'the great unifier', but it turned out that only English would do the job. The Language Act was finally amended in 1967, specifying both English and Hindi as official languages. English has since co-existed with Hindi as the official language, and served as a 'linking language' for the north and the south.

English, however, did not remain an alien tongue for long. The English language absorbed cultural influences, and assimilated an Indian identity with astonishing speed. *The Oxford English Dictionary* first came out in 1884, and by 1886 *the Hobson Jobson Dictionary of Indian English terms* had been released, introducing words such as 'veranda', 'avatar', 'cherrot' and 'typhoon' into the language. The goal of making Indians with "English in tastes, opinions, morals and in intellect" also exposed Indians to the work of European writers and brought them closer to the Western ideas of nationalism, liberty and freedom. Surendranath Banerjee wrote in 1878, "English education has uplifted all who have come under its influence to a common platform of thoughts, feelings and aspirations." This was an unintended result for an imperial tongue.

The English language and the Indian English Press were quickly becoming common ground for the Indian community to exchange ideas and agitate against the British rule. An Indian lawyer had told the British government in its early years, "You cannot talk a person into slavery in the English language," and the British policy soon brought this truth home. During the Congress party's early demands for political representation, they employed the slogan of the 18th century England: 'No taxation without representation.' Which also became the American slogan at Boston Tea Party which demanded freedom. The language did not make Indians more British; instead a shared tongue enabled people from across the kingdom states and British provinces to identify themselves as Indians and unite in resistance. English became the uniter of Indian people divided by language, custom, religion and geography. Critically, English literacy also offered Indians the chance to access the English press. Indians, as a result, became increasingly aware of the struggles for Independence in other countries – the rise of colonies across the world against imperialism, and the surge of European nationalism by the end of the 19th century. The language was offering Indian leaders a window into movements in other countries like theirs.

Language dispute

The three-language formula pitted Indian languages against one another, and states were embroiled in unruly political football. Tamil Nadu's hackles rose up again; its Education Minister, Thiru Thambidurai, declared that the formula was 'an indirect attempt to impose Hindi as a language on the Tamil people'. Both Tamil Nadu and Pondicherry refused to teach Hindi in state schools, and the northern states cheated on the third language requirement by teaching none of the regional languages, opting instead for Sanskrit. The southern states asserted that the regional language should take precedence over English, while to the Hindi-speaking states English was the pretender to the throne, slinking into a national, dominant role that had rightfully belonged to Hindi.

Sulabh focus on English education

Dr. Bindeshwar Pathak believes that language is primarily the medium of communication although it also reflects culture, value system, lifestyle, history and geography – all of which are adequately reflected in its structure, accent, and manners of speech and even in its grammar. But as a language grows, it changes. For instance, the Greek language was never a Romance language, like French, Italian, Portuguese, Romanian and Spanish. But, after Greeks were captured by Romans, the Greek language travelled to Rome, along with booty and Greek mistresses who revolutionalised the way Roman warriors lived and loved. And, thus, a vanquished country became the dominant influence in Roman life. And, quietly the Roman culture became the Greco-Roman civilisation. And, the Greek language was absorbed by Romans to become their own.

Similarly, Dr. Pathak says, no language has a timeless and distinct identity forever. The source languages, including Sanskrit and Latin, produced several languages across the world, but they are not living languages now. But in the case of English, it is not the case. English has never been a pure source language; it is a mixed and mongrel language which evolved as the British Empire expanded to account for one-fifth of the global area during Queen Victoria's time, when English came in contact with many languages, including Hindi, Portuguese, Spanish and French and absorbed many of their words, grammar and spellings. After the British Empire declined and fell following the World War II, English-speaking Americans dominated the post-War world. And, most of the inventions, thought systems, philosophies, technologies and everything that goes into the making of modern world, started in the English-speaking world. No wonder, English is today, the language of science, technology, business and commerce, diplomacy and everything else. And, those who do not know English are likely to be shut out of those areas or remain disenfranchised.

Dr. Pathak says, in seeking to abolish scavenging and finding jobs for liberated scavengers, English helps. For that matter, English is a great facilitator if nothing else. It was with this objective in view, he set up an English medium school in Delhi largely for the children of scavengers and mandated use of English in training centres, including one for liberated women at Alwar who now have the basic knowledge of English, at least enough to operate bank accounts. The logic of the Sulabh Founder is simple: Language is not a patriotism test. In this globalised world, when national boundaries are vanishing, the knowledge of a world language is necessary to join and stay in the global mainstream. And the poor and the disadvantaged people need this language more because English has liberating influence on our lives, bound by age-old customs, rituals, caste system, gender bias and deeply embedded feeling of social prejudices. There is hardly any English-speaking manual scavenger in India.

> *"Who could believe that the founder of modern world would be a British carpenter who invented Spinning-Jenny!"*
>
> *– Edmund Burke*

CHAPTER 22

From Spinning-Jenny to Two-Pit Sulabh Toilet

Both are game-changer technologies

Man has always been searching for new ways to exploit nature and live well. He has succeeded considerably but the mankind is the victim of those successes, some of which don't really serve us. The greenhouse gases are some manifestations to indicate that success has a price tag. Sulabh technologies provide alternatives.

Spinning-jenny and two-pit toilet technologies are among the many which have made substantial impact on the lives of people. Spinning-jenny (1767) marked the beginning of Industrial Revolution while, about two hundred years later (1970), yet another technology of the same seminal genre made a sanitation revolution. The former encouraged setting up and inventing machines while the latter is designed to clean up the mess created by industrialisation, specially in cities whose frightful and unclean living conditions have been described by many writers, including Charles Dickens. Both the innovations arose out of necessity and both of them were developed by chance. James Hargreaves, an illiterate Lancashire carpenter and weaver, saw the spindle rolled down by her daughter, Jenny, and that made him think if there could be more spindles put together to roll out faster and make more money.

Earlier, the invention by an English weaver, John Kay, of the flying shuttle in 1733 accelerated weaving so much that spinners were scarcely able to get supply yarn fast enough to meet the demand. In 1767, James Hargreaves built a machine called the spinning-jenny which advanced the movement towards mass production. Hargreaves first jenny spun yarn on eight spindles simultaneously; a later model had 16 spindles. The spindles were mounted vertically and fed by bobbins containing rovings – loose ropes of fibres. The jennies were worked by hand-turned wheels. In a three-stage operation, the rovings were first drawn out, then twisted and finally wound on to the spindles. Hargreaves patented the jenny in 1770, but the patent was later declared invalid.

However, spinning-jenny was not an overnight invention. Man had been spinning clothes much before the British carpenter found new ways to do it. Spinning was a craft which developed when man began to lead the settled life of a farmer. Sheep were first domesticated in the Zagros region of Mesopotamia (Iraq) and it was easy enough to roll wool into crude yarn for weaving a craft already familiar from basket work. For the first time, people had an alternative to clothing of skins and woollen clothing was much warmer.

In time, spinning-jenny survived until the Middle Ages after which spinning wheel came into use throughout the world. But spinning was still a slow, home-based craft. The more skilful spinner and weavers were employed by merchants to work in their own homes for wages. Richard Arkwright revolutionised spinning when he installed machines in a mill at Cromford, Derbyshire, in 1771 and employed people to work there. Arkwright established the modern factory system and launched the first great manufacturing industry. Samuel Crompton's spinning mule allowed one worker to operate up to 1,000 spindles. By 1812, mules with an output equal to 4 million spinning wheels were in use in Britain alone.

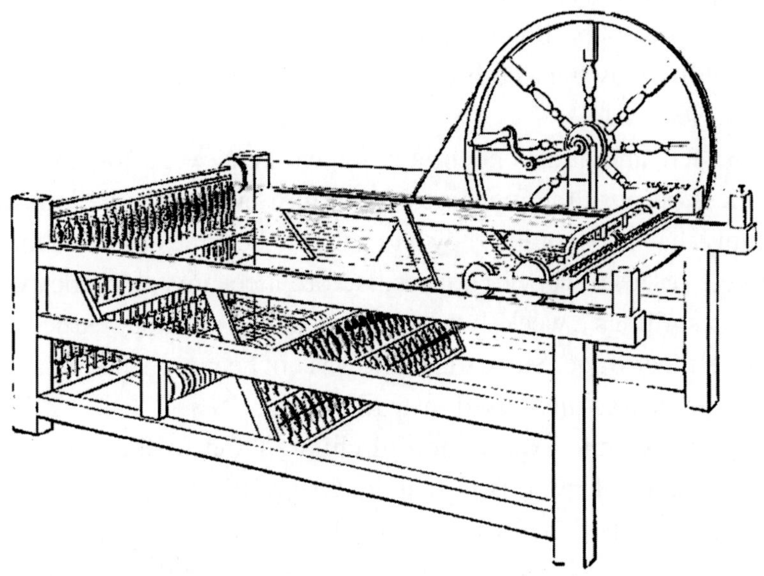

Spinning-Jenny, a simple device that changed the world

Allied inventions

Spinning-jenny triggered off allied inventions, such as the cotton gin to provide the necessary amounts of fibre, and the powerloom to weave the greater quantity of yarn produced. The consequent growth of the cotton industry was phenomenal. The average family could now afford to buy, for example, cotton underclothes which could easily be washed. This led to significant improvement in personal hygiene, health and comfort.

The growth of factories started a shift of population from the villages to towns which, in turn, stimulated development of labour-saving agricultural implements to maintain output. Mill owners set up factories near sources of power, such as flowing water, and later near coalfields. It was near the factories that new towns were hastily built with little thought for comfort, hygiene or sanitation. Mechanisation was bitterly opposed from the start by many textile workers whose livelihood was threatened. Between 1811 and 1816, resentment kept boiling over into large-scale rioting and destruction of machinery by the Luddites – named after their probably mythical leader Ned Ludd.

Skilled and independent textile workers were forced out of business because the machines could turn out yarn and cloth more cheaply than they could. They had either to become unskilled factory workers or go to work in houses. Before mechanisation, they could earn 25 shillings a week, but 18 hours a day in a factory earned them only half that wage. Since the work was not heavy, cheap female and child labour was often used instead of men.

Eventually the exploitation of children and workers in general led to a series of reforms in Britain. One of the most important was the Factory Act of 1833 which banned employment of children under nine, limited working children to an eight-hour day, and ordered factories to provide schooling for them. In the 1800s adult workers banded together and formed unions to fight against exploitation. The rest is a known history.

Sulabh flush compost toilet with superstructure

Sulabh technology: Yet another new idea

The two-pit Sulabh toilet technology also has a story and a very interesting one at that. Like carpenter James Hargreaves, Dr. Bindeshwar Pathak is neither an engineer nor was ever in search of a new technology to make some more money. He was told of a job in the Gandhi Centenary Celebration Committee which he joined in 1968 only to be assigned a job of liberating scavengers by finding ways to do it. A number of organisations and local devices were evolved earlier to dispose of human waste without having to deploy toilet cleaners. These earlier designs included trench latrine, borehole privy, Gopuri-system, *sopa sandas* and simpler still was the one suggested by Gandhiji – *tatti par matti* – (put earth on faeces). But none of these addressed the problem of sanitation adequately and all of them needed services of scavengers. Hence, it was not the kind of technology which Dr. Pathak wanted to develop as a substitute for the tested and established sewerage system.

Two books laid out plan for two pits

As stated in the earlier chapters that it was during this period Dr. Pathak was given two books to read. One published by the World Health Organisation on Excreta Disposal for Rural Areas and Small Communities by two sanitation engineers, Edmund G. Wagner and J.N. Lanoix and another in Hindi by Rajendra Lal Das. The WHO publication was subjected to very close study, and many passages of it left a lasting lifetime impression in young Pathak's mind. "Suffice it to say here that out of the heterogeneous mass of latrine designs produced all over the world, the sanitary pit privy emerges as the most practical and universally applicable type." The WHO publication laid out the following seven conditions to meet the criteria for a sanitary latrine. (Excreta Disposal for Rural

Areas and Small Communities by E.G. Wagner and J.N. Lanoix, WHO, 1958).

1. The surface soil should not be contaminated.
2. There should be no contamination of the groundwater that may enter springs or wells.
3. There should be no contamination of the surface water.
4. Excreta should not be accessible to flies or animals.
5. There should be no handling of fresh excreta. Or when this was indispensable, it should be kept to a strict minimum.
6. There should be freedom from odours or unsightly conditions.
7. The method used should be simple and inexpensive in construction and operation.

These books were like the rolling spindle which made carpenter James Hargreaves to produce spinning-jenny and Industrial Revolution. The technology based on the concept of these books produced the Sulabh Sanitation Movement.

Toilets beyond septic tanks and sewers

In 1970, Dr. Pathak invented, innovated and developed many designs of twin-pit pour-flush toilet and popularised them in the name of Sulabh Shauchalayas. The designs of twin-pit pour-flush toilet can be adopted and adapted for use in different locations. The pits are circular and a minimum of one metre distance has been kept between both the pits to ensure that at the time of cleaning the pit, no water remains at the bottom. There is another design where the two-pits have been separated by the dividing walls, one foot deeper than the other walls, ensuring that the water from the bottom of the pit does not go from one pit to the other, so that the fertiliser is dry. This design is used in an area where there is less space. In the narrow lanes, the pits are kept in single direction and the second pit is connected with the pipe. If there is still less space, then the pan and water seal are placed on the dividing wall itself. Thus in the smallest of places, Sulabh toilets can be constructed, even in the verandah of a house. People can use the covered pit as a pathway, because there is no smell, nor is it visible and no gas pipe is provided.

People prefer using the slab over the pit for various purposes like cleaning foodgrains, cooking food and at times even for offering prayers or even a small shop can be opened on the slab over the pit. This toilet connected with a pipe can even be constructed on an upper floor of a house and can also be constructed where the water table is high. In a high water table area, the upper portion of the pit should be 2 feet above the water table for it to function well. The upper portion of the pit should not be constructed at a par with the water table. Wherever the water supply is through pipelines, there is no chance at all of pollution of water. If the source of water is a tube-well, 15 feet distance from the pits should be maintained. The toilets should be constructed 30 feet away from the open wells. In short, if toilets are constructed with some precautions there is no chance of groundwater pollution.

Sulabh technologies set up new paradigms

Dr. Pathak has thus shifted social service paradigms in many ways. First, he has established that an NGO can earn while serving the people, and remain independent of official dole for survival on one time projects. Sulabh has sanitation network all over the country and abroad, manned by about 60,000 volunters. Second, he has evolved many small, affordable and indigenous technologies to be used at the people's level without much cost, and high level of skill. Dr. Pathak has, thus, proved that social changes are not entirely a social or attitudinal problem, but also of technology. It was the technology and not the civil war, for which Lincoln had to die, that abolished slavery. In the developed countries, the standard practice for the sanitary disposal of human waste is sewerage. Due to exorbitant maintenance and operational costs, sewerage is not the answer to solve the problem of human waste management in India. Sewerage was first introduced in London in 1850, followed by New York in 1860. Calcutta was the next city in the world to have this privilege in 1870, yet out of over 7,935 towns/cities in India only 929 have the sewerage system and that, too, partially and Sewage treatment plants have been installed only in 160 towns. In other towns the untreated sewage is diverted to river, nullah drain etc.

In the developing countries neither the government nor the local authorities, or the beneficiaries can bear the capital, operation and maintenance costs of the sewerage system, which also requires skilled persons. It requires over two gallons of water to clean human excreta. Huge quantity of water is needed to flush it down into an expensive sewerage system into rivers and ponds, most of which are already heavily polluted because of untreated domestic sewage. This has led to deterioration of groundwater aquifers. The septic tank system is also expensive and requires a large volume of water for flushing. There is shortage of drinking water in almost all urban areas; hence water has to be conserved. Septic tank has other problems like periodic cleaning and disposal of sludge. Inadequate effluent disposal leads to foul smell, and mosquito breeding and poses health hazards.

Sulabh technology is eco-friendly

Sulabh two-pit compost toilet technology is eco-friendly, technically appropriate, socio-culturally acceptable and economically affordable. It is an indigenous technology and the toilet can easily be constructed with local materials. It provides health benefits by safe disposal of human excreta on site. It consists of a pan with a steep slope of 25°-28° and an especially designed trap with 20 mm water seal requiring only 1 to 1.5 litre of water for flushing, thus helping conserve water. It does not need scavengers to clean the pits. There are two pits of varying size and capacity depending on the number of users. The capacity of each pit is normally designed for 3 years' usage.

Both pits are used alternately. When one pit is full, the incoming excreta is diverted into the second pit. In about two years, the sludge gets digested and is almost dry and pathogen-free, thus safe for handling as manure. Digested sludge is odourless and is a good manure and soil conditioner. It can be dug out easily and used for agricultural purposes. The cost of emptying the pit can be met partially from the cost of manure made available. Sulabh toilet can also be constructed on the upper floors of buildings. It has a high potential for upgradation, and can later be easily connected to sewers when introduced in the area. Sulabh has so far constructed over a million individual household toilets in different parts of the country.

Sulabh flush compost toilet does not cause water pollution. When constructed in homogeneous soil, horizontally, bacteria do not travel more than 3 metres, and vertically the seepage is not more than 1 metre. To this is to be added the precaution that the toilet is built at a safe distance from the source of water, keeping the above points in mind. If there is a tube well or hand pump sunk, the first joint should be lower than the limit of the vertical seepage.

No vent pipe is needed since the gas gets absorbed in the soil facing the chamber, as the brick lining inside is in lattice formation. The parameters change depending upon the coarseness of the soil and the type of terrain where the

Taking out of manure from the pit of a Sulabh toilet

toilet is being constructed. Depending on the availability of space, the shape of pits may be designed. It may be rectangular, circular or linear in shape. It fulfils all the seven conditions of a sanitary latrine laid down by WHO.

Prevention of pollution

To check pollution of drinking water sources, the pits in fine soils (effective size 0.2 mm or less) should be located at a minimum distance of 3 metres from open wells and shallow hand pumps, provided groundwater table throughout the year is 2 metres or more below the bottom of the pit; if water table is higher, the distance should be increased to 10 metres. In coarser soils (effective size more than 0.2 mm), the same safe distances can be maintained by providing 500 mm thick sand envelope of 0.2 mm sand all round the pit and sealing the pit bottom by some impervious material like puddled clay, polythene sheet, lean cement concrete or cement stabilised soil. Normally bacteria do not move beyond 3 metres horizontally in homogeneous soil and vertically they do not permeate more than 1 metre, however there can be marginal deviations depending upon the types of the soil. It may be noted that chances of groundwater pollution occur due to higher hydraulic load. Since in this system hydraulic load is only 1 to 1.5 litres per use, there is no such chance of groundwater pollution. In water-logged, flood-prone and high subsoil water areas, the pits should be raised so that the invert of pipe or drain is just above the likely water level. The raising of pits will necessitate raising of toilet floor also. Earth should be filled and well compacted all round the pit.

Low-cost and sustainable

The cost of Sulabh flush composting toilets varies widely to suit people of every economic stratum. The cost ranges from US$ 10 to

US$ 1,000 per unit. It depends upon materials of construction of pits and seat as well as of the superstructure. The pits can be constructed with bricks or any locally available materials like stones, woodlogs, burnt clay rings, concrete rings or even used coaltar drums. Similarly, the quality of superstructure ranges from simple gunny bag sheets, or thatch to well finished tiles with R.C.C. roof, doors, wash basin, etc. Cost varies also due to size and capacity of the pits, depending on its capacity for use from 2 to 20 years. Keeping the basic design unchanged, Sulabh has a number of such toilet models for demonstration.

Manure from human excreta

One of the major difficulties for the use of human excreta as manure is the presence of bacterial and other pathogens. Human excreta contains a full spectrum of pathogens causing various infections. It should be free from pathogens before being used as manure. Another problem is psychological/religious taboos associated with it. The studies carried out by Sulabh have revealed that the content of a Sulabh toilet pit is almost free from pathogens when taken out after two years of resting period. To make it completely pathogen-free, digested sludge is sun-dried for 2 to 3 weeks.

During drying of sludge big lumps are formed making it difficult to mix in soil homogeneously. So to granulate such dried lumps into small-size graded granules which look like processed tea leaves, it is processed in a ball mill to break it into small pieces. Then it is passed through the mass mixer where the moisture content of manure is regulated by adding water. Such manure has a good percentage of plant nutrients. Besides, it increases humus and water holding capacity of the soil. Sulabh has carried out experiments to monitor its manurial effects on different vegetables and flowering plants. In all the cases tested, the effect of manure on the growth of plants was very encouraging.

Operation and maintenance

Operation and maintenance of a Sulabh flush compost toilet is very easy and simple:

- Before use, wet the pan by pouring only a little quantity of water.
- After defecation, pour 1 to 1.5 litre of water in the pan for flushing.
- Pour about half litre of water in the pan after urination.
- The pan should be cleaned once a day with a brush or a broom and with soap powder periodically.
- One of the pits is to be used at a time by plugging the drain for the other pit.
- Kitchen, bathroom wastewater or rainwater should not be allowed to enter the pits.
- Other solid wastes like kitchen waste, rags, cotton, sweepings etc. should not be thrown in the pan; this could block the toilet.
- When the first pit in use is full, the flow should be diverted to the second pit and the filled up pit should be desludged after 1.5 to 2-year rest period. The first pit can then be put to reuse, when the second pit fills up.

Sulabh Public Toilet and Bengal Municipal Act 1878*

Provision of the Sulabh public toilet complexes in public places and slums on pay-and-use basis is an important landmark in the field of community health, hygiene and environmental sanitation. Although as far back as 1878, the then Bengal Government had enacted a law to set up toilet facilities in Calcutta, due to many reasons such facilities could not be provided/maintained for the next 100 years. The concept of construction of public toilets and its maintenance on a pay-and-use basis, originated by Sulabh in 1974, was outstandingly

---

**Bengal Municipal Act 1876 as amended in 1878.*

successful throughout the country. For some years the behavioural pattern and attitude of people for not using the public toilets already available in cities/towns was studied. It was felt that the most insanitary and filthy state of public toilets deterred usage. It was felt that along with community toilets, if facilities for bathing and washing clothes could also be provided, maintaining cleanliness all around, people would like to use them and also pay for the use.

In 1978, a national seminar was organised in Patna by the Government of India in collaboration with WHO and UNICEF in which, apart from representatives of the Government of India, Secretaries and Chief Engineers etc. of states participated. In this seminar the system of twin-pit toilets and maintenance of public toilets were discussed and the participants visited households and public toilets to see their functioning.

After a great deal of deliberations, it was unanimously recommended that these two technologies/methodologies be adopted by other states also. The dissemination of information regarding these innovations spread after the seminar and now the technology and its implementation has spread from one local body of Bihar state to 1674 local bodies spread over 26 states and 4 Union Territories of India. Till now more than 8,500 such public toilet complexes have been constructed and are being maintained by Sulabh. One of the biggest public toilet complexes of Sulabh has been constructed at Shirdi, in Nasik district in Maharashtra, having 120 WCs, 108 bathrooms, 28 special toilets (separate for ladies and gents) and 3,000 lockers for the convenience of the pilgrims. Sulabh toilet complexes are located in public places, bus-stands, hospitals, markets and slums. For the construction, operation and maintenance of these complexes, Sulabh plays the role of a catalyst and a partner between official agencies and the users of the toilet complexes. The other bigger toilet complex has been constructed at Pandharpur in Maharashtra which has 1,140 WCs 171, VIP WCs, 350 bathrooms and 136 urinals being used by one lakh people daily.

Toilet-linked biogas plants

Recycling and reuse of human excreta for biogas generation is an important way to get rid of health hazards from human excreta. Sulabh is the pioneering organisation in the field of biogas generation from public toilet complexes. After a series of experiments, the organisation developed a more efficient design of biogas plant that has been approved by the Ministry of Non-conventional Energy Sources, Government of India, for its implementation through state nodal agencies. Human excreta contains a full spectrum of pathogens. Most of these pathogens are eliminated due to anaerobic condition inside the digester. Besides using biogas for different purposes, biogas plant effluent can also be used as manure or discharged safely into any river or water body without causing pollution. Thus biogas technology from human wastes has multiple benefits – sanitation, bioenergy and manure. Based on the 'Sulabh Model' design, 200 biogas plants of 35 to 60 cum capacity have been constructed by Sulabh in different states of the country so far.

Human excreta-based biogas technology remained unnoticed for long due to the fact that the available technology was not socially acceptable, as it required manual handling of human excreta, which contains a full spectrum of pathogens. The design developed by Sulabh does not require manual handling of human excreta and there is complete recycling and resource recovery from the wastes. The digester is built underground into which excreta from public toilets flows under gravity. Inside the digester biogas is produced due to anaerobic fermentation by the help of methanogenic bacteria. The biogas, thus produced, is stored in in-built liquid displacement chamber. One cubic foot biogas is produced from the excreta of one person per day. Human excreta-based biogas contains 65-66 per cent methane, 32-34 per cent carbon dioxide and the rest hydrogen sulphide and other gases in traces.

It prevents greenhouse emission

The Sulabh technology prevents emission of greenhouse gases specially methane. Methane is the only combustible constituent, which is utilised in different forms of energy. Its calorific value is 24 MJ/cum or about 5,000 Kcal/cum. One thousand cft. (30 cum) of biogas is equivalent to 600 cft. of natural gas, 6.4 gallons of butane, 5.2 gallons of gasoline or 4.6 gallons of diesel oil. Biogas is utilised for cooking, lighting through mantle lamps, electricity generation and body warming during winter. Cooking is the most efficient use of biogas. Biogas burners are available in a wide ranging capacity from 8 cft to 100 cft biogas consumption per hour. It burns with a blue flame and without soot and odour. The biogas mantle lamp consumes 2-3 cft per hour having illumination capacity equivalent to 40 kw electric bulbs at 220 volt. Motive power can be generated by using biogas in dual fuel internal combustion (IC) engine.

Biogas burners

Mantle lamp lit by biogas from public toilet complex

Air mixed with biogas is aspirated into the engine and the mixture is then compressed, raising its temperature to about 350°C, which is the self-ignition temperature of diesel. Biogas has a high (600°C) ignition temperature. Therefore, in order to initiate combustion of the charge, a small quantity of diesel is injected into the cylinder just before the end of compression. The charge is thus ignited and the process is continued smoothly. At optimum condition only 20 per cent diesel is required, rest (80 per cent) is substituted by biogas. Biogas consumption by engine is 15 cft/BHP/hour. A public convenience used by about 2,000 persons per day would produce approximately 60 cum of biogas which can run a 10 KVA genset for 8 hours a day, producing 65 units of power. Sulabh has developed a novel technology to run dual fuel genset on biogas alone i.e. without any diesel. Under the system ignition of compressed biogas is done through battery-operated spark system. It is a new method to make biogas-based electricity generation sustainable.

Human excreta-based biogas system has multiple advantages; it improves sanitation, makes available energy, and biofertiliser and reduces greenhouse effect. In addition to conserving and reusing water the system has additional in-built advantage of reducing greenhouse effect arising out of carbon dioxide and methane production due to degradation of human wastes. Due to design of leach pit (Sulabh toilet) produced carbon dioxide is diffused in soil through honey combs. It does not escape in atmosphere as in other

A Sulabh Effluent Treatment System attached with a public toilet-linked biogas plant

cases. During anaerobic digestion of human wastes during biogas production, methane is produced that is used for different purposes. Methane as such is not left to escape in the atmosphere. Thus, both these technologies are helping in reducing greenhouse effect and thus improve environment.

Sulabh effluent treatment (SET) system

Biogas produced from human excreta is being used for different purposes e.g. cooking, lighting, electricity generation and body warming. Since, Sulabh is maintaining over 8,500 public toilet complexes spread all over the country, out of which 200 are linked with biogas plants, it was an important task for the organisation to make the effluent free from odour, colour and pathogens, to use it safely for agricultural purposes. After a series of experiments, the organisation has developed a new and convenient technology by which the effluent of human excreta is burned into a colourless, odourless and pathogen-free liquid manure. The technology is based on filtration of effluent through activated charcoal followed by ultraviolet rays. The filtration unit makes it colourless, odourless and free from organic particles and the UV eliminates the bacteria. It reduces Biochemical oxygen demand (BOD) and Chemical oxygen demand (COD) of the waste water drastically. Since such water is from human wastes, its BOD which is around 200 mg/l, comes down to <1 mg/l after treatment – safe for aquaculture, agriculture, gardening or discharge into any water body. It can also be used for floor cleaning of public toilets in drought-prone areas.

Advantages of biogas plant

Cost of collection of sewage and operation and maintenance of the system is very low; no manual handling of human excreta is required; It is aesthetically and socially accepted; biogas is used for different purposes; treated effluent is safe to reuse for agriculture, gardening, or discharge into any water body; in drought-prone areas treated effluent can be used for cleaning floors of public toilets; and if discharged into the sewer, pollution load will be much lower. Thus, the decentralised system of sewage treatment through biogas technology is more effective for minimising financial burden to combat pollution.

Biogas from dried water hyacinth and other mixed feeds

Water hyacinth is an aquatic, seasonal and problematic weed of national concern. The Government of India formulated a Task Force to get rid of this weed. However, it has an advantage that it is a good substrate for biogas generation. Since this weed is seasonal, biogas plant based on this feed becomes non-functional during summer due to non-availability of this weed. Sulabh has successfully demonstrated that biogas can be produced from this weed throughout the year after harvesting, drying and pulverising it. The pulverised weed can be easily transported and used for biogas generation throughout the year. Sulabh has also carried out a series of experiments on biogas generation from vegetables/fruit wastes and household kitchen wastes with or without mixing with human wastes. Better results were obtained when human waste and vegetable waste were fed in combination. It showed an additive effect.

Use of digester effluent for hydroponics

Biogas digester effluent has a good plant nutrient value. It can be directly used for irrigating grass lawns, flower beds or even for agricultural purposes. Sulabh has successfully demonstrated its use as hydroponics i.e., soil-less culture of plants. The effluent is first dried in earthen pots kept in sunlight where owing to the evaporation of the liquid, the concentration of nutrients increases. It is filtered with a thin plastic mesh. Some trace elements are added in the filtered effluent. Such effluent is completely odourless. Various plants have been grown exclusively on such an effluent when mixed (5 to 10 per cent by volume) with tap water. Plants can be grown in glass bottles or any other jars and kept inside or outside the room. Such technology is useful for the culture of rare plants like cactus and other ornamental plants.

Growth and expansion

Today Sulabh is not merely the name of an NGO; it is a movement. It has a workforce of over 60,000 volunteers covering several districts and towns all over India. Sulabh has also been invited to help out in neighbouring countries like Nepal, Bhutan, Afghanistan and Bangladesh. It has also taken up many programmes in collaboration with the United Nations Centre for Human Settlements, Nairobi, and the International Water and Sanitation Centre, Loughborough University of Technology, UK, through the Water Engineering and Development Centre.

Sulabh has been also closely working in collaboration with national agencies like the NBO, CBRI, HUDCO, and Ministries of Housing and Urban Development, Poverty Alleviation, Social Justice and Empowerment, Rural Development, Government of India and the All India Institute of Hygiene and Public Health, Kolkata. Sulabh's two-pit pour-flush toilet technology innovatively designed and modified over the years, has been evaluated by many international agencies, like the UNDP/World Bank, UNICEF and WHO and recommended for global replication, especially in the developing countries. In addition, agencies like the ODA (Overseas Development Agency of the British Government), BORDA, SIDA (the Danish International Development Agency) and EEC (European Economic Community) have collaborated with Sulabh.

A technology is as good as it delivers.

CHAPTER 23

Economic and Environmental Benefits of Sulabh Technologies

Enough water saved to meet deficit

The Sulabh technology-based toilet system uses only 1 to 1.5 litre of water against 10 litres used by the conventional toilet system, thus, saving 9 litres of water per use per person per day. Mr. Jack Sim, Founder of the World Toilet Organisation, Singapore, said at the Toilet Summit 2007 that every individual goes to toilet, on an average, six times a day; which meant that by changing over to the Sulabh toilet system, every person can save 54 litres of water a day without changing habits, or spending more money; just by making a right choice.

Water saving by implementing the Sulabh two-pit system

Using Sulabh toilet an amount of 9 litres of water per flush is saved per person in comparison to septic tank that requires 10 litres of water to flush toilet (Sulabh requires only 1 to 1.5 litre of water to flush).

If 700 million people, who are yet to have household sanitation facilities, use such a toilet a calculated amount of 6,300 million litres of water will be saved per flush. Taking into account use of flush twice a day, which is bare minimum use by an individual, the figure will be 12,600 million litres per day or 45,99,000 million litres per annum.

Total number of users per day	=	700 million
Water used in Sulabh two-pit toilets	=	1 to 1.5 litre
If Sulabh two-pit toilet is used, then water used	=	700 million × 1 litre = 700 million litres

Had it been septic tank

Water used in septic tank	=	10 litres
Hence, water used per day	=	700 million × 10 litres
	=	7,000 million litres
Water saved in one day by	=	(7,000–700) million litres
700 million people	=	6,300 million litres
If toilet is used twice a day	=	6,300 × 2 million litres
	=	12,600 million litres
Water saved in a day	=	**12,600 million litres**
Water saved in one year	=	(12,600 × 365) million litres
by Sulabh two-pit system	=	45,99,000 million litres

Water saved from existing Sulabh two-pit toilet in one year

Sulabh has so far either converted or newly constructed over 1.5 million two-pit toilets in the country, where per flush only 1 to 1.5 litre of water is required. Assuming 7 persons of a family per toilet it saves 63 litres of water per flush in comparison to septic tank system. Assuming two times flush per day these 1.5 million toilets save 168 million litres per day i.e. 61,320 million litres per annum.

No. of two-pit toilets constructed by Sulabh	=	1.5 million
No. of persons who use one toilet (average)	=	7
Minimum No. of times toilet used (average)	=	2
Total No. of users per day, 1.5 million × 7	=	10.5 million
Water used in Sulabh two-pit toilet	=	1 litres

So, water used by 10.5 million people
per use = 1 litres × 10.5 million
If toilet is used twice a day = (10.5 × 2) million
= 21 million litres

Had it been septic tank
Water used in septic tank = 10 litres
So, water used by 9.1 million = 10.5 million × 10 litres
= 105 million litres

Hence, water saved by existing Sulabh
two-pit toilets = (10.5-21) million litres
= 84 million litres
If toilet is used twice a day = (84 × 2) million litres
= 168 million litre
So, water saved in a day = 168 million litres
Hence, water saved in one year
by Sulabh two-pit system = (168 × 365 million litres
= 61,320 million litres

Cost of manure from existing Sulabh two-pit toilet in one year
No. of toilets constructed by
Sulabh (twin-pit) = 1.5 millions
Average family members = 7
Manure obtained from a person in a year = 40 kg.
Cost of manure = ₹ 10 per kg.
Hence, the cost of manure from
Sulabh twin-pit toilets is = (1.5 × 7 × 40 × 10)
= ₹ 4,200 million
= **₹ 4,200 million per year**

Cost of manure from toilets to be constructed by Sulabh twin-pit toilet for 700 million people. If one person produces 40 kg manure in 1 year, 700 million persons produce

= 40 × 700 million kg. manure
= 28,000 million kg. manure

Cost of manure (in 1 year)
Cost of 1 kg of manure is ₹ 10.00
Cost of 28000 million kg. manure = ₹ 10 × 28000 million
= ₹ 280,000 million

Cost recovered from 1,000 user biogas plant, in the form of energy per year

One person produces	=	1 cft of biogas per day
So, from a public toilet of 1,000 users we get	=	1000 cft of biogas (30 cum)
30 cum of biogas	=	4.6 gallons of diesel
1 gallon	=	4.55 litres
4.6 gallons of diesel	=	4.6 × 4.55 litres of diesel
	=	21 litres

So, in a day we get 21 litres of diesel

Hence, total diesel obtained in a year	=	21 × 365
	=	7,665 litres/year
Cost of diesel @ ₹ 50/- (July 2011 rate in Delhi)	=	7,665 × 50
	=	₹ 383,250/-

per year for one biogas plant of 1000 users

Contribution of Sulabh to save global warming

No. of two-pit toilets constructed by Sulabh	=	1.5 million
Average users of toilet per day	=	7

So, total number of users	=	(1.5 × 7) million
	=	10.5 million
1 person produces 1 cft biogas per day		
So, 10.5 million persons produce	=	(1 × 10.5) million cft biogas per day
	=	10.5 million cft biogas
	=	30,0000 cum
So, total biogas absorbed in soil	=	0.30 million cum biogas per day
In one year total biogas absorbed	=	(0.30 × 365) million cum
in soil	=	109.5 million cum

If 700 million prospective users have Sulabh two-pit system then total biogas produced in 1 day	=	700 million × 1 cft
	=	700 million cft
	=	20 million cum
So, total biogas that can be absorbed in soil in one year (by Sulabh two-pit system)	=	20 million cum × 365
	=	7300 million cum
190 biogas plants constructed by Sulabh average biogas production per plant/day	=	45 cum
So, total biogas production per day	=	(190 × 45) cum
	=	8850 cum
Hence, biogas produced in a year	=	8850 cum × 365
	=	31,20,750 cum
	=	3.1 million cum
Total gas saved by Sulabh technology	=	(109.5 + 3.1) = 112.6 million cum

Since methane damages the ozone layer of the atmosphere, from environmental point of view, it becomes harmless when it is used for different purposes like cooking, heating, or electricity generation.

> *"I would like to live and die for the eradication of untouchability. My concern is the last forgotten man because he is the true face of India."*
>
> *– Gandhiji*

CHAPTER 24

Social Impact of Sulabh Technologies

Of hidden faces and 'missing women'

Nobel Laureate Amartya Sen has popularised the notion of 100 million missing women on account of gender discrimination in China, South Asia, West Asia and North Africa. And, they have escaped the society's radar to remain 'missing'. Truer still is the case of scavenger women who remain uncounted and outside the society's focus; carrying human excreta generation after generation without hope of redemption. Now there seems to be a light at the end of the tunnel; for, they are the focus of the Sulabh Movement. What matters is not the number of scavenger women but the horror of the tragedy.

It is too soon to say that the Sulabh technology is the final solution to scavenging and sanitation problems in India because technology evolves and changes as was the case with T-Ford model car. But from a baby step in 1970, when Sulabh was founded, to now when it strides across the globe, it is safe to argue that the Sulabh technology will solve a great social problem which no one did before since abolition of scavenging in the US more than 200 years ago.

Sulabh technologies have directly impacted the lives of the poor, specially women who earlier could go out to meet the nature's call only before dawn and after dusk, holding the nature's urge for the day, resulting in many health problems. We know these 'hidden faces' sitting along the rail track or moving among shadows facing the risk to their honour and safety. The story of suffering of these 'hidden' faces was lost in the humdrum of modern world, hell-bent on a race to nowhere. Times have changed, economies have grown and people have prospered, but nobody after Gandhiji cared to talk about sanitation and the scavengers, 'the missing women', cleaning, toilets and carrying excreta living on the fringes of society neglected, ignored and disempowered.

Scavengers invariably live in areas of concentrated poverty, the like of which was once identified by the Poor Law in Britain, the only difference being that in Britain it was only poverty; in India it is untouchability. Scavenger is a case apart in the world; we know of slavery, ghettoes, gas chambers and mass killings but the cruelty on scavengers is worse; they are allowed to live in perpetual poverty, destitution and never-ending social discrimination, cleaning excreta of those who do not touch them. The scavengers are forced into this profession by social tradition based on inhumanity and cruelty of the medieval time and they submit to force because they are weak, hungry and illiterate, punished for the birth in the choosing of which they have no hand. *The Bible* says those who light a fire cannot be protected from its flame. No wonder, the caste system has divided India against itself.

All the technologies, which have changed the world, from spinning-jenny to iPod, had huge social consequences but none of them was developed to solve social problems. These technologies are value-neutral. The worst among social exploitation, after slavery in the US, is scavenging when a section of the poor are pushed into the hateful practices of cleaning somebody else's toilet to make a meagre living and live as untouchable outside the social mainstream of society. The story of their sufferings and society's neglect is too shocking to record as a story of human misery.

Scavengers may not be too many to make an impact on this

country but it is not the precision of number that matters but the horror of the tragedy. One man's death is a tragedy and a million deaths are statistics. Francis Ferdinand of Hapsburg was shot at Sarajero in 1914 and the World War I broke out in which about four crore people died. Injured were never counted. Gandhiji was thrown out of the all-White railway compartment in South Africa in 1893 at Pietermaritzburg station and Britishers lost their empire. Back in vintage times, Draupadi was dishonoured and the entire dynasty was destroyed in the Mahabharata War which marked the beginning of new age. The kidnapping of Helen of Troy sparked off Peloponnesian War in which the Greeks lost their empire and became a nation of 7,000 floating islands.

Civil rights and since

In Montgomery, Alabama, (US) in 1955 a bus driver did not give a seat to a black woman, Mrs. Rosa Parks, who refused to leave the bus. And, thus, sparked the civil rights movement led by Martin Luther King Jr. And 54 years later, Mr. Barack Obama, a Black, became the US President. Spartacus (77 BC), a Roman slave and gladiator challenged the Roman power and fought with his army of slaves to be finally captured and nailed on the cross along with his soldiers in the desert of Judea. Spartacus is the history's hero. Many protest movements were launched in Germany in his name and also in other countries of Europe. One of them, Spartacus League, was led

Rosa Parks in 1955, with Martin Luther King, Jr. in the background

by fiery German revolutionary Rosa Luxemburg who was stabbed and killed in Berlin in 1919. Rosa died but Spartacus lives on in history. Ataturk (1881-1939) single-handedly changed Turkey, a Muslim nation, into a modern and secular country, seeking EU membership.

Karl Marx (1818-83) reinterpreted history and the world split into two – one part communist and another part capitalist which later led to global confrontation and the Cold War. Galileo (1564-1642) cried out from the Inquisitor's burning deck stamping on the ground: "Still the Earth moves." And thus, the 2nd century Greek astronomer Ptolemy's doctrine that the Earth was the centre of the universe was demolished and the modern astronomy was born. Einstein (1879-1953) wrote an equation $e = mc^2$ and the atomic age was born. Charles Darwin wrote a book published 100 years ago *(Origin of Species)* and the Christian doctrine was demolished and the world was split into two – believers and non-believers. Darwin said the universe has evolved, and not created by God. Dr. Bindeshwar Pathak is in that league who has come close to abolishing scavenging which is worse than slavery. History is made by individuals and not multitude. Margaret Thatcher, former British Prime Minister, says, "There is nothing like society; it is all about individuals".

To be true great tragedies are about one man or woman and in this case there are about seven lakh scavengers and they don't make a tragedy, so inhuman and insensitive have we become to human suffering. Scavengers' are the untold stories lost in the glitz of modern life created by technology. Scavengers go about practising their profession of carrying human excreta on the head, generation after generation, without protest and representation to the power that be. They have no caste leader to plead for their salvation. Scavengers need not be introduced; we know them but refuse to mention their names. We quietly dismiss them at the backdoors after flinging at them the day's leftovers of the kitchen.

Technology will end scavenging, not law

In small towns, these hidden faces materialise in dark shadows early in the morning, stealthily scurrying between lanes and by-lanes, cleaning dry latrines and collecting human excreta on the head to the tankers which cart it away to disposal spots. Scavengers, as professionals, have been growing in number first, because of the general growth in population and second, because of the rising demand for their services in the fast growing urban and semi-urban settlements, most of which are unplanned and, hence, unsewered.

This situation has also produced ready jobs for them which are hard to come for other untouchables, equally poor, illiterate and outcast. Socially, scavengers are untouchables among untouchables. They are sealed off from the mainstream of social life. The law (Articles 17 and 46 of the Constitution and the Protection of Civil Rights Act, 1955 which was amended in 1976 by making the punishments under this Act more stringent and offences non-compoundable) does not help in this respect at all. The sporadic attempts of private persons or social organisations have not changed the situation either. The question of social acceptability is not entirely a matter of law; it is also an attitudinal problem which has to be solved differently.

In the congested locality, the scavenger has to crawl through a narrow passage, pushing the basket with one hand, resting his (or her) body weight on the other to make way up to the latrine chamber through a narrow opening. And, in the latrine where the seat is deep inside, he or she has to stretch hand to the maximum and thrust the head into the hole to clean the toilet. The scavenger has to bend forward into the narrow space to clean excreta in the antechambers. In the latrines, which have no receptacles, human excreta drops directly on the floor which, with the passage of time, wears out and the brickwork becomes patchy and uneven. In most cases, the sidewalls are also without cement plaster; with the result, human excreta gets stuck up everywhere on the sidewalls and the floor. The scavenger, while cleaning, has to scratch the floor and the side walls to do maximum cleaning. It is also a common sight to see scavengers, mostly women, moving with excreta on the head, stored in bamboo baskets or in leaking drums with the excreta trickling over their faces.

The passers-by avoid such persons. If a scavenger comes close to them, he or she is abused. In many places, latrines are so constructed that the users do not even see their own excreta. They simply squat over the seat and go away without even caring to know who cleans their toilets. The other work of scavengers in the rural areas include carrying of death news from one village to another, removal of carcase, digging burial pits and heating drums at funeral procession, etc. Whenever any scavenger refuses to perform any of these jobs, he is economically boycotted by the villager so that none of the caste Hindus give him any employment. And the scavenger continues to do physical cleaning, being abused, get underpaid, and live a life of degradation unheard of in human history. No human degradation could be more cruel and inhuman than the one suffered by scavengers. This is a human rights violation more serious than any that caused major social revolution. The 2011 Census has revealed that out of 246,692,667 households in the country, 26,06,278 have insanitary latrines in their houses which are serviced as under:

(a) Latrines from which night soil is disposed into open drain - 13 lakh.
(b) Service latrines in which night soil is removed by humans - 8 lakh; serviced by animals - 5 lakh (Total - 26 lakh).

Unlike the spinning-jenny which produced the industrial revolution, the Sulabh two-pit story is focused on toilet which is so mundane and innocuous that many people may be loathe to talk about it. Those who are familiar with Sulabh commitment and contribution to improving and upgrading India's sanitation scenario through the promotion of an appropriate and affordable (low-cost) sanitation technology may vouchsafe how toilets and toilet-related sanitary subjects are important. Toilet as a simple invention of tremendous civilising impact has played a vital role in enhancing the quality of life and in resolving some of the intricate social problems, like the practice of untouchability and the rigidities of India's caste system. The sociological implications of toilet revolution around the world, especially in India, have been most profound. Further, the history of evolution of toilets from 2000 BC to date suggests many notable changes that have been brought about by this supposedly innocuous but realistically important invention.

History shows how an ordinary invention like that of toilet has stirred human mind, evoked passion, inspired imagination and kindled hope and vision of many a social crusader around the world. The invention of toilet is one of the winning ideas which has demonstrated the power course of human history while discussing toilet, one ends up discussing virtually everything–society, culture, economics, technology and even history and geography. Toilet is one single small-time invention that has made us civilised. For that matter toilet is one of the important achievements of mankind. Toilet revolution around the world today has made its mark on the modern civilisation, the advances of which have been truly amazing, inspiring and, at times, terribly horrifying.

India's caste system is a unique method of social classification, dividing society into high-caste and low-caste people on the basis of birth. The persons belonging to lower caste occupying a very lowly position in society are socially, economically, educationally and culturally backward. Scavengers had been subjected to various discriminations and disabilities resulting in their dehumanisation and degradation. India's Constitution came as a redeemer to the socially excluded sections of society, declaring prohibition of untouchability and has led to enactment of laws relating to several affirmative action programmes to bring the low caste people (Scheduled Castes and Scheduled Tribes) into the mainstream of society by initiating policies and programmes for their economic, social and political upgradation, welfare, development and empowerment, with the result, that profound changes are taking place in the hereditary caste system and its pernicious practices that have led to the disability and degradation of such people. Today, the old discriminations and disabilities of the untouchables do not have social approval, nor do they have the old oppressive stranglehold. Many profound social, economic and technological changes have weakened the caste system to a great extent and there is much greater social intercourse amongst different caste groups.

Scavengers most hurt by social prejudices

However, there still remains a class of persons belonging to the scavenging castes, who were traditionally ordained in Indian society to clean and carry human waste. Their appalling hardship, humiliation and savage exploitation have no parallel in human history. Living in the filthiest of surroundings under most trying circumstances, scavengers are hated even by those whose excreta they carry on their heads. Reduced to the depth of degradation as untouchables and forced to lead a subhuman existence, they are the worst victims of a cruel caste-based social order. Theirs is the sordid story of utmost violation of human rights. Their heart-rending plight stretching over centuries is a blot on India's civilisation. Mahatma Gandhi was the first person to take up the scavengers' cause as he was deeply moved by their plight, in his lifetime, though he could not succeed in making India a scavenging-free country.

In contemporary India, the endeavours made by the government and the civil society to liberate scavengers from the suffocating situation have not been able to bear fruit, and therefore, the long shadow of institutionalised discrimination, stigmatisation and marginalisation has still refused to fade out. The atrocious behaviour and treatment meted out to scavengers because of their low social positioning in the caste hierarchy caused deep anger and resentment to Dr. Pathak when he joined the Gandhi Birth Centenary Celebration Committee in Patna as a social worker. He hated to endorse the entrenched injustice of the Indian caste system, especially against the so-called untouchables, who have been the worst victims of the system. His determination to fight it out took a concrete shape when he founded Sulabh International Social Service Organisation in the year 1970, an organisation exclusively engaged in promoting low-cost sanitation technology, eradication of manual scavenging and liberation and rehabilitation of scavengers.

Dr. Pathak took special care to ensure that the subject of sanitation is freed from the popular myth that only low-caste persons had to be employed or engaged in sanitation programmes. He persuaded people from upper castes to join in his efforts and high-caste people now work to promote the programmes and activities. The caste and creed-related barriers find no place in Sulabh. People in India now don't hesitate to talk about toilet and toilet-related concerns. This subject, which was once a taboo, indeed, a detestable and despicable one, has become worthy of public discourse. During his endeavours of four decades in the field of appropriate and affordable sanitation, Dr. Pathak had noticed that a thing as mundane as toilet which has been considered too profane a subject to discuss in both public and private realms of life, has been a tool of many significant social changes.

Toilet is symbol of civilisation

History of toilets is not only about changes in toilet design and technology, but also about its civilising impact, its role in enhancing the quality of life, and by consequence, leading to the redress of some very intricate and pressing social problems which countries like India faced in regard to the practice of untouchability and other demeaning discriminations against a socially disadvantaged section of society, hereditarily engaged as toilet cleaners – manually

Children of the Sulabh Public School, New Delhi

handling and cleaning human excreta from pit/dry privies. The sociological implications arising out of the impact of Sulabh work has been many and most telling in loosening the stranglehold of India's traditional caste system. Some of the major social reform endeavours of Sulabh International, like its social upgradation programme in which upper caste elite closely interact with a family of a scavenger community as part of their social obligation, running Sulabh Public School (wherein children of both high caste and low caste people study under one roof and share meals), and social mainstreaming programmes (wherein efforts are made to prepare scavengers to get connected with mainstream society), have made a dent on the rigidities of the caste system.

No wonder, now Sulabh has been nationally and internationally acclaimed to be a harbinger of a sanitation order in India which has touched social, cultural, health, hygiene and sanitation-related issues, leaving its powerful impact on the pace and progress of a wide variety of current initiatives aimed at breaking the barriers of caste and changing its old traditional structure and system. A large number of community toilet complexes being managed and maintained by Sulabh all over the country are looked after by

ACHIEVEMENTS AT A GLANCE

• Scavengers liberated	2,00,000
• Sulabh household toilets constructed	1.5 million
• Sulabh community toilet complexes	9,099
• Human excreta-based biogas plants	200
• No. of units for housekeeping jobs like hospitals, offices etc.	504
• Towns made scavenging-free	640
• Scavengers trained	11,000
• Number of toilet blocks constructed in schools	19,430
• Towns where Sulabh works	1,968
• Districts where Sulabh works	520
• Local bodies	1,784
• States/Union Territories	26/4
• Persons using Sulabh facilities everyday	>20 million

persons belonging to higher castes. Sulabh has recently undertaken a micro-level programme for the development/empowerment of women from the scavenger community.

Through this, the social status of those women is upgraded by providing them vocational education in economically rewarding occupations. The eatables prepared by these women are being purchased by the so-called touchable people of high caste groups. The wide variety of programmes and activities of the organisation are exclusively focused on social activism inspired and informed by secularist mandate of the Constitution of India which seeks to abolish all forms of caste and creed-based discrimination. Sulabh has successfully pursued its agenda to include India's excluded castes in the social mainstream of society. One outstanding example of this has been Dr. Pathak's visit to a Hindu temple which disallowed the entry of the so-called untouchable persons. He led a group of scavengers and persuaded the priests to allow them to offer prayers and worship. They, however, consented.

His Royal Highness Willem-Alexander, the Prince of Orange of the Netherlands

A new dawn is nigh

Commending Sulabh's good work, His Royal Highness Willem-Alexander, the Prince of Orange of the Netherlands, and Chairman of the United Nations' Secretary-General's Advisory Board on Water and Sanitation (UNSGAB) said in New York on November 21, 2007: "Sulabh International showed me a good example during my recent visit to New Delhi. This organisation has proved how effective small-scale solutions can be and how they can be extended all over India within a short time span. Thousands of 'pay and use' public toilet-cum- bath complexes

'Mission Sanitation' – a fashion show – for a cause. The trainees of Sulabh International's Nai Disha Centre, Alwar, assemble on the dais after walking the ramp with prominent Indian models, in the United Nations in New York on July 2, 2008

and more than a million pour-flush latrines in private houses have been built (and are maintained) and they are used by more than ten million people everyday. By doing so, Sulabh has restored human dignity and given a new future to thousands of untouchables".

From manual scavenging to walking the ramp at UN

The liberated women scavengers were invited to the United Nations in New York to put up on July 2, 2008 a cultural programme, where they walked the ramp with Indian models in dresses embroidered by them. The show highlighted the social transformation process undertaken by Sulabh for scavengers.

"Show me the toilet and I will tell you the educational and income level of the family; its cultural preferences, climate and possibly the level of health. To be true, life begins at the far end in toilet which is the symbol of modern civilisation."

– Dr. Bindeshwar Pathak

CHAPTER 25

The Sewerage System No Longer Self-Sustainable

On-site waste disposal the only answer

For once after the sewer system was laid out in the West, beginning from London City and led by persons such as Edwin Chadwick and Octavia Hill by the end of the 19th century, the rich countries are beginning to realise that transferring city waste to water areas creates more problems than it solves. In which case the alternative is the Sulabh on-site waste disposal system. However, Sulabh is more of a concept of sustainable sanitation practices than a mere technology.

The philosophy behind the Sulabh technology is the sustainability; cultural, financial, social and environmental, none of which is achieved by the sewer system which is simply carrying city sewage from the residential areas to rivers, on the assumption that water will wash it out to nowhere. And, this has happened for a long time. In order to get a perspective of the sewer system, let us see how it all began.

In the West, sanitation has been a state business. John Harington invented WC in the Queen's Palace, and all movements to clean up places after the Great London Fire (1666) were the state-sponsored business. In the 16th century, Harington had invented the Ajax, the first flushing toilet that used moving parts to remove excreta and refill the water tank. His invention, however, didn't take off. Although some of the elite between the 16th and 18th centuries had systems that used water from cisterns to flush their chamber pots, those primitive water closets were hard to install and harder to maintain.

In 1775, Alexander Cummings, an English watchmaker, recognised the economic potential for a functional flush toilet and he drastically simplified Harington's design with a single sliding valve that emptied the bowl released water from a cistern to clean it, and then refilled the cistern. In 1778, Joseph Bramah converted the sliding valve to a hinge flap, simplifying the mechanism even further. By the turn of the century, Bramah's company had sold and installed over six thousand toilets across England.

Significant improvements came in seventy-five years during Queen Victoria's reign. George Adamson incorporated siphonic flush-down, George Jennings improved on it, Thomas Crapper devised the pull-chain method for flushing, and Thomas Twofold encapsulated the whole system into porcelain for easy cleaning and sanitising. While early toilets were by today's measures loud, inefficient, and hard to clean, they sufficed for those who wanted to leave no smear in the WC. In the 19th century, the crap-cleansing capacity of the cities grew ever more strained as population densities skyrocketed. Tenements grew taller, and the excreta productivity of the slums soared. A number of cholera outbreaks including those in 1831, 1849, 1854, and 1866, ravaged the West. The 1849 outbreak killed 35,000 in England and Wales with 15,000 dead in London alone. All over the Western world, as endless waves of migrants flocked to the cities for jobs, cholera followed. 2,200 people died in Quebec City in 1832, 8,000 in Havana in 1833, 5,000 in New York City in 1848-49, and 1,000 in Sacramento in 1850.

A gradual growth

By the end of the 19th century, reforming the sanitary conditions of the poor became a pet cause of the English bourgeoisie. Led by people such as Edwin Chadwick and Octavia Hill, a movement grew to transfer the responsibility for clean water and sewage disposal from individuals to societies and governments. It may be noted that the Chadwick movement was state-sponsored. Between 1859 and 1865, London city engineers led by Joseph Bazalgette built 100 miles of main sewers, 450 miles of interceptory sewers, and 13,000 miles of local sewers, using 318 million bricks and excavating 3.5 million tons of earth in the process. And in the decades following the great cholera outbreak of 1866 in London, the state legislated a number of provisions mandating the same kind of amenities for the working class that the middle and upper classes had long since enjoyed. By World War I, England was a toilet-based society. Paris, the cleanest city in the world, had 'flying toilets' where people wrapped up excreta and flung it around to let it fall on the neighbours' house or in the street. This, in brief, is the growth story of the sewerage system.

America is a different story. It is a country which has no indigenous people of their own traditions. America became the United States as recent as 232 years ago in 1776. People mostly from the English-speaking world, brought their own sanitation practices to a huge land mass four times of India's size with 20 per cent of its population. But sanitation is becoming a problem in the US now as is brilliantly discussed by Dave Praeger in his book, *Poop Culture*. In Europe, the story is more complicated. But, Europeans captured half the world to keep their cities clean. Britain, France, Germany, Italy, Belgium, the Netherlands, Spain and Portugal, with their total population (1950) of 300 million, or half of India's, governed most of Asia, Africa and Latin America. This was not the case with the US.

Storyline changes now

George S. Hawkins, writes in *The New York Times,* (dated 14 March, 2010), "In Washington alone there is a pipe break every day, and this weekend's intense rains overwhelmed the city's system, causing untreated sewage to flow into the Potomac and Anacostia rivers. State and federal studies indicate that thousands of water and sewer systems may be too old to function properly. For decades, these systems – some built around the time of the Civil War – have been ignored by politicians and residents accustomed to paying almost nothing for water delivery and sewage removal. And so each year, hundreds of thousands of ruptures damage streets and homes and cause dangerous pollutants to seep into drinking water supplies. In cities like Detroit, Cincinnati, Atlanta and elsewhere, the situation is the same."

"Water is tied into everything we should care about. Some day, people are going to talk about our sewers with a real sense of pride. And, water is not enough to carry the city sewage. And, sewers have failed," says Mr. Hawkins. The sewer system seems to be failing in the West also because there is not sufficient water in rivers to carry the increasing sewage load from cities which grow rich, resulting in creating more waste per person than before. Or, they are forced to throw the sewage into city spreading diseases and insanitation.

Toilet shortage in London city

Farrukh Dhondy writes in his column (March 20, 2010, Asian Age), "There was a newspaper report which said that 12 urinators had been produced before the magistrate's courts in London for committing a nuisance in Victoria and Soho. The 12 were sentenced and fined a total of £2,000 by the City of Westminster Magistrate's court, with fines for each ranging from £50 to £250. The Westminster Council's strategic director, who had initiated the crackdown on public urinators, said 'not only is it offensive and unhygienic to urinate in the street, it costs a small fortune to clean up the mess and get rid of the putrid smell which seeps into brickwork and paving. I also read a report by an environmental charity whose research showed that

95 per cent of Britons had urinated, or defecated in public places because no toilet was available.

"I recalled writing a column in this very paper years ago extolling the dawn of the public lavatorial revolution in New Delhi where I had seen the first establishment of the Sulabh Shaochalays (sic). I remember discussing the prospective column with a friend at the time and she said 'why would anyone want to read about pubic toilets?' I reminded her of the literary furore that followed the publication of V.S. Naipaul's *An Area of Darkness* in which he wrote at some length about the Indian habit of urinating and defecating in public places and cultivating a social blindness to the undesirability of the tradition. He, unlike his critics who called his book a gutter-inspector's report, thought this almost universal habit worthy of mention as a national trait.

"After the column was published a few people complained that there were revolutions and transformations more important than the lavatorial one. The slogan that I had coined for the Sulabh Shaochalays at the time, with apologies to W.B. Yeats was:

Ode to Sulabh
"I must go down to Sulabh
again
To the Sulabh Shaochalay!
A rupee a pee,
Two for a poo,"
(Farrukh Dhondy - Asian Age, March 20, 2010)

"The truth about London today is that despite the fines and the alertness of police to the nuisance makers, the scourge of public urination is set to continue and increase. Between 2000 and 2005, the number of public toilets in London dropped by 40 per cent. There are now 415 public toilets in London serving a population of 7.5 million and the additional 28 million people a year who visit the capital. The creative strategy of people who dodge into a pub, pretend to be looking for a friend and when you've evaded the barman or barwoman's eye to go into the toilet. There are also always the McDonald's, the Kentucky Fried Chicken and other fast food joints which I only enter in extreme circumstances to use the loo. Coffee shops, supermarkets and department stores also have public toilets but in the department stores it is more than likely that one has to tackle five floors, escalators and vast trading areas before one finds the facility," adds Dhondy.

Sources of water shortage

The toilet crisis is looming in the West also because of water shortage in rivers to flush out city waste, agricultural, industrial and household. Virtually all of these human uses require fresh water. As many as 97 per cent of water on the Earth is salt water, leaving only 3 per cent as fresh water of which slightly over two-thirds is frozen in glaciers and polar ice caps. The remaining unfrozen fresh water is mainly found as groundwater, with only a small fraction present above ground or in the air. Fresh water is a renewable resource, yet the world's supply of clean, fresh water is steadily decreasing. Water demand already exceeds supply in many parts of the world and as the world population continues to rise, so does the water demand. Awareness of the global importance of preserving water for ecosystem has only recently emerged as more than half the world's wetlands have been lost along with their valuable environmental services. Biodiversity-rich fresh water ecosystems are currently declining faster than marine or land ecosystems.

Water sources under pressure

The concept of water stress is relatively simple. According to the World Business Council for Sustainable Development, it applies to situations where there is not enough water for all uses, whether agricultural, industrial or domestic. Defining thresholds for stress in terms of available water per capita is more complex, however, entailing assumptions about water use and its efficiency. Nevertheless, it has been proposed that when annual per capita renewable fresh water availability is less than 1,700 cubic metres, countries begin to experience periodic or regular water stress. Below 1,000 cubic metres, water scarcity begins to hamper economic development and human health and well-being. The following are the major sources of water overuse resulting in stress condition :

POPULATION GROWTH: In 2000, the world population was 6.2 billion. The UN estimates that by 2050 there will be an additional 3.5 billion people with most of the growth taking place in developing countries that already suffer water stress. Thus, the water demand will increase unless there are corresponding increases in water conservation and recycling of this vital resource.

EXPANSION OF BUSINESS ACTIVITIES: Business activities ranging from industrialisation to services such as tourism and entertainment continue to expand rapidly. This expansion requires increased water services including both supply and sanitation, which can lead to more pressure on water resources and natural ecosystems.

RAPID URBANISATION: The trend towards urbanisation is accelerating. Small private wells and septic tanks that work well in low-density communities are not feasible within high-density urban areas. Urbanisation requires significant investment in water infrastructure in order to deliver water to individuals and to process the concentrations of wastewater – both from individuals and from business. These polluted and contaminated waters must be treated or they pose unacceptable public health risks. In 60 per cent of European cities with more than 100,000 people, groundwater is being used at a faster rate than it can be replenished. Even if some water remains available, it costs more and more to capture it.

CLIMATE CHANGE: Climate change could have significant impacts on water resources around the world because of the close connections between the climate and hydrologic cycle. Rising temperatures will increase evaporation and lead to increases in precipitation, though there will be regional variations in rainfall. Overall, the global supply of fresh water will increase. Both droughts and floods may become more frequent in different regions at different times, and dramatic changes in snowfall and snowmelt are expected in mountainous areas. Higher temperatures will also affect water quality in ways that are not well understood. Possible impacts include increased eutrophication. Climate change could also mean an increase in demand for farm irrigation, garden sprinklers, and perhaps even swimming pools.

DEPLETION OF AQUIFERS: Due to the expanding human population, the demand for water is growing. Many of the world's major aquifers are becoming depleted. This is due both to direct human consumption as well as agricultural irrigation by groundwater. Millions of pumps of all sizes are currently extracting groundwater throughout the world. Irrigation in dry areas such as northern China and India is supplied by groundwater, and is being extracted at an unsustainable rate.

Water pollution

Water pollution is one of the main concerns of the world today. The governments of many countries have striven to find solutions to reduce this problem. Many pollutants threaten water supplies, but the most widespread, especially in underdeveloped countries, is the discharge of raw sewage into natural waters. This method of sewage disposal is not only the most common method in underdeveloped countries, but also is prevalent in quasi-developed countries such as China, India and Iran. Sewage, sludge, garbage, and even toxic pollutants are all dumped into the water. Even if sewage is treated, problems still arise. Treated sewage forms sludge, which may be placed in landfills, spread out on land, incinerated or dumped at sea. In addition to sewage, nonpoint source pollution such as agricultural run-off is a significant source of pollution in some parts of the world, along with urban stormwater run-off and chemical wastes dumped by industries and governments.

Water conflict

The only known example of an actual interstate conflict over water took place between 2500 and 2350 BC, between the Sumerian states of Lagash and Umma. Yet, despite the lack of evidence of international wars being fought over water alone, water has been the source of various conflicts throughout history. When water scarcity causes political tensions to arise, this is referred to as water stress. Water stress has led most often to conflicts at local and regional levels. Using a purely quantitative methodology, Thomas Homer-Dixon successfully correlated water scarcity and scarcity of available arable lands to an increased chance of violent conflict.

Water stress can also exacerbate conflicts and political tensions which are not directly caused by water. Gradual reductions over time in the quality and/or quantity of fresh water can add to the instability of a region by depleting the health of a population, obstructing economic development, and exacerbating larger conflicts.

Conflicts and tensions over water are most likely to arise within national borders, in the downstream areas of distressed river basins. Areas such as the lower regions of China's Yellow River or the Chao Phraya River in Thailand, for example, have already been experiencing water stress for several years. Additionally, certain arid countries which rely heavily on water for irrigation, such as China, India, Iran, and Pakistan, are particularly at risk of water-related conflicts. Political tensions, civil protest, and violence may also occur in reaction to water privatisation. The Bolivian water wars of 2000 are a case in point.

Water supply status report

Food and water are two basic human needs. However, global coverage figures from 2002 indicate that, of every 10 people:

- Roughly 5 have a connection to a piped water supply at home (in their dwelling, plot or yard);
- Three make use of some other sort of improved water supply, such as a protected well or public standpipe;
- Two are unserved;
- In addition, 4 out of every 10 people live without improved sanitation.

At the Earth Summit 2002, governments approved a plan of action to:

- Halve by 2015 the proportion of people unable to reach or afford safe drinking water. *The Global Water Supply and Sanitation Assessment 2000 Report (GWSSAR)* defines 'Reasonable access' to water as at least 20 litres per person per day from a source within one kilometre of the user's home.
- Halve the proportion of people without access to basic sanitation. The GWSSAR defines 'Basic sanitation' as private or shared but not public disposal systems that separate waste from human contact.

As the scenario shows, by 2025 water shortages will be more prevalent among poorer countries where resources are limited and population growth is rapid, such as the Middle East, Africa, and parts of Asia. By 2025, large urban and peri-urban areas will require new infrastructure to provide safe water and adequate sanitation. This suggests growing conflicts with agricultural water users, who currently consume the majority of the water used by humans.

More developed countries of North America, Europe and Russia will not see a serious threat to water supply by the year 2025, not only because of their relative wealth, but more importantly their populations will be better aligned with available water resources. North Africa, the Middle East, South Africa and northern China will face very severe water shortages due to physical scarcity and a condition of overpopulation relative to their carrying capacity with respect to water supply. Most of South America, sub-Saharan Africa, Southern China and India will face water supply shortages by 2025; for these latter regions the causes of scarcity will be economic constraints to developing safe drinking water, as well as excessive population growth. As many as 1.6 billion people have gained access to a safe water source since 1990. The proportion of people in developing countries with access to safe water is calculated to have improved from 30 per cent in 1970 to 71 per cent in 1990, 79 per cent in 2000 and 84 per cent in 2004. This trend is projected to continue to be aligned with available water resources. This is good news.

The United Nations, during the Millennium Summit in New York in 2000 and the World Summit on Sustainable Development in Johannesburg in 2002, developed a series of Millennium Development Goals (MDGs) aiming to achieve poverty eradication and sustainable development. The specific target set for the provision of water supply and sanitation services is to halve the proportion of people without access to safe drinking water and adequate sanitation by 2015. WHO and UNICEF reported in 2004 that the number of people lacking basic sanitation services rose from 2.1 billion in 2001 to 2.6 billion by 2004. The UNDP Human Development Report (2006) has shown the progress towards meeting the MDG sanitation target is however much too slow, with an enormous gap existing between the intended coverage and today's reality, especially in sub-Sahara Africa and parts of Asia. The reasons for this are numerous. A major issue is the fact that sanitation rarely benefits from the political attention given to other topics despite its key importance on many other sectors and on all other MDGs. Political will has been sorely lacking when it comes to placing sanitation high on the international development agenda. This has pushed sanitation into the shadows of water supply projects, for example, and limited innovation in the sector.

Sustainable sanitation system

The main objective of a sustainable sanitation system is to protect and promote health by providing a clean environment and breaking the cycle of disease. In order to be sustainable, a sanitation system has to be not only economically viable, socially acceptable and technically and institutionally appropriate, but it should also protect the environment and the natural resources. When improving an existing and/or designing a new sanitation system, sustainability criteria related to the following aspects should be considered:

- *Health*: It includes the risk of exposure to pathogens and hazardous substances, that could affect public health at all points of the sanitation system from the toilet via the collection and treatment system to the point of reuse or disposal. The topic also covers aspects such as hygiene, nutrition and improvement of livelihood achieved by the application of a certain sanitation system, as well as downstream effects.
- *Environment and natural resources*: It involves the required energy, water and other natural resources for construction, operation and maintenance of the system, as well as the potential emissions to the environment resulting from use. It also includes the degree of recycling and reuse practised and the effects of these, for example, reusing the wastewater, returning nutrients and organic material to agriculture, and the protecting of other

non-renewable resources, for example through the production of renewable energies (e.g. biogas or fuel wood).

- *Technology*: It incorporates the functionality and the ease with which the system can be constructed, operated and monitored using the available human resources (e.g. the local community, technical team of the local utility etc.). It also concerns the suitability to achieve an efficient substance flow management from a technical point of view. Furthermore, it evaluates the robustness of the system, its vulnerability towards disasters, and the flexibility and adaptability of its technical elements to the existing infrastructure, to demographic and socio-economic developments and climate change.
- *Financial and economic issues*: It relates to the capacity of households and communities to pay for sanitation, including the construction, maintenance and depreciation of the system. Besides the evaluation of investment, operation and maintenance costs, the topic also takes into account the economic benefits that can be obtained in 'productive' sanitation systems, including benefits from the production of the recyclables (soil conditioner, fertiliser, energy and reclaimed water), employment creation, increased productivity through improved health and the reduction of environmental and public health costs.
- *Socio-cultural and institutional aspects*: They are the criteria in this category to evaluate the socio-cultural acceptance and appropriateness of the system, convenience, system perceptions, gender issues and impacts on human dignity, the contribution to subsistence economies and food security, and legal and institutional aspects. Most sanitation systems have been designed with these aspects in mind, but in practice they are failing far too often because some of the criteria are not met. In fact, there is probably no system which is absolutely sustainable. The concept of sustainability is more of a journey rather than a stage to reach. Nevertheless, it is crucial, that sanitation systems are evaluated

carefully with regard to all dimensions of sustainability. Since there is no one-for-all sanitation solution which fulfils the sustainability criteria under different circumstances to the same extent, the system evaluation will depend on the local framework and has to take into consideration existing environmental, technical, socio-cultural and economic conditions.

Human dignity index

Taking into consideration the entire range of sustainability criteria, it is important to observe some basic principles when planning and implementing a sanitation system. These were already developed some years ago by a group of experts and were endorsed by the members of the Water Supply and Sanitation Collaborative Council as the "Bellagio Principles for Sustainable Sanitation" during its 5th Global Forum in November 2000: Human dignity, quality of life and environmental security at household level should be at the centre of any sanitation approach; In line with good governance principles, decision making should involve participation of all stakeholders, especially the consumers and providers of services; Waste should be considered a resource, and its management should be holistic and form a part of integrated water resources, nutrient flow and waste management processes; and the domain in which environmental sanitation problems are resolved should be kept to the minimum practicable size (household, community, town, district, catchment etc.).

But, sanitation problems in the poor countries are different. They have different waste disposal systems; hand ablution and open defecation in India and stone and bricks are used in many countries of Africa. A large number of different sanitation practices are prevalent in 52 inland countries of Africa, 14 major countries of Latin America and many more countries in Asia and South-East Asia where they developed their cultural practices in their own ways. But, all these poor countries suffer from insanitation following influx into cities. Now it is an established fact that growing population in poor countries and the expanding consumption level in the West have put the natural resources under stress when there will not be enough water in rivers to flush out the city waste. This may not happen in the West in the next 20 years or so, but the sewerage system is beginning to show its deficiency even in the West. In which case what do we do to achieve the MDGs in these poor societies and also avert crisis in the West? The only answer is to find an alternative to the sewer system which has already become redundant in poor countries. In that context, the Sulabh technology idea becomes relevant.

Sulabh, a role model

The Sulabh technology was a revolutionary change, shifting from storing to composting and on-site disposal, instead of transferring it to water areas through sewer. Nor is the Sulabh technology a consequence of the evolution process but a paradigm shift which is why it is a game-changer. It is a whole new idea evolved through invention, development and experiment with in-built design adaptability and change to suit different climates, cultural preferences, income levels and choices unlike the previous designs which were fixed and unchanging. It disposes excreta on site instead of transferring to water areas where sewer system creates more problems than it solves. The earlier designs were Dug-well latrine, Ulta Matka, Privy Gopari System, Sopa Sandas, Hagebu latrine, Barpalli-type latrine, PRAI and VIP models aqua privy and many others. They did stand the basic test of good hygiene and phased out.

Nowhere in the world any non-government organisation (NGO), like Sulabh, has worked for sanitation to achieve the level of success which Sulabh has achieved. Sanitation is now a slogan, a rallying cry of the poor countries to join together and take up the broom to clean this exploited planet which is the common heritage of mankind.

> *Technologies have modernised the world.*
> *– Thomas L. Friedman*

CHAPTER 26

Science and Technology Trigger Social Change

A divide between old and new worlds

Technology is the defining feature of the modern world, marking it out from the previous age. Remove technology from our lives and we become primitive species which we had always been before fire was produced accidentally by tribals. The modern world is all about technology which doesn't only mean iPods, DVD and the Internet but a lot more. For thousands of years, technology has been the means by which people secured food and shelter, established social order and shaped their ways of life. The story of technology impact on social life and values remains unfinished.

From the time of the great voyages of the 15th and 16th centuries, it had been possible to talk of one world. Yet getting to know more of this world took time. In the name of religion and trade, the European powers acquired colonies in distant parts of the world, carrying with them their own ways of life and often clashing violently with local inhabitants who had their own distinctive customs. China and Japan long remained isolated, and Australia and New Zealand, reached by travellers in the 18th century, were at first sparsely settled.

In North America, modern times were ushered in when 13 British colonies broke away from rule by Britain and fought for independence, pledged to the goals of freedom and the pursuit of

AMONG THOSE WHO HAVE CHANGED THE WORLD

Albert Einstein (1879-1955) *Theory of Relativity*	**J. Robert Oppenheimer** (1904-67) *Atomic bomb*	**Jonas Salk** (1914-95) *Polio vaccine*	**James Watson** (1928-) *Structure of DNA*	**Ed Moses** (1949-) *Nuclear fusion*

human happiness that were to attract immigrants from many lands during the 19th century. The French Revolution, also proclaimed in the name of 'the people', was a more violent revolution, culminating in the march of Napoleon's armies through Europe. Aristocrats lost their privileges and many of the long-standing grievances of the peasants were met, as the ideals of liberty, equality and fraternity were proclaimed. It was second revolution.

The third revolution, the Industrial Revolution, which began in Britain, was to have far-reaching economic, social and political consequences. As machines were devised to supplement or replace human skills, and as new forms of power were developed to augment human and animal strength, ways of work were transformed. Behind the transformation was a huge increase in population. The numbers of Europeans more than doubled in the 19th century as industrialisation proceeded, from around 200 million to 430 million. These were still, however, a minority in terms of the total world population, which also doubled during the century. All the three revolutions brought permanent changes to human prosperity, expectations and daily life, but none was without its human costs. In its first stages, the Industrial Revolution depended on the labour of women and children, and in many centres of industry it created class conflicts between employers, living on profits, and employees, living on wages. It thereby stimulated revolutionary ideas and movements. There were sharp contrasts between the everyday lives of rich and poor, the latter creating trade unions and, in time, political parties. The industrialising process also damaged the environment, darkening the skies and polluting the rivers.

Old values, particularly religious values, were challenged. In the long run, however, material standards of living were raised, along with human expectations. Over large parts of the world there was a movement, too, towards democracy – the granting of the vote to all men, although in most countries still not to women, who were beginning at last to fight for their rights.

Even in autocratic Russia, which in 1900 was still ruled by a tsar, the serfs had been liberated and industrial growth had begun. It was Russia, which had escaped revolution during the 19th century that was to become the first nation to experience revolution in the 20th century. The repercussions were to be felt throughout the world, as the new century progressed. So, too, were the repercussions of growing American wealth and power. These all happened because of technology. Technology is a great power, and a greater killer. It destroys and builds both, depending on how it is used. And, thereby hangs a tale of growth of science and technology and how they have changed the life and social values since ancient time.

James Hargreaves, born in Oswaldtwistle, England, in 1720, was a carpenter who received neither formal education nor was taught to read or write. Legend has it that Hargreaves' daughter Jenny knocked over a spinning wheel and, as Hargreaves watched the spindle roll across the floor, the idea for the spinning jenny came to him. This is how it is called spinning-jenny. Who could imagine that an illiterate carpenter and weaver would produce an Industrial Revolution which has finally created technology-driven world in which we live today? The Industrial Revolution was a period between the 18th and 19th century during which major changes happened in agriculture, manufacturing, mining, and transport which had a profound effect on the socio-economic and cultural conditions in the United Kingdom. Starting in the later part of the 18th century, there began a transition from manual labour and animal-based economy to machine-based manufacturing.

It started with the mechanisation of textile (spinning-jenny) industries, the development of iron-making techniques and the increased use of refined coal. Trade expansion was enabled by the introduction of canals, improved roads and railways. The introduction of steam power fuelled by coal, wider utilisation of water wheels and powered machinery underpinned the dramatic increases in production capacity. The development of all-metal machine tools in the first two decades of the 19th century facilitated the manufacture of more machines for use in other industries. The effects spread throughout Western Europe and North America during the 19th century, eventually affecting most of the world, a process that is called Industrial Revolution. The impact of this change on society was overwhelming.

In the 19th century, Gregor Johan Mendel (1822-84), an Austrian botanist, pioneered genetics, Charles Darwin (1809-82) helped develop the Theory of Evolution and Charles Babbage (1792-1871) made the first mechanical computer. As the last century closed, scientists studied the atom and motion at the speed of light in space. Here Newton's rules did not apply: Einstein's theory of Relativity and Planck's Laws of Quantum Mechanics were needed. In the last century, nuclear power was born, so also the transistor and modern computer. Later the space age began and men stood on the Moon in 1969.

Until about 7,000 years ago, there was almost no technology apart from simple tools, clothes and shelters. From then on, human civilisation needed new farming tools, more housing and new materials to make them from. The most important invention was the wheel, in use from about 5,000 years ago. Ancient people learnt how to make metals by heating ores found on the Earth's surface and then manufactured useful objects. Much of the early technological development occurred in the Middle East and the Far East. The Egyptians and Indians were advanced in making things from pottery, glass and a range of different metals. Europe did not begin to catch up until the 14th century, when the Church's opposition to new scientific ideas began to decline. Development in printing, mining, processing materials and scientific instruments made Europe the most advanced technological region.

Technology was transformed by the production and control of energy to power machinery during the Industrial Revolution. The steam engine and later the internal combustion engine provided reliable sources of power for manufacturing, transport, agriculture and processing. The development of electronics made communications and small powerful computers possible and triggered a new revolution in the 20th century.

Science is philosophy, technology is fact

Technology is the systematic study of techniques for making and doing things; science is the systematic attempt to understand and interpret the world. While technology is concerned with the fabrication and use of artefacts, science is devoted to the more conceptual enterprise of understanding the world which depends on the sophisticated skills of literacy and knowledge, which became available only with the emergence of the great world civilisations. Science began with civilisations, from 3,000 years BC, while technology came later. Science and technology developed as different and separate activities, the former being for several millennia, a field of abstruse speculation practised by a class of aristocratic philosophers, while the latter remained a matter of essentially practical concern to craftsmen of many types. One is philosophy; the other is fact.

Michael Faraday, Henry Ford and Thomas Edison

The role of Thomas Edison is significant in deepening relationship between science and technology, the prodigious trial-and-error process by which he selected the carbon filament for his electric light bulb in 1879. The application of scientific principles to technology grew rapidly. It led easily to the engineering rationalism applied by Frederick W. Taylor, workers in mass production, and to the time-and-motion studies of Frank and Lillian Gilbreth at the beginning of the 20th century. It provided a model that was applied rigorously by Henry Ford in his automobile assembly plant and that was followed by every modern mass production process. It paved the way for the development of systems engineering operations research, simulation studies, mathematical modelling, and technological assessment in industrial processes. This was not just a one-way influence of science on technology, because technology created new tools and machines while scientists were able to achieve an ever-increasing insight into the natural world. Taken together, these developments brought technology to its modern highly efficient level of performance. But, science is the mother of technology.

Steam engine

Although the qualification regarding older sources of power is important, steam became the characteristic and ubiquitous power

JAMES WATT (1736-1819)

Watt was a British engineer and inventor whose improvements to the steam engine made it into a useful source of power. In 1764, he invented an outside condenser (which turned waste steam back into water). He then designed engines in which the steam acted on both sides of the piston. The watt (unit of power) was named after him.

source of the British Industrial Revolution. Little development took place in the Newcomen atmospheric engine until James Watt patented a separate condenser in 1769, but from that point onward the steam engine underwent almost continuous improvements for more than a century. Watt's separate condenser was the outcome of his work on a model of a Newcomen engine that was being used in a University of Glasgow laboratory. Watt's inspiration was to separate the two actions of heating, the cylinder with hot steam and cooling it to condense the steam for every stroke of the engine. By keeping the cylinder permanently hot and the condenser permanently cold, a great economy on energy used could be effected.

Moral value of an idea, theory or technology is judged by its social utility.

– Jeremy Bentham

CHAPTER 27

Philosophy of Sulabh Technologies and System

Greatest good to the largest number

"Man assuredly needs to rise above the humdrum of the world. Wisdom shows him the way. Man tends to create monster technologies which may destroy the world if only to seek fantastic satisfaction, like landing on the Moon. But the question is how to save this planet from human greed".

– E.F. Schumacher

The morally superior position is the one that would result in the 'the greatest good to the largest number.' The term, coined in 1781 by Jeremy Bentham, is the concept of utilitarianism which replaces rationalism that says reason, not utility, is the determinant of moral value of goods and services. Utilitarian philosophers say that the moral worth of an action should be judged by its consequences – in this case, its social utility.

The pleasure or satisfaction a consumer derives from using a product, service or technology, has its root in classical economics referring to the utility, or usefulness, of a commodity. The theory originated in the early 19th century which was later developed by economists known as *marginalists.* According to this theory, consumer satisfaction can be numerically represented in terms of *'utils'* or units of satisfaction. In principle, the more someone consumes, the more utility she or he derives, but as total utility increases, marginal utility – the satisfaction derived from each additional consumption of a commodity – decreases.

The goals of utilitarianism were almost assailed as unquantifiable: How can happiness or utility be measured? How can the outcome of an action be predicted? Which is preferable – more bliss for many and more agony for some, or a better balance of both for all? In his *'Evolutionary Utilitarianism,'* Herbert Spencer tried to reject this argument by focusing on the cumulative effects of moral ideas, like altruism, over the whole history of societies. John Stuart Mill sought to quantify utilitarianism by distinguishing between 'higher' and 'lower' grades of happiness and between those capable of appreciating them: "It is better to be Socrates dissatisfied than a pig satisfied," he said.

Whatever the consequences of the philosophical polemics, the concept of utilitarianism has set a standard to judge the utility of an idea or technology. For instance, space science or atomic bomb technology may be great scientific achievements, but they have no moral legitimacy, which the small Sulabh technology may have because it serves the greatest good to the largest number criterion. It is easy to measure the utility of, say woollen garments, for those who shiver in cold, but what is the utility or moral value of the altruistic action of a glass of water being given to a thirsty man? Or, the satisfaction a woman, who has to wait from sunrise to sunset to go for open defecation, gets when she is given a very inexpensive and culturally acceptable Sulabh toilet in her home? It is not hard to judge the difference in the moral value of both technologies–one of space science, and another as mundane as Sulabh toilet. Hence, the Sulabh technology has a much higher moral legitimacy than the technologies of mass destruction.

The term 'philosophy' is derived from the Greek word for 'love of wisdom' which implies the worldview and its implications for the good of humankind. While philosophy seeks to determine the ethical basis of social action, (or technological innovation) the core value of philosophy is rooted in moral action which defines the best ways to live in a happy relation with others. While philosophy is largely an abstraction, defined by different philosophers differently, there is total agreement that this discipline of knowledge (epistemology) is based on knowledge, universal values, reason and humanism.

Philosophy has subfields, including philosophy of religion, law, economics, biology, physics, mathematics, technology, psychology, art, politics, music, literature, and so on. Any or all of these topics can be studied in a philosophical way by making inquiry into their moral values. When such disparate topics are raised, conflicts and paradoxes also arise. Science, for instance, leads us to believe that every act is determined by a prior cause *(a priori),* cause and effect phenomenon.

Philosophy has different interpretations in different countries and different times. We have medieval philosophy, Renaissance philosophy, Chinese and Indian, so also many other philosophies with different focus and emphasis. But all of them seek an inquiry into moral questions of right and wrong. For instance, Greek and the Renaissance philosophies were based on reason *(Averroism),* medieval philosophy is based on faith; Chinese philosophy is rooted in Confucianism. But, Indian philosophy is all about *'dharma',* differently defined in different ages by different rulers. The Indian philosophy refers to several traditions of philosophical thoughts that originated in the Indian subcontinent, including Hindu philosophy, Buddhist and Jain philosophy. All these philosophies have a common underlying theme of *dharma.*

Philosophy and technology may be very different from each other, but all technologies have been assessed for their moral values. For instance, when Einstein discovered that $e = mc^2$ was a way for mass destruction, he gave it up, leaving it for Oppenheimer, another physicist, to build atomic bomb in New Mexico in 1943-45 to be finally dropped in Japan. Einstein was a German Jew who fled to England and later to the US only to develop a weapon which could defeat Hitler. But when he found one, he flinched and stopped research. On the first explosion of atomic bomb, Einstein exclaimed: "If I had known this equation may destroy human race, I would have loved to remain a watch maker." It was his moral revulsion that made him campaign for peace the rest of his life. It was philosophy. Similarly, technologies have social and political implications.

How technologies won empires

The modern world is, as a matter of fact, the product of the Industrial Revolution which started in the late 18th century. And today our entire life, value system, and social relationships are governed by technology which has made Europe master of the world. Until 1820, India and China were the largest economies in the world, but then came the Industrial Revolution and we lost the global primacy to the West which had high technology and we had none.

Historian Niall Ferguson says in his book, *Empire,* that the one gun, *Maxim,* invented by an American in a London underground, helped the West conquer all the 53 countries of Africa within weeks. Cecil Rhodes, son of a clergyman of Stafford, who migrated to South Africa when he was 17, virtually conquered the entire African continent, from Cairo to Cape, in weeks, working with other predator, looter, adventurer and financier Nathaniel de Rothchild, who captured South African goldmines. Rothchild and Rhodes virtually owned all the wealth of Africa between 1882 and 1888. Ferguson writes: "The key to the phenomenal expansion of the British empire in the late Victorian period was the combination of financial power and fire power." The Maxim gun, says the historian, "looked to the Matabele (chief tribe ruling North Africa under Lobengula), like heavenly fire. It seemed that the white men came with guns that spat bullets from the heavens which spit hails, while the naked Matabele soldiers stood against these guns to die like animals." Around 1,500 Matabele warriors were wiped out in one day while only four of the 700 invaders died. None of them was British. *The Time* reported smugly that the Matabele took the British victory as witchcraft, saying that *Maxim* gun was a pure work of an evil spirit. Thus, one gun technology was developed and entire Africa was lost. For that matter, Plassey was also never a battle fought between two equals in 1757. Robert Clive had brought some crude guns from Mysore and gardeners who fought the Nawab soldiers, riding horses and fighting with spears and swords. Not one Englishman was killed because they never came in contact with the enemy. And the battle was lost. So also India's freedom. This is the story of all the empires in Asia, where the West ruled for centuries with technology, cunning and deceit. They built empire with technology.

Small technologies cause big change

Technology has also redefined our daily social life and political relationships and reinvented values. Household devices like VCR, CDs, Internet, Laser Discs, Fax Machine, Facebook, Twitter, cellphone and many other small and affordable devices have changed the world beyond recognition. Lately, Twitter, and Facebook have caused political revolutions in Iran, Tunisia, Egypt, Libya, Yemen and Lebanon. Twitter and Facebook connected people without coming to street to organise themselves in protest agitations. President Ben Ali of Tunisia fled the country without a bullet being fired or man being killed. Power changed hands in Egypt and Libya. Earlier, to bring about a change of this magnitude, France had to launch a revolution and fight a bloody war for 26 years (1789-1815) when Napoleon was finally defeated and exiled. After which the world was never the same again.

Sulabh technologies rooted in values

Technology has also brought social changes which have moral implications; Sulabh technologies are ones. They are simple devices of human ingenuity which have changed the lives of millions of people, especially the poor, in the way only spinning-jenny did before. However, Sulabh technologies are different from many others, in that they are affordable and universal and have a much larger human and environmental impact than most others. Let us first take the simple two-pit, pour-flush on-site human waste disposal technology. The poorest among the poor can, on his own, dig up two pits with primitive tools and avail of toilet privacy and healthy living. It will benefit 2.6 billion people in the world, who have no access to toilets and sit out in the open. Besides other implications, 50 or more types of diseases are caused by open defecation which diminishes the production and productivity of a nation, resulting in deeper poverty and many disabilities. This technology throws excreta into the pit where it matures to become pathogen-free manure to be used in fields to grow crops. The septic tank system was developed by the Portuguese but it has vent pipe which is the source of environmental pollution. The Sulabh technology has none; it is clean, environment-friendly, culturally appropriate and adaptable in different climes and cultures.

Where West is no guide

The West had developed the sewerage system in early 19th century which flushes out human waste through the pipe into water areas. When this raised *'Great Stink'*, the West invented technology to treat sewage, reduce BOD and again discharge the treated sewage water into water. This system is adopted in the West because they have enough water to pollute and enough money to spend. Now that the people in the developing countries are migrating to cities for jobs, education and good life in large numbers, there is not enough water to carry sewage into water areas nor money to set up treatment plants. In which case, the poor are facing serious health problems which have been highlighted at many national and international meetings, the most important being the Johannesburg millennium mega conference in 2002 which has clearly set out the Goal Number 7 (target 7.C) to reduce the number of people without toilets by half by the year 2015.

Imagine, if the excreta of 80 crore people in India (assuming that 20 crores have flush system) are thrown out, all the water of ocean cannot clean it. And, if one adds the number of the rest of the toiletless people of Asia, Africa and Latin America, the human waste disposal problem will become catastrophic, threatening the planet. In this context, the Sulabh technology becomes globally relevant with a moral message. No wonder, Sulabh technologies are catching up with UN-Habitat and other global and national agencies declaring Sulabh toilet systems as the Best Global Practices to be adopted globally after appropriate changes. The two-pit technology, thus, serves the social purposes of providing toilets to all, rich and poor, without having to spend lots of money.

The Sulabh biogas system extracts nutrients, collecting methane gas for cooking and street lighting. The water is also treated and reused. The low-cost toilet can be specially used in slums where the poorly disposed waste spreads diseases. Sulabh has so far built 1.5 million household toilets, 8,500 community toilets and several school toilets and they are being used by more than 20 million people everyday. Such toilets will be built in 50 other countries and Sulabh plans to set up 500 toilets in each country as models. Sulabh has already trained people from 14 countries of Africa in collaboration with UN-HABITAT, so that they may replicate it on their own. (For details, access www.sulabhinternational.org)

Sulabh technology is emancipator

Apart from these, the great social objective that the Sulabh technologies have achieved is the liberation of scavengers through them. So far, more than 2 lakh scavengers have been thus liberated and rehabilitated after education and training. This is a great social reform achieved by any technology. If new airplane, car, phone or any high-end technologies have been developed, they have benefited only those who use them. But consumption and excretion are the basic biological features of all humans, rich and poor. And, for that matter, Sulabh toilet technologies benefit the mankind. The scope and extent of social change caused by Sulabh technologies far exceed any that we have known today since spinning-jenny, which has provided affordable clothes to all, the rich and poor.

For that matter, to be true, the Sulabh technology is an agent of social change. The technology which replaced slave labour in American plantations and, not entirely the Civil War, helped abolish slavery in the US. Similarly Sulabh toilet has ended scavenging, besides promoting the environmental sanitation, human rights, economic productivity, health and happiness. This is the philosophy behind Sulabh technologies. This is the *dharma* that it seeks to promote. Dr. Bindeshwar Pathak, a man of faith, takes a moral view of things and does not take up the project which he finds without moral perspective. By his social and family background, he is very sensitive to social and human problems, defining them in terms of *dharma* which, for him, is a comprehensive view of right and wrong.

Dr. Pathak's view of economic philosophy

Dr. Pathak explains his philosophy also in economic terms and quotes Prof. Jagdish Bhagwati and Prof. Amartya Sen. Prof. Bhagwati says that economic growth must come first to provide the money required for social development. Prof. Sen says, "If 85 per cent of money spent for public benefit is wasted prior to the economic reforms, as Mr. Rajiv Gandhi has said, attention should be focused to redesign institutions and organisations to be able to produce more bang for the buck." Of course, the two opinions are not contradictory, but priority is different. It is about chicken and egg.

Some economists say that the quality of public services will improve by handing them to the private sector which, with its focus on efficiency and profits, will cut out waste. Another section believes that environmental damage is caused by the 'tragedy of the commons' which no one owns. Creation of private property rights (including tradable rights to pollute the atmosphere) will induce human beings to behave irresponsibly. The basic premise of this school of thought is that the market, in which self-interested persons can trade, will always produce good results while the others say that institutions for progress must be founded on principles of rights and wrong, (*dharma*) judged in the context of the greatest good to the largest number. Free market is insensitive, amoral, valueless and inquisitive; it cannot deliver social good.

Re-inventing wheel

The West says why they must re-invent the wheel which is already there. India's problem is the delivery system. Prof. Amartya Sen says: "There are two reasons why India must find new and innovative solutions. The first is that the wheel of progress that has been invented in the West has put more pressure on the Earth than it can bear. Hence, the Western technologies are not compatible with environmental conditions in the poor countries which have large population and relatively scarce resources. The Western goal of progress seems to be that all must aspire to attain the lifestyle of American consumers. If all the people of the world were to live at the standards of middle class Americans, we would need one more planet to support them. But we have only one; so it is imperative we find a sustainable way for economic growth." Dr. Pathak, an admirer of E.F. Schumacher, quotes the German economist and the writer of the great book, *Small is Beautiful,* to say: "Adam Smith's theory of perpetual 3 per cent compound global growth of the peoples of the world whose number is rising exponently, will be devastating. This is not sustainable because while population grows along with the awesome technologies to exploit nature's resource, the 'global commons,' remain unchanged, though renewable. So sustainability should be the core philosophy of economic growth if we want this planet to continue to provide life support to the coming generations. Our ambition to consume resources is limitless, while natural resources are limited. Hence, the Club of Rome's appeal for 'Limit to Growth'."

MDG benchmark

During the last 20 years, there is an increasing consciousness of universal human rights as expressed in the UN Millennium Development Goals. These rights include the right to food, health, sanitation, and education. Through ubiquity of information through media, cell phones, and the Internet, people know what others do. They wonder why it should be their destiny to wait while others already enjoy the fruits of progress. These two forces are stirred up further by rapidly proliferating numbers of civil society organisations which have made people much less patient than they used to be earlier. Therefore, for more rapid inclusion and sustainability, we need to re-invent the wheel and make development sustainable. And, institutions are the wheels on which the cart of progress moves. The need to redesign institutions to ensure inclusion and sustainability is important also to promote public interest, social entrepreneurship, and larger good of society.

When Ms. Elinor Ostrom was awarded the Nobel Prize in Economics, she said the solution to social problems is not only the government, but good institutions managing shared resources efficiently as well as fairly, and blended capabilities of public-private partnerships. Ms. Elinor Ostrom is an American political scientist. She was awarded the 2009 Nobel Memorial Prize in Economic Sciences, which she shared with Oliver E. Williamson, for "her analysis of economic governance, especially the commons."

Dr. Pathak adds to it and says system of social service delivery has also to change to be able to take the benefits to the largest number of people. He says institutions have to be developed to improve human development index which in India is lower than in Bangladesh. He does not, however, take a doctrinaire position and says, the role of civil society should be promoted to ensure a synthesis of private profit and public good. They must work together. "As long as the greatest good to the largest number happens, the system is not important. Life does not offer many choices. The one which serves the moral purpose, *dharma,* of serving the poor is the system good enough to be adopted." This is what Sulabh technologies and system seek to achieve.

"I may not be born again, but if it happens I will like to be born in a family of scavengers, so that I may relieve them of the inhuman, unhealthy and hateful practice of carrying night soil."
– Mahatma Gandhi

CHAPTER 28

Scavenging: A Flawed Social Construct

A historical injustice revisited

One cannot argue that scavenging being a historical injustice, cannot be corrected by law or social reforms, or both, because it is beyond both. It is like arguing that since injustice against the Jews is of biblical vintage, hence, we cannot discuss Holocaust and Hitler's concentration camps. The analogy is false.

The scavenger cannot choose anything when they have only one thing to choose from, i.e., toilet. Henry Ford said: "You can choose any colour as long as it is black". They can choose any job as long as it is toilet in any city, town, individual house; they are free to choose anything as long as it is toilet. German philosopher Hegel (1770-1831) distinguishes between abstract and concrete freedom. The former means the freedom to do whatever you want. Women can choose between different kinds of clothes, to look smart but none of them will allow you to walk. Such was the freedom of capitalism.

For Hegel, this is a false freedom because our wants and desires are determined by society, not by ourselves. By those standards, a Western fashion victim is as much a sartorial prisoner as a woman in a burqa. By real freedom, Hegel meant not doing whatever one wants to but having the freedom from societal conditioning. In other words, the real freedom is when a scavenger can say 'no' to toilet and take up other jobs with full social acceptance. If you come across someone who manages to be really free in this sense, we can really celebrate his escape. But it does not happen; our freedom is restricted by society, its rulers and *Pandits* as is the case with scavengers and our social customs and religious rituals, which have divided society into two – touchable and untouchable.

None of us is really free in that sense. One would rather see a headscarf ban than Muslim ghettoes. Or a scavenger in toilet than a scavenger dying of hunger. Liberating people from their social shackles would make us free but not by robbing them of their living. We love such abstract freedoms and not the concrete freedom which is harder to ensure because it will mean changing attitude and destroying faith, which is hard to do. For Hegel, this was the basis of the French Revolution's collapse into the terror in which individuals were sacrificed to the ill-conceived pursuit of abstract freedoms. The US is an exception because of the manner of its birth, the system of its belief and huge resources. France has venerated abstract freedom for 210 years, no wonder it is out of steps with most EU countries.

America is a constantly evolving society that never ceases to change unlike France and India which are frozen in time. Plurality, multi-culturalism and republican ideals are the founding ideas which have made America far too different a society than any we have known before. For that matter, India also gets along by accepting diversity, and you feel a glow of pride at India's impressive effort to live in unity amidst mind-blowing diversity. True, our efforts break down every now and then and we descend into vengeful ways in fits of madness. But as we master the art of making up and reconciliation, the madness will fade away and we'll move on.

Social justice: A fallacy

In case of scavengers, the concept of social justice is also a fallacy. Prof. Amartya Sen in his book, *The Idea of Justice,* says there are two lines of reasoning about justice – the utopian approach, which concentrates on the nature of a perfectly just society, and the comparative approach, which focuses on the actual realisation of justice and the prevention of the manifestation of severe injustices. Prof. Sen argues that the first approach, which he has named "transcendental institutionalism" is redundant; "it is neither necessary nor efficient," because it is a remote search for an ideal. There is also a problem that at the level of principle, one may not be able to reject certain claims that may all seem equally just. "The idea of justice demands a comparative approach." To explain this, Prof. Sen gives the analogy that the knowledge that Mona Lisa is the ideal picture in the world is of no importance, when one has to make a choice between cinema posters. They are two entirely different things.

Mona Lisa

'Niti' and 'Nyaya'

Drawing on the ancient jurisprudence of India, Prof. Sen makes a distinction between the two approaches using the two Sanskrit words for justice – Niti and Nyaya. "While Niti is the organisation of propriety and behaviour correctness, Nyaya is a comprehensive idea of justice." Again, scavengers do not fit in this template of comparative or absolute justice. Very clearly this is absolutely a transcendental injustice, the like of which has never been known in history. "We know of massive genocide, and all kinds of cruelty on man by man. But nothing like this has been known because hurt is deep and it is just that a class of people are condemned to live a life of filth and all conceivable type of degradation without anybody knowing or telling about it under the system of democracy, freedom, rule of law, social justice, freedom of free choice and other platitudes. This is because nobody knows what the problem is about and the victims are too defenceless, poor, weak and untouchable to be heard by those who claim to lift the world so that people can breathe free. It is both a tragedy and a farce.

Freedom of choice – a flawed concept

The ongoing theories of justice in mainstream political philosophy are very strongly dependent today on a way of thinking largely initiated by Thomas Hobbes in the 17th century, with an overwhelming concentration on a hypothetical 'social contract' that the people of a sovereign state can be imagined to have endorsed. This presumed contract is supposed to identify the 'just institutions' needed. This 'contractarian' approach is the dominant influence in the contemporary political philosophy of justice, and its limited focus has narrowed the analysis of justice unduly, and in particular distancing the theories of justice from the actual lives of people. According to this interpretation, scavengers clean toilet as a consequence of social contract. This is ludicrous.

A number of other enlightenment theorists (Adam Smith, Marquis de Condorcet, Mary Wollstonecraft, Karl Marx and John Stuart Mill, for example), however, had a variety of approaches that shared a common interest in the people's actual lives, rather than on institutional perfection. What happens to people depends not merely on the institutions that exist but also on other influences, in particular people's behaviour and social interactions. This alternative approach has much to offer to contemporary political philosophy and also to our actual practices and policies.

If it is important not to be restricted by the reading of freedom within institutional libertarianism, the need to go beyond the utilitarian concentration on the mental metrics of utilities in the form of pleasures or desire fulfilments is no less strong. Even if chronically deprived persons – the hopelessly poor, or long-term unemployed – learn to come to terms with and accept cheerfully their deprived lifestyles, that cultivated or contrived cheerfulness will not eliminate the real loss of freedom. One cannot argue that just because the poor laugh, play and live a normal life, they have accepted their status in society.

When dealing with the issue of torture, and rejecting it as anti-freedom, the concept of libertariansim is easy to understand. It is outright wrong but when the focus is on issues of economic and social inequality, the concept of freedom can be captured better by a fuller assessment of what is called, in the new literature, 'capabilities', which reflect the actual opportunities of a person. The real opportunities that different persons enjoy are very substantially influenced by variations of individual circumstances (for example age, disability, talents, gender, maternity) and also by disparities in the natural and the social environment (for example epidemiological conditions, pollution, prevalence of crime). An exclusive concentration on inequalities in income distribution cannot be adequate for an understanding of economic inequality.

Consider an example. Being disabled has a double effect, in reducing the person's ability to earn an income ('earning handicap') and in making the conversion of income into good living that much harder, thanks to the costs of assistance, and the impossibility of fully correcting certain types of disadvantages caused by disability ('conversion handicap'). A person who happens to be physically disabled may need to pay for assistance, and even then may not become able to move around freely. The conversion handicap is routinely missed in poverty relief programmes that concentrate only on the lowness of incomes.

What about power, a concept that closely relates to the idea of freedom? To say that a person is powerless in reversing the kind of neglect that they have been experiencing can also be expressed in the language of capability; they are not capable of reversing the neglect from which they suffer. And yet there is some evocative strength and rhetorical force in the language of power, particularly in dealing with powerlessness, that the word capability, which is really a term of art, cannot really match. Analysing power and powerlessness can help to generate a better understanding of the divided world in which we live. Mary Wollstonecraft's wrath and bitter irony about the subjugation of women complemented her cool reasoning against gender hierarchy in her 1792 classic, A Vindication of the Rights of Woman.

Or take Steve Biko's remarks on 'powerlessness' in the apartheid-based South Africa in the 1970s. "Powerlessness breeds," Biko said, "a race of beggars who smile at the enemy and swear at him in the sanctity of his toilet; who shout 'bastard' during the day and call the white man a dog in their buses as they go home." If capability failure of any kind is a matter of concern, those related to people's inability to act freely or speak openly because of the power of others have special urgency. This is an important concern in the advancement of freedom and capability, since societies involve conflicts as well as togetherness and mutual support. The pursuit of justice in enhancing freedoms and capabilities in people's lives has to be alive to both. This can be possible by social and economic action and not by theoretical models. *(Source: Amartya Sen, a Nobel prize-winning economist).*

Scavengers need opportunity, not patronage

We live in a new information society which has destroyed many myths, most important of which is the misconceived notion that revolution produces social change. Not necessarily, not any more. Change will come only through information, so also social reform to end discrimination, prejudices, violence, religious radicalism and so forth. All political systems address social development issues which involve social justice, education, economic growth, equitable distribution of resources and a whole range of human relationship issues as determined by tradition, cultural preferences, the environment and political choice. For that matter, the world was set for Great Transition at the end of last millennium which presented more complex situations and greater uncertainties than any that the humankind had faced before.

The rapid communication system, television, radio and hundred other scientific inventions have destroyed national boundaries, aggressive nationalism and cultural identity – they all have been globalised. Mastery of digital information now determines success or failure of a society; and low-cost, high-speed communications will make citizenship in the global village possible. The Internet, that began as a means of exchanging information between scientists in the Pentagon, has emerged as a challenge to traditional societies.

Everything has changed except the conditions of scavengers, who still manually clean and carry human excreta to make a meagre living. Their entire life revolves round toilets where they are born and where they die. Scavengers seldom grow old; they die young from diseases and unclean living conditions. The 'scavenger' concept was introduced by the British (earlier they were called *Chandals*, *Doms* etc.) for whoever cleans up human excrement. Since it was an impure job and, therefore, he was treated as untouchables. Within the group of untouchables, the scavenger finds himself at the bottom of the hierarchy. Untouchables with other jobs like cremation of corpses or selling animals skin have a higher position in society. Nothing has been able to change this: neither a resolution in 1932, approved by Mahatma Gandhi and proposed by the Hindu leaders after the Poona Pact nor the Constitution which has officially abolished untouchability. Many do not even know that 15 per cent of all state jobs are reserved for persons belonging to the lowest castes. Gandhiji had said no one will have to clean excrement to earn a living and no one should be treated as an untouchable. These two promises of Mahatma Gandhi have remained unfulfilled until today. Even now hundreds of thousands of men and women have to empty toilets without flush with their hands and carry off the faeces in containers. The few rupees they earn are sufficient to eke out a livelihood but only to live in remote ghettos.

Socially, scavengers are untouchables among untouchables. They are sealed off from the mainstream of social life. The law (Articles 17 and 46 of the Constitution, the Employment of Manual Scavengers and Construction of Dry Latrines (Prohibition) Act, 1993 and the Protection of Civil Rights Act, 1955 which was amended in 1976 by making the punishments under this Act more stringent and offences non-compoundable) does not help in this respect at all. The sporadic attempts of private persons or social organisations have not changed the situation either. The question of social acceptability is not entirely a matter of law; it is also an attitudinal problem which has to be solved differently. Scavengers, as professionals, have been growing in number; first, because of the general growth in population; and, second, because of the rising demand for their services in fast-growing urban and semi-urban settlements, most of which are unplanned and, hence, unsewered. This situation has also produced ready jobs for them which are hard to come for other untouchables, equally poor, illiterate and outcast.

Ironically, persons from all the religions, viz., Hindu, Sikh, Muslim and Christian are scavengers today. Once a scavenger, always a scavenger. The people, who were pushed into this profession as a consequence of lost wars or joblessness, never came out of it. They became untouchables forever. Thus, once the defenders of our land and faith have become scavengers of today! Surnames like Chauhan, Bisen, Bhadwaria, Thakur, Rout and Bundela are tell-tale clan names of scavengers as well as of Rajput warriors who fought and fell for the country and its glory.

The truth is that scavenging and untouchability are a man-made social contract which has neither moral legitimacy nor social justification. They are the inevitable consequences of the feudal system introduced during the imperial days when the foreign rulers divided society into many layers and those at the bottoms became untouchable scavengers to remain in a frozen social status since. Religion, spirituality, social reforms, and democracy's tall talk of equality, justice and human rights have bypassed them; even Five-Year Plans ignored them also because they don't fit into any stereotype, SC, ST, OBC, and other reservation tags which have produced many parties, some of which have seized power.

Scavengers are deeper into degradation, deprivation and backwardness more than any other class. Even other Harijans and scavengers have nothing in common. They don't intermarry nor eat together. Scavengers don't have anything to do with the tribes, castes, religions, or cultural groups described in the Constitution or recognised by society. Scavengers are also divided among themselves, coming as they do from different castes – Rajputs, Rawat, etc and religious groups, Hindus, Muslims, Christians and Sikhs. Scavengers don't have anything in common among them, except miseries, deep poverty and social neglect. No wonder, they don't make any voting bloc to get political influence. The fact is that nobody knows how to identify them because all social indicators and studies have bypassed them. And they are no class either.

Scavengers are essentially an occupational group united by their common job profile of cleaning somebody else's toilet and live a sub-human life. No rule can list the measures which is specially focused to help scavengers living in a comprehensive social injustice network when it is hard to say who is the sinner. We know the sin but not the sinner. In a free society like India, we are free; so are scavengers. But what does freedom mean for scavengers whose entire life revolves round toilet from cradle to grave. They don't look beyond toilet, so freedom is an abstract idea, meaning nothing for scavengers.

They have no common caste or religion

Scavengers have no caste identity, they are often called Shudra, but among Shudras are also *Dusadh*, *Chamar*, and Pasi etc. There is no Jati to which scavengers can be identified. Their profession is their identity, the profession of manually cleaning and carrying human excreta. Prof. Shyamlal says in a case study: "A caste of the removers of night soil and the cleaners of latrines belongs to a well-defined group in the Indian social order. All such workers in India are today included under the general nomenclature 'the Bhangi'. For this occupational group, there are various names and titles in use in different parts of the country but this is the better known term. They are known in South India as Hela (meaning cry) and that they were called so because they had to cry out to demonstrate their identity while moving on the roads. According to another theory it is derived from the world Hilna meaning 'be domesticated'. Another source of derivation is from Hela, meaning basket-load or Hel or Hil meaning filth mud".

The scavenging castes professing Hindu, Buddhist or Sikh religions are included in the list of Scheduled Castes in their states. The scavenging communities belonging to Muslim or Christian religions have been included in the list of Other Backward Classes (OBCs). There are some tribal communities engaged in scavenging whose names find place in the list of Scheduled Tribes like *Kabui Nagas*, *Kurubas*, etc. There are still some communities which do this work because of poverty and they do not find any place either in the list of SC/ST or OBCs. They are scavengers with all the disadvantages and social stigma without having any constitutional protection or the benefits flowing from it. Scavengers come from different racial and social groups.

The variations in their physical features show that the members of various castes have joined this profession at different points of time owing to economic compulsions. Stephen Fuchs in his book

At the Bottom of Indian Society, has pointed out that, "the endogamous sub-sections of this lowest of all low castes are not without a certain social gradation. Within the scavenging castes, some sections are considered superior to others and their social status is determined according to their birth, or the type of work they do. The lowest place is occupied by those who carry night soil and the highest among them are those who have given up scavenging. Among the lowest scavenging sections, which clean night soil, there is still a distinction. Those who serve in private houses consider themselves higher than those who clean public latrines."

Caste-based profession

The caste system is traditionally associated with occupations. It is so striking that one can say that caste is nothing more than the aggregation of occupational groups. Caste system is also among Muslims, though there is no religious sanction. Syeds rank as the highest and sweepers, the lowest. Equality is basic to Sikhism also, but this has not prevented the existence of castes. Sikhs are broadly divided into *Sardars* and *Mazhabis*, the former are of high castes and the latter are sweepers. Ibbetson has recorded that the terms *Mazhabi* and *Rangreta* denote *Chuhras* who have become Sikhs. The *Mazhabis* take the '*pahul*' (or formula of initiation), wear their hair long, and abstain from tobacco and they apparently refuse to touch night soil, while doing all the other work hereditary to the *Chuhra* caste. Their great guru is Tegh Bahadur, whose mutilated body was brought back from Delhi by *Chuhras*, who were thereafter admitted to the faith as a reward for their devotion. However, taint of hereditary pollution is upon them; the Sikhs of other castes refuse to associate with them. Caste divisions occur among Indian Christians also. Similarly, there are caste distinctions among Indian Jews. The concept of pollution plays a crucial role in maintaining a distance between different castes and dividing people into social groups based on occupation.

Thus, the religion of sweepers and scavengers is a curious mixture of various faiths. They profess to be Hindus, Muslims, Christians, Sikhs and tribals. Though all religions, except Hinduism, preach equality, they refuse to recognise them as equals. Scavengers not only suffer from the extreme form of untouchability but even their sight is avoided. In some parts of South India, bells used to be tied round their necks so that upper caste people could avoid coming across them. In order to escape untouchability, a large number of sweepers and scavengers, mostly in northern India, abandoned Hindu religion, and embraced Islam, Christianity or Sikhism. But the change of religion has not brought any significant change in their occupation or social status. This has, however, infused a feeling of greater solidarity among them towards their own community than towards their religion. For example, a Hindu *Chuhra* will readily marry a *Chuhra* girl belonging to Muslim or Christian religions and vice versa. Earlier, they did not marry in the same faith.

Scavengers are worst among untouchables

Cleaning toilet is where scavengers come in direct contact with human excreta and his (or her) hands are soiled by it. In the congested locality, the scavenger has to crawl through a narrow passage, pushing the basket with one hand, resting his (or her) body weight on the other to make way up to the latrine chamber through a narrow opening. The passers-by avoid such persons. If a scavenger comes close to them, he or she is abused. In many places, latrines are so constructed that the users do not even see their own excreta. They simply squat over the seat and go away without even caring to know who cleans their toilets. And the scavenger continues to do physical cleaning, being abused, get underpaid, and live a life of degradation unheard of in human history. No human degradation could be more cruel and inhuman than the one suffered by scavengers. This is a human rights violation more serious than any, that caused major social revolution.

It is believed that scavenging started in India during the Puranic period when people were divided into 15 castes and one of the castes, called *Chandal*, was allotted the work of cleaning and carrying human excreta. The number of dry latrines increased during the Mughal period when women in purdah were provided with this indoor facility. Later, it spread to other communities as well because of increasing insecurity of women. Warriors made captives in wars were also forced to clean latrines and, later, there emerged a class of scavengers who belonged to different castes and social backgrounds only to unite in the work of scavenging, which became an institution and is now a running sore on India's social structure.

Society divided along structural fault lines

The division of Hindu society is built into its structure. The so-called superior castes enjoy a wide range of choices which the lower castes don't. The lower castes do unclean jobs, including excreta cleaning, sweeping and leather processing. Sweeping streets, cleaning drains and sewers, removing human and animal waste, raising pigs, etc. are included in their jobs. Since latrines in most cities don't have flush, the sweepers or scavengers (*Valmikis*) have to carry buckets of human faeces on the head or in carts. Leather work includes handling dead animals, removing their skin and curing it to make leather goods. By assigning these tasks to scavengers, society has saved other people from doing dirty work. Besides the scavengers' jobs being undesirable, they are also low-paid; they eat kitchen left-overs and live far out of the habitat centres. Sweepers and scavengers collect everyday one or two chapatis from each house to make for the day's meal. This practice is gradually disappearing in big cities but is still prevalent in small towns.

It may be noted that the Hindu society has never been united by

Hinduism which remained divided, (maybe for good reasons in the beginning) along arbitrarily defined caste structure based on birth, in the choosing of which victims had no hand. Viewing the world in terms of caste has diminished (or destroyed) the growth potential of Hindu society, which is at war with itself. Since, there could not be any high moral ground to defend the caste system, the high-caste *Brahmins* called it a divine dispensation, quoting (or misquoting) books of religion, including the *Ramayana and the Mahabharata,* which have considerable influence on the Hindu way of life, under which the self-styled upper castes carry the 'burden of civilising' *Shudras* (scavengers) by making them carry their excreta on the head. There is some historicity about this exploitation. Ashamed to justify slavery in America on crude economic grounds, the slave-owning states of South America felt "it is a natural form of society – good for the slave, good for the master." When one sees these sad and helpless scavengers cleaning excreta, one begins to wonder how ruthlessly history is repeating itself in India. And, without resistance and remorse.

Day begins in the life of a scavenger with a broom and a metallic pan

Sociologists argue, that caste-based discrimination is not comparable to racism. How do we know who is from which caste when everyone looks alike? It is this apparent reason for the caste system and the ability of upper caste to claim victimhood as one-time subjects of colonial racism, that help elude the question of caste. Such interpretations suffer from a facile biological reading of racism, failing to see racial discrimination and caste discrimination as sociologically and politically constructed. Indians practising caste do know how to place the other person's caste within minutes of a meeting or conversation. Surnames, accents, food habits, place of origin or residence and other personal preferences are not discriminatory. Yet the caste system persists.

As long as the fight against caste is seen as the problem of only Dalits as victims, it shall not be possible to abolish it. Dr. Ambedkar said in his book *The Annihilation of Caste (1936)* that the destruction of caste demanded the destruction of Hindu religion that sanctioned caste. It was rejected by Gandhiji himself and later by all leaders. In other words, it is not enough for Dalits to be anti-caste. Unless the Brahmins down to Shudras recognise that clinging to caste negates the human spirit and humanity, the fight against caste may not be won.

All great civilisations had been built on social discrimination and exploitation, including Romans, Greeks and Ottoman, but none of them made the exploited class untouchable. But this is what still happens in India, the land of Ashoka and Gandhiji.

> *"Society has been created by our need and the state by our wickedness."*
>
> – *John Locke*

CHAPTER 29

Scavenging is Breach of Social Contract

The state has failed the untouchables

Society has been created by our need and the state by our wickedness. As part of a social contract, citizens surrender part of their sovereign rights to the state, (of which the government is the executive wing), in return for good governance, social justice, non-discrimination and fair play. If the state does not deliver on the terms of social contract, it loses legitimacy and ceases to be an instrument of social justice. The state has failed scavengers on all these counts; no wonder scavenging continues.

The social contract is an intellectual device to explain the relationship between individuals and their governments. Social contract theorists assert that individuals unite into political societies by a process of mutual consent, agreeing to abide by common rules and accept corresponding duties to protect themselves and one another from violence, injustice and discrimination. Social contract theory played a historical role in the emergence of the human rights and the idea that political authority must be derived from the consent of the governed.

Socrates was the first thinker who refused to flee jail, saying that he had entered into a social contract with the state and he would rather love to honour the terms of social contract than live on in remorse for violating the contract. Plato, who watched Socrates die, says in his book, *The Republic,* what his Guru said, "Let the state live on while we don't. I have seen enough of this life; now let me see what lies beyond it". Socrates took days to die almost alone in the dark cave (a tourist spot in Athens now) after taking hemlock (*dhatura*), a slow poison. After his death, the Greeks discovered that they killed the greatest philosopher that ever trod on the Earth. This is the hallowed tradition of social contract theory.

Thomas Hobbes (1651), John Locke (1689), and Jean-Jacques Rousseau (1762) are among other most famous social contract theorists. Each drew quite different conclusions from the theory. Hobbes advocated absolute monarchy, Locke was for natural rights, and Rousseau supported collective sovereignty in the name of 'the general will'. The Lockean concept of the social contract was invoked in the United States Declaration of Independence in 1776. Social contract notions have recently been invoked by American thinker John Rawls.

According to Thomas Hobbes, human life would be 'solitary, poor, nasty, brutish, and short' in the absence of political order and law. In its absence, we would live in a state of nature, where each person has unlimited natural freedoms, including the right to plunder, rape, and murder; there would be an endless 'war of all against all'. To avoid this, free men establish civil society through a social contract in which each gets security in return for subjecting himself to an authority. Rousseau argues that we get civil rights in return for accepting the obligation to respect and defend the rights of others, giving up some freedoms in the process. According to the social contract theory, law and political order are not natural, but they are human creations.

The social contract and the political order it creates are simply the means towards an end – the benefit of the individuals involved is legitimate only to the extent that they meet the general interest ('general will'). For many social contract theorists, this implies that failings discovered in laws or political structures can be changed by the citizens through elections or other means, including, if necessary, by violence. And, this provision was quoted to justify the American War of Independence in 1776.

New and old

Locke believed that individuals in a state of nature would be bound by the law of nature, not to harm each other but without government to defend them against those seeking to injure or enslave them; people would have no security in their rights and would live in fear. Locke argued that individuals would agree to form a state that would provide a 'neutral judge', acting to protect the lives, liberty, and property of those who lived within it. While Hobbes argued for near absolute authority, Locke argued for inviolate freedom under law. In his book, *Second Treatise of Government,* he says that government's legitimacy comes from the citizens' delegation to the government of their right of self-defence ('self-preservation and dignity').

The government, thus, acts as an impartial, objective agent of that self-defence, rather than each man acting as his own judge, jury, and executioner – the condition in the state of nature. In this view, government derives its "just powers from the consent of the governed," in the language of the declaration. For Jefferson, as for the other American founding fathers, Locke was the most important and most esteemed author on political philosophy. In sum, the entire structure of democratic institutions is based on the concept of social contract. Today, the social contract theory is under siege.

The present crisis of liberal capitalism is threatening to become the crisis of social contract and democracy. However the level of social disquiet sweeping advanced economies is not surprising. Slow growth, high unemployment, social discrimination, uncertain financial future, are the consequence of the breach of social contract. The form and shape of these protests are, as yet, not clear but it is their very lack of cohesion that indicates the crisis has deep historical root.

Welfare capitalism

The fact is that social contract has broken down, undermining capitalism based on three main claims – that in the welfare capitalism, inequality in income will be justified on grounds of merits, not inheritance, and that the benefits of inequality should also go to the deserving people, not speculators and fixers. Second, the poor and disempowered will not be allowed to fall below a benchmark when the social service network will take care of them. Third, the highest and the lowest income will be regulated through tax system or other executive measures.

That the capitalism has not lived up to its promises is evident in the *'Occupy Wall Street'* protests which reached new heights in October, 2011, when thousands thronged Times Square in New York City as part of a wider 'global day of rage' against the West's unjust economic systems. The agitations decried what they see as the collusion of the state with corporate and financial interests. And they taped into the widely-shared belief that the bankers, speculators, and traders, responsible for the economic recession, have escaped it unscathed, leaving behind a vast hinterland of despair and struggle.

Indian analysts, including Pratap Bhanu Mehta, saw agitation as a protest against not just Wall Street but the breaking of the old social contract of welfare capitalism. This social contract accepted high inequality because the poor will be better off. This contract, say critics, has been violated with middle class and working class stagnation, which now challenges the very fundamentals of liberal democracy. The Tea Party conservatives in the US have also criticised the Barack Obama administration for encouraging overborrowing and overspending by home owners, discouraging saving, and then asking prudent Americans for more taxes to bail out the imprudent bankers. This represents a social split not between the rich one per cent and the remaining 99 per cent, but between prudent taxpayers and others. The numbers suggest that this split runs deeper than the old rich versus poor conflict. This agitation is also all across Europe from Greece to Spain. This is the collapse of social contract in the capitalist West which won half the world, holding it hostage to its glory.

Worse than slavery

Mulk Raj Anand, in his famous book, '*Untouchable*', says, "The scavenger is worse off than a slave; for the slave may change his master and his duties and may even become free, but the scavenger is bound to scavenging forever, born into a state from which he cannot escape and where he is excluded from social intercourse and the consolations of his religion. Unclean himself, he pollutes others when he touches them." Bakha, the scavenger character in the book, is a real individual, lovable, thwarted, sometimes grand, sometimes weak, and thoroughly Indian. "Even his physique is distinctive; we can recognise his broad intelligent face, graceful torso, and heavy buttocks, as he does his nasty jobs, or stumps out in artillery boots in hopes of a pleasant walk through the city with a paper of cheap sweets in his hand. But he cleans toilets and nobody can touch him. He is scavenger".

Scavenging is the consequence of a breach of social contract; for scavengers, like all others, have surrendered their rights to constitute the state which will deliver fair treatment and social justice to all. In case of scavengers, it was not done. They are enslaved to carry somebody else's excreta to make a living and are made to do it because of traditional practice, social and religious orthodoxy or because scavengers are too disorganised to protest or because the institutions of state, like the press, judiciary or executive are managed by those who are not scavengers. Hence, they are not sensitive to this blatant breach of social contract also because the wealthy or high-born castes know that scavengers are too poor, weak, and discriminated to shout at the breach of social contract on the basis of which the state has been constituted in the first place.

"When beggars die, no comet falls," says Shakespeare

The miseries of scavengers make no news; their suffering is part of the Indian culture and accepted social practice and political acceptance. This injustice is built deep into our mind; we see people defecate in the open and women sitting along the railway tracks struggling to hide their honour. We don't accept it. The Dalits, the OBC, or other ethnic or caste groups demand and get special treatment in terms of the social contract but not scavengers because they are not of one ethnic, caste or religious group to be a vote bloc. They have no local identity either nor property, land or house to establish; they have no address and no postman goes there. They migrate to wherever there are toilets to clean. Scavengers are the dregs and froth of society, left out of the development loop united in their sufferings, humiliation and early death.

Had it only been a problem of poverty, standard anti-poverty programmes would have been enough to help scavengers out of the trap. But it is about their social exclusion and untouchability which is extensively practised even today. How many of us are ready to dine with manual scavengers? No one. Democracy is about social contract and not about generosity or entitlement or patronage. It is about equality and setting up an inclusive social structure which is fair, non-

ULTIMATE DEGRADATION – A scavenger cleaning a sewage pit.

discriminatory, and just. If the high dining table cannot find seats for scavengers, there will be another table around where will be sitting the disenfranchised people who will have no stake in social stability which is a threat to civilised society. Touchables and untouchables cannot have any other relation except of hate and disaffection which will be dangerous for society.

The empowered men and women have taken shelter (excuse) of objectivity in order not to be involved in social activism and to protect their good living and privileges, leaving the poor, weak and the voiceless alone to suffer. In the entire human history, wrongs have been committed on the defenceless people because strong and rich persons have not stood up for them.

Safety of silence

George Clemenceau (1841-1929), French Prime Minister, during the World War I, said while standing at the dinner table at the Versailles Peace Conference in 1919, "I want a strong France and weak Germany. Look at the chicken in the plate. They are dead and we are eating them because they could not resist our power of oppression. I don't want France to become a dead chicken". Now that poor and defenceless scavengers cannot resist the power of oppression of the high-born and rich, they are as good as dead chicken in Clemenceau's plate. This is the historical analogy, true then, and truer today.

Prof. Howard Zinn, a political philosopher, calls this as the 'safety of silence' designed to protect the privileges of the few at the cost of many. Prof. Zinn re-interpreted history to say that until we take a moral position, based on social contract, the mere narration of events about kings, queens and the stories of their rise and fall doesn't add up to anything; it has no social value more than that of folk tales. The value-neutral attitude is amoral, unjust and inhuman. In Roman times the entire city saw the gladiators being devoured by lions and they enjoyed it. Today, we see an equivalent of this injustice, but we don't have the tears to shed. We are reliving history. This is the tragedy of our times.

His concept of social contract and a moral approach to social problems highlight the need for social change through pressure, persuasion, education, campaigning and technology which empower the weak and poor. In this situation, neutrality, objectivity or academic analyses have no social value except reading and forgetting it. If social sciences, history or any other subject has to stay a credible profession, it has to find a social context. Scavenging also has the historical context of the master-servant relationship of which scavengers are the worst victims. We have to examine it to know the mystery of scavenging which has been there for centuries, surviving revolution, war, rise and fall of kings and queens. Everything changed since Christ but not scavenging. Why?

The Alwar model

Sulabh has mounted two-front attack on scavengers' problems; first, to end their poverty and, second, to socially mainstream them. The Alwar project is quite an appropriate model. Scavengers have been taken away from scavenging and then given jobs after training. Now, they are fully mainstreamed and people buy their products. The households where they worked earlier, now freely accept them as co-equals and invite them to their houses on festivals. These houses have been provided scavenging-free Sulabh toilets and hence they have no complaint either. This is social rehabilitation of scavengers. The Alwar model needs to be expanded.

Scavenging is a complex, political, social, economic, anthropological, cultural and historical problem which has evolved over 2,000 years or more, in different disguises, names (scavengers have different names in different regions), various levels of social degradation, different castes, religion and everything else. In sum, they have no single identity, nor any common social status, economic benchmark, facial features or language. They are just united by the common profession of degradation which has received political and religious acceptance as a result of which they persist even today, thousands of years after scavenging was first mentioned in ancient books or folklore.

Scavenger presents the sad face of humanity, made sadder following social neglect, criminal attitude and worst kind of cruelty of man against man. Scavengers come from all deprived sections of society whose conditions have been made worse after industrialisation and urbanisation which brought greater sufferings, and degradation to them specially in developing countries where city slums and urban poverty have raised their numbers which have never been counted because they are too unimportant to count, less important than caste and religions which the census staff count.

The classical argument is that all civilisations are built on exploitation and social injustice. Romans and Greeks supported and practised slavery, Europeans rampaged Africa, and Asia, hunting down slaves to work in their fields and factories, America trapped slaves in western Africa, sold in Haiti, and made them work in plantation to grow rich. The story is long and horrible told by historians and story tellers (read *Uncle Tom's Cabin*). And still the last words on their miseries have to be told.

A new name for slavery

Scavenging is only the extension of the idea that a section of people have to suffer so that others could stay clean and enjoy life. Gandhiji was the first who highlighted the miseries of scavengers and undertook fast in 1933 to end untouchability. He wanted a scavenger girl to be head of the state. Other leaders took the cue and followed him. But still manual scavenging persists because there was no big idea for their redemption. The Sulabh Founder has provided one when he said, there is no one way to address a very old and complex problem of scavenging. He has provided a package consisting of new on-site waste disposal affordable and culturally appropriate technology, education, economic empowerment (not social entitlement alone) and social mainstreaming. These and many more simultaneously happening social measures, continued to be taken up over a period, will alone end scavenging. And, not any one-time measure, however, revolutionary.

The 'big idea' of the Sulabh Movement is a shift from the traditional poverty-based, compassion-driven half-measures to the assertive claim on the resources of the country and the social justice system. Dr. Pathak challenged the basic assumption that scavenging was the consequence of social outgrowth and economic development; it is deliberate human attempt and the consequence of skewed social justice system and religious superstition that have created the scavenging system which can be abolished if only a 'big idea' has been accepted to replace old, cruel and immoral practices.

Class division in West

A hundred years ago, domestic servants constituted Britain's largest source of employment. That simple statistic reveals, better than anything else, the inequality in a class-driven society, and the partnership between wealth and power in Victorian and post-Victorian Britain. The British upper classes were not cruel to servants, although there were strict distinctions; in a grand house, servants were permitted to eat and drink as much as they wished, but could only live downstairs. The meltdown of the ancient regime was evolutionary in Britain, rather than revolutionary, as in Russia which swept out the old social order in the October Revolution of 1919. And three generations suffered the consequences of it. Even though British democracy has been an evolving process, there were 'rotten boroughs' and in-built inequity; women got the vote even later than the 'lower classes'. It took two World Wars and the death of millions of the poor in the service of the Empire before the privileged system crumbled to become history after 1945 where Great Britain became a small England.

The 19th century America did not have servants, it had slaves; and slavery reinvented itself in many forms before it ended. Slavery produced the bloodiest civil war in the US which later claimed the life of Lincoln (Read *Uncle Tom's Cabin* by H.B. Stowe – the one book that produced the civil war).The British attitude towards colour was far more sophisticated, and there were many nuances of racism. Today the word servant or slave has disappeared from the popular lexicon of both America and Europe. If it survives it is only within the construct of a 'civil servant' – who is definitely not a servant, but a boss, and very often not civil either.

Neill Ferguson says in his book, *Empire,* that 1,200 civil servants kept the British Empire together and ruled India with a population not less than 300 million. Of course, in the West there is the huge demand for 'illegal' immigrants as servants. But the terms of reference have changed in favour of servants. The largest source of employment in contemporary India is also domestic servants, including scavengers. In that sense, we are today, where Britain was a century ago. There is a world of difference between the service economy and a servants' economy; India claims the first and lives in the second. In urban India, servant cleans utensils and scavengers clean toilets only because there is a necessity. The rewards are pitiful; the treatment pitiable. The threat of servant violence is the regular diet of the media; but cruelty towards servants is largely ignored. Developed societies in the West created robotic machines, like the dishwasher, to fill the gap, even as they lifted the poor into an expanding middle class, loosely defined as a group with enough for food, clothing, shelter and basic education.

But in India we hire servants to use washing machine. Some

overlap is understandable in the transition phase, but the incremental rise in upward mobility of the poor, or scavengers is not a sustained reality. The tension is evident on the visage of those servants and scavengers who haven't reconciled to their fate. It's true that the majority of servants and scavengers have no dispute with their destiny, because this arrangement at least prevents starvation. But, surely, that is not a happy reality in a democracy because it is a potential threat to the social structure.

Joe the Plumber

The changed status of scavengers (called plumber in the U.S.) came in high focus when Joe the Plumber (Samuel Joseph Wurzelbacher of Ohio) became mascot of Mr. Barack Obama's election campaign in 2008 which marked a change in the master-servant relationship. We have not made a scavenger girl Governor-General of India (now, President) as conceived by Gandhiji, but Joe the Plumber has filed papers (October 2011) to run for Congress as a Republican candidate from Ohio, 9th US House district. He has done it without reservation or any social entitlement while the super-rich Dalit leaders in India still fight elections from the reserved constituencies. This is where the two societies are different.

In India, also plumbers and electricians are becoming expensive. The rising cost of skills is proof of some transfer of wealth. To be true, India will become a modern economy only when domestic service and toilet cleaning are treated as civil service that brings salary equal to government jobs. This may be high rhetoric but this is the India which lives in many parts; we are democrats and feudal at once. We oppose exploitation yet do not hesitate to exploit servants, particularly scavengers. Besides being a poverty problem, scavenging is also a social problem which has to be addressed differently. Servants are not untouchables but a scavenger is and thereby hangs the tale of the Sulabh Movement and its philosophy.

Old value system

This being the source of untouchability and scavenging, how can it be effectively cured by one solution alone? The Sulabh philosophy is, thus, based on action which is all about working out ideas of social contract into action. Dr. Bindeshwar Pathak says it is not necessary to demolish the old value system and cultural practices to build new ones. Both of them can co-exist in happy relation. After all, culture is not produced overnight; it evolves over a long time. Now we can bring about this change faster because of technology, information revolution and globalisation which together tend to produce a new social contract in which discrimination of any kind has no place nor relevance.

To talk of social contract in terms of social justice is, however, not to suggest that it will produce justice or non-discrimination. No, it will not. Hobbes talked of social contract to support dictatorship, Rousseau just wanted people to get out of their caves and live in organised society constituted on the basis of social contract; John Locke talked of social contract to justify the American War of Independence and capitalism – a dispensation in which, as Jeffrey Sachs says, one per cent Americans possess 25 per cent of the national wealth, resulting in America being among the most unequal societies in the world.

Human rights defined

The concept of social contract was re-interpreted in the Declaration of Human Rights in 1948 which has a long history of evolution. Human right is a concept derived from the doctrine of natural rights, which holds that individuals, by virtue of their humanity, possess fundamental rights beyond those prescribed in law. It was first incorporated in the US Declaration of Independence (1776). A Declaration of the Rights of Man and the Citizen was adopted by the French National Assembly (1789). Most written Constitutions contain a bill of rights. Although having no legal standing, the UN General Assembly adopted a Universal Declaration of Human Rights in 1948, detailing individual and social rights and freedoms, followed in 1953 by the European Convention on Human Rights. The European Court of Human Rights was established within this framework. India has signed this convention to commit itself to abolishing social discrimination, including those of scavengers. But, it is over sixty years now and still we see scavengers carrying excreta, bent in poverty and hated even by those whose toilets they clean. And, we are the mute spectators. Gandhiji wanted a scavenging-free India, but when we see scavengers deep into the stinking toilet pit, we discovered now we have betrayed the Father of the Nation.

The caste system was a social contract, according to which each person was given a job based on birth, not ability. Scavenging is the consequence of this skewed, unfair and sinful social arrangement.
– Dr. Bindeshwar Pathak

CHAPTER 30

Scavengers are Worst Victims of Caste System

A birthmark no reform could remove

Enormous research work has been done to find out the sources of the caste system since Vedic times and the origin of scavenging but it could not be traced to any specific period. This skewed social system evolved, mutated and changed, always adapting itself seamlessly along the path of its evolution during the periods in which different rulers ruled in different times. And all of them practised discriminations differently which finally hardened into the caste system which is neither rational nor moral.

A conception of Indian society in terms of genus (*Varna*, here synonymous with *Jati*) appeared first in *the Rig Veda,* the oldest collection of Vedic priestly hymns, composed in Punjab in about 1200-1000 BC. The Vedic people saw themselves as members of a single 'genus of respectable men' (*Aryavarna*), 'the humans' (*Manusa*). Their code enjoined them to offer sacrifice (*Yajna*) to members of another genus of beings, the Vedic gods (*Devas*); it also enjoined them to enslave their enemies, 'the non-humans' (*Dasyuvarna*), who were naturally and morally fit for service. The Varna system in ancient India functioned as the larger framework within which the caste society was formed. According to *the Rig Veda,* the oldest of the four *Vedas,* the distinction between the four Varnas dates back to the origin of the human race. That is to say, at the time of creation, the Brahmins were born from the mouth of Purusha, the Kshatriyas from his arms; the Vaishyas from his thighs and Shudras from his feet.

The upper caste category included Brahmins, Rajputs, Baniyas or Vaish. All castes belonging to upper caste category exercised control over different sources of power. The Brahmins enjoyed ritual supremacy and as priests controlled access to sacred Sanskrit texts, they were also a source for reinforcing the caste system. At the bottom of the caste hierarchy was the category of untouchable castes who came to be designated as the depressed/exterior castes during the British rule. It included *Chamars, Bhambhis, Meghwals, Balais, Raigars, Jatavas, Dhobi, Dom, Buntar, Khatiks, Valmikis, Bhangis, Mehtars* etc. in Rajasthan. There are other names for these castes in other parts of the country like *Paky, Paide, Malkana, Korar, Zadamall* etc. These castes are mainly agricultural labourers. Some of them also worked as sweepers, folk musicians, basket makers, cloth weavers, meat sellers and they performed various manual jobs for their higher-caste patrons. They were considered to be untouchables and, therefore, were neither allowed to enter the temples of the high-caste Hindus nor were they admitted to educational institutions. Financially, they were serfs and in some cases even slaves. In villages and towns, they did not have any access to the streets used by the upper castes. Nor were they allowed to use public tanks and wells. Socially, there were many forms of discrimination. They were also prevented from dressing in Caste Hindu style and from wearing gold and silver ornaments, use of umbrella, ride on horses or putting on chapplas, shoes etc. The stories of their suffering are unmatched by any such discriminations suffered in any other countries.

The origin of the caste system has been defended with high pretention of religious sanctity and moral posturing to give the impression that violating the caste code is anti-religion and a sin.

And, to respect and practise the caste system and untouchability is the bounden duty of all right and religious persons. This fallacy was re-enforced by the religious Guru like Manu who later became a part of political terminology Manuvadi. But the fact is that the caste system is a sanctimonious humbug and an invention of evil mind.

When caste becomes an ideology

At times caste becomes an ideology and a cover for rigidity of textual certitudes and for craven hero worship. The caste identity in politics and social relations is openly practised and shamelessly flaunted. Poverty is defined in terms of castes (SC, ST, Dalit etc.) not to end poverty but to perpetuate it for the rich and powerful to seize power and retain it. Nor is caste or community-based solution the way to end poverty and backwardness. Mr. Salman Khurshid, Union Minister of Minority Affairs, said in June 2009 that the reservation only creates "envy, hostility and resistance and does not inject an ability to compete." This is what Dr. Ambedkar had also said when he provided for reservation in the Constitution only for ten years which has how became a permanent feature very clearly. The Union Minister had also suggested that there should be 'affirmative action' and not reservation. He defined 'affirmative action' as a way to create additional ability, empowerment and making the disadvantaged groups compete in the open market, instead of having to perpetually depend on 'supporting stick' or official assistance. The long-term social cost of quota will far outweigh the benefits of the reservation which created a reverse caste system; the earlier 'high castes' are wanting to be 'reserved' and get the benefits without working for it. For this reason, the so-called higher castes are condescending and moralising more than rationalising the caste system which is an absolute social evil and anti-modern.

This evil system is continuing because of political patronage and social acceptance, becoming an instrument of power and its misuse. It may be noted that while opposing the Communal Award in 1932 which Dr. Ambedkar had demanded and against which Gandhiji had gone on fast resulting in the Poona Pact the Father of the Nation had said, "I would prefer Hinduism dead to untouchability living forever". Gandhiji's fear has come true and the caste system, in its new political avatars, has become the defining feature of Indian society. Sadder still is the fact that there is no way to avert the disaster. Caste system is India's nemesis.

New world, old mindset

We live in a world of competing beliefs, conflicting political systems and claims. In such a world, it is rare for a struggle to emerge that speaks something universal about humanity but the caste system is an universally accepted evil and its abolition alone will ensure the progress of India. Victimhood and rejection of ordinary decencies cannot be allowed because of a permanent feature of our social structure. Casteism is an equivalent to the medieval disavowal of social outcasts. The caste system, however, has been changing spots and colours like a chameleon as is manifest in discriminations in all societies and religions. It is class in Britain, marked by stuffed shirts and plummy accents, colour in the US, sects in Muslim world (Shia and Sunni), tribal divides in most African countries, fascism, communism etc.

All societies, in all ages, have been divided along their fault lines and, hence, extensive social unrest. The evolutionists say that the human mind is not designed to accept equality. Or else, there would not have been conflict or the evolution of human species. And Charles Darwin would not have been born at all. But in India, these discriminations are a shade darker and rooted deeper into our social system and culture.

Rudyard Kipling's 'Lesser Breeds'

Although the 19th century idea of non-Western countries being incapable of attaining modernity is put to rest, the tribal behaviour, religious fanatism, caste system and ritualism make this fear surface again. When the West says India is a great civilisation, or that Cairo is the timeless city or that Afghans and Pashtuns are warrior races, growing poppy and fighting for warlords, the West simply means that these countries are incapable of modernising themselves by learning science, technology and other ways necessary to change. Let them live with the past prejudices and suffer while the rest of the world continues to grow. Among the literary bards who advocated this line of thinking is Rudyard Kipling who romanticised the Afghan warrior figure. Kipling wrote such lines as "take up the white man's burden" or "East is East and West is West and never the twain shall meet". Kipling had said the Asiatics are tribals (white man's burden) and the West has divine right to rule them without law. Different people have described caste system in India differently. But Kipling associated it with tribalism which cannot change and hence, India will always remain hard to modernise. When we see poll analysis being made today in terms of caste and reservation, we begin to rediscover the 'timeless wisdom' of Kipling. Let us know about Kipling a little more to put the historicity of caste in perspective.

Joseph Rudyard Kipling (1865-1936) was an English writer, born in India. He wrote *Plain Tales from the Hills (1888)*, and his Anglo-Indian society, contains the earliest of his masterly short stories. His books for children, including *The Jungle Book (1894-95), Just So Stories (1902), Puck of Pook's Hill (1906),* and the picturesque novel *Kim (1901),* reveal his love for the exotic. He was given the Nobel Prize for Literature in 1907. Born in Bombay, Kipling was educated in England. At the age of 17, he returned to India as sub-editor of *The Lahore Civil and Military Gazette.* He was posted later in *The Pioneer* of Allahabad in 1887. Kipling advocated 'Englishness and imperialism' and used his rich experience in India to say forcefully that India cannot be saved because of its caste system, which is cut too deep into the societal structure to be removed. Hence, the West must rule India without law – all because of the caste system. Modernity, however, is not the immature rejection of old habits and traditions; both can co-exist together.

Caste system also in regional societies

To be true, castes are social systems that differentiate and rank the whole population of a society in corporate units (castes) generally defined by descent, marriage, and occupation. Elaborately differentiated, caste systems have developed in the regional societies of India and among adjacent populations in the territories of what is today modern Pakistan, Bangladesh, Nepal, and Sri Lanka over the past 2,000 years. So intricate are the connections of caste systems in South Asia with regional systems of ideas regarding such matters as genetics, physiology, kinship, ethics, and cosmogony that they have been equated by some scholars with the whole culture of Hinduism. Caste systems resemble the much more widespread systems of social and economic classes occupationally linked, hereditary, and endogamous (marrying within a group). Corporate caste units differ from social classes in being clearly defined rather than by birth, descent, and marriage.

What we seek to achieve by abolishing caste is the economic equity and cultural freedom of a modern nation state. Poverty is anti-modern; it stinks of a colonised past, flood, famine and epidemics which we would rather love to forget. But modernity is much more than caste and money. There are countries that have money beyond the definition of avarice, or resources beyond the limits of good fortune (as in West Asia) but, they are neither modern, nor casteless nor do they show any sign of trying to become ones by ending social and economic discriminations. The truth is that we have a new horizon in old skyline.

There is no difference in skin colour, or in DNA, or in any other physical characteristic, between a Dalit and a Brahmin. Yet the social chasm between the two has remained unabridged for millennia. So Indian officialdom is right when it says that racism and casteism can't be equated. They can't. For the simple reason that casteism is far more overtly rampant, more widespread and more socially accepted (at least in India) and more deeply ingrained in our polity than racism anywhere in the world. And there is one particular caste in India which, in some ways, is as equal if not more oppressed as Dalits. It is a caste that is routinely burnt alive, killed in the womb, beaten, sexually violated and often subject to life long abuse and deprivation. It is a caste called woman.

Portuguese first called it caste

The Portuguese seafarers who traded mainly on the west coast of India in the 16th and 17th centuries were first to describe groups, which they called castes (from which derive the English and French words caste), meaning 'species' or 'breeds' of animals or plants and 'tribes', 'races', 'clans', or 'lineages' among men. Only in the 18th century did the distinction that is now made between unranked tribes and ranked castes that begin to be drawn clearly in the usage of the French and English. The inequality and exclusiveness of the castes, as well as the peculiar occupational division of labour prescribed for them, generally produced a sense of shock in Western missionaries and officials of the turbulent 19th and 20th centuries. Attempts were made to explain the castes as a self-serving invention by the system's top-ranking priestly castes, or (after Charles Darwin) as 'the unplanned evolution' of successively higher castes through the growth of superior technological specialisation.

The South Asian society was set up on the cultural assumption that all living beings are differentiated into genera or classes, each of which is thought to possess a defining coded substance. The commonest word for genus *Jati* is derived from an Indo-European verbal root meaning 'genesis', 'origin', or 'birth.' It is applied to any species of living things, including gods and humans. Among humans, *Jati* can designate a distinct sex, a race, a caste, or a tribe; a family, a lineage, or a clan; an ethnic group, a regional population, the followers of an occupation or a religion, or a nation. The South Asian Society was founded in 2003 in Devon and Cornwall, United Kingdom. Its main aim was to create a cultural, social and mutual support network for increasingly large South Asian community. It had a wide membership base of people who were drawn from countries surrounding the Indian subcontinent or were part of the Asian diaspora.

Every human genus (and therefore every caste) is thought to have as the shared property of its members a particular substance (e.g. *Sarira*, 'body', *Rakta*, 'blood') embodying its code for conduct (*dharma*). Each caste's inborn code enjoins it to maintain its substance and morality, its particular occupation, and its correct exchanges with other castes. Indian thought does not separate 'nature' and 'morality' or 'law', so that castes are, in Western terms, at once 'natural' and 'moral' units of society. These units make up a single order, one that is profoundly particularised.

Money decides caste, says Max Weber

In writings published posthumously in 1922, the German sociologist Max Weber made a distinction between class, status, and power, arguing that these represented forms of stratification that co-existed but did not necessarily coincide in modern societies. According to Weber, class situation was mainly determined by the ownership or non-ownership of property (more or less along the lines that Marx had described); status situation was determined by the 'social honour' on the basis of consumption or style of life; and the power was determined by possession or non-possession of the means of command. The predominance of one or the other would depend upon economic and cultural conditions that affect the extent to which men become class or status-conscious. Moreover, political power is relatively independent of both class and status; it is not regarded, as in Marx's theory, as being merely a consequence of class position.

The introduction of the notion of social status (which was developed from the feudal idea of legal status) led to the formulation of a distinctive theory of social stratification. In contrast to the Marxist conception according to which society was divided into major classes engaged in economic, political, and cultural conflict over the basic structure of society itself, the new theory viewed society as a hierarchy of status levels with each level determined by a social evaluation of the importance or worth of the activities carried on by individuals at that level. The emphasis was upon the placement of individuals in the social hierarchy, not upon the formation of groups and their interrelations.

Caste perspective

In the earliest human societies, differences of class and status as one of the principal types of social differentiation may have emerged in various ways partly as a result of the accumulation of property or the monopolisation of leadership positions by particular individuals and families and partly by means of conquest and the enslavement of other social groups. Once established, these differences are maintained by inheritance and strengthened by the deepening of cultural distinctions in dress, education (initially a distinction between literacy and non-literacy, and later, differences in quality and duration of education), and style of life as a whole; they are also consolidated by legal and religious codes. Occupations may become hereditary (either in a formal way, as in the Indian caste system, or on a customary basis); property is transmitted through the family;

and political power is inherited by the members of royal and noble families. Political dynasties today may have historical roots.

Vilfredo Pareto (1848-1923), the Italian economist and sociologist, however, exaggerated when he wrote in *The Mind and Society* that "history is a graveyard of aristocracies," but it is certainly true that in all societies there has been some circulation of individuals and families between different social levels. Even in the Indian caste system, which was a particularly closed form of social stratification, it was possible for individuals, and especially for caste groups, to rise in the social hierarchy by various means. In the European feudal societies, there were considerable opportunities for mobility, particularly after commerce and the towns began to develop. Many commoners became conservative leaders in Britain, including John Major, and vice versa. In India, also, we have cases of social mobility but only in profession but not in caste.

> *"As long as there are castes, there will be outcaste."*
> *– Dr. B.R. Ambedkar*

CHAPTER 31

Caste is Rooted in Past, False Beliefs and Religion

India remains a wounded civilisation

Human institutions are sticky – they are hard to change. The caste system was the one which was created to meet a set of demands when each village was a 'mini-republic', and self-sufficient with its own social network of warriors (Rajput), scholars (Brahmin), farmers, carpenters and traders. But the caste system has stayed on even while the situation has changed with a super national institution, the state – controlling everything comprehensively. The caste system has done more damage to society than any conqueror or killer did before.

The caste system has exposed us to two thousand years of defeat and stagnation. It has left us fragmented and vulnerable. Its philosophy of exclusion has diminished us intellectually; it has stifled growth making us incapable to face challenges. It has left the country invaded, plundered, and defeated with a quarter of its population always in the serfdom of untouchability – the people who have no country, but only masters. India needs a new social code, but it has none.

Francis Fukuyama, one of the greatest intellectuals of our time, says in his book, *The Origin of Political Order*, "The self-organising character of Indian society was noted by many intellectuals, including Karl Marx, who said that the king owned all land and that villages were self-regulating units, a practice which was also widespread in

Britain in Victorian times". The Indian village was a little republic that could survive the ruin of empires. The panchayat was the source of political order until it was undermined by the British colonial administration. (To revive that tradition, Rajiv Gandhi in 1989 sought to decentralise power transferring it to be bottom level through Article 40 of the Constitution.) "The actual nature of local governance in early India was not, however, democratic and secular, but based on *Jati* or caste. Each village tended to have a dominant caste that numerically outnumbered others and owned the greater part of the village land. The panchayat was simply the traditional leadership of that caste", says Fukuyama.

Villages had their governance institutions and did not depend on a state to provide services from the outside. The panchayat decided disputes based on customary law. Property rights within the village were based on a complex patch work of ruling caste families. The king did not 'own' the land but he was nominally sovereign. Commercial activity was also based on *Jatis*. A great deal of trade in southern India from the 9th to the 14th century was controlled by merchant guilds like the Anyvole, which had representatives throughout the subcontinent and dealt extensively with Arab merchants outside India. Gujarati merchants, both Muslim and Hindu, have long dominated trade across the Indian Ocean, in East Africa, southern Arabia, and into South East Asia. The merchants of Ahmedabad were organised into a large, city-wide corporation on which sat members of all of the major occupational groups. In China, trade networks were based on lineages but were not nearly as well organised as their Indian counterparts, according to Fukuyama.

A building block of society

Sociologist Satish Saberwal says: "The *Jati* provided defence against aggression and secured the village from outside dominance by resisting the larger states and empires to capture it. The *Jatis* provided their members with opportunities for physical and social mobility. For example, the Kaikolar, a Tamil weaver caste, shifted to trading and soldiering when the opportunity arose under the Chola kings; Sikh carpenters and blacksmiths left their native Punjab for Assam and Kenya in the late 19th century. These decisions would be taken collectively by groups of families who would rely on one another for support in their new surroundings. In northern India, the Rajput *Jati* was particularly successful in expanding its domain and came to control substantial territory".

The Brahmanic social order limited political power by controlling literacy and, thus, consigned huge numbers of Indians to poverty and illiteracy. Even today, while a number of extremely well-educated Indians have risen to the top of global rankings in a variety of fields, most others are trapped in ignorance.

The historical roots of these disparities and social inequality is rooted in the caste system. The Brahmins, of course, controlled access to learning and knowledge. According to Saberwal, "memorising the hymns for use in ritual – for oneself and for one's clients – has been the most characteristic form of Brahmanical learning. Efficacy in the ritual, and therefore the process of learning, did not necessarily require that the meanings of the hymns is understood. A great many Brahmins devoted large parts of their lives to the memorisation of the Vedic texts and to have their desired ritual effects. Small mistakes in recitation, it was believed, could lead to disaster.

The Brahmanic commitment to the oral transmission of the Vedas reinforced their own social supremacy by creating additional barriers to entry into their Varna. Unlike Jews, Christians, and Muslims, who were all 'people of the book', the Brahmins strongly resisted the introduction of writing and technologies related to it. Chinese travellers to India in the 5th and 7th centuries AD, looking for sources of Buddhist tradition, were hard-pressed to find any written documents. Long after both the Chinese and Europeans had switched to writing on parchment, the Indians were still writing on palm leaves and bark. The aversion to durable parchment was religious in origin, since it was made from animal skin. But the Brahmins were also slow to adopt paper when that technology became available in the 11th century. In rural Maharashtra, paper was not used in routine administration until the middle of the 17th century, and when it did arise, it immensely improved the efficiency of accounting and oversight.

Monopoly of learning

It wasn't until the second millennium AD that writing became more common and spread beyond the Brahmins to other groups in Indian society. Merchants began to keep commercial records, and individual *Jatis* (*Bania*) recorded family genealogies. In Kerala, the *Nayars* 'of royal and noble lineages' began to learn written Sanskrit, and the political class in that state began to produce voluminous records of political and commercial transactions. No wonder Kerala, under a local Communist government, emerged as one of the best-governed states in India because its performance had deeper roots in the tradition of literacy of the political class in earlier centuries.

Compared to the Chinese, the Brahmins' monopoly on learning and their resistance to the adoption of writing had an incalculable impact on the development of a modern state. From the Shang Dynasty onward, Chinese rulers used the written word to communicate order, record laws, keep accounts, and write detailed political histories. The education of a Chinese bureaucrat centred on literacy and immersion in a long and complex literary tradition. Training for administrators, while limited by modern standards, involved prolonged analysis of written texts and the drawing of lessons from earlier historical events. With the adoption of the examination system beginning in the Han Dynasty, recruitment into the government was based on mastery of literary skills and was not restricted to people of a certain class. While the effective access of ordinary Chinese to high government office was limited in many practical ways, the Chinese were long aware that education was one important route to upward social mobility. Lineages and local communities therefore invested heavily in educating sons to take advantage of the system.

Illiterate rulers

Nothing like this existed in India. Most rulers were themselves illiterate and relied for administration on a similarly uneducated cadre of patrimonial officials. Literacy was a privilege of the Brahmin class, which had a strong self-interest in maintaining their monopoly over access to learning and ritual. As in the case of the military, the hierarchical system of *Varnas* and *Jatis* severely restricted the access of the great majority of the population to education and literacy, and therefore reduced the pool of competent administrators available to Indian states. The final way religion affected political power in Indian development was through the establishment of 'the rule of law', which was a body of rules reflecting the community's sense of justice that is higher than the wishes of the person, even of the king. Law has been laid out in the different *Dharmasastras,* not created by kings but by Brahmins acting on the basis of ritual knowledge. The laws make very clear the fact that the *Varnas* are not there to serve the king; rather, the king can gain legitimacy only by being the protector of the *Varnas*. If the king violates the sacred law, the epic Mahabharata explicitly sanctions revolt against him, saying that the king is not a king at all but rather a 'mad dog' if he did not respect *Dharmasastras*. In the Laws of Manu, the locus of sovereignty lies in the law and not in the person of the king.

The social system that grew out of Indian religion, thus, severely constrained the ability of states to concentrate power. Rulers could not create a powerful military instrument capable of mobilising all sections of the population; they could not penetrate the self-governing, highly organised *Jatis* that existed in every village; they and their administrators lacked education and literacy and they faced a well-organised priestly class that protected them. Only one caste, Rajput, fought war while the others were outside the state fighting system. This social exclusion weakened the Indian state and no wonder, all wars between Kalinga war in 262 BC and 1971 AD were lost to invaders. (The above narrative is excerpted from Fukuyama's book, *'The Origin of Political Order'*.)

The caste system has thus exposed India to thousand years of defeat and stagnation. The defeat, poverty and humiliation because of caste system have made India a 'wounded civilisation', as V.S. Naipaul says, condemning the great country, its versatile people to a perpetual sense of doom and despair.

Caste grew out of religion

Caste system in India is *sui generis* to Hindu religion. The orthodox Hindus believe that an early hymn in *The Rig Veda* (*The Purushasukta:* 10.90) and much later *the Manava Dharma Sashtra* (Law of Manu) are the sources of the caste system. Manu, the law-giver, cites *The Purushasukta* as the source and justification for the caste division of his own time. Among the Aryans, the priestly caste was called the Brahmins, the warriors were called the Kshatriyas, the common people occupied in agriculture, pastoral pursuits, trade and industry were called the Vaishyas and the *Dasas* or non-Aryans and the people of mix blood were assigned the status of Shudras. The *Chaturvarna* system has been gradually distorted in shape and meaning and has been replaced by the prevalent caste system in the Hindu society. The caste system kept a large section of people in the country outside the fold of society who were called the untouchables. Manu required that the dwellings of the untouchables shall be outside the village, their dress and the garments will be those of the dead, and food should be given to them in a broken dish.

When Aryans came to India as conquerors, they retained for themselves the religious and military functions in the social order. As the time passed on, they held the functions of the priests and nobles to become great landed property holders. The conquered people performed the lowly tasks of life. They reduced them to the position of serfs and assigned to them those duties which it was thought beneath their own dignity to perform. Therefore, Stanley Rice says: "There is strong probability that the outcastes were the survivors of the conquered people, who became the drum-beating, leather and farm labouring classes to which as serfs they had been relegated from early time."

The caste system as projected by Manu and accepted by Hindu society has proved to be the biggest curse for this country. The *Chaturvarna* system under the Aryans was more of an occupational order projecting the division of labour than the division of society. Prof. Harold A Gould in his book, *'The Hindu Caste System,'* says "the Brahmins were at the top of the occupational order, and occupationalised the sacred order". With the passage of time, the caste system became the hellhole of the Hindu society.

Caste gave stability?

J.H. Hutton, Census Commissioner (1931), and an anthropologist has described the Indian subcontinent as 'a deep net' into which various races and people of Asia drifted over time and were caught. The tall Himalayas in the north and the sea in the west, east and south isolated this net from the rest of the world, which led to the development of a unique plural society, in which diverse people of different colours, languages and customs have lived together in reasonable stability and they had no way to escape. It is unlike in Europe which is one flat plain in which innumerable people lived, fought and freely moved about between Atlantic and Pacific oceans. And, created a large number of states, kingdoms and principalities

S. No.	Group name	Percentage of total population
	I - Scheduled Caste and Scheduled Tribe	
A-1	Scheduled Castes	15.05
A-2	Scheduled Tribes	7.51
	Total of A	22.56
	II - Non-Hindu Communities, Religious Groups etc.	
B-1	Muslims (other than STs)	11.19
B-2	Christians (other than STs)	2.16
B-3	Sikhs (other than STs)	1.67
B-4	Buddhists (other than STs)	0.67
B-5	Jains (other than STs)	0.47
	Total of B	16.16
	III - Forward Hindu Castes and Communities	
C-1	Brahmins (including Bhumihars)	5.52
C-2	Rajputs	3.90
C-3	Marathas	2.21
C-4	Jats	1.00
C-5	Vaishyas – Banias etc.	1.88
C-6	Kaysthas	1.07
C-7	Other forward Hindu Caste Groups	2.00
	Total of C	17.58
	IV - Backward Hindu Caste Communities	
D	Remaining Hindu caste/groups which come in the category of "Other Backward Classes" (OBC)	43.70
	V - Backward Non-Hindu Communities	
E	52 per cent of religious groups under section B may also be treated as OBCs	8.40
F	The approximate derived population of other Backward Classes including non-Hindu Communities (Aggregate of D & E rounded)	52 per cent

which Europe has become today. According to him, the caste system made it possible for people of great diversity to live together in a single system over thousands of years. Caste was, thus, a consequence of historic migrations of many people and tribes who came to India over thousands of years and made it their home. Every time a new intruder arrived, a new Jati or 'sub-caste' was created based on profession, colour and faith.

As stated above, in the classic four-caste hierarchy the Brahmin (priest and teacher) is at the top, followed by the Kshatriya, landholder, warrior and ruler. The Vaishya, businessman, comes the third, and the Shudra, labourer, is last. Below the four are the casteless untouchables (or Dalits) and tribal people. The others are sub-castes. The three upper castes constitute roughly 12 per cent of today's India but they have ruled the country for millennia. About half of India is Shudra, depressed classes divided among hundreds of sub-castes. About 20 per cent of Indians are untouchable Dalits. (The remaining 18 per cent Indians belong to other religions – 13 per cent Muslims and the rest Sikhs, Christians, Parsis, Buddhists, Jains etc.).

The Mandal Commission (1989) has given in its report the following distribution (in percentage) of Indian population by caste and religious groups:

The NSSO (2009-10) 66th round had estimated the OBC population to be 41.7 per cent as against 52 per cent estimated by Mandal Commission.

Foreign rulers specified more than 6,000 castes and sub-castes in the gazetteers and fixed caste allegiances in the census operations from 1881. As the Census Commissioner for the 1911 Census, Sir Herbert Risley, said, it was not enough merely to record the caste preferences of individuals. To make life easier for policy-makers, the census had also to identify "social precedence as recognised by native public opinion." In other words, the administration had to locate a caste in the social hierarchy and determine which caste was high, intermediate or low. Risley's attempt to define caste precedence triggered an upsurge in civil society. Caste groups mobilised to redefine their *Varna* status, undertake changes in ritual practices and even press for changes in caste names.

Risley went a step further and ranked the *Jatis* in the local hierarchy and *Varna* affiliation of each. The ranking of *Jatis* and castes by the census created an unprecedented situation. Whatever their de facto status, most of the communities at the lower rung of the caste ladder felt that it was a good opportunity for social climbing by laying claims to higher status and registering a higher ranking in the census documents to have an official stamp, indicative of their higher social origin. Thus, a process of social mobility was set in motion whereby a caste claimed a higher social status by 'Sanskritising' its religious beliefs and rituals. A number of caste associations were formed and overnight honorific caste names were adopted, showing descent from Brahmins or Rajputs etc. The census led to a government-induced process of, what M.N. Srinivas was later to call 'Sanskritisation', social changes premised on the belief that Brahmins were role models.

Troublesome profiling

While medieval rulers also created lists of castes and occupations, such as those in the *Ain-i-Akbari* or *the Rajatarangini,* the urge to map every single caste is commonly attributed to the British colonial need to know about population they have to govern. Every caste in India has its own dialect, behaviour pattern and attitude to life. Caste and religion were considered as key determinants to help in the recruitment of martial races to the army or other occupations. Yet successive Census Commissioners, like Herbert Risley in 1901 and Yeatts in 1941, described the caste tables as the most troublesome and expensive part of the census. Risley complained: "If the person gives the name of a well-known tribe or caste...all is well. But he...

may give the name of a sect, of a sub-caste, of an exogamous sect or section... his occupation or the province from which he comes." In 1881 in Madras Presidency alone, the inhabitants reported 3,208 different castes, which the census then regrouped into 309 castes.

Herbert Risley came up with the amazing theory that castes could be distinguished in accordance with the average nasal index– those with the finest nose will be at the top, and those with the flat at the bottom. His classification made a systematic attempt to isolate the physical types and lend support to racial affiliation or the racial basis of castes. The main criticism of his classification was that (a) he took into consideration only a limited number of characteristics, (b) used linguistic terminology like 'Aryan' and Dravidian in racial classifications and (c) had no place for such important tribal groups as 'Australoid' or 'Kolarians'.

Census data

In the 1921 Census, for 'low castes', the term 'depressed classes' was used for the first time but no standard list of such castes was available for want of an adequate definition. Population data were collected and published for each individual caste and tribe separately at the state and district levels. In the 1931 Census, these figures were confined to exterior castes and primitive tribes, besides all other castes except those whose number fell short of 4,000 of the total population and for those whose figures were considered unnecessary by the local government. The 1941 Census data on populations of tribes were presented on a somewhat modest scale. Since then compilation was restricted due to the World War II. It was also felt by the then Census Commissioner, Yeatts, that in the then prevailing circumstances the scope of enquiries on castes and tribes would be dissociated from the Census.

Caste was not the only identity, but religion and language were equally explosive. For instance, in 1941 the Dalit Chuhras in

Punjab complained of pressure to be recorded as Sikhs or Hindus but Sikh and Hindu enumerators demanded that their religion be entered as *Adh Dharmi* instead. Given such battles, and the concern that India's innumerable castes and religions were used to justify colonial rule, the Constituent Assembly framing the Census Act of 1948 decided to exclude caste returns (except for SCs and STs). Similar debates have taken place over the counting of race and ethnicity in the U.S. and U.K. census respectively, with some people pointing to the unscientific nature of race, and others arguing that "in order to get beyond racism, we must first take a count of race."

If India has not won any battle since the Kalinga War, it was because the country was divided, layer upon layer, by caste, religion, and ethnic loyalties. And, there was no common ground for the entire country to unite against the enemy. British rulers sought to unite India through a common language (English), land tenure, civil service, educational system and cricket. But they united just enough to ensure that the Raj was not endangered. They kept the society divided in order to rule it.

The 1857 Mutiny was, for instance, not fought by British troops but by the Sikh Regiment. The Battle of Plassey was fought in 1757 by Mysore soldiers and farmers; the Rajputana soldiers fought for British Raj all over the world, from France and Flanders to Indonesia, North Africa and to Central Asia. The story of India being divided against itself is a sad chapter in history. However, generations of Indians have been taught to believe that the colonial rulers sought to divide India. Valentine Chirol, a distinguished journalist, in 1926 observed: "Hinduism could not build up a nation because caste was the negation of everything that constitutes a nation." National allegiance, he said "was secondary to the loyalty each (Hindu) owed to his caste since his caste was his Karma, determining much more than his present life."

Fixed customs and ideas

We have been living all these centuries in a world of fixed ideas, customs, cultural and social practices. No wonder, we have never grown out of caste mindset when each caste or social group was given specific role to play – Rajput to fight and rule, Brahmin to read holy books and teach, Vaishya to trade goods and services and scavengers to clean toilets. It is unprofitable to discuss the sources of these evil practices which prevailed in all societies in all times in virulent forms. Inquisition was ordered in Europe for those who disagreed with the Gospel and they had to burn at stake. Those who belonged to a dissident group had no right to state protection. Strangely enough, women virtually in all societies and cultures had been treated as objects of pleasure without any right and were traded in some societies as chattel.

Slavery and caste system

The caste system is worse than the slavery system which had never been a social or cultural practice; it was imperialism. It was exploitation of the defeated by the conquerors. It is a different kind of exploitation which ended in different countries at different times. Britain was the first to pass on March 22, 1807 an 'Act for the Abolition of Slave Trade.' The slave trade in the British Empire, however, continued until it was finally abolished by yet another Act, the Slavery Abolition Act, 1833. In the United States, slave labour existed as a legal institution in North America for more than a century before the founding of the United States in 1776, and continued mostly in the South until the passage of the 13th amendment to the United States Constitution in 1865 after the Civil War.

The first English colony in North America, Virginia, acquired its first Africans in 1619, after a ship arrived, unsolicited, carrying a cargo of about 20 Africans. Thus, the practice established in the Spanish colonies as early as the 1560s, was expanded into English North America. But in India, there has never been slavery but the castes and there was no such law which directly identified the caste system built layer upon layer in our cultural and social consciousness. Of course untouchability was abolished by free India in 1950 under the Constitution, but it is still practised today. The social prejudices run deeper into our social and religious psyche, many of which continue even today despite social awakening, education and economic development.

Social exclusion

Thus, casteism remains politically and socially based on exclusion, bias and injustice. An anti-Semite will ask, for instance, why the Jews do so well in business and a white racist will fear apparent black physical prowess. Prejudice against outcastes is built on the idea that one will be polluted if one goes near them. The caste system is a uniquely powerful form of social controls, since it is total and self-replicating. The higher castes can only remain high if they have others to look down upon as low. So when a boy touches a scavenger, his mother whispers to him; "Don't touch, you will be polluted!" This would lodge in the child's memory, and as he grows older and less traditional, the flinch remains. This was also the experience of Dr. Bindeshwar Pathak who had once touched a Dom (untouchable) in his house and he had to swallow cow dung and urine (It is mentioned earlier). And, such outcastes are enormous in number. "To equal the number of Dalits in India, one would need to add together the population of Albania, Australia, Belgium, Israel, Kuwait, Libya, the Netherlands, Rwanda, Sri Lanka, Sweden and the United Kingdom. To put it still more simply, every sixth person on the planet is Indian, every sixth Indian is Dalit," says Patrick French in his book, *India*, to give a global magnitude to the Indian caste problem.

Birthmark, says Dr. Ambedkar

Throughout his life, Dr. B.R. Ambedkar tried to figure out why Caste Hindus had an obsession with defilement. He discovered that the laws of Manu specified that anyone touching a Buddhist or a member of other outcaste groups should purify himself with a bath. Dr. Ambedkar's theory was that old wars between the settled and nomadic tribes, and between Brahmins and Buddhists, had led to the expulsion to the edge of villages of 'Broken Men', (Dalits) who followed the teachings of the Buddha and ate beef. They became untouchables. His thesis about Broken Men and their social, cultural or religious origins shows how he was attempting to understand the historic position of groups that had been recorded mainly by others. Dr. Ambedkar was part of a wave of people of similar background, examining the origins of the caste system and trying to create a new social contract.

Dr. Ambedkar was not among the worst suffering untouchables. Mahars were respected in the region around Bombay for their military service. Dr. Ambedkar had won a scholarship sponsored by the Maharaja Gaekwad of Baroda, studied at Columbia University and the London School of Economics, published books, including *The Problem of the Rupee*, and by the late 1920s was both a legislator and a professor at the Government Law College in Bombay, which would not have been possible if he were among the worst kind of untouchables, like scavengers. A related movement for social reform and self-respect had started in the South by Periyar E.V. Ramaswamy, but most untouchables in India remained oppressed and the situation did not change much, which Dr. Ambedkar found even more frustrating as he grew older. Modern education made all the difference in the Ambedkar movement.

Sir William Jones and Manu Law

Sir William Jones, an 18th century British judge, who had translated *The Manusmriti* from Sanskrit says, "It is the Indian system of duties, religious and civil". Jones says that Europeans did not know about

SIR WILLIAM JONES

Sir William Jones

Sir William Jones (September 28, 1746–April 27, 1794) was an English scholar of ancient India, particularly known for his proposition of the existence of a relationship among Indo-European languages. He was also the founder of the Asiatic Society. Jones was born in London at Beaufort Buildings, Westminster. His father (also named William Jones) was a mathematician from Anglesey in north Wales, noted for devising the use of the symbol pi. The young William Jones was a linguistic prodigy, learning Greek, Latin, Persian, Arabic, Hebrew and the basics of Chinese writing at an early age. By the end of his life he knew thirteen languages thoroughly and another twenty-eight reasonably well, making him a hyper polyglot. Though his father died when he was only three, Jones was still able to go to Harrow in September 1753 and on to Oxford University. He graduated from University College, Oxford, in 1768 and secured M.A. in 1773. Too poor, even with his award, to pay the fees, he gained a job tutoring the seven-year-old Lord Althorp, son of Earl Spencer and as such an ancestor of Princess Diana. He embarked on a career as a tutor and translator for the next six years. During this time he published *Histoire de Nader Chah* (1770), a French translation of a work originally written in Persian by Mirza Mehdi Khan Astarabadi. In the subcontinent, he was entranced by Indian culture, an as yet untouched field in European scholarship, and on January 15, 1784 he founded the Asiatic Society in Calcutta.

Indian society and, hence, a different kind of Indian behaviour was hard to regulate. Since their ability to exert physical control over Indian behaviour was limited, the British rulers have "to leave the natives with their own laws", and the British administration should only govern politically. Hence, *The Manusmriti* was adopted as the principal source of Indian jurisprudence, which the British rulers accepted. The Manu Law also helped British to divide the already divided Indian society. It was for that reason that although we had English education, we had not the benefits of the Enlightenment and Reformation which were happening in Europe at the time when Jones gave this advice to British rulers. True, the caste system existed before Jones discovered it but *The Manusmriti* got British approval for the caste system. And, since then, it has had much deeper consequences in politics and society than Judge Jones or Dr. Ambedkar could imagine.

No caste gene; it is contrived

There is no scientific basis to say one could have a caste gene. Indian people fall into four major language families: Indo-European, Austro-Asiatic, Tibeto-Burman and Dravidian. The first group is spread across the upper and middle reaches of the country; the Austro-Asiatics (the tribals or *Adivasis*) were clustered in the centre and east, the Dravidians are spread as far as Andhra Pradesh and the Tibeto-Burmans were confined to small border areas to the north. There have been, however, membership exchanges within these four groups. It's all mixing up. Hence, no caste purity, say Dr. Arijit Mukhopadhyay and Dr. Mitali Mukerji of the Institute of Genomics and Integrative Biology (IGIB), New Delhi, who have done extensive genomics study of the caste system and India's social structure.

In Kashmir, there were people who were genetically similar to Dravidians. In Gujarat and eastern Orissa, the same was true. In parts of Andhra Pradesh and Karnataka and in the south of the country, the situation was reversed: here were Indo-Europeans. In Madhya Pradesh, there were ancestors who had come from the Himalayas. So people who thought they were product of a place where their family lived for infinite generations, as a matter of fact, were genetically closer to Indians who lived a thousand miles away, and spoke a different language. "For that matter, the unity of species is not of caste or groups", says Dr. Pathak. The population group test of DNA sequence variations has indicated that we have nearly a 100 per cent chance of knowing if they are tribals or not, and an 85 per cent chance of establishing their language group. The data, however, would not indicate the caste, because there is no basis. One can't say who is 'superior' or 'inferior'. People in India have come in from places that are now Iran, Burma, Central Asia, and Afghanistan in waves of settlers from various directions. There are many admixtures; while Caucasians are homogenous, others are not. India was like a melting pot compared to other Asian countries. Mitochondrial DNA shows that women moved around and reproduced with other communities. Marriage within one group is more recent in India, according to the Institute of Genomics and Integrative Biology (IGIB).

Purity of blood is a dangerous doctrine

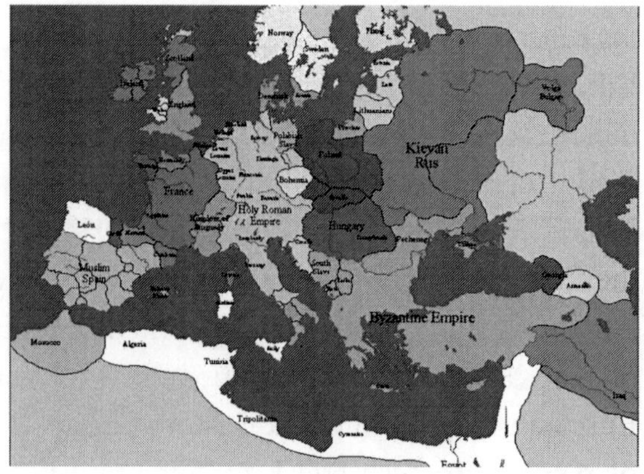

Yet another historical controversy persists about the purity of blood, which is associated with caste superiority and thus right to rule. Nazis claimed they were product of the pure Aryan blood. This misconception resulted in war and massacre in World War II. An equivalent of it persisted in India with some castes, including Kshatriyas, claiming the right to rule because of the 'purity of blood'. Historian Arnold J. Toynbee in his book, *A Study of History* says, "The Greeks had been the most talented people in the world and they were most mixed". This view has been repeated in a thesis put forward in a judgment delivered on January 5, 2011 by the Supreme Court. The court says: "While North America (USA and Canada) has new immigrants who came mainly from Europe over the last four or five centuries, India is a country of old immigrants in which people have been coming in over the last ten thousand years or so. Probably about 92 per cent of the people living in India today are descendants of immigrants, who came mainly from the North-West, and to a lesser extent from the North-East. People migrate from uncomfortable areas to comfortable areas. This is natural because everyone wants to live in comfort. Before the coming of modern industry there were agricultural societies everywhere, and India was a paradise for these because agriculture requires level land, fertile soil, plenty of water for irrigation and so on, which were in abundance in India."

Medieval Europe

In medieval Europe, the Church and priests also taught the people to spurn work and material progress and aspire for spiritual attainment. Like St. Francis of Assisi, many Christian saints suffered and starved themselves to death, hoping this was the greatest spiritual attainment. And, ascetism developed in the West as a branch of Christianity. This included meditation, fasting, renunciation and mortification of the flesh. No wonder, the western civilisation did not develop until the Renaissance, beginning from the 18th century, broke the spell of priestly influence and civilisation started progressing. Thus, in Europe, idleness and exploitation did not permanently become part of a socially accepted ideal life which continued to be so in India where, this mentality (aristocracy) has become second nature of the people. This was the source of caste system in India.

The difference between Europe reborn (Renaissance) and India rolling unawakened still, resulted in the material progress in the West, and advanced their civilisation. In India, this did not happen and the Brahmins, and later the non-Brahmin landlords, developed the habit of living on exploitation which became an accepted social practice and was morally defended. The caste system became worse and civilisation did not grow to compete with Europe. This is the main source of all our misfortune.

The progress made by European civilisation is attributed to the superior knowledge, especially in science and mathematics, which empowered them to conquer the world. Some people believe that brute force alone enabled the Europeans to conquer the world but it was also because of their mastery over science which also produced guns and other superior weapons. The knowledge which India had developed at one time in astronomy, algebra, geometry, mathematics, botany and medicine, musicology, inductive logic, etc. was gradually forgotten and finally lost. The mathematician, Ram Chandra of Delhi College, and Mahendra Lal Sarkar in medicine are great names, lost to us. The Europeans became wiser by reading them only to later capture our textile market which was once India's monopoly. Thus, our decline began with the creation of the caste system that finally destroyed our national unity, and so we remained a defeated nation until 1947.

Technology causes change

Now, the philosophical question is why these prejudices don't go and, what do we do to bring about a change. In this context, it may be noted that social changes come with economic changes which largely happened during the two hundred years of industrialisation in the West. With massive across-the-board application of technology, human behaviour, value system and cultural preferences have changed. And most changes came in those countries where technology was most used – namely in the US and, in the countries specially in the Third World, where technology was least used, least social change happened. Yet another source of change has been education and global interaction as a consequence of communication revolution. Mobile phone, fax machine, TV and a range of other information gadgets have destroyed national boundaries and globalised the world which seems headed to produce a common culture, common language, a common value and belief system and lifestyle in a manner and on a scale unheard of before.

Still more changes happened after the internet was born in a motor garage in California, some 30 years ago which now helps us to talk to the world while sitting in our bedrooms. Yet another source of change is education. While laying out the future agenda, former British Prime Minister Tony Blair shouted from rostrum: "Education, education and education again. This is the only way to save Britain from falling out of the global race for growth and retain its primacy in world affairs." Despite what we have done, the education gap remains the single most important cause for social disparity and poverty. Amartya Sen says: "There is no inequality in India, except in education. Once this gap is bridged or narrowed, the rest will be all right." A backward nation like Kenya has more than 70 per cent literacy while we are still far behind it, though the recent government initiatives, including the bill on compulsory education, will go a long way in bridging the education gap.

Sulabh intervention

According to Newton's First Law, every material body persists in a state of rest until it is forced to change through external intervention. This is true of social change also which is neither inevitable nor automatic; there have to be external stimuli which the Sulabh

Founder has provided in the hallowed tradition of previous social reformers who worked to abolish caste and unite the multi-cultural and multi-ethnic society that we live in today. For that matter Dr. Pathak is a leading change-maker of our time marked by frozen values, stale debate, old ideologies and divided social order most of which are pre-modern and antediluvian.

Because the political system tends over time to institutionalise dominant values, change usually comes from outside the political governance system. Social movements, therefore, are 'the sources of social innovation,' while political governance systems provide the 'instruments of social bargaining' through which the institutionalised norms of the state may be challenged. Thus, through the process of conflict and cooperation, a city evolves. At the root of social change are individuals, who together form social movements. Thus, in order to understand social change, one must also understand what motivates the behaviour of individuals. "The purpose of all human behaviour is to meet needs". People have many different needs, but all fall into two categories: survival and personal growth. All people share common survival needs for food, shelter and safety. However, different people may have very different personal growth needs such as love, approval from others, self-worth and creativity.

Sulabh works to inspire, build and support inclusive partnerships that address the systemic causes of poverty and inequity. By 'inclusive partnerships', Dr. Pathak means collaborative initiatives that are as representative as possible of all or most significant stakeholders in an issue and that ensure a significant role and voice for communities, the poor and marginalised in determining their own future and finding solutions to their problems. Dr. Pathak believes that collaboration among government, business and civil society is a necessity if the world's massive and complex social deficits are to be overcome. More effective dialogue, 'bridging leadership' and partnership building are required to bridge deep socio-economic divides. All sectors need to recognise the necessity for sustained engagement between social partners, and in particular, to amplify the less powerful ‘voices’ of the poor and the civil society sector; to protect and expand the public spaces in which the poor can access power and mobilise as citizens; and to create a more level playing field in which civil society organisations and citizens can play a meaningful role in multi-sector partnerships.

Now the question is: Will India ever become a casteless society? Although it is hard to look into the future, it is safe to believe that there cannot be any fixed idea, class or caste in a world which is constantly moving literally and figuratively. Man tends unceasingly towards unmeasured greatness at the end of the long track which humanity has yet to tread. To be true, changes are happening. As the caste system seems to be disappearing a new model of society is emerging when the caste profile is not as conspicuous as before. No class, caste or society can claim infallibility. Human history is the story of man forever seeking to improve the social order, forever falling, forever rising again, often disappointed but never ceasing to try. This flux will mark the end of the caste system when hereditary wealth, the privileges of rank and the prerogatives of caste will vanish and man will derive his social status and wealth from himself alone and not from the caste to which he was born by chance.

Religion has always been the identity of people which, earlier in India, determined the social status. The 'untouchables', therefore, sought to change their identity by seeking entry into temples. The temple entry movement began in 1924, in Travancore and it continues today, with Dr. Pathak taking scavengers to holy places in order to upgrade their social status.

CHAPTER 32

Temple Entry Movements Led to Social Awakening

Sulabh initiatives a link in the long chain

The Temple Entry Movement started first in the South where untouchability was most brutally practised. The untouchables were robbed of their land and honour. Dr. Bindeshwar Pathak took up the temple entry projects so many decades after the ban on temple entry was ended in Travancore State in 1936, while it still continued in the North. Hence, the Sulabh initiative is a link in the series of temple entry movements which, one hopes, will mark the end to this anti-social practice.

The Temple Entry Movement has a long history because it also indicated a new social order which was, in fact, nowhere in view of happening. It first started in 1924 with *the Satyagraha* in Vaikkom Mahadeva Temple of the northern part of Travancore State. Travancore was a princely state which merged with another princely state of Cochin to form Travancore-Cochin. After the states reorganisation on linguistic basis in 1956, the present Kerala State was formed by merging Travancore-Cochin with the Malabar area of Madras Presidency, now known as Tamil Nadu.

Maharaja Marthanda Varma was maker of Travancore, and under his reign, Travancore emerged a centre of political, cultural and social activities. He signed an accord with the British and abolished the supremacy of the feudal landlords (Ettuveetil Pillamar) and seized the small kingdoms of Kollam, Attingal, Ambalapuzha, Kayamkulam and Kottarkara to expand his rule. In 1753, Marthanda Varma signed a treaty of peace with the Dutch accepting their supremacy. But he maintained his sovereignty for a time. In 1757, yet another pact was signed between Travancore and its northern neighbour, Cochin, to ensure peace on the boundary. He developed proper tax system, built many irrigation facilities and introduced social reforms.

The ban on temple entry was, however, not confined to the untouchables only. Even Swami Vivekanand was denied entry into the 2000-year-old Bhagavathi Kali Temple, situated at a place called Kodungalloor, 38 km south of Trichur. Before he left for Chicago in 1893 for the World Parliament of Religions as a wandering mendicant, then unknown to people as Swami Vivekanand, he toured India and came to Kodungalloor in November 1892. He tried to enter the Kali Temple but the temple guards prevented him because he refused to disclose his caste identity. Without getting annoyed, he prostrated before the deity from outside, and sat under a banyan tree. His ochre robes and brilliant eyes attracted the attention of two princes who had come to the temple. When the princes approached him, the monk asked them why he was refused entry into the temple. The princes replied that, according to the local tradition, a person whose caste was not known could not enter the temple. A few months later, when the news of the World Parliament of Religions was reported by all leading newspapers with the photograph of Swami Vivekanand, the princes regretted the decision.

The depressed communities of South Travancore had demanded the right of temple entry in order to raise their social status. Originally a Temple Entry Movement was started in Travancore State. The

His Highness 'Padmanabha Dasa' Sri Chithira Thirunal Balarama Varma Maharaja

Ezhavas, who formed the major lower caste Hindu community in Travancore, launched the Vaikkam Satyagraha. Their organisation known as SNDP drew the attention of the government and demanded the removal of Tindal Palakas (the prohibition boards) placed near the temples.

At this juncture, the Nayar Service Society and the Harijan Seva Sangh recommended to the government for granting temple entry right to the lower-caste Hindus. When the Satyagraha movement became vigorous, the government opened the roads on three sides of the Vaikkam Temple to the lower caste Hindus. But these communities were not permitted to have a glance *(darshan)* of the deity in the *Garbhagriha*. It was only a selective entry permission.

It may be recalled that in 1896, an Ezhava memorandum signed by more than 13,000 representatives of the Hindu Ezhava community of Travancore was submitted to the government seeking recognition of the right of the Ezhavas to enter government service jobs. The upper caste Hindus of the state prevailed upon the then Maharajah not to accept the petition.

Sir C.P. Ramaswami Iyer who served as the Dewan of Travancore from 1936 to 1947

In protest, many Ezhavas embraced Christianity, making the Christian population of Travancore increase from six lakhs in 1901 to 17 lakhs by 1931. When it seemed that the fight for justice had not gone too far, the leadership threatened to convert en masse, rather than stay as untouchables in the Hindu society. Sir C.P. Ramaswami Iyer, Dewan of Travancore, realising the imminent danger, prompted the Maharajah of Travancore to sign on November 12, 1936 the Temple Entry Proclamation, ending the ban on temple entry. This was a historic declaration. The proclamation introduced revolutionary changes in the Hindu society. It was also an act of justice to the poor Hindus in the state and Magna Carta of a resurrected Hinduism purified, ennobled and equipped to prosper and conquer. The proclamation created a healthy spiritual life and helped the advancement of the various castes and classes among the Hindus. The proclamation sanctioned the rights to enter temples, use roads, public wells, tanks, guest houses etc for lower caste Hindus.

Gandhiji's intervention on behalf of untouchables

It was after the intervention of Mahatma Gandhi and his negotiations with the government, the latter promised that the roads at

Suchindram Temple

Suchindram Temple of Travancore State would also be opened to the *Avarnas* (untouchables) but the strong pro-*Savarna* attitude of the government and opposition of the orthodox *Savarnas* (touchables like Brahmins etc.) made the government to ignore the promise given to Gandhiji. Therefore on May 12, 1926 the *Satyagraha* which was originally started in 1924 was resumed. The *Satyagrahis* challenged the government restrictions, faced the *lathi-charge* and proceeded towards the temple that spread alarm in the temple areas. Hard-pressed by the agitations, the ruling sovereign on November 8, 1932 appointed a committee, known as the Temple Entry Enquiry Committee.

Though the appointment instilled hope among the *Satyagrahis*, the failure intensified the agitation. Throughout the state the *Satyagrahis* decided to use all roads, tanks and wells used by other caste Hindus. In response, the government gave orders to open forty roads in the Travancore State to all classes of people. A conference of Devaswom Commissioner and engineers was held which decided that those public roads, wells and tanks, maintained out of public funds, should be immediately thrown open to all the people, but those which were maintained out of Devaswom temple funds would be closed to non-caste Hindus.

The Nayar Service Society and other Hindu Missions began to reconvert those who were not allowed in the Hindu fold. Thus, the outcaste *Parayas* and *Pulayas* gained the right to stand along with Brahmins before the sanctum sanctorum of the Hindu temples after their conversion. Further the proclamation radiated a fusion of sub-castes which, in turn, fostered intermarriages of different castes. It ushered in a new era of equality and freedom. But this was shortlived due to protest by high-caste Hindus.

A. Srivathsan writes in *The Hindu* (November 12, 2011): "On November 12, 1936, the Maharajah of Travancore signed the historic Temple Entry Proclamation, and in one bold stroke, the age-long injustice of barring lower castes from entering temples was removed. And, a tidal wave of joy and rejoicing passed through every nook and corner of Travancore. The action attracted attention and admiration from the whole country.

Two decades of struggle

"Such an 'epoch making' event was the culmination of two decades of struggle. In 1919, T.K. Madhavan, a prominent social reformer and the Editor of *Deshabhimani,* the Malayalam newspaper, took up the issue of temple entry with the Travancore Government. So did Kunju Panicker in 1920, and again Madhavan in 1921. But none of these had any effect on the government. Gandhiji, who was anguished by the 'very feeble response' of south Indian temples to reform efforts, agreed with Madhavan, during a meeting in 1921, that Kerala was ripe for a temple entry agitation. He insisted on peaceful protest and found that there was no swifter remedy than a real Satyagraha properly handled."

Satyagrahas largely Kerala-centric

As stated earlier, before Trivandrum became the epicentre of the temple entry campaign, protests had begun in Vaikom, in 1924. Though this struggle did not succeed in lifting the bar to *Avarnas*, or lower castes, entering the Mahadeva Temple, it managed to open the roads around the temple for their use. The Temple Entry Movement gained momentum after this. The action was later shifted to Trivandrum. The temple entry agitation was formally launched in the city on April 3, 1926. However, before the campaign could move on to the next stage, the Satyagraha started at the Guruvayur Temple.

On November 1, 1931, a large number of Dalits and upper caste Hindus assembled at the Guruvayur Temple to demand that the *Avarnas* be allowed inside the temple. The 10-month long protest, and fasting by K. Kelappan, popularly known as 'Kerala Gandhi' (which he dropped on Gandhiji's advice on October 2, 1932), drew national attention to the Temple Entry Movement. The call to open temples for Dalits grew louder. Shortly afterwards, in November 1932, the Travancore Government appointed a Temple Entry Enquiry Committee. The committee, which submitted its report after a year, did not recommend the opening of temples, but suggested roads and tanks could be opened for all.

The reformers rejected the report as it 'did not meet the present need.' They insisted that appropriate action alone would meet 'the test of the hour.' On May 9, 1936, an All-Kerala Temple Entry Conference was held in New Theatre Hall near the Trivandrum Central Railway Station, and it was resolved to step up the agitation. Speakers at the conference pointed out that, of the nearly 30 lakh Hindus living in the state, as many as about 20 lakh were being prevented from entering temples. They decided to convert 'all the passive goodwill in the state' into an 'irresistible demand,' and simultaneously appointed a committee to take up the issue with the Maharaja.

Chowdar Tank Satyagraha

Dr. B.R. Ambedkar had launched a movement against the untouchables being barred from temple entry or taking bath in public tank. Apart from publication of various journals and books in this direction, he launched the Chowdar Tank Satyagraha in Mahad for Dalits' right to draw water in 1927 and the Kalaram Temple Satyagraha, which continued for five years.

A mass meeting of the untouchables was held at Mahad on March 19-20, 1927, over which Dr. Ambedkar presided. It was decided that the untouchables would march on the public tanks. Fearing a breach of peace the authorities promulgated prohibitory orders. Thus the proposed march had to be abandoned. *The Manusmriti* was publicly burned on December 25, 1927, at Mahad. Ambedkar demanded that the *Sastras* be proscribed as they lowered the dignity of the whole people in sanctioning untouchability.

The next major agitation in which the untouchables were involved was the Temple Entry Movement launched in 1930. It began with the Satyagrahis demanding entry for the untouchables into the Kalaram Temple at Nasik in Maharashtra, which was opposed by the upper caste Hindus. Finally, to appease the agitators they agreed to include a few untouchables in the select group that carried the idol in the annual procession. But at the last moment they backed out of the agreement. The temple was closed for a year when the untouchables continued to agitate for the right to entry.

Gandhiji had congratulated C.P. Ramaswami Iyer, Dewan of Travancore, for advising the Maharaja to issue the proclamation on temple entry though what actually motivated the proclamation was the fear of mass conversions to Christianity. The scene of action was subsequently shifted to the princely state of Cochin. The little kingdom found itself in the vortex of a controversy, which was closely linked to the Travancore Temple Entry Proclamation. On April 15, 1937, the Cochin Government issued an order which declared that the priests who had officiated in Travancore temples after the Temple Entry Proclamation and participated in ceremonies at the temple at Kudalmanickam, near Irinjalakuda in Cochin, had polluted that temple. The Raja of Cochin had issued the order against the advice of his Dewan but under pressure from the Nambudiri Brahmins. Which indicates that the Temple Entry Proclamation was not a voluntary act but the one forced by fear of conversion or social pressure.

Dr. Bindeshwar Pathak solved the problem of entry of Harijans into the Nathdwara Temple in Udaipur, Rajasthan, for prayers in 1988, while several attempts, made by others, had failed. Even the then President of India, Mr. R. Venkataraman, wanted himself to lead Harijans into the temple. However, Dr. Pathak with 100 scavengers and orthodox Vedic Maithili Brahmins, entered the Nathdwara Temple, offered prayers and recited Bhajans and Kirtans. The scavengers and the whole group took their meal together. This programme was performed without police protection. On return from the Nathdwara Temple, Dr. Pathak, along with the scavengers and the Vedic Brahmins, was given audience by Mr. R. Venkataraman, the then Vice-President, Dr. Shankar Dayal Sharma and the late Prime Minister, Mr. Rajiv Gandhi. This act of Dr. Pathak was quite in line with Dr. Ambedkar's who had led a group of Harijans to draw water from Chowdar public tank, in Mahad and led another Satyagraha for Kalaram Temple entry in 1930.

Casteless Puja

On his return from Nathdwara, Dr. Pathak launched a campaign to help the Scheduled Castes offer prayers in temples and performing Puja at their homes by Vedic Brahmins in 1989. Also, he started common Puja and dining programmes where members of the Scheduled Castes did fasting, sat on the Puja and prepared 'prasad' and also food which were distributed to all, including Vedic Brahmins, who also ate with them. This programme, which is continuing since then, has got wide acceptance.

When high and low meet

It was a proud and unthinkable moment for the erstwhile untouchable scavenger families from the remotest parts of India, when they were led by Dr. Pathak and allowed to enter the local Jagannath Temple at Alwar, Rajasthan by the priests on December 21, 2008 and dined with families of the people of the 'upper social strata'. A history of sorts was created when people witnessed an unprecedented event of common dining in Hazoori Gate colony of Alwar, where families of erstwhile untouchable scavengers live. That those, who thought even the shadow of a scavenger befalling upon them will pollute them, have now participated in common dining, is no less than achieving almost the impossible. Mahatma Gandhi and Dr. Bhimrao Ambedkar had dreamt of such a happening. Now, the dream has come true.

Kashi Vishwanath Temple

Usha and Dolly, along with other 200 women of the scavengers' community, made history in Varanasi on June 20, 2011 by offering prayers at Kashi Vishwanath Temple (KVT) and sharing food with Brahmins and other upper caste people. Before going to the temple, they took a holy bath in the Ganga at Dasaswamedh and adjoining ghats. They also went to Sant Ravidas (*Sarva Dharma*) Temple at Rajghat. Later, they shared meal with *pandits* and upper caste people at Patel Dharmashala amidst chanting of Vedic *mantras* by the students of Panini Kanya Mahavidyalaya. They also went to Vindyavasini Temple in Mirzapur district and offered prayers. While working as a scavenger like other family members, Dolly

Former 'untouchable' women with Dr. Pathak at Varanasi where they visited Kashi Vishwanath Temple and offered prayers before *Jyotirling* of Lord Shiva. (June 20, 2011)

had to face discrimination in school. But her father encouraged her to pursue her studies. After rehabilitation by Sulabh International Social Service Organisation in 2008, she engaged herself in carpet weaving like other members of the community. Over 150 erstwhile scavenging women of Tonk were associated with carpet making.

At Ajmer Sharif Dargah to offer Chadars by way of homage to Khwaja Gharib Nawaz. (June 24, 2011)

Visit to Dargah, Pushkar, Church and Gurudwara

The liberated women visited on June 24, 2011 the Ajmer Dargah and performed rituals at a temple in Pushkar. Usha Chaumar, who

In front of the Sacred Heart Cathedral, New Delhi, where a special prayer meeting was arranged for the former 'untouchable' women. (June 25, 2011)

At Bangla Sahib Gurudwara, New Delhi, where former 'untouchable' women offered prayers. The head of the Gurudwara also offered *Siropas* to all of them

once worked as a manual scavenger and is a member of Nai Disha, Sulabh's rehabilitation wing, performed rituals with upper caste Hindus at the Kashi Vishwanath Temple. After performing rituals at the Dasaswamedh Ghat for nearly two hours, they proceeded to the Vishwanath Temple, carrying earthen pots filled with water from the Ganga.

The former 'untouchable' women were also taken to the Gurudwara Bangla Sahib, New Delhi, and then to the Sacred Heart Cathedral where they attended a prayer meeting specially organised for them.Thus, the erstwhile scavengers can now freely enter temples and pray to the deities and break the centuries old barriers of society by eating together with the families of 'upper strata', thanks to the Sulabh Founder, who has been in his own humble way attempting since 1968, to realise, in no small measure, one of the dreams of Mahatma Gandhi.

Civil society is an idea as old as hills; it averts conflict between the state and society while indicating the ultimate manifestation of people's power.

CHAPTER 33

Power Back to People: Role of Civil Society

Sulabh, a new self-sustaining civil society model

Harold Laski says, "James the 1st and Louis XIV taught that the King could do no wrong, and their successors lost their heads; Hegel and his disciples taught that the State could do no wrong, and plunged the world into war; Our doctrinaire democrats teach that the majority can do no wrong, and they bid fair to wreck our civilisation completely." Therefore, civil society was created.

Among civil society's rediscovered symbols, none were so pronounced as Neila Chaabane of Tunisia, Wael Ghonim of Egypt, Mohammed Nabbous of Libya, Razan Ghazzawi of Syria, and Bushra al Mugtari of Yemen–the faceless women who led social action to topple the autocratic regimes in North Africa. No one could have known that when a Tunisian fruit vendor, Mohamed Bouazizi, set himself on fire on January 4, 2011 in a public square in a small town near Tunis, he would spark off protests that would bring down dictators in Tunisia, Egypt and Libya and rattle regimes in Syria, Yemen and Bahrain. Or, this social action would spur Mexicans to rise up against the terror of drug cartels, or Greeks to march against irresponsible leaders, or Americans to launch Occupy Wall Street protest against income inequality. In 2011, protests occurred in the countries whose populations totalled at least 3 billion people, and the civil society action was reported in newspapers more prominently than at any other time in history. They very evidently proved that civil society action can bring about a colossal change, political and social.

One of the defining features of modern governance is the diminishing role of the state or a union of states like the European Union. In which case, the role of civil society becomes important; for, it provides the critical mass for democracy to grow. In simpler terms, democracy can grow not only in the framework of elected institutions, but also in the regime where civil society is strong enough to provide a forum to counterbalance hubris of the government and the venality of elected representatives, both of which are in full display all over the world, most specially in the developing societies. Civil society actors include charitable societies, churches, neighbourhood organisations, social clubs, civil rights lobbies, parent-teachers associations, unions, trade associations, and a wide range of other agencies. Civil society actors can be distinguished from the government and business sectors on a number of dimensions.

While government seeks to provide public order and public goods, and uses its authority to raise the money and create the desired public conditions, and business works to provide private goods and services through the mechanisms of voluntary exchange, civil society actors seek to actualise the values and purposes of citizens and citizen groups through their independent voluntary efforts, as well as through the influence that citizen groups can exert on both business and government. If governments mobilise resources through legitimate coercion and taxation and businesses mobilise resources through resource exchanges, civil society organisations mobilise resources through appeals to values and social purposes. While businesses are oriented to private interests and governments are oriented to public interests, civil society actors focus on the interests of social groups within the society – including those groups disadvantaged by existing arrangements.

The civil society is often referred to non-governmental organisations (NGOs), that focus on issues like poverty alleviation, human rights, environmental degradation, and other issues of social, economic and political development. These NGOs carry out a range of activities, such as providing services to poor populations, building local capacity for self-help, sanitation, analysing and advocating policies that support disadvantaged constituencies, or fostering research and information sharing. Some NGOs focus on serving their members, and others focus on serving clients outside the organisation. Some operate domestically, working on projects whose impacts may be felt from the village level to national policy to international arenas.

The Grameen Bank began as a Bangladeshi NGO experiment in micro-lending to poor entrepreneurs who had no collateral for bank loans. After demonstrating that small groups who shared responsibility for the loans had a repayment rate vastly superior to ordinary borrowers, the Grameen Bank expanded its operations to serve more than 2,000,000 poor, mostly women entrepreneurs in Bangladesh, and catalysed an international micro-credit movement supported by major donor institutions around the world.

Sulabh International Social Service Organisation has turned sanitation from what was primarily about waste disposal and water supply into a mass movement. Both these examples describe initiatives launched by NGOs in developing countries that have expanded to affect international policies and programmes. The micro-credit movement promises to foster grassroots participation in developing economies, and the struggles over large dams have produced changes in international policies and decision-making institutions that have effects far beyond any single country or region.

International NGOs and NGO alliances have been responding to disasters and delivering services for many years, and this is still the most common international NGO role. Most of these organisations originated in industrialised countries; many have branch organisations and large projects in developing countries. A conference of the eleven biggest international relief and development organisations (e.g., CARE, OXFAM etc.) identified a number of challenges associated with globalisation processes.

Civil society and NGOs are often used as synonyms but they are different although in detail. While a civil society organisation may be a mass movement without any legal obligation and covenanted commitments, the NGOs are the home-grown legal vehicle to carry out projects, and social objectives, working outside the state control and without any profit motives (non-profit outfit). The NGOs are regulated by different national laws and regulations. Not the civil society.

For instance, the Indian social and religious movements like Arya Samaj, Brahmo Samaj or other social movements were civil society initiatives but they were neither registered bodies, nor were they accountable to the government. The Rose Revolution in Ukraine, the Velvet Revolution in Georgia, the Tulip Revolution or the Polish Revolution were among many civil society mass mobilisations against their governments.

The concept began with Romans

From a historical perspective, the actual meaning of the concept of civil society has changed twice from its original, classical form. The first change occurred after the French Revolution, the second during the fall of Communism in Europe. The concept of civil society in its pre-modern classical republican understanding is usually connected to the Age of Enlightenment in the 18th century. However, it has much older history. Generally, civil society has been referred to as a political association governing social conflict through the imposition of rules that restrain citizens from harming one another.

In the classical period, the concept was used as a synonym for good society. For instance, Socrates taught that conflicts within society should be resolved through public argument using 'dialectic', a form of rational dialogue to uncover truth. According to Socrates, public argument through 'dialectic' was imperative to ensure 'civility' in the polis (city) and 'good life' of the people. For Plato, the ideal state was a just society in which people dedicate themselves to the common good and practise civic virtues of wisdom, courage, moderation and justice. It was the duty of Plato's 'Philosopher king' to look after people in civility. Aristotle thought the polis was an 'association of associations' that enables citizens to share in the virtuous task of ruling and being ruled.

The concept of *'societas civilis',* however, is Roman and was introduced by Cicero. The political discourse in the classical period places importance on the idea of a 'good society' in ensuring peace and order among the people. The philosophers in the classical period did not make any distinction between the state and society. Rather, they held that *'civility'* represented the requirement of good citizenship. They held that human beings are inherently rational so that they can collectively shape the nature of the society they belong to. In addition, human beings have the capacity to voluntarily gather for the common cause and maintain peace in society. By holding this view, we can say that classical political thinkers endorsed the genesis of civil society in its original sense. The Middle Ages saw major changes.

Due to feudalism, the concept of classical civil society practically disappeared from mainstream discussion. Instead conversation was dominated by problems of a just war, a preoccupation that would last until the end of Renaissance. The Thirty Years' War and the subsequent Treaty of Westphalia marked the birth of the sovereign states system. The treaty endorsed states as territorially-based political units having sovereignty. As a result, the monarchs were able to exert control domestically by emasculating the feudal lords and to stop relying on the latter for armed troops. Henceforth, monarchs could form national armies and deploy a professional bureaucracy and fiscal departments, which enabled them to maintain direct control and supreme authority over their subjects. This gave birth to absolutism. Until the mid-18th century, absolutism was the hallmark of Europe.

Enlightenment and after

The absolutist nature of the state was disputed in the Enlightenment period. As a natural consequence of Renaissance, humanism, and the scientific revolution, the Enlightenment thinkers raised fundamental questions such as "What legitimacy does heredity confer?", "Why are governments instituted?", "Why should some human beings have more basic rights than others?", and so on. These questions led them to make certain assumptions about the nature of the human mind, the sources of political and moral authority, the reasons behind absolutism, and how to move beyond absolutism. The Enlightenment thinkers believed in the inherent goodness of the human mind. They opposed the alliance between the state and the Church as the enemy of human progress and well-being because the coercive apparatus of the state curbed individual liberty and the Church legitimatised monarchs by putting out the theory of divine origin. Therefore, both were deemed to be against the will of the people.

Hobbes – when life was "solitary, poor, nasty, brutish and short"

Hobbes and Locke

Strongly influenced by the atrocities of the Thirty Years' War, the political philosophers of the time held that social relations should be ordered in a different way than in natural law conditions. Some of their attempts led to the emergence of social contract theory that contested social relations existing in accordance with human nature. They endorsed that the nature of human beings should be encompassed by the contours of state and established positive laws. Thomas Hobbes (1588-1679) underlined the need of a powerful state to maintain civility in society. For Hobbes, human beings are motivated by self-interests. Moreover, these self-interests are often contradictory in nature. Therefore, in state of nature, there was a condition of a war of all against all. In such a situation, life was "solitary, poor, nasty, brutish and short". Upon realising the danger of anarchy, human beings became aware of the need of a mechanism to protect them. As far as Hobbes was concerned, rationality and self-interests persuaded human beings to combine in agreement, to surrender sovereignty to a common power. Hobbes called this common power, state, (Leviathan). State was created out of this thinking and philosophy. And, thus begins the story of civil society.

The social contract theory of Thomas Hobbes set forth two types of relationship. One was vertical, between the Leviathan (state) and the people; therefore, the latter submitted themselves to the former. The second system was the realm of horizontal relationship among the people. In that system, people, under the surveillance of Leviathan, were compelled to limit their natural rights in a way that would not harm the rights of others. The first system denotes the state and the second represents civil society. In Hobbes's paradigm, the formation of the civil society led to the formation of government, state, and laws. Therefore, in his view, the state is imperative to sustain civility among men. Thus, Hobbes's concepts of the 'state of nature' and the 'sovereignty of the state' led to the later realism that defined the nature of the relationship between the state and civil society.

John Locke's idea of state

Locke – the man who was behind Glorious Revolution in England

John Locke (1632-1704) had a similar concept to Hobbes about the political condition in England. It was the period of the Glorious Revolution, marked by the struggle between the divine right of the Crown and the political rights of Parliament. This influenced Locke to forge a social contract theory of a limited state and a powerful society. In Locke's view, human beings led also an unpeaceful life in the state of nature. From that major concern, people gathered together to sign a contract and constituted a common public authority. Nevertheless, Locke held that the consolidation of political power can be turned into autocracy, if it is not brought under reliable restrictions.

Therefore, Locke set forth two conditions with reciprocal obligations. First, people submit themselves to the common public authority which has the power to enact and maintain laws. The second condition contains the limitations of authority, i.e., the state has no power to threaten the basic rights of human beings. As far as Locke was concerned, the basic rights of human beings are the preservation of life, liberty and property. Moreover, he held that the state must operate within the bounds of civil and natural laws.

Both Hobbes and Locke had set forth a system, in which peaceful co-existence among human beings could be ensured through social contracts. They considered civil society as a community that maintained civil life, the realm where civic virtues and rights were derived from natural laws. However, they did not hold that civil society was a separate realm from the state. Rather, they underlined the co-existence of the state and civil society. The systematic approaches of Hobbes and Locke (in their analyses of social relations) were largely influenced by the experiences in their period. Their attempts to explain human nature, natural laws, the social contract and the formation of government had challenged the divine right theory. In contrast to divine right, Hobbes and Locke claimed that humans can design their political order. This idea had a great impact on the Enlightenment thinkers who argued that human beings are rational and can shape their destiny. Hence, no need of an absolute authority to control them. Both Jean-Jacques Rousseau and Immanuel Kant said that people are peace lovers and that wars are the creation of absolute regimes. As far as Kant was concerned, this system was effective to guard against the domination of a single interest and check the tyranny of majority.

Hegel's civil society

The leading thinkers of the Romanticism era considered that civil society stood for individual interests and private property. Hegel held that civil society served its interests: individual rights and private property. Hence, he used the German term *'bürgerliche Gesellschaft'* to denote civil society as 'civilian society' – a sphere regulated by the civil code. For Hegel, civil society manifests opposite forces. Being the realm of capitalist interests, there is a possibility of conflicts and inequalities within it. Therefore, the constant surveilance of the state is imperative to sustain moral order in society. Hegel considered the state as the highest form of ethical life. Alexis de Tocqueville, after comparing despotic France and democratic America, contested Hegel, putting weight on the system of civilian and political associations as a counterbalance to both liberal individualism and centralisation of the state. Hence, Hegel's perception of social reality was followed by Tocqueville, who distinguished between political society and civil society.

The relations between civil society and democratic political society have their roots in early liberal writings like those of Alexis de Tocqueville, who argued that the political element of many voluntary organisations facilitates a more informed citizenry, who make better voting choices, participate in politics, and hold government more accountable as a result. The statutes of these organisations have often been considered micro-constitutions because they accustom participants to the formalities of democratic decision making.

State is needless, says Marx

This was the theme taken further by Karl Marx. For Marx, civil society was the 'base' where productive forces and social relations were taking place, whereas political society was the 'superstructure'. Agreeing with the link between capitalism and civil society, Marx held that the latter represents the interests of the bourgeoisie. Therefore, the state as superstructure also represents the interests of the dominant class; under capitalism, it maintains the domination of the bourgeoisie. Hence, Marx rejected the positive role of state put forth by Hegel. Marx argued that the state cannot be a neutral problem solver.

The post-modern way of understanding civil society was first developed by political opposition in the Soviet bloc East European countries in the 1980s. From that time, stems a practice within the political field of using the idea of civil society instead of political society. However, in the 1990s with the emergence of the non-governmental organisations and the civil society as a third sector they became a key area of strategic action to construct 'an alternative social and world order.' Henceforth, post-modern usage of the idea of civil society became divided into two, as political society and civil society.

Civil society's big role in the West

The number of associations has increased substantially in recent years. In France, over 60,000 associations were created in 1990 alone, compared to less than 18,000 in 1961. Similarly, in Germany, the number of associations per 100,000 population nearly tripled from 160 in 1960 to 475 in 1990. Even Hungary, within two years of the fall of communist rule, boasted over 13,000 associations. And Sweden, often regarded as the prototypical welfare state, displays some of the highest participation rates in civil society worldwide: most Swedes belong to one or more of the country's close to 200,000 membership associations, creating a dense social network of 2,300 associations per 100,000 population.

Such organisations also appear to be increasingly widespread in the developing countries as well. Some 45,000 non-profit organisations are functioning in Sao Paolo, Brazil, for example, and another 16,000 in Rio de Janeiro. In Brazil as a whole, the number of non-governmental organisations is close to 200,000. In Egypt, a survey found some 20,000 such organisations in existence as of early 1990s. In Thailand, Bangkok alone boasts approximately 2,200 non-profit organisations, and close to 11,000 have been identified countrywide. India has one of the most complex and diverse civil society sectors in the world, including a rich tapestry of Gandhian rural development organisations as well as numerous 'empowerment-oriented' associations tied to various political, religious and ethnic movements.

Wide network in U.S.

The United States has a dense and complex network of voluntary organisations: churches, professional societies, charitable institutions, private schools, universities, and hospitals, and, of course, a very strong private business sector. This complex associational life was noted first by Alexis de Tocqueville, during his visit to America in the 1830s. This aspect of American society was also observed by the sociologist Max Weber after visiting the United States around the end of the 19th century: “In the past and up to the very present, it has been a characteristic precisely of the specifically American democracy that it did not constitute a formless sand heap of individuals, but rather a buzzing complex of strictly exclusive, yet voluntary associations”.

The destruction of civil society was perhaps most thorough in the Soviet Union. Russian civil society before the Bolshevik Revolution, weakened by centuries of absolutist rule, was not strong. What existed, such as the small private sector and social structure like the peasant commune, was ruthlessly eradicated. By the time of Stalin’s consolidation of power in the late 1930s, the Soviet Union exhibited a ‘missing middle’: the complete dearth of strong, cohesive, or durable intermediate associations. The former Soviet state was very powerful, and there were many atomised individuals and families, but in between there were virtually no social groups whatsoever. The ironic consequence of a doctrine designed to eliminate human selfishness was that people were made more selfish. It was a common observation, for example, that the Soviet Jewish émigrés to Israel were much more materialistic and less public spirited than Jews who had come from bourgeois countries. Virtually everyone in the Soviet Union had become cynical about public spiritedness as a result of a state that constantly hectored and coerced them into ‘voluntarily’ giving up their weekends for the sake of Cuban or Vietnamese people or some other such cause.

The civil society organisations (CSOs) nomenclature has acquired popular currency in recent years, but there is no agreement on what constitutes ‘civil society’ because the term was mindlessly borrowed from the West. While the term ‘civil society’ has a long history, the nomenclature, ‘civil society organisation’ is of recent vintage. For example, a Google search on ‘civil society’ shows that the definition and legitimacy was provided by the World Bank, which uses the term CSO as synonymous with NGO (non-governmental organisation).

Civil society role in India

Social movement has a hallowed tradition in India. The Independence of India itself was the consequence of the social action launched by Allan Octavian Hume, a liberal ICS man, in 1885 to educate Indians and encourage them to oppose Asian apartheid. It may be noted, Netaji Subhash Chandra Bose's father, Janaki Nath Bose, and Jawaharlal Nehru's father, Motilal Nehru, attended the first Congress meeting, called by Hume in 1890. The Congress was a civil society organisation before it became a political party.

The last century has been a time of immense social innovation. Paradoxically, however, one of the social innovations for which the 20th century may deserve to be best known was the civil society sector, and the plethora of private, non-profit, and non-governmental organisations that provide vehicles through which citizens can exercise individual initiative in the private pursuit of public purposes. The power and outreach of the civil society has been reinforced by media which has united the world against unjust state action. Anything happening in, say, as far apart as Iran and Ireland, will have ripple effect across the globe. Together, media and civil society constitute a supranational compact of the willing which sets the national agenda, fixes policy priorities and influences public opinion. Together, they can also make war and peace – a very lethal combination at that!! They are also major game changers in politics today. No wonder, politicians desperately seek to influence media and win their favour by whatever means – fair or not fair. Their working together has been made easier by communication explosion. We know the twitter revolution in Iran which sent the entire civil society into streets, protesting against the government.

The media attack is much harder to stop than the invasion troops. How can one stop people talking on cell phones in homes across the country and exchange opinion through 'twitter'? Radio Free Europe destroyed the Soviet empire, before Berlin Wall fell in 1989, without a bullet being fired and man being killed, which the entire US army could not. Today it is the battle over who reaches media first and how much he or she is able to influence it. It is a colonial reflex to believe that the government knows better than the citizen about how best to improve his life.

Various avatars of NGO

The term NGO was coined by the UN in 1945 to refer to organisations not under the direct control of the government or any political party. But it became popular in the 1970s, following a larger influx of Western donor agencies as well as various agencies of the UN, offering funds to the organisations and individuals willing to adopt their development agenda. This agenda depoliticises poverty by attributing it, not to God's way of managing the world or one's fate, but to bad governance and consequent backwardness of the people compared with the West, which provides resources and guidance on how to overcome poverty and backwardness in underdeveloped countries.

Before being called NGOs, civil society organisations were known as voluntary organisations (VOs). They were renamed because donor agencies could not justify giving large salaries to those who claimed to do 'voluntary' work. In the last decade, the VOs-turned NGOs adopted yet another identity when the World Bank took the lead by giving them their new name, civil society organisation. Barring a few, most CSOs have no roots in society rather, it remained a concept or abstraction and not a tool for policy traction. A genuine civil society organisation should necessarily draw financial sustenance on its own or from the social groups it serves.

But most CSOs get grants from Western agencies and promote their social, cultural, economic and political agendas.

Sulabh has redefined role of civil society

Sulabh has not conformed to any template; it has gone its own way, setting up a new work model, combining best and honest business practices with social services. For instance, Sulabh does projects at a 15 per cent premium as service charge and take up the responsibility to keep it in state of good repair for a period, ranging from 10 to 30 years. It is not like building a road and giving repair bills next year. This is a good business practice of accountability and spending the surplus from projects on social services like education, campaigning, research and other social work and not on giving dividends. For that matter, Dr. Pathak has re-invented the role of NGO, making it an agent of social change, working without government help or assistance from any quarter. Sulabh is an exception, not the norm.

Dr. Bindeshwar Pathak has redefined the role of NGOs, (or CSOs) making it a dependable social service delivery system in a self-sustainable way. He has made social service a career option, making professionals and engineers join the voluntary social movement while making a good living and a career. NGO is a lucrative option because there is good remuneration today; there is also a large opportunity to express oneself through work, workshops, seminars and trainings. Sulabh International is one of the largest NGOs in the country which was formed 47 years ago. No civil society organisation has touched the human lives so intimately nor has any exceeded the sweep and network of Sulabh International which is a global phenomenon. True, greater impact has been made by CSO working in politics with leaders like Jayaprakash Narain (J.P.) or Anna Hazare, or many more abroad. Political CSOs have seized the political agenda and influenced the functioning of the system, for good or bad. But getting the global eminence through service to the poorest among poor, scavengers, is Dr. Pathak's great achievement which he could do by redefining the role of NGOs (read CSOs). The non-government organisations, including Sulabh, are registered under the 150-year-old Act, the Societies Registration Act 1860, which was enacted largely to set up contact groups between the British rulers and Indian subjects. During the long period, NGOs have been through many avatars to finally become today as a major social service delivery system.

This is Sulabh's third avatar – the first was Sulabh Shauchalaya Sansthan, the second Sulabh International and now a comprehensive name, Sulabh International Social Service Organisation. The name changing has been done to fully indicate the areas of work. Sulabh Shauchalaya Sansthan was to strictly build toilets based on new Sulabh technology; community toilet building started after 1970 and in the last decades of the last century, comprehensive programmes for social reforms, including education, training in different skills, social upgradation, and social campaigning, were launched. Thus the juggernaut rolled on to new areas of human concern. Hence, the change in name, although the core areas, including liberation of scavengers, remain the same.

However, the case with Sulabh is different. It does not accept donation, aid or contribution but only takes up projects and gets nominal service charges to run the Sulabh network. It has not taken any help from anywhere or anybody, national or international to run the system. Sulabh has no debt or claim of any other kind on its sources. It is a fully self-supporting and sustainable NGO system. For that reason, it is free to make choices without being under pressure of the donors because there are none. It works alongside a team of professionals who previously held jobs in highly respected corporate firms and quit to join Sulabh. Now there is a more scientific and established methodology to solve issues and problems in the social work industry. A lot of emphasis is placed on planning and monitoring. Sulabh also cannot be categorised as a work-specific

NGO, but it works in wide-ranging fields, including abolition of scavenging and untouchability, social reform, education, technology research and women's empowerment. It is essentially a technology-based organisation, still in a process of evolving on national and international scale.

'Servant leadership'

Sulabh organised World Toilet Summit-2007 in New Delhi. Its Founder, Dr. Bindeshwar Pathak, addressing delegates from 44 countries, besides a large number of Indian NGOs and other civil society organisations

Dr. Bindeshwar Pathak has subscribed to the idea of 'servant leadership'. It is a simple idea that recognises that good leaders should serve their followers, not the other way around. As with other large social initiatives, companies have the resources to make a positive societal impact. Their organisational resources and ability to market and deliver products can be applied in many creative ways to make a difference in society. In fact, multinational companies are especially well equipped to have a profound impact. The bottom line is that Sulabh has the wherewithal and the know-how to help reignite the passion of volunteerism, beginning with its own good work. Volunteering benefits the individual, the company, and society. It empowers employees to share their talents. It builds character, leadership capabilities, and new skills, and fosters cross-cultural understanding. This creates stronger, better-rounded individuals. For the company, this means a higher performing and more committed workforce. More important for society, the power of volunteerism unites people and restores hope to those in need. In good times and bad, employees want to give back. They want to work in a company that's truly connected with their communities.

It's all about people's power

NGOs and NGO alliances have identified emerging problems, articulated new values and norms, created or reformed institutional arrangements, fostered innovations in international practice, and helped resolve conflicts and manage differences. These contributions to international governance, in turn, highlight problems of democratic and institutional accountability of international NGOs and NGO alliances, and the possibilities of multispectral cooperation to solve complex problems of international governance.

In conclusion, the civil society organisations are important actors in national and international development work. Their emergence during the last few decades is associated with the forces of globalisation, which have contributed to the personal, economic, political and social dynamics that give rise to expanding people's power. The growth of international NGOs and NGO alliances has also been shaped by the global impacts particularly visible in providing services and disaster relief, policy analysis and advocacy, social learning and problem-solving.

> *"Small steps by people somewhere, turn into giant strides everywhere."*
> *– John F. Kennedy*

CHAPTER 34

Landmark Years in Sulabh Movement

A long journey of many small steps

Sulabh grew into a massive people's movement in stages, beginning from very low profile. No wonder, the trek was neither smooth nor regular. The following are the landmark years of the Sulabh Movement which were also the turning points in the story that is at once amazing and true.

Nikkei Asia Prize 2018

The Sulabh founder, Dr. Bindeshwar Pathak, has been honoured with the Nikkei Asia Prize 2018 for his contribution to Asia's development. Dr. Pathak is among the three who have been awarded. According to the Nikkei Asia Prize Secretariat, Dr. Pathak has been described as "an Indian social reformer tackling two of his country's biggest challenges, poor hygiene and discrimination".

Mr. Naotoshi Okada, President & CEO, Nikkei Inc. presenting the Award to Dr. Bindeshwar Pathak

Nikkei Inc., one of the largest media corporations in Japan, has been

Dr. Bindeshwar Pahak has a message for the Japan's Prime Minister, Hon'ble Mr. Shinzo Abe, when they met in Tokyo on June 11, 2018 before receiving the Nikkei Asia Prize. On the extreme right is Mrs. Amola Pathak.

presenting the awards since 1996 to honour people in Asia who have made significant contributions in one of the three areas: Economic and Business Innovation, Science and Technology and Culture and Community. The prize was awarded on June 13, 2018 in Tokyo to Dr. Pathak who works to promote human rights and environmental sanitation among other social services. Sulabh International has built flush composting toilets throughout India, contributing to better sanitation and safety for rural women, who are freed from the demeaning job of manual removing of human waste.

Dr. Pathak also met Japan's Prime Minister, Mr. Shinzo Abe, at a dinner at the 24th International Conference on the Future of Asia, which was hosted by Nikkei and presented him the coffee table book, *"Narendra Damodardas Modi: The Making of a Legend,"* an illustrated biography having images and text depicting Prime Minister Narendra Modi's life journey, his struggles and his achievements. Prime Minister Abe was delighted to see in it his photographs with Mr. Modi. The photographs capture Mr. Abe's visit to India in December 2015.

Earlier

1968: Sulabh technology

Dr. Bindeshwar Pathak joined the liberation of scavengers' cell of the Bihar Gandhi Centenary Celebration Committee in 1968 when he was entrusted with the task of finding out an alternative to scavenging. Dr. Pathak modified and developed a technology of two-pit pour-flush toilet (popularly known as Sulabh Shauchalaya). He also succeeded in demonstrating the effectiveness of the two-pit pour-flush toilet system. Today, engineers not only from India but even from the World Bank have accepted that the on-site excreta disposal toilet system is an alternative to scavenging, open-air defecation and unhygienic, unsafe systems of human waste disposal like trench and borehole latrines, in the developing countries of the world.

Miracle technology: Sulabh twin-pit toilet model

1970: Sulabh organisation registered

By the time Dr. Pathak found the alternative to scavenging, the Bihar Gandhi Centenary Celebration Committee was dissolved by the government. That year, he founded the non-profit making voluntary social organisation, Sulabh Shauchalaya Sansthan (now known as Sulabh International Social Service Organisation), to carry out the work of liberation of scavengers. Thus, the seeds of the Sulabh Sanitation Movement were sown in 1970. The mass movement by Dr. Pathak started spreading all over the country with a cadre of about 60,000 Sulabh volunteers, now working from right atop the mountain at Vaishno Devi, to deep down in South and in the farthest corners in the east and the west of the country.

1972: Catalytic Agent

After developing a technology, Dr. Pathak evolved a methodology which also spelt out how a non-profit making social organisation could work as a catalytic agent between the government, local bodies and the beneficiaries. It was felt that the government alone could not liberate scavengers from the subhuman occupation. House-to-house contact and campaigns in local languages for their liberation were suggested as part of the methodology which was adopted by the Bihar Government. Later on it was adopted by many state governments. During the past 40 years, Dr. Pathak brought the scavengers' liberation programme from the micro-level to the macro-level. In 1973, he had put up just two Sulabh Shauchalayas for demonstration in the compound of the Arrah Municipality, a small town of Bihar. Since then Sulabh has constructed and converted about 1.5 million bucket latrines into Sulabh Shauchalayas throughout the country; and more than 2 lakhs scavengers have been liberated and over 640 towns have been made scavenging-free.

1974: Pay-and-use system

In 1974, the Sulabh Founder gave another concept of maintaining the community toilets and bath on the pay-and-use basis. Before 1974, public latrines in India were regarded as hell holes. Nobody was able to find a solution to this problem. Dr. Pathak found one and, on that basis, over 8,500 public toilet complexes are now being maintained absolutely clean, spick and span in al the states and Union Territories. Sulabh household community and school toilets are thus used by over 20 million people a day.

1978: Historic seminar

Seeing the success of the scavengers' liberation movement in Bihar, the Ministry of Works and Housing, Government of India, in collaboration with the WHO and UNICEF, organised a national seminar in Patna in 1978 on conversion of bucket latrines and liberation of scavengers. In this seminar, representatives from the Planning Commission, Ministry of Health, Ministry of Works and Housing, international agencies like WHO, UNICEF, World Bank, and the Secretaries and Chief Engineers of all the state governments participated. They all approved the Sulabh technology and methodology for adoption by individuals as well as institutions. And, thus the work of liberating scavengers and the maintenance of public latrines and baths started from Bihar to spread throughout the country in due course.

1980-81: Legal protection

Dr. Pathak persuaded the Ministry of Home Affairs, Government of India, to include liberation of scavengers and their rehabilitation programme on the 'whole-town approach' basis. Under the scheme, implementation of the Protection of Civil Rights Act 1980-81, was taken up in two towns of Bihar, Biharsharif and Purnia. In 1981-82, two more towns of Bihar, Daltonganj and Chaibasa now in Jharkhand, were taken up. Later, the programme was moved on to other states. The state governments agreed to provide alternative employment to liberated scavengers and hence all of them got jobs. No one has become unemployed so far. The Ministry of Welfare, Government of India, later took charge of this programme.

1984: Biogas from public toilet

The first Sulabh public toilet-linked biogas plant was set up at Adalatganj, Patna. It produced electricity from biogas which was supplied to the 3 kms long Bailey Road, Patna. Now over 200 such biogas plants are in operation all over the country.

1985: Training and rehabilitation

With the help of the Ministry of Welfare, Government of India, the Welfare Department, Government of Bihar, and the Bihar State Scheduled Castes Development Corporation, Sulabh started a training and rehabilitation programme for the wards of scavengers in different trades like shorthand, typing, motor driving, mechanics, masonry work, carpentry, canework, etc. A large number of children of scavengers have already been trained. This programme is being extended to cover the entire country. The programme was later expanded to include regular education and technical training.

1985: Technology evaluation

The UNDP and the World Bank after evaluation of the Sulabh technology of the pour-flush toilet and the methodology of the maintenance of public toilets and baths on pay-and-use basis, passed it on to the countries of South-East Asia, Africa and Latin America for their adoption.

1986: Protection of Civil Rights (PCR) Act

Dr. Pathak persuaded the Ministry of Welfare to give stipends to the wards of Muslim and Christian scavengers also for training and rehabilitation. Earlier, these were available only to Hindu scavengers. Without this, the wards of Muslim and Christian scavengers would have been left out and the movement for their liberation and rehabilitation would have suffered a setback.

1988: Scavengers in temple

Dr. Pathak solved the problem of entry of Harijans into the Nathdwara Temple in Udaipur, Rajasthan, for prayers in 1988. The controversy of entering the temple had taken a serious turn and so many attempts made by others had failed. The situation became so serious that the then President of India, Mr. R. Venkataraman, wanted himself to lead Harijans into the temple. Even the political leaders and the state government officials had to go to the temple with police protection. This attracted Dr. Pathak's attention who with 100 scavengers and orthodox Vedic Maithil Brahmins entered the Nathdwara Temple, offered prayers and recited Bhajans and Kirtans.

Dr. Pathak leading liberated scavengers into a temple

The scavengers and the whole group took their meal together. This programme was performed without police protection. On return from the Nathdwara Temple, Dr. Pathak, along with the scavengers and the Vedic Brahmins, was given audience by Mr. R. Venkataraman, the then Vice-President, Dr. Shankar Dayal Sharma and the late Prime Minister, Mr. Rajiv Gandhi. This act of Dr. Pathak was quite in line with Dr. Ambedkar's who had led a group of Harijans to draw water from a public tank, Chodor Talen, at Mahad in Kolaba district of Maharashtra in 1927 and led another Satyagraha to establish the right of the untouchables to enter the famous temple of Kalaran in Nasik in 1930.

1989: Casteless Puja

On his return from Nathdwara, Dr. Pathak launched a campaign to help the Scheduled Castes offer prayers in temples and performing Puja at their homes by Vedic Brahmins. Also, he started common Puja and dining programmes where members of the Scheduled Castes did fasting, sat on the Puja and prepared 'prasad'. They also prepared food for lunch or dinner. After the Puja was over, the 'prasad' and food were distributed by Scheduled Castes to all, including Vedic Brahmins, who also ate with them. This programme, which is continuing since then, has got wide acceptance.

1990: Social upgradation of scavengers

To improve the social status of scavengers in India, Dr. Bindeshwar Pathak launched a movement to socially upgrade them. This was a novel concept. There was a question mark as to whether after liberation, training and education, scavengers and their children will have upgraded status in society to be on par with the so-called upper-caste people. To socially upgrade the scavengers' status in society, Sulabh started a social upgradation campaign, calling upon high-status family in society to 'socially adopt' a scavenger family who will be treated like family members. Association with these high-status people would raise the status of the scavengers. This programme took off very well. So far, 10,000 scavenger families have been 'adopted' by high status people, including judges, advocates, journalists, ministers and planners. Among them were the then Union Deputy Commerce Minister, Mr. Salman Khurshid, Planning Commission member Ms. Chitra Naik, *Times of India* Editor, Mr. Dilip Padgaonkar, and the former Prime Minister, Mr. I.K. Gujral.

1992: Awareness campaign

In February 1992, Sulabh organised a 'National Seminar on Liberation and Rehabilitation of Scavengers' in New Delhi in which Vice-Chancellors, professors, planners, and administrators passed a resolution to make it a people's movement. The seminar was inaugurated by the former President of India, late Giani Zail Singh. Dr. Pathak regularly took such steps to create social awareness against unfounded beliefs and prejudices. He organised conferences, seminars, workshops, plays and folk dances on these themes. The attempt was to involve a large number of people from all walks of life in order to speed up the pace of the movement.

1992: Educate, organise and agitate

On the 'educate, organise and agitate' principle of Baba Ambedkar, Sulabh set up an English medium school in Delhi for the sons and daughters of scavengers wherein education was given in three principal areas: General and theoretical education, compulsory vocational education (knowledge of office management, shorthand, typing and computer training), and optional vocational education (intensive training in specific vocations) so that they may not have to wait in long queues for employment. This will also enable them to be self-employed or get jobs. Sixty per cent of the school's enrolment was of scavengers' children and the rest was from other families to visibly obliterate discrimination. This unique experiment was extended to other states also. The idea is: Education alone can empower the weak and poor.

1994: Sulabh International Museum of Toilets

The first of its kind in the world, the Sulabh International Museum of Toilets was set up in Delhi. The museum, through artefacts, pictures, posters and other available materials, tells the story of the development of toilets through the ages. This is the star attraction at the Sulabh Service Centre, Mahavir Enclave, Palam, New Delhi.

1996: Duckweed project

Sulabh demonstrated an eco-friendly low-cost technology for waste water treatment through duckweed. The technology, besides having low operational and maintenance costs, gives economic return in terms of pisciculture.

1997: STAC

A new technology for composting of biodegradable wastes, known as Sulabh Thermophilic Aerobic Composting (STAC) was developed in 1997. It requires only 8–10 days to degrade any biodegradable materials without churning.

1998: People's commission

Sulabh set up a People's Commission on the Abolition of Scavenging. The then Prime Minister, Mr. Atal Behari Vajpayee, inaugurated the commission at a function organised on November 26, 1998 to honour him with the Honest Man of the Year Award, 1997. Justice M.N. Venkatachalliah, former Chief Justice of India, and Chairperson of the National Human Rights Commission, was the Chairman of the Advisory Board of the Commission.

2000: Sulabh towards villages

Sulabh Towards Villages, a national campaign to improve rural sanitation, was started in 2000.

2001: Training of women

Sulabh started a countrywide programme for involvement of women in sanitation, health and hygiene.

2002: SET technology

Sulabh developed a new and convenient technology to make biogas plant effluents free from colour, odour and pathogen. The technology known as SET (Sulabh Effluent Treatment) lowers BOD (Biochemical Oxygen Demand) of effluent to less than 1 mg/l, making it suitable for agriculture, aquaculture or safe discharge into a river or any water body or cleaning of floors of public toilets.

2003: Sulabh University

Steps were taken to establish a Sulabh University of Sanitation; Compilation of Encyclopaedia on Sanitation has also started;

WASH campaign launched in collaboration with the Water Supply and Sanitation Collaborative Council, Switzerland; Sulabh started another Vocational Training Centre for liberated scavengers (Nai Disha) at Alwar, Rajasthan. UNDP recognised Sulabh technologies in its Human Development Report 2003; a Sulabh delegation visited Afghanistan to take up sanitation work.

2004: UN Task Force

Members of the U.N. Millennium Project Task Force on Water and Sanitation visited the Sulabh Campus.

2005: Workshop on sanitation

International Academy of Environmental Sanitation was registered under the Societies Registration Act 1860 by the Registrar, Government of Delhi.

23 professionals from five countries attended the 'International Workshop on Sanitation Technologies' organised by Sulabh International Academy of Environmental Sanitation in collaboration with UN-Habitat; Sulabh activities find mention in President APJ Abdul Kalam's book *'Mission India – A Vision for Indian Youth 2006'*. UNDP re-recognises Sulabh technologies in its Human Development Report. 24 professionals including representatives of UN-HABITAT covering 14 African countries attended the International Capacity Building Workshop, organised by Sulabh International Academy of Environmental Sanitation in collaboration with UN-HABITAT; Stanford University includes article on Sulabh – *'That Gandhi may not be born again'* – in its curriculum and five public toilets with biogas plants were set up in Kabul, Afghanistan, with the financial support of the Government of India.

2007: World Toilet Summit 2007

Sulabh organised the World Toilet Summit 2007 in collaboration with the World Toilet Organisation (WTO) in which representatives of 44 countries participated. And after the three-day conference, a Delhi Declaration was issued for a cleaner world; 'Mission Sanitation–a fashion show for a cause' was held at the Embassy of Bulgaria in New Delhi when the trainees of Sulabh's Nai Disha centre in Alwar assembled on the dais after walking the ramp with prominent Indian models, showcasing their talent.

2008: Liberated scavengers of Alwar visit New York

The United Nations Department of Economic and Social Affairs (DESA) invited Sulabh International Social Service Organisation to host 'Mission Sanitation', a special cultural event in collaboration with UN-NGO-IRENE Network at the United Nations, New York, on July 2, 2008, to seek and raise awareness and accelerate the progress towards improved sanitation worldwide; A fashion show was organised where rehabilitated women scavengers, accompanied by prominent models wearing Indian garments embroidered by them, walked the ramp in the United Nations with great pride and grace. The liberated women scavengers also visited the Statue of Liberty at the New York harbour to declare their liberation from the subhuman, demeaning and humiliating profession of cleaning dry privies and physically carrying human excreta (night soil) of others, to make a living for their families; and on coming back home, they paid tributes to Mahatma Gandhi at his Rajghat Samadhi, in New Delhi, on July 15.

The President meets liberated scavengers

The President Mrs. Pratibha Devisingh Patil, met Mrs. Usha

Hon'ble President Mrs. Pratibha Devisingh Patil received liberated scavenger Usha Chaumar and her colleagues at Rashtrapati Bhavan on July 25, 2008 after their return from New York where they were invited by the UN.

Chaumar and other liberated scavengers at Rashtrapati Bhawan on July 25, 2008 on their return from New York. She wished them a happy and prosperous new life, after being freed from age-old social prejudices. The President said that only after more scavengers are liberated Mahatma Gandhi's dream would come true.

2008: Untouchables enter temple

The liberated women scavengers visited Jagannath temple in Alwar along with their families and the families of those in whose houses they had earlier cleaned bucket toilets and they all jointly performed Puja in the temple. This was followed by a community lunch in which all of them participated jointly. A history of sorts was created on December 21, 2008 when people witnessed an unprecedented event of common dining in Hazoori Gate colony of Alwar, where families of the erstwhile untouchable scavengers used to live. That those who thought even the shadow of a scavenger befalling them will pollute them have now shared common dining is no less than

A Brahmin priest accepting sweets offered to the deity by liberated scavengers at Hazoori Gate Colony, Alwar, on December 21, 2008.

achieving almost the impossible. Mahatma Gandhi and Dr. Bhimrao Ambedkar had dreamt of such a happening. Now, the dream has come true. This act helped to remove, to a considerable degree, social untouchability and discrimination from the caste-ridden Indian society – a shameful practice attached to 5,000 years of social prejudice. It was the beginning of lighting of a candle in the darkness and a first step in the journey of miles.

2009: Prof. Rajmohan Gandhi takes food with liberated scavengers

It was a proud moment for liberated 'untouchable' scavenger families from Alwar, Rajasthan, when they were invited to the national capital to share meals with families of 'Upper Social Strata (of those in whose houses the scavengers had earlier cleaned toilets)' in the presence of Prof. Rajmohan Gandhi, the grandson of Mahatma Gandhi, on January 5, 2009. Some of

Dr. Bindeshwar Pathak, Prof. Rajmohan Gandhi, liberated women scavengers, some upper class family members and the temple priests dining together at the lawns of the Sulabh Campus, New Delhi, on January 5, 2009.

them have earlier even travelled to New York for a special UN session programme.

Stockholm Water Prize (2009)

Dr. Bindeshwar Pathak was given the 2009 Stockholm Water Prize by the Royal Swedish Academy of Sciences. This is world's most prestigious prize for outstanding achievements in water-related activities. The prize includes $ 150,000 and a crystal sculpture.

Swedish PM's visit

Swedish Prime Minister His Excellency Mr. Fredrik Reinfeldt, and his wife Mrs. Filippa Reinfeldt visited Sulabh on November 6, 2009.

A MOMENT TO REMEMBER: Dr. Bindeshwar Pathak receiving the 2009 Stockholm Water Prize on August 20, 2009 from H.R.H. Prince Carl Philip of Sweden

Belgium envoy's visit

His Excellency Jean M. Deboutte, Ambassador of Belgium and the Second Secretary, Mr. Jochen Anthierens, visited the campus on December 21, 2009.

2010: US envoy visits Sulabh

US Ambassador His Excellency Timothy J. Roemer and his wife Sally visited the campus on January 15, 2010.

Dr. Bindeshwar Pathak, Swedish Prime Minister His Excellency Mr. Fredrik Reinfeldt, his wife Her Excellency Mrs. Filippa Reinfeldt, with students and teachers of the Sulabh Public School in New Delhi, on November 6, 2009.

The Ambassador of the US in India, Mr. Timothy J. Roemer, Mrs. Sally Roemer, Dr. Bindeshwar Pathak and Mrs. Pathak along with students of the Sulabh Public School on January 15, 2010. The school is the first of its kind in India, having 60 per cent of students from scavengers' families and 40 per cent from those of upper castes studying together.

Her Royal Highness Princess Mathilde of Belgium and Dr. Bindeshwar Pathak along with students of the Sulabh Public School on March 23, 2010.

Belgium Princess visit

Her Royal Highness Princess Mathilde of Belgium visited the Sulabh campus on March 23, 2010.

2011: General Consultative Status with Economic and Social Council of the United Nations

The United Nations Economic and Social Council granted 'General Consultative Status' to Sulabh International Social Service Organisation for its outstanding contribution in the field of sanitation, human rights, removal of untouchability and improving the living conditions of millions of people. The Council had earlier granted Special Consultative status to Sulabh.

2012: Reward for brides who revolted against lack of toilet

Mrs. Anita Bai Narre, a newly married bride who revolted against the lack of a toilet at her in-laws' house, was honoured and awarded by Sulabh International at Mavalankar Hall, New Delhi, on March 19, 2012.

Mrs. Priyanka Bharti, Mrs. Priyanka and Mrs. Kumari Jyoti, newly-wed brides from Uttar Pradesh, who also revolted against lack of toilet in their in-laws' place, were awarded by Sulabh at a function held in village Vishnupur Khurd, District Maharajganj, Uttar Pradesh, on June 28, 2012.

Sulabh takes up the cause of the widows of Vrindavan

The Supreme Court of India directed the National Service Legal Authority (NALSA) to contact Sulabh to find out whether it could help the widows living in four government shelters in Vrindavan. Consequently, Dr. Pathak and Sulabh volunteers worked hard for the widows providing them

Dr. Pathak listening to the hardships of the widowed mothers

succour, relief and financial helps. Sulabh provided a stipend of ₹ 2000 to nearly 800 widows every month, besides medical and ambulance facilities, and vocational training in garland making, tailoring, agarbatti making etc to make them self-reliant. The widows were also taught English, Hindi and Bengali. To bring cheer and happiness in their lives, Sulabh celebrated the festivals of Holi, Durga Puja, Diwali and Christmas with them and also took them on regular excursions to Delhi, Kolkata, Agra etc.

The high point came when these widows of Vrindavan met Prime Minister Narendra Modi and tied Rakhi on his hands.

2013: National Conference on Sociology of Sanitation

The National Conference on Sociology of Sanitation, organised by Sulabh International Centre for Action Sociology in collaboration with Sulabh International Social Service Organisation, was held at Mavalankar Auditorium, New Delhi on January 28 and 29, 2013.

Dr. Pathak presented his Theory of Sociology of Sanitation, which is a "scientific study to solve the problems of society in relation to sanitation, social deprivation, water, public health, hygiene, ecology, environment, poverty, gender equality, welfare of children and empowering people for sustainable development and attainment of philosophical and spiritual knowledge to lead a happy life and to make a difference in the lives of others."

Support to flood victims of Kedarnath

In the Kedarnath deluge, Deoli-Bhanigram was the worst hit village. Dr. Pathak launched the Sulabh Sahayata Yojana mainly for the young and middle-aged women from Deoli, many of whom had become widows. Sulabh started giving a monthly stipend and other facilities to the sufferers, mainly the widows and the old people.

Baby Sukanya was barely two months old when she lost her father in Kedarnath's deluge. Dr. Pathak adopted her as his granddaughter and promised her life time care and upbringing.

Sulabh set up a Vocational Training Centre at Deoli-Bhanigram village, where training was imparted in tailoring to women and computer education to children.

Miss Universe on Sulabh Campus

Miss Universe Ms. Olivia Frances Culpo (2012) visited the Sulabh

Dr. Pathak and Ms. Rajini Vaidyanathan of the BBC at the human excreta-based Sulabh biogas plant situated on the Sulabh Campus

campus and interacted with the liberated untouchable scavengers and also saw the various technologies invented by Dr. Pathak.

2014: Sulabh technologies as one of the five unique inventions of the World

BBC Horizons declared Sulabh technologies as one of the five unique inventions of the world. This was featured on the BBC Horizons programme telecast on October 27, 2013 and March 30, 2014.

Toilet construction in Nepal

Sulabh signed an agreement for construction of toilets at Pashupati Nath Temple and other places in Nepal.

International Toilet Festival

A series of events spread over 3 days (November 18-20, 2014) was organised by Sulabh as part of the International Toilet Festival keeping with the spirit of 'Swachch Bharat' campaign of Prime Minister Narendra Modi's government. The World Toilet Day was celebrated at the Constitution Club Annexe, Rafi Marg, New Delhi.

2015: Union Minister's visit

Mr. Thaawarchand Gehlot, Union Minister of Social Justice and Empowerment, visited the Sulabh Campus and saw the various Sulabh technologies and activities and also interacted with the former manual scavengers, the widows and schoolchildren.

Sulabh Purified Drinking Water

Sulabh started its purified drinking water roject. Impure water from rivers, ponds, water bodies and taps is purified through Sulabh technologies and made safe for human consumption. Sulabh installed water treatment plants at three sites in West Bengal, Madhusudankati (24 Parganas, near Bangladesh border), Mayapur and Murshidabad. Raw water is drawn from the river Ganga in Mayapur and Murshidabad, while in Madhusudankati it is taken from a local pond. After its treatment at the Sulabh Water Treatment Plant, the water becomes pure and safe for drinking. Sulabh is bottling this water which is available for ₹ 0.50 paise per litre. It is also available in the Sulabh Water ATM, installed at the entrance of the Sulabh Campus in New Delhi.

Breaking the taboo: Untouchability No More

Mr. Rajnath Singh, Union Minister of Home Affairs, shared meal

Hon'ble Shri Rajnath Singh, Union Minister of Home Affairs, shared meal with the erstwhile untouchable scavengers

with the erstwhile untouchable scavengers on the occasion of the National Function 'Untouchability No More' organised by Sulabh to mark the 150th birth anniversary of Dr. Babasaheb Bhimrao Ambedkar. The families of the higher caste and untouchable scavengers exchanged greetings and ate food together.

Portsmouth University invitation

Dr. Pathak was invited as a main speaker by the British Association for South Asian Studies (BASAS) at the University of Portsmouth, United Kingdom. He spoke on 'Sanitation and Women's Rights in India'.

'Clean India' Campaign

Sulabh joined the 'Clean India' campaign launched by Prime Minister Narendra Modi who asked the people during the election campaign to build "toilets first, temples later".

'BBC Impact' Programme

Dr. Bindeshwar Pathak and former untouchable scavenger Mrs. Usha Chaumar were interviewed on the BBC World News channel on April 9, 2015. The programme known as BBC Impact was compered by the world famous television commentator, Ms. Yalda Hakim. She referred to Dr. Pathak as 'Mr. Sanitation' for his efforts in bringing about a change in the sanitation scenario in India.

US envoy's visit

His Excellency Mr. Richard Rahul Verma, US Ambassador to India, visited the Sulabh Campus on August 13, 2015 to observe the technologies and social change programmes.

'One Year of Cleanliness'

Sulabh International Social Service Organisation celebrated 'One Year of Cleanliness' on September 17, the birthday of Prime Minister Narendra Modi, at a function at FICCI Auditorium in New Delhi. The Prime Minister lighted the candle of cleanliness and asked the people to restore the culture of sanitation which the Indians had during the Harappan Civilisation. Sulabh and the Founder, Dr. Bindewshar Pathak, wholeheartedly joined hands with the Prime Minister with all the might and resources to make the country clean and free from open defecation. Sulabh also spread the message among the masses to be civilised and cultured and make India clean and standout in the row of civilised nations and thus fulfil the dreams of Mahatma Gandhi and the Prime Minister by October 2, 2019, the 150th birthday of the Father of the Nation.

The Minister of State (Independent Charge) for Tourism and Culture, Dr. Mahesh Sharma, unveiled a giant 365 kg "ladoo" at the function to mark the 'One Year of Cleanliness'

Safaigiri Award

Sulabh was presented the 'Safaigiri Award' on October 2, 2015 by *India Today Group* in the category of 'Cleanest Ghat' of the country. On behalf of Sulabh, its President Mrs. Usha Chaumar received the award from Prime Minister Narendra Modi.

Visit by New York Global Leaders Dialogue officials

Mr. Phil Scanlan, Chairman, and Ms. Pam Kwatra, Executive Board Member, New York Global Leader Dialogue, Harvard Club, USA, toured Varanasi and New Delhi during October 11–13, 2015 and interacted with hundreds of liberated untouchable scavengers, widows, community women and activists and professionals of Sulabh Sanitation and Social Reform Movement. They also addressed scores of media professionals.

Bosnian envoy

Dr. Sabit Subasic, Bosnia and Herzegovina Ambassador to India, Mr. Andrés Barbé Gonzales, Ambassador of the Republic of Chile, Mr. Georges de La Roche Du Ronzet, Ambassador of the Republic of Guatemala and Mr. Vladimir Maric, Ambassador of the Republic of Serbia, visited the Sulabh Campus on October 27, 2015.

Top Global Diversity figures

Ranked by *The Economist* Dr. Pathak was recognised amongst World's Top 50 diversity figures in public life along with US President Barack Obama, Angelina Jolie and Bill Gates.

Toilet Day celebration

Sulabh organised a two-day National Conference on 'Fulfilling the Dream of the Hon'ble Prime Minister to Provide Toilet in Each Household by 2019: Challenges and Way Ahead' and celebrated the World Toilet Day. The programme among others was attended by actress Hema Malini, Member of Parliament, as Guest of Honour.

2016: New York Global Leaders Dialogue Humanitarian Award

The 2016 Prestigious 'New York Global Leaders Dialogue Humanitarian Award' was bestowed upon Dr. Pathak in recognition of his effort to enhance quality of life for millions of fellow human beings. Dr. Pathak has been recognised as a "humanist, social reformer and diversity champion".

".....I, Bill de Blasio, Mayor of the city of New York, do hereby proclaim Thursday, April 14, 2016, the city of New York as: Dr. Bindeshwar Pathak Day..."

'Dr. Bindeshwar Pathak Day' in New York

Hon'ble Mayor of New York City, Mr. Bill de Blasio, honoured Dr. Pathak with a proclamation declaring April 14, 2016 as *"Dr. Bindeshwar Pathak Day"* in New York City, for being a "pioneer" in championing human rights in India through campaigning for social reforms and developing innovative and environmentally sound sanitation technologies.

World's biggest toilet complex

The clusters of three-storey mega-toilet buildings of the world's largest toilet complex at the pilgrim centre of Pandharpur in Maharashtra which cater to the need of 1.5 lakh people were opened in July, 2016. The complex consisting of 1,417 toilets in eight clusters was constructed by Sulabh International and financed by the Government of Maharashtra. Terming the project as a landmark Sulabh Founder Dr. Pathak expressed hope that the project would give a boost to the Prime Minister's ambitious 'Clean India' campaign.

Brand Ambassador, Swachh Rail Mission

Railway Minister Suresh Prabhu made Dr. Pathak the "Brand Ambassador, Swachh Rail Mission" on November 2, 2016.

Honorary Citizen of the French city of Montier

Dr. Bindeshwar Pathak was honoured as the "Honorary Citizen of the French city of Montier" by the Mayor, Mr. Jean Jacques Bayer, on November 19, 2016 during the four-day International Festival of Animal and Nature of Montier-en-Der.

NALSA member

Dr. Bindeshwar Pathak was nominated as a Member of the Central Authority of the National Legal Services Authority (NALSA) by the Ministry of Law and Justice, Government of India.

Amit Shah's visit

Mr. Amit Shah, National President of the Bharatiya Janata Party visited the Sulabh Campus on December 20, 2016.

Chief Justice visit

Mr. Justice Tirath Singh Thakur, Chief Justice of India, who had set a new benchmark of judicial probity and excellence, visited Sulabh Gram on December 31, 2016.

2017: Book on Modi launched

The Coffee Table book *"Narendra Damodardas Modi: The Making of a Legend"* written by Dr. Pathak, was launched by RSS Sarsanghchalak, Dr. Mohan Madhukar Bhagwat, at a function attended by BJP President Amit Shah in New Delhi on July 12, 2017.

This illustrated biography has the images and text depicting Prime Minister Modi's life journey, his struggles, his achievements and his various pro-people initiatives since he took over as Prime Minister in 2014.

18th Lal Bahadur Shastri National Award

Dr. Pathak was decorated with the coveted "18th Lal Bahadur Shastri National Award for excellence in Public Administration,

Dr. Bindeshwar Pathak received "18th Lal Bahadur Shastri National Award for excellence in Public Administration, Academics and Management 2017" from the hands of President Shri Ram Nath Kovind

Academics and Management 2017" by President Ram Nath Kovind at a function held on October 10 at Rashtrapati Bhavan.

Dr. Pathak was awarded in recognition of his distinct and outstanding contribution in the field of social reform.

"The weight of the dreams is heavier than the baggage of past memories."

– Thomas Hardy

CHAPTER 35

Bihar: Always a Nursery of Social Movements

A land where great things happened

For many centuries, Bihar has been the leading light of the East where great ideas, movements, and religions were born. This rich inheritance has influenced Dr. Bindeshwar Pathak, whose philosophy of pluralism, tolerance and nationalism is manifest in the Sulabh Movement. Let us briefly know about the land and the legends of Bihar to put the Sulabh story in perspective.

The present is always rooted in the past. What we have today biologically, historically, spiritually and socially began in the misty past which is hard to identify and harder still to determine its influence on the future. But the problems of today don't emerge from nowhere; they have a long history. It is truer for Bihar than of any state or region of the country.

Ancient Bihar was to the Indian subcontinent, what Greece was to Europe. Greece, a country of 1,400 islands, was virtually a nation of one city Athens, where great thinkers, philosophers and scientists lived, including Herodotus, Homer, Archimedes, Socrates, Plato, Aristotle and Pericles, to make the city centre of art, science and culture. Edward Gibbon Says: "What was discarded in the Greek backyard has become the rich heritage of Europe". Name any original thinker and he is Greek. In sum, what is great and glorious in Europe is Greek! About the same time before Christ, (Socrates – c399, and Buddha – c460 were almost contemporaries). Bihar also had become the centre of power and acquired the peak glory in learning, culture and philosophy.

During the time the people in the West were learning to read and write, Bihar was talking of philosophy and religion. It was here that great religions were born and scholars launched the endless search for truth and universal brotherhood. No wonder while talking of Bihar, one is talking of ideas and not a state of Indian republic – so great has been its history, so fascinating its culture as a land of glory. In the early stages of human civilisation, when not much of culture was known to outside world, Bihar was the hub of intellectual and spiritual activities.

Mystics and sophists roamed about the Ganga Valley, all advocating mental discipline and asceticism as a means to salvation; but the age of Buddha, when many of the best minds were abandoning their homes and professions for a life of asceticism, was

Nalanda – when it was the 'Light of the East'

also a time of advance in commerce and politics. It produced not only philosophers and ascetics, but also merchants, princes and men of action.

The ruins of Nalanda represent only a part of the extensive establishment. Excavations have uncovered nine levels of occupation and construction of six monasteries. Ruins of the university complex, where the total area of excavation is about 14 hectares, contain a number of Buddhist stupas and Chaityas, monasteries, hostels, cells or rooms on four sides with a central courtyard and lecture halls and amphitheatre. The places of interest at Nalanda are the Archaeological Museum, Nav Nalanda Mahavihar, Hiuen-tsang Memorial Hall, Nargaon, Kundalpur and Silao.

Prof. Ramchandra Prasad, a renowned Professor of English, stated in his book,*'Bihar'* that Bihar is named after Buddhist monastery (Vihara) which is the birth place of Mahavira and Guru Govind Singh. This is also the place where Buddha, Mahavira and Mahatma Gandhi started their movements. Dr. Rajendra Prasad, Dr. Shrikrishna Sinha, Jayaprakash Narayan and Babu Jagjiwan Ram belonged to Bihar and Raja Rammohan Roy had studied at Patna. Bihar produced revolutionaries like Khudiram Bose and has been the land of Chandragupta, Kautilya, (Chanakya), Ashoka, Aryabhatta and Patanjali. Kautilya's *'Arthshastra',* Aryabhatt's *'Aryabhattiye'* and Patanjali's *'Mahabhashya'* establish the fact that Pataliputra (modern Patna) produced great authors, scientists and spiritual leaders, who led a *dharma*-based way of life. Dr. Bindeshwar Pathak also launched the Sulabh Movement from Arrah in Bihar, which later became a global phenomenon.

Pataliputra was the capital of the Kingdom of Magadha. Dr. Pathak belongs to Vaishali, the *Janmabhumi* of Lord Mahavir and *the Karmabhumi* of Lord Buddha. Gandhiji started his first *Satyagraha* from Champaran in Bihar. Pataliputra was also a centre of educational excellence. It had 12 names, including Pushpapur, Kusumpur, Azimabad, Udantpur, Patiligram and Bankipur. (Book

'Bihar', Author Dr. Ramchandra Prasad, Professor and Head of the Department of English, Patna University, Patna).

For many centuries Bihar has been the leading state of the East. H.G. Wells in his book, *An Outline of World History,* says: "Ashoka shines like a luminary in the galaxy of the kings of the world". His capital was Pataliputra. Megasthenese in his book *'Indica'* talked high about this place. He spent a decade from 302 BC to 291 BC at Pataliputra in the court of Emperor Chandragupta Maurya. Bihar, as a matter of fact, has always occupied an important position in the history of India; for centuries it was the principal seat of imperial powers and the main focus of Indian culture. Under the British, it was a part of the Bengal Presidency until 1912, when the provinces of Bihar and Orissa were formed. In 1936, Bihar was separated from Orissa and made a separate province. After India's Independence in 1947, it became a state. In 1948, the small states of Saraikela and Kharsawan were merged with Bihar. In 1956, when the Indian states were reorganised on linguistic basis, a large chunk of territory was transferred from Bihar to West Bengal.

Profile of the people

People of Bihar have neither sub-nationalism nor do they go about flaunting their identity. They don't suffer from egocentricity, chauvinism or exclusiveness. Bihar has a large number of cultural groups identified by their distinct languages, cultural practices, and social customs, but they don't claim to be separate or assert superiority over others. They proclaim only one identity that they are Indians, first and last. No wonder, Prof. Amartya Sen says that Bihar has

Prof. Amartya Sen

always been a uniter of the country, even when the dividing forces were in high prominence. Bihar has a rainbow culture with people of different backgrounds, language groups and habits, living together, fiercely loyal to their beliefs, family values and social commitments. They share and care, easy to be seduced and easier to be provoked into violent action. This sense of national consciousness flows from Bihar being the confluence of Indian culture and sub-cultures which has also a historical root. When Magadha was the centre of the greatest Maurya empire, cultural, social, spiritual, political and intellectual streams flowed in from all over the empire which stretched beyond India. Hence, a composite and cosmopolitan world view emerged, much of which is manifest in the birth of many religions, including Buddhism and Jainism, which found Magadha a fertile ground for growth. The Maurya Empire originated from Magadha with its capital at Pataliputra in 325 BC. Mauryan Emperor Ashoka, who was born in Pataliputra, was said to be one of the greatest rulers in the history of the world.

A centre of power

When Ajatshatru founded the city of Pataliputra in 5th century BC, Lord Buddha came to inaugurate the city. Looking round, Lord Buddha said: "This city will suffer from flood, fire and feud". Lord Buddha did not curse the city by saying this; he was only talking geography; the city is situated at a level lower than the Ganga's and hence it has the tendency to get flooded. The multi-racial demographic structure had caused many feuds in the Magadha empire after which Ajatshatru became king. And the fire incidence took place as often as flood because nomadic tribes recklessly burnt forests to clear the land for cultivation and grow food.

Ajatshatru's son Udayan made it the capital of the empire, with which it remained until the 1st century BC. The second Magadha dynasty, the Maurya, ruled in the early 2nd century BC until the city was sacked in 185 by Indo-Greeks. The Sun dynasty ruled until about 73 when Pataliputra became a centre of learning to remain so until 4th century. Later, it declined and was deserted by the people in 'fire, flood and feud'. The city was re-founded as Patna by an Afghan ruler in 1541. Pataliputra was Athens of the East, which saw the rise and fall of India's first major empires. Sprawled on the bank of the Ganga, Pataliputra, 'the eternal city of the East', is a lineal descendant of the ancient metropolis relics of five periods, beginning from 600 BC.

Pataliputra saw the rise and fall of India's first major empires. The Patna Museum presents several historical glimpses. From Golghar one gets a panoramic view of the city and the Ganga. It is also the birth place of Guru Govind Singh, the tenth and the last Guru of Sikhism. The Gurudwara, which was originally built by Maharaja Ranjit Singh, is next to the Golden Temple of Amritsar in sanctity. Pathar-ki-Masjid, built by Parwez Shah, son of Jahangir and Governor of Bihar in 1621, is also a place of attraction.

In 475 BC, the capital of Magadha Empire was located in Pataliputra with which it remained under Ashoka (274 to 232 BC) and the Guptas (4th and 5th centuries AD) until the onslaught of the Huns in the middle and late 5th century. In the 6th-7th century AD, the city was devastated by the Son river. The other place of tourism is Rajgir, 102 km from Patna, known in ancient times as Rajagriha, meaning home of royalty. Rajgir had very close association with the life and work of Buddha. He not only spent many rainy seasons here but also delivered many sermons and it was the sacred Griddhakoota Hill where he converted Emperor Bimbisar to Buddhism. The places of interest at Rajgir are Griddhakoota Hill, pagoda and monastery, aerial ropeway chairlift, Saptaparmi Cave, Cyclopean Wall, Bimbisar-ka-Jain, Swarn Bhandar Cave, ruins of fort, and hot water springs.

The next is Pawapuri, known as Apapuri. It is a very sacred Jain pilgrimage centre. It was here that Lord Mahavira attained salvation.

Hundreds and thousands of his followers took away the ashes after his cremation here. The rush was so great that even the soil of the area was taken away and it became a tank. Later a beautiful temple of white marble was constructed in the centre of the tank to consecrate the Lord's Nirvana. It is now known as Jalmandir. Samosharan is another beautiful temple of white marble. Here, Lord Mahavira had delivered his last sermon.

On the map of Bihar, there exists one place which attracted the whole world. It is Bodhgaya, situated on the bank of the Niranjana river now known as Phalgu. It was here, 2,500 years ago, the Sakya prince first spotted places where Lord Buddha spent seven weeks. The places have seven shrines. Buddhists from Burma, Tibet, China, Thailand, Sri Lanka and Japan have raised monasteries in their native architectural styles. The tree that stands today is said to have grown from the original Bodhi tree under which Lord Buddha meditated and attained enlightenment. The Mahabodhi Temple in Bodhgaya is the most sacred shrine for the followers of Lord Buddha.

The golden age

Bihar remained an important place of power, culture and education for over one thousand years. The Gupta Empire, which again originated from Magadha in 240 AD, is referred to as the Golden Age of India in science, mathematics, astronomy, religion and philosophy. The peace and prosperity attained under leadership of the Guptas enabled the pursuit of scientific and artistic endeavours. Historians place the Gupta dynasty alongside the Han Dynasty, Tang Dynasty and Roman Empire as a model of a classical civilisation. The capital of the Gupta Empire was also Pataliputra. The Vikramshila and Nalanda universities, were among the oldest and best centres of education in ancient India. A National Geographic edition reads, "The essential tenets of Buddhism and Hinduism arose from similar ideas best described in *the Upanishads,* a set of Hindu treatises set down in India largely between the eighth and fourth centuries BC."

The Buddhism in Magadha was finally swept away by the Muslim invasion under Muhammad bin Bakhtiar Khilji, during which many of the Viharas and the famed universities of Nalanda and Vikramshila were destroyed, and thousands of Buddhist monks were massacred in 12th century AD. However, after the Battle of Buxar (1764), things changed; the British East India Company obtained the Diwani rights (rights to administer, and collect revenue or tax) for Bihar, Bengal and Orissa. From this point, as stated earlier, Bihar remained part of the Bengal Presidency of the British Raj until 1912, when the provinces of Bihar and Orissa were carved out as a separate province. In 1936, certain portions of Bihar were reorganised into the separate province of Orissa. The state of Jharkhand was carved out of Bihar in the year 2000.

Geography is history

The state is geographically divided into two parts – the alluvial plains of the Ganga in the north and the Chota Nagpur plateau in the south (now known as Jharkhand). But this new divison has not changed the cultural pattern of Bihar except that Jharkhand has primarily aboriginal tribe culture.

Originally, Chota Nagpur was mostly forest-clad area and was ruled by chiefs of various aboriginal tribes. Though British authority was only established gradually in the plains to the north during the second half of the 18th and the beginning of the 19th century, occasional revolts against them took place in Chota Nagpur, the most important being the Ho revolt of 1820-27 and the Munda uprising of 1831-32.

In the early Vedic period (1500 BC), several kingdoms existed in the Bihar plain. The capital of the ancient kingdom of Magadha was Rajagraha (modern Rajgir); to the east was the kingdom of Anga, with its capital at Champa (near Bhagalpur). A new kingdom later arose in southern Videha with its capital at Vaishali. By 700 BC, the kingdoms of Vaishali and Videha were replaced by a confederacy of the Vijjis, said to be the first republican state known in history. Hiuen-tsang, a Chinese traveller, who visited India two hundred years after Fa-hien, also a Chinese traveller, recorded in his diaries in 637 AD that Pataliputra had only a few inhabitants. It regained some of its glory, but it is doubtful that it ever served as the capital of the Pala Empire (775 to 1200). During the Muslim period (1200 to 1765), Bihar had little independent history, remaining a provincial unit until 1765 when it came under British rule and, together with Chota Nagpur, was merged with the state of Bengal.

Land of resistance

The peasants movement was an important aftermath of the freedom movement. The Kisan Sabha movement started in Bihar under the leadership of Swami Sahajanand Saraswati, who had formed in 1929, the Bihar Provincial Kisan Sabha in order to highlight peasants' grievances against the zamindari attacks on their occupancy rights. Gradually the peasant movement intensified and spread across the rest of India. All these radical developments on the peasant front culminated in the formation of the All-India Kisan Sabha at the Lucknow session of the Indian National Congress in April 1936 with Swami Sahajanand Saraswati being elected as its first President.

Babu Kunwar Singh of Jagdishpur and his army, as well as countless other persons from Bihar, fought India's First War of Independence (1857). Resurgence in the history of Bihar came during the struggle for India's Independence. It was from Bihar that Mahatma Gandhi launched his pioneering civil disobedience movement, the Champaran Satyagraha in 1917. People in Champaran had earlier revolted against indigo cultivation in 1914 (Pipra) and 1916 (Turkaulia) and Pandit Raj Kumar Shukla took Mahatma Gandhi to Champaran and the Champaran Satyagraha was

Dr. Rajendra Prasad, the first President of India, was born in Saran district in Bihar

Jayaprakash Narayan, the great freedom fighter, scholar and committed Gandhian, was born in Sitabdiara of Siwan district of Bihar in 1902

launched. Raj Kumar Shukla drew the attention of Mahatma Gandhi to the exploitation of the peasants by European indigo planters. The Champaran Satyagraha received support from many Bihar leaders including Sri Krishna Sinha, first Chief Minister of Bihar, Dr. Rajendra Prasad, and Anugrah Narayan Sinha who later became the state Finance Minister.

Dr. Rajendra Prasad and Jayaprakash Narayan were among the many who played crucial roles in the Independence Movement. Dr. Prasad, a true disciple of Mahatma Gandhi, was associated with him since 1917, when he joined the Champaran struggle. A brilliant student and an able advocate, Dr. Prasad was introduced by Gandhiji to a Gujarat audience in 1918 as follows: "My own brothers are dead; but we have here Shri Rajendra Babu, on seeing whom I forget their loss. He has given me love such as I can never forget." The Congress President in 1934, 1939-40 (after Subhas Chandra Bose was obliged to leave), and 1947-48, Dr. Prasad, unlike Rajagopalachari and Nehru, refrained from questioning Gandhiji. Mildness and an appearance that was even milder were his identity.

The movement aimed at overthrowing the feudal (zamindari) system instituted by Britishers under the Permanent Land Settlement Act. It was being led by Swami Sahajanand Saraswati and his followers, Pandit Yamuna Karjee, Rahul Sankrityayan, Pandit Karyanand Sharma, Baba Nagarjun and others. Pandit Yamuna Karjee, along with Rahul Sankritayan and a few others, started publishing a Hindi weekly, Hunkar, from Bihar, in 1940. Hunkar later became the mouthpiece of the peasant movement and the agrarian movement in Bihar and was instrumental in spreading the movement.

The other outstanding people who took part in the freedom struggle include Sri Krishna Sinha, Dr. Anugrah Narayan Sinha, Brajkishore Prasad, Maulana Mazharul Haque, Satyendra Narayan Sinha, Basawon Singh, Rameshwar Prasad Sinha, Yogendra Shukla, Baikuntha Shukla and Sheel Bhadra Yajee, who worked for India's freedom relentlessly and helped in the uplift of the underprivileged masses. Khudiram Bose, Upendra Narayan Jha 'Azad', Prafulla Chaki and Baikuntha Shukla were also active in revolutionary movement in Bihar.

Maithili also a cultural group

Bihar is the land of many cultures, the most notable among them being Mithila, which once covered an area larger than the present Madhya Pradesh (a large part of it later went to Nepal and West Bengal). The Mithila culture has many salient features like Mithila paintings, Maithili

Mithila painting

language, Maithili script (Tirhutta), Mithila folksongs and most famous Panjikaran system. Mithila figures in the Hindu mythology and also in *the Ramayana*. Mithila has been a centre of learning. Chanakya, Yagyavalkya, Udyanacharya, poet Vidyapati and Ayachi Mishra were born here. Maithili is a language spoken mainly in Bihar and in the eastern Terai region of Nepal. It is an offshoot of the Indo-Aryan languages which are part of the Indo-Iranian, a branch of the Indo-European languages. Linguists consider Maithili to be an eastern Indian language and thus, a different language from Hindi which is Central Indian in origin. According to the 2001 Census, 12 million people speak the Maithili language in India alone.

Once, Maithili was considered a 'dialect' of both Hindi and Bengali but in 2003 it got the status of an independent language. A movement was carried out to give the language an official status through its inclusion in the Eighth Schedule of the Constitution, so that it may be used in education, government, and other official dealings. In 2004, Maithili was given an official status. A very sweet language, Maithili has a very rich literary and cultural heritage.

The name Maithili is derived from the word Mithila, the ancient kingdom of which King Janak was the ruler. Maithili is another name of Sita. The medieval age of Maithili was during the Karnat Dynasty when the names of many scholars got prominence. They include Gangesh, Padmanabh, Chandeshwar, Vireshwar, Vidyapati, Vachaspati, Pakshdhar, Ayachi Mishra, Udayanacharya, Shankar etc.

Vidyapati is said to have lived in the period from 1350 to 1450. Vidyapati, though a Sanskrit scholar, wrote innumerable poems (songs) on *Bhakti* and *Shringar* in Maithili. Though equally accepted in Bengal and Mithila, his songs are the soul of Mithila and no celebration is complete without his songs. His songs are best sung by Maithili womenfolk. Verses of Vidyapati are given religious importance in the Mithila culture.

Vaishali was visited three times by Lord Buddha. In his lifetime,

Lord Buddha had announced his approaching Nirvana and preached his last sermon here. Amrapali, a courtesan, presented a mango grove to Buddha here and later became a Buddhist nun. Vaishali was the venue for the second Buddhist Council which was held 100 years after the passing away of Buddha. It was believed that Vaishali was the birthplace of Mahavira Tirthankar. Other attractions in Vaishali are the pillar built by Emperor Ashoka, Buddha stupas, Raja Vishal-ka-Garh, Abhishek Pushkarni, Chaumukhi Mahadev, Miranji-ka-Dargah, Balsan Pokhar Temple, archaeological museum etc.

There are many language groups in Bihar, major among them being Bhojpuri, Magahi, Angika and Bazzika. They are derivative groups, branching out of Maithili which is spoken in about 20 districts while Bhojpuri remains the dominant spoken language in many districts, including Chapra, Siwan, West and East champaran district, Arrah and Buxar. (Bazzika, the derivative of Maithili, Bhojpuri and Angika, is spoken in Rampur Baghel, Dr. Pathak's birth place). These languages have created their own cultural practices. Dr. Pathak was born in Mithalanchal, where Maithili language and culture prevailed. His mother, wife and other relations are also in the same Maithili language and culture group, distinctly marking out the cultural preferences and attitude. He has, thus, inherited a rich cultural legacy which is manifested in his attitude and personal life even today.

Language has been a great uniting (or dividing) factor in history. Prussia, once a small German-speaking kingdom on eastern fringe of Europe, expanded to become a huge German empire in central Europe after a series of struggles over the language led by Fredrick the Great and Bismark, the Founder of modern Germany. Many small nations between Germany and France are fighting even today over languages. The English-speaking empire has been the dream of Churchill. Back home, Bangladesh separated on the basis of language; common religion with West Pakistan could not prevent the split in 1971. In India also, states were reorganised on the language basis in 1956. No happy decision at that. This kind of linguistic division exists in Bihar but Biharis are celebrating diversity, instead of fighting over it. This is because the art of living together of diverse language groups has been the inheritance of the imperial Pataliputra. Biharis live their past without knowing it.

Gandhiji appreciated the simplicity of Biharis and wrote in his autobiography that he couldn't go a single step ahead in the Champaran Satyagraha against indigo growers without the support of Rajendra Prasad and Braj Kishore Prasad. *Chura dahi* (curd), *Chini* (sugar) and *sathu* are special dishes and Biharis are rice-eaters. Indentured labourers of Bihar settled down in Mauritius, Suriname, and Caribbean Islands and they developed those countries.

Now that Bihar is emerging from its past failings, a new future awaits its people who have the ability, honesty and commitment to build a modern state with a glorious past. This, in brief, is the profile of the people and the land where the Sulabh Movement was born.